Awkward Silence

A self-help Autobiographical Novel

By

Jack Taylor

Jack Taylor

All Rights Reserved

Awkward Silence
A Self-Help Autobiographical Novel
By **Jack Taylor**

Copyright © 2025 by Jack Taylor

LCCN: 2024950031
ISBN: 978-1-965408-64-3

Published by
Book Writing League

Trigger Warnings

✓   Child Abuse

✓   Violence

✓   Depression

✓   Dissociative Identity Disorder

✓   CPTSD

✓   Dissociative Disorders

✓   Emotional Apathy

✓   Child Confinement

✓   Police Brutality

✓   Guns

✓   Suggested Abortion ✓ Murder

✓   Suicide References

✓   Alcohol Consumption

✓   Drug Consumption

✓   Sexual Abuse

✓   Bullying

✓   Profanity

✓   Abusive Relationships

✓   Emotional Abuse

✓   Physical Abuse

✓   God and Spiritual Themes

Dedication 1

This is dedicated to the beginning and the end. It is enthusiastically devoted to He that was, that is, and that is about to come. Working with Him on this project has been the joy of my lifetime. He is decisive. He knows exactly the word He wants me to use and, at times, will riddle me through it. I have worn out the pages of the thesaurus to adjust for my complacency. We are not finished with that as I write this. My mind wouldn't absorb all the details He wants to reflect, and when I can't see any deeper, He lifts another blindfold. It is clearly my work with its imperfections that do surface. However, it is written to accomplish a greater deed, and that is my healing. That would be self-serving if I didn't continue to say, His purpose is bigger than mine. He wants this to serve others in their individual healing and, through that, social healing. I recognize His desire to use this infrastructure to encourage a change in the state of mind, which is repentance and to promote forgiveness, which is self-healing.

I dedicate this story of my life to He who gave me life, and because of that, not only is the story His, but the life itself I dedicate to God!!!

Dedication 2

Some say that if you allow the magic to drift away, there is very little left. I disregard that statement because if it were true then it is a hopeless theme. Every relationship loses its magic at some point for a period. I believe that at the end of the day, three things should always remain: hope, faith, and love. I believe that you kindle the fire. I believe that you make every effort to keep the magic alive, but sometimes it feels like it has dimmed to a point of no return, and it is then that you step up to the plate and knock it out of the park. The truth is that I read a Facebook post that stated that a real man does not love multiple women but instead finds multiple ways, new and creative ways, to love the same woman.

I dedicate it to you, Candice; it is a way, maybe not the best way, but a way to love the same woman in another creative way. As I will, as I hope to uncover depths that I have not known, I hope that it is the actions that stand out. The words, I hope, are creatively placed in ways never done before so that it is a showing of deeper love than you have ever known.

Dedication 3

As swiftly as the wind sweeping across the empty field, stirring up the dust, you rode your broom into my desert terrain. You disrupted the deterioration of my wretched life with tidings of the most petrifying and, at the time, most repressive predicament imaginable. I had deep engravings of abhorrence in my soul, and I targeted you with all that hate, but I could not use this dedication page to heighten and acknowledge my wonderful, amazing daughter, Katie and not give thanks to you. Thank you, Tonya! I, apprehensively, hand over my shame. You were the one who made the right choice. We did make a beautiful child and I love you for that! Oh, and just playing about the riding the broom thing.

Dedication 4

Jennifer, in my most transcendental pipe dream, I could not have imagined the savory bouquet that has become our friendship! Words like savory and bouquet may give people the wrong idea about what it is that we are! That, of course, is the fun part. Did you know that we've been best friends for over 20 years. It astounds me to speculate, but only one of two things can be true. You were either as nutty or nuttier than I am, or you are the most compassionate individual on the face of this planet. It seems that the latter is true.

Table of Contents

Foreword

"The objective is Healing."

Judith Lewis Herman, a psychiatrist and Harvard researcher, coined the term Complex Post-Traumatic Stress Disorder (CPTSD) in 1988. Despite this, CPTSD is still not a separate diagnosis from PTSD in the DSM. There are nuances that, in my opinion, often escape the attention of clinicians. One significant aspect is that trauma experienced at different developmental stages profoundly affects natural development. From my perspective, these complexities stem from the impact of trauma across these stages. However, a barrier to recognizing CPTSD as a separate diagnosis is the idea that the complexities could be limited to individuals who experienced trauma during their formative years. It is important to note that symptoms of complexity are also evident in cases of severe adult trauma.

The symptoms of CPTSD form an extensive list that includes flashbacks, hypervigilance, memory lapses, suicidal ideation, self-destructive and self-sabotaging tendencies, a distorted sense of self, risky sexual behavior, autoimmune issues, dissociative disorders, difficulty regulating emotions, extreme apathy, gastrointestinal problems, poor interpersonal relationships, avoiding people or places, substance abuse, self-blame, low self-esteem, a distorted perception of reality, excessive sense of responsibility, and more. When trauma occurs during developmental periods, additional signs of underdevelopment may be present, such as a lack of self-care or means of emotional expression.

Treatment for CPTSD often involves a combination of psychotherapy and medication. Medications are typically used to manage elevated symptoms, such as anxiety or depression. Therapy focuses on developing coping skills to address ongoing symptoms, such as identifying triggers and adopting new behavioral responses. However, creating new responses to deeply ingrained triggers can take countless hours of therapy, especially when conditioned responses have become natural reactions over a lifetime. Progress can also be hindered by other symptoms, like dissociation, which may create conflicting barriers. Ultimately, building trust and fostering love is crucial to the healing process.

The symptoms of CPTSD share common underlying themes. Dissociation and extreme apathy act as protective mechanisms, while self-destructive and risky behavior often stems from feeling undervalued. Physical health issues are frequently linked to the prolonged stress implied by these symptoms. Flashbacks and memory "ruts" reflect the trauma at its core. The journey toward healing requires patience, kindness, and, most importantly, love.

Through my memoir, I aim to demonstrate how and when these symptoms developed. The journey may be challenging to understand, but it is logical. Some symptoms require close observation to notice, while others are more explicit. Treatments are often tailored to individual symptoms; for example, alcohol and drug abuse treatment programs have found success with the twelve steps of AA. I conclude that this approach is effective across a wide range of symptoms. From a Christian perspective, forgiveness and repentance can help loosen the grip of the past. While the physical scars may have faded, it is the lingering thoughts and feelings that create ongoing dysfunction. True healing comes when you change your mind and reshape your perceptions.

My path to healing was less straightforward than the twelve steps of AA. I approached the process from multiple directions, often overcomplicating it. However, I believe that sharing my experience can offer valuable insight to those interested in healing. We all carry burdens, regardless of their size. I am no different from you—you are special, and if I can heal, anyone can!

Awkward Silence

Chapter 1
Seed of Desperation

Genesis 1: 1, "Now the earth was formless and empty,
darkness was over the surface of the deep,
and the spirit of God was hovering over the waters."

"When inspiration is led by desperation
it is best followed by dedication."

Inspiration is sublime. It can be ignited by a chance encounter, a word, a look, or even a smell. The connection to this stimulus runs deep, rooted in the soul. When inspiration strikes, it releases a powerful energy, like a tornado that reduces everything in its path to splinters. Nothing can stand in its way once it takes hold in the heart. It is the driving force behind all great works— paintings, poetry, architectural marvels, and even the words that fill the pages that follow. Inspiration clears the way, allowing thoughts to swirl until, like a puzzle, the message comes together piece by piece.

You never know when or how this spark will ignite, but once it does, it is all-consuming. It triggers a series of small explosions, each one building upon the last, like a fireworks display leading to a grand finale. It feels like a dog chasing a squirrel—full of excitement, unstoppable. Yet inspiration is not born from randomness. Every moment connects to the next, illuminating a path that brings hope and direction to life.

My own path has been filled with shadows—abstract hallucinations that served as barriers, resisting my connection to inspiration. These hallucinations were false impressions planted in my mind long before I discovered an alternate reality. That reality, the miracle of Christ, set me free. True inspiration brings hope, instills faith, and gives you the power to move mountains. It equips you to deflect the arrows of doubt and opposition. To me, inspiration is the aspect of love that calls us to action.

For a long time, I felt lost at sea, rowing a lifeboat with a broken oar that only sent me in circles. Everything around me felt empty, dark, and void. Despite the emptiness, I learned to smile and found a semblance of life. I was diagnosed with CPTSD, but the real cause for concern came with IBS-C. Stress was literally eating away at my body, determined to kill me slowly through anguish and pain.

I was blind to it. While these poisons crippled my thoughts and aspirations, I was busy chasing butterflies through rainbows. I lived in a seemingly safe space, yet pieces of my existence were being tossed into the flames. I existed in a state of shock—an overloaded system forced into a shutdown, offering only fleeting relief from the chaos. Shock provided distance from tragic events and, in my case, numbed the dissonance caused by the destructive deeds that severed my connection to myself and to reality. I pretended everything was fine, ignoring the shortness of breath, the heart palpitations, and the pervasive hopelessness, clinging instead to an illusory world of unicorns and candy.

Despite it all, the inspiration that has found me now is undeniable. It pushes me to face my reality and navigate through the shadows. True inspiration gives us more than just hope; it equips us to confront and transcend even the darkest of circumstances.

Meanwhile, fragments of my identity and purpose lie scattered across fields as vast as the universe. Dissociative Identity Disorder (DID) is often misdiagnosed or conflated with Multiple Personality Disorder. I don't intend to discredit this clinical perspective by calling it hogwash, but my experience is not based on an outward analysis of someone else's soul—this is my story. I am the one who was once a fragile vessel, shattered and scattered. I am more than a clinical evaluator. My identity, my purity, splintered into countless shards that washed ashore like slivers of glass. Yet, as these fragments begin to come together, like pieces of a puzzle, a picture slowly takes form. This shattered vessel once carried a message for humanity—or at least for those willing to take the time to read and comprehend as the pieces reunite. It's as though the message in a bottle yearns to reveal itself, emerging from behind the veil of healing.

Desperation has led me just far enough to peek through the windows of my soul, searching for love—something to ignite that spark of inspiration. And then, like a bolt of lightning, love reached out from my heart, igniting the fuse of inspiration that fuels the words on these pages. For now, the field is empty, void of form. Not even a sapling breaks through the earth, but there is a cry from deep within the soil—a seed of desperation buried and waiting to emerge. Love knows no boundaries, exceeding even the depths of the abyss. It reaches through the cold stone and earth, pulling the script from the ground. Love, unselfish in its intent, transcends borders, and my hope is that this inspiration will bridge the gap between my altered reality and yours.

No one wants to be seen as desperate. Desperation is unattractive; it repels others. Desperate men are perceived as weak. But what if you are desperate? What if you are desperate for that one smile, desperate just to see that special someone move across the room? What if you are desperate for oxygen itself because missing it makes it feel like the air has become unbreathable? What if you're desperate for a connection that feels real, if your entire life hinges on your ability to love and be loved? What if you're desperate for healing?

Desperation is often seen as a red flag. But no—desperation is a white flag. It is surrender; it is humility. Humility brings a person to their knees in prayer. It is what brings a man to his knees in a proposal of love. Desperation, when truly understood, is a beautiful image of surrender and humility. In a world filled with arrogance, boasting, and pride, the humility of desperation is like a breath of fresh air.

I may have gotten ahead of myself. Let's start again. Love—it is sublime. It embodies the very character of God, for God is love. I would not worship a God who lacks the essence of love. The communication of love is mysterious, profound, and the driving force behind this inspiration. Love shows up in the synchronization of our breaths, in the subtle movements we make in unison. It's reflected in our mirroring facial expressions. And sometimes, it's in something as magical as the fragrance of lilacs and lavender that seems to materialize from the chemistry between us. Alone, neither of us carries the scent of lilacs or lavender, but together, it emerges—bigger than life—as if our pheromones combine to create that exquisite fragrance.

She awakens this fantasy realm, filling it with inspiration. She is the spark that shortens the fuse, drawing closer to an explosion of thoughts and emotions that ignited the moment we first met. When our eyes locked for the first time, words leaped from my heart onto the page without hesitation. Without her inspiration, perhaps I would have continued soaring through the clouds, never expecting to come back down.

The sublime intricacy of our connection was immediate and rare, at least for me. We met in a bar—an ordinary place by most standards. But where it becomes extraordinary is in the circumstances that led me there. I found myself here, driven by compromise and conflicting desires, chasing an illusion, an imaginary pot of gold at the end of a rainbow. It almost felt like there was an angelic purpose behind me being here tonight.

The bar is called Stew's—a rough-and-tumble watering hole, where by the time I walk in, my co-workers are already seated, glasses in hand. A double whiskey on the rocks awaits me, and a pizza is in the brick oven. I notice a woman across the room trying to catch my attention—giving me that look as if I'm the juiciest hot dog at the stand. She tries to gain my attention subtly at first. When that doesn't work, she pulls one of my buddies aside.

"Hey Jack, this is Trish. She asked me to introduce you," he says.

"Nice to meet you, Trish," I reply politely.

I had no intention of letting this go beyond the exchanged pleasantries. My mind is elsewhere, committed to stepping out of the patterns of my past—leaving behind the impulsiveness of sexual immorality. Besides, I can't help but think that tomorrow, there will be someone else to catch her eye, and I'm not interested in competing for that. I drain the whiskey in one swift movement, feeling the heat spread through me as it slides past my Adam's apple. I stand, ready to leave, but I feel her hand lightly pushing me back down. It's not forceful—gentle, even, but there's a hunger in her eyes. She wants me to stay. But I know all too well how whiskey and bad decisions are companions, so I get out of there before I falter—determined to resist the temptation.

Next door is another bar called "The Derail." It's fitting, as it's where my plans are completely derailed. I enter through a door near the alley, my friends trailing behind me. The place is alive with action—the pool tables are surrounded by people, and the league night energy buzzes throughout the room. Yet my focus narrows, tunnel vision locking in. There, across the room, I see her.

A woman who, with just one glance, seizes my every sense. The world around me blurs—she has me detained, captured, chained. My every fiber of desire belongs to her now. When our eyes meet, it's electric—intense. Her gaze holds a depth that reaches into me, and in those eyes, I see something profound, something that draws me in. She moves like magic, an effortless, fluid grace that's impossible to look away from. She doesn't need to say a word or even lift a finger—there's no force on Earth that could make me look away.

Feathers hang from her ears, swaying gently, adding to her ethereal presence. Her eyes are like pure emeralds—bright, deep, and alive. She is the most beautiful woman I've ever seen, and that says a lot for someone who has spent a lifetime admiring attractive people. There it is again, that familiar scent—gardenias? No, it's lilacs and lavender. I need to know her.

Her braid, resting against her chest, frames her face perfectly, highlighting her jawline with an effortless elegance. She is a vision of beauty, and I can feel myself veering off track from every plan, every agenda I thought I have had. And I'm okay with it. No, more than okay—I'm elated. I am happily derailed. In an instant, my life feels like it's changing, and I know that with absolute certainty. It's as if I'm looking into a mirror, seeing a reflection of my innermost self in her eyes.

This moment feels like a scene from an old dream replaying itself. In that dream, I was standing at a crossroad, and here I am again. I can see her as if she were an image carved in the rustling leaves of a tree—her silhouette moving with the breeze, feathers dangling just like now. It's elusive yet deeply familiar as if the spirit of that dream has materialized before me. The road that led me here has been dark and twisted, marked with sin and regrets. I've traveled it many times before, but this time, something feels different—maybe it's the recent decisions I've made that have begun to shed light on this path. Even in the darkness, that light has led me right here, standing in front of the most beautiful woman I could ever imagine.

"What's your name?" I ask, my voice almost trembling.

"Candice," she replies.

"Hi, Candice. I'm Jack," I say, trying to steady myself.

She smiles, her eyes holding mine, and she asks, "What do you want to know, Jack?"

Everything. Everything about her. "I want to know everything there is to know about you, Candice," I say, feeling like all the air in my lungs has left me in that one breath.

Some conversations are filled with words yet lack substance, like empty vessels. But this one—this is different. It is sparse but profound, each word laden with meaning. From that first night, I took her words into my heart, weaving them into poetry. Her words became the spark for the beginning of this book, changing my perspective on life itself. That is conversation. Real, deep, and transformative. Every word she spoke, I heard—not just with my ears but with my soul. They resonated deep within, becoming a part of who I am.

Her slight southern drawl, particularly when she says words like "can't" or "light," wraps around me like a melody. There's a quality to her voice that reassures her, something that feels like home. I am captivated by her, entirely enamored by every small nuance. The way she speaks, the way she moves, even the way her words seem to carry a warmth and a promise—I am drawn in, unable and unwilling to look away.

Chapter 2
Lemonade or Sweet Tea

Proverbs 18:22 "He who finds a wife finds a good thing and obtains favor from the lord."

"Romance is the songs that the stars sing that are heard through the eyes."

There's a charm and depth to an old-fashioned courtship that feels rare and timeless, something that resonates with the core of what love should be. I can see her now, sitting on a chair swing, her silhouette framed by the soft glow of moonlight, while I serenade her with music and dreams. The simplicity of star-gazing, where our thoughts meander into realms far beyond ordinary conversation, becomes more than just a date—it's a connection where dreams spawn dreams of their own. Ice-cold lemonade in hand, we talk about the possibilities of a future, while the symphony of crickets serenades us, joining in harmony with the whispers of the breeze and the invisible choir of angels.

There's beauty in the silence too—in those quiet moments where I sit, simply watching her smile, as peace fills every corner of my heart. I let go of all thoughts that might try to pull me out of this moment, surrendering entirely to the present. It's in this surrender, in this stillness, where love's true essence reveals itself. It's as if, by laying down all the weapons life has forced me to carry—those defenses forged from the struggles of the past—I am surrendering to God, to the divine conditions of love. That is the path I want to walk in courtship and marriage—a path of peace, respect, and purity.

I want nothing more than to take her on this journey, to offer her something real, grounded in honor and intention. The idea is pure, wholesome, and exactly the kind of love I want to dedicate my life to. Yes, I want an old-fashioned courtship.

But getting there—getting from where I am now, with the shadows of past mistakes clinging to me like smoke—seems like the hardest part. I've spent so much of my life in relationships that started in bed, thinking passion could replace the deeper bond I was truly searching for. And every one of those relationships left me empty. They expanded the darkness instead of bringing light. If I'm going to date, it should be with the intention of building something lasting, something meaningful. Otherwise, what's the point? The breath I waste asking her father's permission to court her would be hollow if my intentions weren't pure. And yes, even at my age, I believe asking for that blessing is important. To begin with integrity sets the foundation for a future that's strong and resilient.

Infidelity is a thought I wouldn't even want to entertain. If a relationship begins impurely, it weakens the structure from the start, making it more susceptible to distrust. In an old-fashioned courtship, you build desire slowly, with respect and patience. You learn each other—really learn each other, not just in a physical sense, but emotionally, mentally, and spiritually. There's something deeply sacred about that process. It's almost ceremonial. I believe in the idea that marriage, like all things good and holy, should be arranged by God. Just as Eve was made for Adam, I believe that for each of us, there is a partner God has chosen, someone created as a helpmate, a companion through life.

Yes, I am a romantic. And yes, I am unapologetically old-fashioned. I want to do this the right way.

"I'm sorry I called so late, but I won't apologize for wanting to hear your voice or for wanting to spend time with you,"

I said, feeling a bit sheepish about last night's late-hour call. I hadn't even been away from her that long, but it just felt too late for a call after nine. I continued, "That being said, I really enjoyed your company. I'd love to keep learning about you, if that's okay with you." I didn't want to assume anything. "And if you were serious about letting me check out your lawn mower? I'd be happy to help. It would be the perfect excuse to see you and look into your eyes again."

She smiled, brushing it off. "It's fine. It wasn't that late, and we can talk more later. I've got to get back to work."

"Can I take you to dinner?" I asked, trying to keep her attention for just a bit longer.

She paused just long enough to kiss me on the cheek, flashing me a beautiful smile. "We'll talk about it later. Gotta go."

"I want to see you!" I called out as she walked away, trying to catch her before she slipped out of sight.

She glanced back, teasing. "Let me see when I can get away. I'll let you know."

"Awesome! I'll be looking forward to hearing from you!" My heart surged with anticipation—it was a powerful feeling.

I couldn't help myself. I didn't want a whirlwind romance, but everything I did, every word I spoke, was to get closer to her. I worried that I might scare her off with how quickly I was falling, but even more, I worried that I was scaring myself. The pull between us was undeniable, like a magnetic force stronger than anything I'd ever felt.

The next morning, I sent her a text: "Good morning, Candice," just to let her know she was on my mind.

Jack Taylor

That day, I was headed out of town because my mom was finally going in for knee replacement surgery—a procedure that had been postponed countless times. At first, COVID caused delays. Then there was the dental work, scheduling conflicts… but today was the day. I had only mentioned it to Candice briefly in passing, not expecting her to remember.

To my surprise, I received a text from her: "Good morning! Hope all goes well with the surgery and that she has a speedy recovery."

My heart lifted. She had remembered! It wasn't even a big conversation, just something mentioned in passing. But for her to recall and check in on me… it meant the world. Sometimes, it's these small things that reveal someone's heart.

Later in the day, she reached out again: "Hope things went well for your mom today?"

Another sweet, thoughtful message from her—giving me a second glimpse into her caring nature. It was clear I wasn't wrong about her.

"Thank you! Yes, it went really well! It's amazing what they can do. The entire surgery only took an hour and a half," I replied, eager to share the good news with her.

"Wow, the whole thing?" she asked, sounding impressed.

"Yep, full knee replacement in just an hour and a half!" I confirmed.

"That's incredible."

I couldn't resist making a joke. "The next one will probably be at a drive-thru window, and she'll be able to order a milkshake with it!"

Awkward Silence

She laughed, indulging my humor. "How's she feeling?"

"She's doing great so far. You'd never know she had surgery. They say the pain won't hit for a couple of days, though." I added, "I really appreciate you asking."

In building this relationship, I've come to realize how powerful words can be—words of comfort, edification, and encouragement. I understand, to some degree, the creative force of words. After all, He created the universe by the power of His word. And in the beginning of my relationship with her, my words matched my actions. I held her close during our beer mug dance lesson, where I awkwardly led, just trying to stay near her. It wasn't about dancing perfectly—it was about connection. I'm no dancer, and she knows it, but I'd learn for her. I'd make any sacrifice just to be by her side.

But as time goes on, I find myself challenged by the subtleties of her words.

"Just like a man," she quipped one day, leaving me unsure of what to make of it.

When she introduced me to her dog, she warned, "Be careful, Bear doesn't like men."

I realized then that men had hurt her in the past. I could hear echoes of that pain as I grew closer to her. I want to be the man who changes her perspective, who helps heal those wounds, but I'm starting to feel the weight of her past experiences bearing down on us. As she instinctively pulls back, I fear that I might inadvertently reinforce her guardedness. I try to stay positive and supportive, but each time I hear something that reminds me of her hurt, I feel fragile, uncertain. The closer I get, the more I tread carefully, fearing that I'll end up fulfilling her doubts instead of dispelling them. I want to push forward, to connect, but I find myself holding back, afraid of being hurt. I'm not myself when I walk on eggshells like this, but the fear of rejection is something I'm not ready to confront.

"So, toots, how's the day?" I text her, trying to keep things light and playful. "Toots? Just trying it out for size... I don't think it works."

"Lol, maybe not in text form... It's going well," she responds, keeping things casual.

"Are we still on for tonight?" I ask, eager to spend time with her but realizing I don't have a plan yet.

"I'm exhausted... I need some rest. Tomorrow?" she replies. I can't hide my disappointment, but I know she's busy, and I respect her need for rest.

"Oh, I get it... Have a wonder-filled night. Sweet dreams!!!" I send, still feeling connected to her even through text, imagining her standing right in front of me as I type.

"Hope you have a great evening as well!" she closes the conversation.

The next morning, I wake up to a message that makes my heart skip. "Good morning, thank you for your kind words and positive thoughts. I'd really like to spend more time with you."

I was worried that she was pulling away after breaking our plans, but now she's making it clear she wants to keep seeing me.

"Awe!!! Yes, I'd like that very much!!!" I reply, unable to hide my excitement.

Awkward Silence

"And by the way, I was just watching some of your music videos and reading the writing you posted on Facebook. You're really good."

Her compliment sends a rush of warmth through me. Wow. Her words are like magic to my ears.

"Awe, thank you!!! You know, it's hard to stay modest when I'm so excited about a compliment from YOU. It truly means a lot!" I say, feeling like she's starting to see that I'm not the typical man. I'm here because I want to be, because she's the reason I want to be. But she's still unaware of the internal forces I'm battling just to stay here, to stay vulnerable.

"I honestly believe I can play the guitar better with the confidence your compliment gave me!" I lean into this moment of connection, but I decide to reveal a little more, a confession that's been simmering inside me.

"I have a confession I'm not sure I should say... Remember Saturday, the day after the second time I stopped by? It was the Friday following my birthday... I found myself inspired to write because of you. I hope that's not too bold of a statement, considering the content." My cheeks grow hot. "It was, well, sexual in nature. Of course, I pulled scenes from movies and past experiences, but after that beer mug dance lesson... the inspiration was alive. I hope that isn't too forward. I really mean it as a compliment, as an unveiling of truth. Like I said when we first met, I want to learn everything about you. I feel a little embarrassed that my imagination leapt forward like that, but I don't know why I feel the need to tell you this." My face is bright red, and I can feel the heat of it. But that's okay. I want her to know that, yes, I desire her in every way. I don't want that message to get lost in the process. The fact that I'm blushing shows I'm alive, that I'm not some desensitized guy who expresses sexual desire without thought.

This is different—this desire is layered with something deeper, something that yearns for more than just fleeting passion.

"I'm absolutely flattered," she replies. "That makes me smile. And I'm glad you shared that with me. Thank you. My confession is that I'm starting to really like a lot about you. I like your passion, your protectiveness... and not to mention, I find you very attractive." Her words reach me like a symphony, striking every chord of hope.

"I want to see you soon!!! The anticipation of seeing you again is stirring in me and leaving me breathless!" I admit, feeling my eagerness rising.

"My crazy schedule..." she begins, explaining her packed weekdays and limited free time. "I work Monday to Friday, 8-5. Tuesdays are my long days. Then there's the shop, kids, homework, dinner, chores... but I can usually get away Thursday evenings. Weekends are better. I don't have to wake up early— unless, of course, the kids are sick, projects are due, yard work needs to be done, or I just need a day in bed, lol."

Her busy life only makes me admire her more. I can hear her voice as I read every word. "I, despite my anxious desire to see you, am very patient... but, in the same shortness of breath, today and tomorrow *are* the weekend... Just saying," I tease, my heart full of hope.

"I'm going to try to get away this evening... I just have to help my son with a book report and finish laundry. After that, I'll see what I can do."

She's amazing.

"If you can get away, I would love to see you!!!" I reply, holding onto the possibility.

"Okay, I'll let you know," she texts back.

"I like your adventurous spirit, your spunkiness, and your commitment to the people around you," I tell her. "I love the glimpse I've gotten of your sense of humor, and I admire how much people seem to enjoy being around you. I like how intelligent you are and how you can hold a great conversation. And more than anything, I like how I feel when I'm around you—or even when I text you. You make me want to step out of my comfort zone. You've seen me dance, so you know I'm not good at it," I joke. "But I wasn't dancing to impress you. I just wanted to be near you. I'm going to take a nap, but I hope to talk with you later! And of course, I find you very attractive too!!!" I close the conversation, always wanting to leave her with something positive, something that sets the tone for more connection in the future.

I'm hopeful. Hopeful that we've turned a corner, that I'm no longer seen as a threat but as someone worth getting closer to.

"I'll let you know, possibly around 8... but I'll confirm," she replies.

The mention of time feels like positive assurance.

Chapter 3
The Ambush of Insecurity

1st Samuel 9:21 "Saul didn't feel qualified to be king and he hid the day of his coronation."

"Feed yourself with security and let no one poison it."

The night was wonderful, and I just can't stop thinking about it! She is amazing! But the cataclysmic events that followed our encounter opened a portal, through which raging demons—my insecurities—have climbed. These insecurities are rushing into the natural world. I am now in conflict with myself, as an internal war begins to corrupt the purity of my heart. The dating climate today is rooted in instant gratification, but if I'm being true to myself, I believe that dating should be about building a relationship based on serenity, kindness, and trust. I showed no patience and gave in to the temptations of lust.

Relationships should be enjoyed as an adventure. There's no need to rush to the finish line. There are so many wonderful experiences to share, both as a couple and as a family. With the right attitude, life can become a journey of mystery and excitement—filled with activities like hiking, fishing, concerts, and travel. The imagination opens up new possibilities every day. There's no legitimate reason to become stagnant. Even marriage isn't the end of the journey.

Being with her was a transcendental experience. I felt our souls collide in a mystical encounter. It feels like a part of me has left to live within her. My breath is short, and I feel lightheaded, as if my endorphins are taking my heart on a wild ride, pounding in my chest like the feet of a stampede slamming against the ground. I really dig her. She turns me on. Yet, instant gratification weakens the concept of a lasting commitment. It weakens the bond, taking away the focus on the long term and parking it in the short-term. The key to building a lasting relationship is thinking long-term, and I believe this is why divorce rates are so high. All I know is that if the past predicts the future, I've messed up in a big way.

Instant gratification is not the path to paradise. Sin invites darkness to creep in. Insecurities, born from slanderous whispers, slither out from beneath the lily pads, causing a detour from life's original plan. Finding a rattlesnake under a lily pad is unexpected—but it has to be a rattler because the rattle is the distraction before the strike. It's the temptation that diverts us from a life of wholeness and holiness, diminishing the potential for a life filled with mystery and excitement.

What weighs heavily on my mind is that I'm not setting myself apart from any other guy who wants to be with her. I'm not distinguishing myself from the men who have hurt her in the past. I'm not building trust. I'm not keeping my eyes on Jesus, and either the water is rising, or I'm sinking. I can't dwell on this. What's done is done. I'm committed, even if she's not ready to take that leap. I made that choice when I slept with her. My integrity isn't worth a plum nickel if I don't follow through on that decision with a commitment to her. The truth is, that commitment is ultimately to God. He loves her with a love that surpasses all understanding, and He's made that abundantly clear to me, even if she doesn't realize it. That alone is reason enough for my unwavering commitment.

Still, I'm in awe of our night together! But experience is like a Q-tip—it has a variety of uses.

"Good morning beautiful!!! Today may be a short day for me!!! We need the sun to shine to do some testing and it doesn't look like we're gonna get that!!! As I go through the day I'm going to hold you close in my thoughts!!! I feel a little like Gomez Adams and the French, speak French to me thing because every time I say

21

hold you close or cuddle I'm stimulated!!! Is that a strange thing to say? Anyway, I am going to hold you close in my thoughts!!! There I go again… seriously, have a fantastic day!!!" That is ridiculous banter. I am trying way too hard.

"Good morning hope you have a wonderful day. Been thinking about you too.."

A tiny sprout is breaking through the earth's crust, where the seed of desperation was planted. In this field, these words are taking root, and the tree is beginning to grow. Soon, the background will fill in—a brushstroke of information forming her very essence through the lights shining from the backdrop. Behind the tree are memories, like distant, smoking factories bombed in an act of war. The picture is unclear, the backdrop blurry, but one thing stands out above all else: she is the flame that has ignited my soul and is leading me out of the cul-de-sac corridor where I've been stuck, lost in a maze of false beliefs.

This maze in my mind was created in my youth. The walls are built from false beliefs—about the world around me, about the spiritual world, and about myself. Every failure I've experienced reinforces those beliefs, affirming their original existence. Any success that challenges them is quickly quashed through self-sabotage. These walls are deceptions, disguised as truths. And here I am, stuck as a hostage to these lies, which perpetuate themselves and make me a liar. I know this maze is, in some way, a coping mechanism, but it has kept me trapped for decades.

I've been so hungry for someone real. Now I'm catching feelings like you might catch a fever or a cold—it comes with nausea, dizziness, and cold sweats, or it strikes with a heart-pounding intensity. I couldn't decipher the jungle-drum beat of my heart. Was it a warning shot from another tribe across the plains? Was it my heart communicating with hers? Or was it something simpler? I don't know why I make everything so complicated. To reconcile this overthinking, I lean on one simple answer: I believe in love at first sight.

This analytical thinking clings to the edge of every cliff, rappelling down with each twist and turn of cognition. It's like a winding road created by the slithering tongue of a snake, bringing confusion to the simplest of topics. You take the limited information you have, dissect it, turn it in every direction, and still try to complete the puzzle, even with pieces missing.

The blurry outline of her silhouette gives me little definition of who she is, but insight is another matter. I know her through my own reactions in her presence. I know I'm home. She represents the world to me—she holds that level of importance, and now I understand why. I'm finally ready to face myself. I'm ready to heal. I'm ready to put away childish ways and become a man. But being ready in desire doesn't make it so, and I don't even know where to begin. My insecurities are rummaging through the walls of false beliefs, trying to concoct a potion of destruction. Like so many in today's world, I never had the role model I needed to truly understand what it means to be a man. I've been acting—observing the strengths and weaknesses of those who raised me—and though I hold nothing against them, I know I need to do better. And she has inspired me to become a better man.

I fear that my perception of reality may be distorted. Two trains are on the same track, heading toward each other. I close my eyes—I can't bear to watch the collision. It's enough to know it's happening, and there's not a damn thing I can do to stop it. My insecurities are popping my own balloons while inflating the next one too much. My authenticity is trapped between a facade of false beliefs, buried beneath the ore of grief. It's tortured, deformed, and when it comes out of my mouth, it's filtered and disconnected. I don't even know who I am anymore. The masks I've worn hide the lies I've told. The last person I want to introduce her to is myself.

Jack Taylor

I've been living with this version of me for so long, and I'm painfully aware that once my insecurities show their ugly faces, I can't regain my composure. I can sense things that most people wouldn't. This gift—or curse—comes from childhood trauma. But right now, I don't want to face this problem. In its purest form, it's a gift, but it has the potential to cause an avalanche in the Mojave Desert. It's a pure gift until the trauma tightens its grip on my mind, wringing it out like a sponge in a death grip.

They say confession is good for the soul, but it's hard to see that before the words leave your mouth. Humility always seems to get stuck in the throat. Confessing a lie feels humiliating. I didn't lie as part of some con or manipulation—I lied because I'm afraid of rejection. If I show my authentic self, I'm a likable person. Those who truly know me actually adore me. But those aren't the voices I hear when I lay my head down at night. Instead, I hear the shouting, screaming, terrifying voices of the demons that haunt Jansen Avenue. The sin clouding my conscience is heavy with remorse.

Trying to control how she perceives me is wrong. She caught a few glimpses of my authenticity before fear took over. She actually saw me more clearly than anyone ever has in my life. If the planets had aligned in that brief moment, just as the sun was setting, and that flash of authenticity had appeared, it would have affirmed God's divine plan. My true self is trying to break through the hardened layers of lava. It's a struggle to keep myself buried under the ash and dust. I want to know her, and I want her to know me—but I don't even know who I am. I'm so buried beneath the rubble that all I can hope for is a miracle. Beneath the charismatic showman, I'm a mess. If she could see my soul in the natural world, it might look like a man lying in the aftermath of a natural disaster or war zone, with my parts and pieces scattered everywhere.

Awkward Silence

I've learned that she owns a wine shop, a little beer and wine bar. That she enjoys history. That her grandmother was a bit strict with her, especially when it came to charm school training. I listen with the intent of learning everything there is to know about her. We connect because we're both compassionate, generous, smart, strong, and courageous—but I'm still plagued by the demons of my past.

I'm starting to hear the voices of self-sabotage, those self-destructive "blue orbs." It's not literal—I just mean I'm becoming more alert to the warnings of my behavior, things I seem unable to control. I try too hard, or I get too concerned and worried about how I appear. These are habitual responses, signs that my insecurities are about to strike. It's like watching all the birds take flight because a predator is near.

Her eyes reveal that she's endured pain. There's been an outward cry for the supernatural reach of God. I wish I could absorb some of that pain. I want to be a light in her world. But something shifted in my perspective—I think it happened the first moment I saw her.

This universe is not real. I should just pull the pin and let the anti-matter fall away.

There's a powerful urge to give in to the "blue bastards" of self-sabotage, but an even stronger force behind me pushing me to climb back up—to resurrect what has died within me. The desire for revival is stronger than anything I've ever felt. I will no longer be the person I've been. I can't just pull the pin and let the anti-matter fall away. I can't walk away—she means too much to me. I'm filled with hope, motivation, and a drive to change my world and make things right.

She has a way of filling me with anticipation. She seems to be offering subtle hints—the keys to her heart. I have to get control of the feelings of boastfulness, jealousy, and envy. While I haven't acted on these darker emotions, I can feel them bubbling up, ready to cross into the physical world.

A glass is raised to those lips—those lips I must kiss. The subtle nuances of unspoken romance magically dance in the resonant tones of the soft music filling the room. The flowery aroma and the way her face glows in the flickering candlelight are almost more than I can bear. Yes, I have to kiss those lips! The smooth texture of her skin, and the way her braided hair rests flawlessly along her neckline and upper chest, is stunning. Her eyes are locked on mine. My breath catches, and my heart pounds in anticipation of that kiss. The nectar of the vineyard swirling in our glasses sets the tone for romance—wine might just be the spirit of romance itself!

There we are, and my lips are upon her skin. I used my teeth to lower her zipper, just as I had imagined. The uncontrollable thoughts that begin to take over are like flies in August—annoying and impossible to ignore. I shoo them away, but less than a second later, they're back in my face. They're not crippling, just a nuisance—until I start swinging at them, not knowing what might get broken in the process.

Thoughts of pride lay faithless in the pools of molten lava that are my emotions, fueled by wounds that were never acknowledged or healed. It's a thought born from the overwhelming fear that shakes the ground beneath me. Instead of asking her if she needs help with something, I take control, overshadowing her with my swollen male ego.

This fear is the dragon that lives within me. The dragon sits on a throne in a room of my mind, shouting blasphemous words— words of destruction, discouragement, and distrust. In this banquet hall, he feasts on words that steal, kill, and destroy. The irony is that within me is where the enemy perpetuates strategies to pull me away from experiencing heaven on earth. It's telling me to take flight. It's a fight or flight situation. Part of me wants to run for her sake. I've already begun to separate myself from authenticity because of my insecurities. All the historical relics of my life begin to scream at me, and I somehow know she won't like my authentic self. I want to run, but I can't bring myself to do it. The first look into her eyes made me too attached to run. So, I start lying to her about who I am. I boast and exaggerate my accomplishments. The guilt from my deceptions begins to eat away at me, making my communication feel strange. She isn't even in this room of deception, but I'm trying to drag her in while simultaneously pushing her out.

"Do you think that you can support me and my boys?"

I'm not a wealthy man, but I make over 100k a year. I don't live in poverty, but I don't have anything to show for it either. I give away more than I spend. I know there are deeply buried monsters that have been twisting my priorities. I can't solve the problems of the homeless. I can't fix the world's issues, but if I'm not trying, I can't look at myself in the mirror. I'm already having trouble looking at myself as it is. I led her to believe I have more than I do. I lied to her, and no matter how I try to soften the confession, there's no excuse or justification. My narrow mind shortens my response. I can't see past the financial aspect of the question, and my arrogance speaks up, "Of course!" If my arrogance would just calm down, I'd have considered the question more carefully. I would have said something more like... "I don't know. I am willing but what would you need from me." No matter what her needs are I am willing.

It is the words of my own inadequacies that I must confront to drive out fear. Protecting her from the dragon means overcoming the beast that lives within me. I will do everything in my power to shield her from my boasting, lies, and arrogance, but that animal is already rabid. In the tree of my dream, where I first saw her silhouette, I saw a dragon hovering over her. I wanted to save her, but I realized it was just a dream, filled with illusions.

The feel of her lips as I kiss them takes me away to distant places. There is nothing more real, more beautiful, more satisfying than that. Ah, shucks, I could crawl into a cast iron stove. I'm so pathetic!!!

Chapter 4
Deafening Silence

Mark 9:34 "The silence was deafening- they had been arguing with one another..."

"Dark things hide in disguise and silence is just another way of masking."

We are in her wine bar, deliberating on who is going to break the rack. Candice has owned this place for about three years, and she's grown it into something special. I'm proud of her efforts. She and I share a similar adventurous spirit. When I opened the music store, I approached it the same way. I pointed the skis down the mountain with no idea how to navigate them, but I knew I would figure it out. She started with a building that used to be a mechanic's shop, a garage. She had walls built, a bar top installed, and a rough but inviting decor. She even bought a pool table so that we can find ourselves here, debating who's going to break the rack.

Then he walked in, like a whirlwind of arrogance that could be mistaken for confidence if you weren't paying attention to the dilation of his pupils. He made gesture after gesture as I sat there, in disbelief, unable to react. One gesture was particularly inappropriate. As he squatted down to put quarters in the pool table, he turned his face toward her zipper as Candice walked by. I would have liked to defend her, but jealousy raged inside me. I just wanted her to give me that sign, that go-ahead, but when she didn't, I was stuck. I heard his words, each one violating my trust. He made sure I heard every single word. He spoke about a rendezvous he planned with the woman—the woman I was beginning to fall for.

I would have considered it an honor if she trusted me to defend her. That's my duty as a man in a relationship. I would

29

never have violated that trust. I would have simply asked him to step aside so we could talk. I would have asked him to treat her with the respect she deserves. We would have come back in as friends. I know it would have required a lot of trust in me, not to overreact and turn it into a physical altercation. This is the moment when I realize I am more invested in this relationship than she is. Since she didn't ask me to handle it, all I could do was remind myself that she didn't belong to me. I had no claim.

I've never thought of a woman as something to claim. I've always believed that in a relationship, you honor each other, and it naturally grows together. Of course, I've never had great success in relationships. But I've also never faced a challenge like this. I tried to control the turmoil now spinning in my head. I felt my heart sinking into the lava that's always simmering beneath the surface. Those would have been my tears, if men could cry and if I hadn't been hardened by life's events. But my tears still lie deep beneath the surface.

The dragon breathes out the flame from its nostrils, and agony cries out in pain. As the smoke clears just enough, I catch a glimpse of the dragon's underbelly. It's unmistakable, and all logic shatters like a giant among dwarfs. It becomes inarguable that, since the injuries have always been so close to the surface, the boy must still be near the flames. Not only do I see him, but now I begin to feel the fear—fear that is certainly the remnants of smoldering debris. It's like the smoking factories with their bright lights, revealing the dragon overhead. For a moment, it feels as if the chains of discouragement are tightening around my chest. I am frozen in time, unable to put a word on the page. But this is not the time to remain immobile. This is the instant that will define the outcome:

Flashes of memories from our first encounter appear before my eyes. I was captured. I was intrigued. I couldn't stop my thoughts from spilling out of my mouth. It was the moment when I could no longer consider my heart as mine. The bells, whistles, and sirens were cranked up to level 10, the speakers ready to blow. Something is happening. It's completely internal. There's a war raging, and I have to subdue the outward desolation.

"She did nothing wrong. In fact, she did everything to bring me comfort. I am out of control." I try to cast reason upon how I am feeling.

The light bounces off the obstacles in the room like a pinball off bumpers. It picks up fragments of color, dispersing them as a radiant glow. Yet, that glow is stifled by a shifting fog that clings to my attention like a leech. This fog obscures the light, consuming it with darkness. Thoughts perpetuate through the storm, appearing symmetrical in the absence of light, making a kind of sense.

There seems to be some logic, but it lacks integrity. It lacks sound moral judgment. When placed in the company of love, these thoughts become confused. Shame, guilt, bitterness, and fear slither away from the attributes of love. The tattered response of the teenager following the child's reaction indicates that I am weighed down by the shame of the disgraceful actions imposed upon me. The shame was worn like a cloak, ripped and frayed, as I dragged it along on my belly. I have never felt so opposed to logic, nor have I been so conflicted in my heart. Who am I that she should trust me with such a heavy responsibility—to defend her? That would mean trusting me with her heart. The turmoil is harrowing, ripping me to shreds. The confetti left behind is the shrapnel, lodged and displaced with the remnants of other memories.

I should have spoken to the school nurse when she measured the bruises. I should have spoken up. I should advocate for myself. But after that, it becomes incredibly difficult to even glance in the mirror, let alone hold a gaze. The shame that grips me feels like a self-deprecating burden. I feel as if I have no backbone, and so I slither. I am still the emotional child, now stunted in the behaviors of my early teens. I am tortured by the loss of my innocence. I know nothing of love. I only know the curse of shame. "Upon your belly you shall go, and dust shall you eat all the days of your life."

The pulse of the room and its surroundings cause my mind to wander, searching for something. As I gaze at the relics around me, a realization hits. I look at the license plates hanging in configurations, questioning their truth or lack thereof. I see the writing on the wall and it reminds me of the biblical story of Daniel. I notice things I had never noticed before—artifacts of a dark time. And it dawns on me that I am sitting in the manifestation of her inner world. I am in her mind. I am in her soul. I recognize both its beauty and its hardships.

I widen my thoughts to encompass her entire world—the one she has created. I think of the implications of this world. It could be said of every bar across America, yet there is something calling out from within this place. I can't quite put my finger on it, but I feel it, as if it grew from trauma. The faint, undisclosed relics confirm the presence of that trauma. In this moment, I am learning more than she may want me to know. Then again, maybe I've lost touch with reality. There is nothing here that is overtly personal, yet everything feels deeply personal. I am undeniably connecting to something that screams from within, but perhaps it's just me who is dislodged. It might have nothing to do with the relics or the decor. Maybe I'm simply at my breaking point.

I remember again the words that spewed from my mouth the day I met her, "I want to learn everything there is to know about you." I haven't stopped learning.

Awkward Silence

I consider the castle and the sweet princess trapped inside, with the dragon as her guard. It makes me realize how she has become a prisoner of this circumstance. It's a coping mechanism. She has locked herself in her fortress, guarded and, in many ways, discontent with the life she has created. Yet, it offers her comfort as an escape from the pains of reality. Here, she has control—and she must exercise that control, which points to a time of trauma and complete lack of control. This suggests that the inciting incident happened early in her life, but her rebelliousness speaks of a teenager thrown into an adult world. There have been multiple instances of trauma, and the first one set the mindset that normalized tragic behavior.

I sense that much of our communication comes from this deep, spiritual place she is hesitant to share. She has created this divine fortress that gives her a sense of control. She still connects to the violations, but now she holds the power to determine the outcome. It's her way of reclaiming power. However, she's stuck, reliving the transgression every day, which keeps her trapped within these walls. She's unsettled. There is no peace, and because of that, everything feels like a battle.

In my mind, I gather the evidence that reinforces the similarities between us. We're not that different, her and I. Now, as I reflect on my dream, I know what I must do: I have to save her from the dragon. I won't leave her in this endless curse. The cherubim have lifted their flashing swords enough for me to glimpse the life that was meant for us. I can see the tree of life, and I know what I must do!

The bells are still ringing in my ears. Time has stood still through these observations. I flash back to my youth, and the enemy artillery begins firing again. The sounds of bazookas and machine guns rage through my mind. The blood-colored tiles on the checkered floor, the stench of rotting flesh, are burned into my memory. The fruit cellar and the hand that forcefully covered my mouth, leaving bruises on my face, haunt me still. "You say a word and your a dead man," were the words piercing my flesh. The dirty sock that was stuffed in my mouth to mute my cries still lingers with the taste in my mouth. The music of Black Sabbath, turned up loud enough to drown out any sound I could make, plays violently in my head. Everything from my past is projected in my mind like a horror movie.

I stand here, unable to respond to this man's disrespectful behavior. I saw it — him trying to press his face against the zipper of her pants. I felt the event in my chest. My blood boiled, but I couldn't respond. No acceptable response came to mind.

"Why aren't you talking tonight?"

My emotions stay hidden behind walls of stone. I just cannot respond. They want to step forward, but they get caught in the flypaper of memories. The hand covering my mouth squeezes so tightly that it bruises my cheeks — the same hand that once left bruises on my face. "You say a word and you're a dead man," I am defensive and hurt, but I have no way to convey what's going on inside of me with a healthy demeanor. Disoriented, I struggle to maintain my balance, which only causes me to react in ways that are uncalled for. Instead of letting it go, I grabbed onto her to assert dominance. Animal instinct took over unexpectedly. I think, if I could have justified it, I might have marked my territory with urine.

I feel helpless and vulnerable to my emotions. Vulnerability shakes me to my core, throwing me out of balance so easily. Normally, I become apathetic, but the problem is I am not numb. In this moment, I am feeling a lifetime of emotion all at once. I've opened my heart, and there's no way to seal the door again. Emotions are shifting the alignment of every cell and fiber of my body. My thoughts are racing so rapidly that it's impossible to hold onto just one. My life is flashing before my eyes. This is the moment that will define me. This exact second will determine my future happiness. It's a momentous time, a declaration. This is the split second when I must decide whether or not I'm worth taking the steps to heal from my past. Inspiration has struck me with a force beyond my control. I have no choice but to heal. I must reconfigure the shattered remnants that lead a life of apathy. I have to stitch back together my identity and purpose. The images flash before me quickly, seemingly at random. I see myself with Snowball. There's a flash, and I'm running through a forest. The songs of heaven ring in my ears. A tear is ready to fall, but all I can do is stand here in awkward silence.

Chapter 5
Thicker than a Milkshake

Mathew 18:3 "Except ye be converted and become as little children, ye shall not enter into the kingdom of heaven."

"Before a problem can be solved it must be clearly identified and understood."

The beginning of my life, from an outward view, would present itself as typical. I have a mom, a dad, and an older sister. I have a family that loves me— aunts, uncles, and cousins who delight in me. It seems like the entire world loves me. I have been blessed. When I walk to the store with my mom, every stranger we pass becomes an unplanned opportunity to reinforce a positive belief in my identity. I am happy and free to explore the world.

"He is so adorable, look at those eyes." One stranger after another affirms and reaffirms that God made me adorable.

"Thank you!" I have grown quite comfortable with this routine.

"Wow, even your voice is adorable."

"Thanks."

My imagination is vivid. I'm aware that there isn't much distance between imagination and reality. God made me very creative— maybe even a little top-heavy when it comes to creativity. In fact, my reality is just a few shakes and a hiccup away from my imagination.

Awkward Silence

In the world I live in, angels are as common as regular folk. The whole world seems lit up by the fluttering vibrations of their wings. There is nothing I want more in my daily life than to hear the voice of God, and I did. He spoke directly into my heart. I had an abundance of joy, and I tried to spread it.

"Mom, guess what?" I run through the entry door.

"What?" she asks, standing by the ironing board, getting ready for her morning workout as she presses the iron over the clothes.

"God said you should treat me to a MoonPie!"

"Oh, He did, did He? I thought I told you not to use God like that." It doesn't sound like I'm going to get that MoonPie.

"He did, though," I say, disappointed.

"I'm going to get you one this time because your imagination is..."

"Thicker than a milkshake," I finish, repeating what I'd just heard the Holy Spirit say. I think He's protecting me from whatever harsh words might have come out of her mouth next.

She tries many times to quash my imagination. It's not out of malice; she's just so tied to a carnal reverence for God. She's Mormon, and I don't think they see God for who He truly is. They can't see that He is joyful and playful. They lost me at an early age with the near-legalism of their faith. Their belief that Jesus is Satan's brother almost makes it seem like you have to go through Satan to get to know Jesus when it's framed that way. Reverence and fear of the Lord is important to my faith. However, that fear is mantled with love and it is that love that is the focus of my relationship with the Father and it is the relationship that I have with the Father that should be emulated in all of my relationships. This is not meant to be a jab at Mormonism. My view becomes tainted in Minnesota by those that call themselves Mormons but punish me without cause and without love. And still I know that my relationship with God is not determined by who I choose to fellowship with. That fellowship or the church I attend is not the set of rules that gets me into heaven. My relationship with God is the key. I am certain with this notion that there are many that are in fellowship within the Mormon church that know this truth.

The incarnation of my inventiveness causes me to see God more as the Creator than as any of His other amazing qualities. When He takes on the role of the Healer, I view His healing through the lens of His creative power. In my mind, His identity as the Creator distinguishes Him as the ultimate Healer. I believe God to be the creator of all that exists, and my mindset is such that if He didn't create it, it doesn't exist. In His perfect work as the Creator, He did not create disease. Therefore, disease is merely a lie that seeks to discredit His role as Creator. It's a deception passed down through generations, so convincing that it requires the keen sight of an eagle to discern how the message is spread. I tread carefully with these words. I would never suggest that someone who is ill shouldn't seek medical help if they believe that's what they need to do.

There is a correlation between reality and imagination, and most certainly, one influences the other. Reality is not a one-way street. My perception is different from yours because our experiences are different. We can close the shades and turn off the lights, but the truth will likely shift both of our realities toward a more centered perspective.

This is the time in my life when I'm reconnecting with my true identity. I believe my true identity is who I was created to be before the carnal influences of the world corrupted and tainted my view. This is who I am returning to. I don't want to be a rock star. I don't want to be the know-it-all who has all the answers. I just want to be the compassionate child who sheds a tear for the injured sparrow.

I want to see all of humanity through the same lens I'm using at this moment in my life. I'm not sure if that means looking through filters or removing them entirely. Sometimes, I catch glimpses of it. I see a person of any age, and I can't see beyond their innocence. In those moments, that person has the power to destroy me because I can't perceive them in any other light. I just want to make mud pies, fly kites, and play laser tag with them.

There are other sources that directly influence both your imagination and your perception of the real world. Love provides balance to all things, bridging the gap between imagination and reality. If love is jeopardized, ego becomes inflamed. Ego can stand at the threshold, obstructing a clear view in either direction. As I focus on reconnecting with my true identity, I remember how love used to pour out of me.

If these attributes—imagination, creativity, compassion, love—are truly who I am beneath the sin and darkness I will soon inherit, then I finally know what I want to be when I grow up. God made me imaginative, creative, compassionate, loving, courageous, strong, generous, protective, and passionate. God made me amazing, but by my actions, I nearly destroyed His good work. Thanks to love, I might be able to reclaim that title.

"Come on, hunting dog. We've got to tell everyone the good news," I say as I gallop down the sidewalk with my toy poodle, Snowball. Snowball has been my faithful hunting dog for as long as I can remember. Considering that I'm three years old, that memory might only span a couple of days or weeks.

Jack Taylor

I lead Snowball into the unlit forest where the bears and tigers live. We are cautious but brave as we proceed on our hunt. I crawl on my belly into the cave, where I encounter the bear for the first time.

"Be careful, Snowball. He's ferocious!" A funny thing about me is that my voice has never changed— even as a three-year-old, I speak in a deep man's tone.

The bear is about the size of one of the trucks at my grandma's trucking company. I go there on weekends with my dad to help him fix the trucks. When I get worn out from all that tough labor, you'll likely find me asleep on the capital H— a concrete block shaped, as you might guess, like a capital letter H.

One of this bear's claws is bigger than Snowball's entire body. He swings at Snowball, but Snowball is quick and agile. The bear charges at me, and I know I won't be able to defend myself unless I can leap over him and attack from behind. As he rushes toward me, I jump, and he passes right under my feet. Now I'm on his back. I pull out my cardboard saber and drive it into the ground an inch away from his head.

"Now you listen here, bear. I don't ever want to see you around here again. You've been mean to all the other animals, and you're no longer welcome. Get out!"

When I reflect on my life from a prophetic perspective, I can see that the bear represents evil. I recognize myself as a protector who has compassion even for my enemies, and I see victory.

It was a successful hunt. Snowball and I dance our victory dance all the way back to the house. I see the neighbor lady watering her lawn. I pick her some dandelion flowers. She's special to me; I see her out here every day, caring for her yard and flowers. I don't know her name, but I'm sure she'll appreciate the flowers.

"These are for you," I say, feeling my cheeks warm. There's something about giving flowers to a woman that makes me blush every time, and this time is no different—the feeling just wants to burst out of my chest.

"Oh, aren't you the sweetest little guy! Be careful, though, you might make my husband jealous!" She smiles, and I grin back before continuing on my way.

"Come on, hunting dog! We've got to tell everyone the good news!" I say, and once again, there's a gallop in my step and joy in my heart.

I have an invisible friend, as many children my age do, but this friend is soon to become my little brother. I'm three years old, and the invisible friend I'm telling you about is named Mark.

Mark and I do all sorts of things together. We climb Mount Everest, rappel down the Rockies, dig our way to China, and even build a leaning tower. We are inseparable, as you might imagine. But soon, Mark will be visible. That's part of the good news I'm supposed to tell everyone. The other part, He said, I'll understand when I'm older.

After all our adventures, Mark, Snowball, and I have worked up quite an appetite. You wouldn't believe how exhausting it is to dig all the way to China.

"Mom, can me and Mark have a cookie?" I ask as I burst through the front door. It's the front door now, but just a little while ago, it was the entrance to Tiny's Saloon, where I had a gunfight earlier. It's been a busy day.

"Jackie, how would you like a little brother or sister?" Mom asks, handing me a cookie.

"It wouldn't be fair if you didn't give Mark one too. After all, he's going to be my brother," I say, quite matter-of-factly.

"Is Mark going to eat it, or are you?" she asks with a smile.

"I told you, Mark can't eat right now because it would fall right through him, but he still wants to be part of this family," I explain earnestly. I'm not trying to manipulate her—I believe every word I'm saying.

"What if it's a little sister?" Mom questions my certainty about Mark becoming my brother.

"It's not, it's Mark! I already have a sister," I reply, defending my belief.

"I'm pregnant! You're going to have a baby brother or sister!" she says, trying to contain her excitement.

"What does pregnant mean?" I ask, unfamiliar with the word.

"It means I have a baby in my tummy," she says, rubbing her belly.

"That's more good news to share!" I exclaim, feeling an overwhelming urge to sing.

"Jackie, stop. What other good news do you have?" she asks, amused.

"First, Jesus came to see me, and now Mark is coming—just like Jesus said," I explain, filled with excitement. She tolerates my vivid imagination. To her, everything I say comes from my imagination, but she's blissfully unaware that I've been given a gift.

"Jesus?" she asks, a little surprised.

"Yeah, Jesus! He's the guy who visited me today," I say, beaming.

"A guy visited you?" She reaches out to adjust the brim of my baseball cap.

"Yep!"

Mark may have shuffled my priorities a little. Before I found out I was going to have a baby brother, Jesus was the absolute only thing on my mind. Well, that and the bear and the leaning tower.

"He told me to share the good news! He told amazing stories, and the stories came to life."

"What stories?" Mom asks, dismissing it all as part of my imagination.

"The cloud shaped like a boy and his dog flew by, just like He described."

"Mark walked into you like Casper the ghost walks through walls," I add, not quite sure how to explain it all.

I didn't see Jesus again for a long time after that day. The truth is, I'm not sure if I've seen Him since, but I now see evidence of Him all around me every day. We talk, and sometimes He tells me stories that later come true. I share them when I can, though there were blockages for a long time that made it hard to hear Him. But now, many of those obstacles have been removed, and I can hear Him again.

"Jackie, what should we name your little brother?" Mom asks.

"I told you, his name is Mark!" It's like they're not even listening to me.

Mark was born, and I had an amazing little brother! But I no longer had an imaginary friend named Mark.

Chapter 6
River of Gold

Psalm 119:105 "Thy word is a lamp unto my feet and a light unto my path."

"I'm on the top of the world looking down on creation but falling rapidly."

The colors move with an ebb and flow, like the choreographed grace of a professional ballet. Water shoots up as if through the blowhole of a killer whale. A ball flies swiftly over the net from the fingertips of a beautiful young woman, bouncing from one pair of hands to another. The motion of the ball mirrors the snap of a bikini. Inflatable animals float like rafts, drifting lazily on the water. Miniature dunes form as sandals dig into the sand, flipping it up with each step. All this commotion sends sound waves rippling through the air, nearly drowning out the music playing in the background. The breeze is a fresh breath sweeping across the surface of the water.

A familiar woman lies on a beach towel, soaking up the sun. She's the one who wakes me up every morning with that rhythmic knock on the door, "shave and a haircut, two bits." Her willingness to fix me breakfast far exceeds my mom's. My mom sleeps well into the afternoon, making her difficult to wake. If I expect breakfast from her, I'll go hungry. But Karen, just a short walk across the street, is always willing.

Shandon and Kristi are busy building sandcastles, but Steve notices us. These are Karen's kids. None of them had any idea we'd show up, and as I size up the situation, I'm certain they'd have bet their lives against us pulling into that parking lot. My dad is likely the most surprised of all by our arrival. Like I said, Karen is willing, and it's just a short trip across the street.

45

Jack Taylor

I watch as my mom rushes out of the car, kicking up sand and destroying micro dunes in her wake. A bikini top clutched tightly in her hand leaves Karen exposed, her hair coming out in fistfuls. Before I can even get out of the car, I see my dad tearing the two women apart. As they race back to the car, my mom leads, followed closely by my dad. All of this activity is almost overwhelming for a six-year-old boy.

"Jackie, you're the man of the house now. Take care of your mom."

Yeah, way to go, Dad—offloading your responsibilities onto your six-year-old son. Sarcasm courses through my veins like tadpoles swimming upstream to reach an egg. I'm confused, both in my thoughts and emotions. These were the last words my dad spoke to me as my father. After that, I became a visitor in his home during the summer months.

When he spoke those words, it felt like the universe was created. It was tantamount to God saying, "Let there be light." For all intents and purposes, my dad's words might as well have been spoken by God Himself. He was my hero. His words created a new reality for me, opening up the heavens and revealing a world I hadn't known could exist. I was now the man of the house, responsible for my mom's safety and well-being. Wrap your head around that. Protecting her honor became my daily habit. I had a duty to shield her from enemies—both real and imagined. I felt obligated to provide comfort, to free her from her inner demons. My new role was to sacrifice myself to the world he had created with just a few short words.

This turning point began to take shape from those ignorant words. They might have eventually faded if not reinforced. But now they loomed large in my mind, an expanse in the heavens without form. Darkness hovered over the surface of these words, but actions soon solidified them.

Awkward Silence

"Who do you want to live with? Your mom or your dad?" These words echo through space and time, overloading my mind at the worst possible moment. It's the sound of bells and whistles, an overstimulation that paralyzes me. How could I possibly answer that question? If I choose one, I dishonor the other. *Honor your mother and father.* Answering feels like betrayal. Since I refuse to choose, the decision is made for me. Just a couple of months later, I find myself here.

The blooming flowers greet us at my grandparents' house. The marigolds, shining brightly, form a golden river flowing around the brim of the dwarf cottage where they live. If you watch the flowers carefully, their gentle sway will lead you to the back of the house, where they introduce you to a beautiful vegetable garden. The sweet corn stalks stand tall and dense, perfect for hiding—unless the radishes give you away. Berries dot the ground and bushes, with little red currants that make your face pucker. Hidden beneath the thorny blackberry bushes is a chicken coop. It's like having grocery store aisles in their backyard. There's a gigantic food pantry, and no one's telling me to stay out of the fridge.

Idaho is quite different from California. The mountains in the distance are majestic, their peaks illuminated by the morning sun in colors I've never seen before. Birds and squirrels seem to bring me gifts throughout the day. And at night, the sunset tucks you into bed with even more vibrant hues as it disappears behind the mountains. There's nothing more beautiful. If we hadn't just left my dad to tend to his new family, this place would be amazing—but the larger part of my heart is still with him. I'm hurting from his reckless betrayal, though I don't know how to express it. I'm just sad.

My grandparents' house could easily be the home of the seven dwarfs from *Snow White.* My grandpa isn't Dopey or

Sleepy—he's more like Happy. He doesn't work in a diamond mine; he's a chemist at a sewage treatment plant. It's not exactly the same thing, and he's not literally a dwarf—he meets the height requirements for the rides at the fair, but not by much. I've never heard him sing, but I'd pay good money to hear him belt out the "Hi Ho" song.

My grandma, Wanda, is an artist. She pours her love into everything she does. Her paintings are beautiful, her crafts are creative, but her poems are my personal favorite. Sometimes she's so corny that she makes me laugh. She's a bit divided, though— either joyful and full of cheer, or laid up in bed with a migraine, unbalanced sugar levels, or some other painful ailment. One minute she's singing corny sunshine songs, the next she's crying out for God's mercy.

Grandpa spends almost every moment outside of work in the garden. He waters each plant individually to ensure it gets exactly what it needs. He tests the pH of the soil and makes adjustments as required. He guards the plants from encroaching weeds. He raises them like his own children, pouring his love into them—and it shows. He's a good man with strong moral character.

We stay in this paradise for about a month. I miss my dad. I spoke to him on the phone a few times, but before my cousins arrived, life here was mostly peaceful. Grandma introduced me to simple crafts, and Grandpa recruited me for small garden projects. These kept my mind focused, free from the damaging clutter of thoughts.

Kippy is quiet and blends in easily, but in a charming way. Corine, Nick, and Cherie, on the other hand, bring chaos and turmoil with them. Nick wasn't around for long and is absent from this particular night of recollection.

Awkward Silence

There were just the five of us kids left after Nick's departure. But that is five kids and four adults living in this cottage, this tiny little cottage. I am amazed that there is enough oxygen to go around. Mark is two years old. Cherie and I are six. Monica and Kippy are ten. I am outnumbered three girls to one boy. We are leaving Mark out of this because he sleeps where my mom did. There are the four of us stacked up to share a room.

Tonight, once the chirps of the crickets had faded and the blanket of night fell upon us, I lay here trying to sleep. Monica and Kippy are going on and on like someone had just pumped adrenaline into their veins. They are talking like ten year old girls with curiosity about boys. The later it got the more their curiosity crept in like a slow moving fog bank. That fog began to take over the room.

"Jack, we want to see you hump Cherie." The walls are closing in. This room is not big enough for me and these three girls. Monica, my sister, says it again,

"Take off your underwear and Hump Cherie." Her curiosity is strongly over developed for a ten year old.

"Just let me go to sleep. Leave me alone!" Cherie is my cousin.

"Hump her." We are never going to get to sleep. She is a bulldog after a bone. Apparently, I have the bone. It feels like hours and hours of this shenanigans.

"Leave us alone!" I plead.

"I want to go to sleep!" I beg.

"Stop!" I insist.

"Just do it Jack, so we can get to sleep!" Cherie exclaimed.

With reluctance I mount her. I don't know what I am doing. We are naked and our privates are touching but what do they want? They took my little limp penis and rubbed it on Cherie's vagina. And that was it. We did not lose our virginity that night. We were six years old. I assure you that I remained limp but even if I would have gotten a boner the fact still remains that Cherie is only six as well.

The next morning, I wake up just in time. Today is the Snake River Stampede's buckaroo breakfast, and we're going to see Lynn Anderson sing at the rodeo tonight. I'm excited. I don't know who she is, but the thought of horses and bulls is enough to make me eager for the day. The breakfast is fun. Some of the bronco riders are here, signing stampede booklets for us kids. Overhead, a Frisbee takes flight, and an amazing dog leaps to catch it.

"Whoa! Did you see that, Grandpa? That dog jumped ten feet in the air to catch the Frisbee!" I say, brimming with excitement.

"That dog didn't jump ten feet in the air," Cherie immediately chimes in, correcting me.

"Maybe not, but he jumped so high!" I reply.

"It wasn't ten feet. Mom, that dog didn't jump up ten feet, did he?" Cherie, now determined to prove me wrong, asks her mom.

"No, that dog did not jump ten feet in the air," Corine confirms.

I'm already feeling defeated, and we've only been around them for a couple of weeks. I'm not fond of Nick. His brief visit was enough time for him to kick me in the balls several times, as if they were a soccer ball. He even gave me a new nickname—one that I hate. Corine has been relentlessly antagonistic, scolding and demeaning me every chance she gets.

"Mom, I don't think I want to go to Minnesota with them," I tell her. "You don't have a choice," she replies.

Later that night, Corine corners me in the room where us kids are sleeping. "So, you don't want to come to Minnesota with us? Just so you know, anything you say to your mom, she tells me. Do you get it? She's my sister, and that means I win," she says smugly.

I don't understand what's happening. I'm just a kid, but they take every opportunity to humiliate me. They never do it when Grandma or Grandpa are nearby, but as soon as they step away, Corine belittles me.

If my dad were here, they wouldn't get away with this. I had almost forgotten how much I miss him. Tears begin to stream down my cheeks. "Stop crying. I didn't even touch you. What is it Nick calls you? Oh yeah, Jack-a-puss. Stop crying, Jack-a-puss," Corine sneers.

"I miss my dad," I manage to say between sobs.

"You little pussy. Stop crying," she mocks again, putting her hand near my face.

Just then, I hear the back door open.

"Jackie, come give me a hand," Grandma calls from the other room. Her timing couldn't have been better. Whether she heard anything or not, she saved me.

51

Jack Taylor

The day of reckoning arrives. The marigolds and tulips wave goodbye as I climb into my aunt's station wagon, beginning the long journey to Minnesota. My dad feels so far away now—I wonder if I'll ever see him again. The trip is uncomfortable. I'm stuck in the back with the luggage, but at least it's a safe place to be. My aunt is mean, and Cherie is an instigator. I have no allies in the war zone ahead. Every one of them has alienated me, even my own mom. I overheard Corine telling her not to baby me because it would just turn me into a wimp.

2346 Jansen Ave. is the end of the line.

Chapter 7
Tears of Condensation

Psalm 56:8 "Record my misery, list my tears on your scroll; are they not in your record?"

"A dancing flame is different than a dance that ignites a flame."

It only takes two steps down the stairs to realize I am descending into the pits of hell, but it's too late to turn back. I *can't* turn back. It's not my decision—evil has entered the minds of the shot-callers. I'm scared. I can feel the presence of the evil that crept in, nesting in the wound left by betrayal and divorce. That betrayal, that sin, has swept the broom of wickedness into this stairwell. I feel the evil surging up from below, like crude oil rising from a well. I hear the devils chanting in monologue, declaring some sort of victory below.

Have you ever tried to imagine what happens in hell? The nightmares wasted on Chucky amaze me—he isn't scary at all compared to this. This is the closest I've ever been to hell. The scars from these two burning years have lasted a lifetime.

At first glance, I sense the pull from below, where the red and white checkered floor lies. The red tiles are the color of dried blood—and dried blood is exactly what comes to mind whenever I picture them. An unfamiliar odor hangs in the air, one I've never encountered in any other basement. It smells like a slaughterhouse—not the stink of animal dung—but the stench of death, decay, and raw misery.

At night, I lie awake, listening to the house wail. The vibrations of screams, absorbed by the walls during past miseries, are now released into the atmosphere. These screams send chills down my spine. Strangely, the walls shed real tears—condensation—for the victims. The horrors that occurred here are so profound that they manifest orbs and demons, convincing me this place is hell itself.

The things that happen in this basement are cruel. This is the last time I'll venture into this infernal place. What I wrote before was done with poise, minimizing the emotions by skimming over the obstacles in the room. I told my truth plainly but kept myself numb. Now, I have no intention of sparing anyone or sugarcoating anything. My purpose is therapeutic, and I will not hold back.

This isn't comfortable for me. I return to confront the enemy and reclaim everything he has stolen from me. I'm entering the promised land.

Avoidance seizes me, slinging me around like a rag doll. I can't sit still to write. The words are jumbled. "No, sir—you're out of order."

I smear ink across the pages, mindful of the circular direction of my thoughts. I scrape the words off again, trying to reverse their flow, as if I'm performing some strange ritual—wax on, wax off. These words are written in avoidance. I need to get them out, but avoidance is like Dobby from *Harry Potter*: it seems to be trying to protect me, but instead, it paralyzes me.

I lie frozen, terrified to move, as I hear footsteps descending the staircase. I fix my eyes on a knothole in a cedar plank on the wall. It seems to stare back at me. I must stay perfectly still—even the sound of my eyeballs moving could attract his attention. I want to disappear.

I know this isn't who I was created to be. And I know this isn't who Nick was meant to be, either. Yet, he has trained himself to be vicious, and it seems every thought in his head is focused on new and creative ways to torment me. Still, I believe the pictures in his mind are very different—he probably thinks he's doing me a favor, that he's toughening me up, making me a man.

Just as Nick has been trained to be vicious, I now face the same training. I hope I can resist internalizing it. I want to be kind. I want to grow up loving.

I am screaming at the top of my lungs, but you could hear a pin drop over my silence. I am crying—no, *wailing*—but you would never see a tear fall. Fear and anxiety have consumed my every thought, but if it weren't for the cuts, scrapes, and bruises, you'd never know I've been at war.

I want to resist the mindset that prevails in this house, along with all of its so-called training. There is no love here. That may be a controversial statement—others in this house might argue otherwise. But I know one thing for certain: there was never any love for me.

"Hahaha... He's coming to get you!" The demonic orbs taunt me, warning of the beating to come.

"You can't run, and you can't hide," another blue orb zips across the room, feeding the dread.

"Stand against the wall with your hands at your sides," Nick commands.

Everything in me screams that this isn't right. The muscles in my legs begin to tremble. I move to the wall, turn away from it, and back into it. The cold, damp concrete presses against my back and shoulders. Fear, once a stranger to me, now feels like a familiar companion. I remind myself, *God made me courageous.*

I stand there, hands at my sides, as Nick drives his fist into my chest with brutal force. He's aiming for the wall—but my chest just happens to be in the way. The dull thud resonates deep and painfully inside me.

"I have to do it again. Don't flinch," he says.

Another punch slams into my chest.

"You can't move, or I'll have to do it again," Nick shouts.

I don't flinch. I don't move. But the blows keep coming, fist after fist, until he is somehow satisfied. If only I could understand what brings him that satisfaction—maybe I could control it. If I'd known what was coming next, I would've flinched. I would've moved. I would've invited his dissatisfaction. I would've let him punch my chest all night to avoid what followed.

When a flame touches your flesh, there's a moment of connection—an instant that can stretch into eternity. A second divides infinitely in that space, and if you sync with this timeless moment, you might even feel the strange romance of the flame.

At first, it dances gently along my hip, tender and whispering sweetly in my ear. I don't understand its words, only that they're soft and hypnotic. The heat draws my breath, exciting my endorphins. But soon, the gentle warmth turns to searing pain. My muscles contract violently, and my heartbeat pounds in my chest as the flame digs deeper. The illusion of romance vanishes, replaced by the harsh truth: this flame never intended kindness.

It rises out of the fire, nostrils flaring and neck stretching impossibly long. A creature is forming from the flame—a beast with reddish scales, snake-like in texture. As its eyes lock onto mine, it shatters through the windows of my soul. The broken glass paves the way for the beast to enter.

Awkward Silence

It bursts into full form, overtaking the room and my mind. This may have been the moment the dragon seized control of my soul.

A scream is wrenched from deep within me, driven out past my lips by sheer pain. As the flame burrows further into my flesh, a blister rises—a wound that will scar, not just physically, but emotionally, mentally, and perhaps even spiritually.

The scream isn't just mine—it echoes across dimensions, aligning with versions of me in every alternate universe. Together, these screams form a sound so powerful it breaks every synaptic chain in existence, birthing the first black hole. As the cry tears through the barriers of time, it becomes the first of its kind—a singularity of suffering.

The instant the scream leaves my body, it implodes, sucking in all the pain of the world. But no one comes to my rescue.

My skin deformity is on my hip. No one will ever see it. The flame's path creeps closer, threatening to burn off my penis if I flinch or cry. It will remain hidden beneath the underwear I wear—underwear that is already too tight. The elastic cuts painfully into my hip, but now it will dig even deeper. Past that fleeting, dimension-shattering scream, no one would ever know I was in pain. There was only a brief window to pull me away from this dragon—a chance for rescue—and that moment has passed.

"Men don't cry."

Our spirit, made up of conscience, fellowship, and intuition, falls into jeopardy when the soul can no longer express emotions. The programming I've been fed tells me that emotions belong to women—that showing them makes a man weak. But a messenger, like a carrier pigeon, whispered a truth: repressing emotions clogs the flow of information, making fellowship with others—and with God—stagnant.

God created me for fellowship, especially with Him. He gave me a conscience to keep the pathways clear, to regulate this flow. When emotions are trapped, the drainpipe gets blocked, distorting intuition. I used to trust my female friends' intuition more than my own, thinking they had a natural gift I lacked. But I've learned that men, too, can cry—when they no longer hold back tears behind the stigma that warps the true nature of gender.

The tortures continue through the night.

At the stroke of midnight, I hear the next command:

"Jack-a-puss, say it: 'Women are nothing but a pain in the neck, thorn in the side.'"

"Women are nothing but a pain in the neck, thorn in the side," I repeat obediently.

"Again."

"Women are nothing but a pain in the neck, thorn in the side."

"Say it louder."

"Women are nothing but a pain in the neck, thorn in the side."

Over and over. My eyes start to roll back, heavy with exhaustion, but I am not allowed to stop.

"Keep repeating it."

Awkward Silence

The phrase echoes through the hours, twisting its way into my mind. I drift in and out of sleep, my head slumping forward until a fist strikes me back to awareness.

"Say it again."

"Women are nothing but a pain in the neck, thorn in the side."

I hear the clock strike three. I've been repeating this for three hours now, and the words are blurring into meaningless static.

"Repeat it."

"Women are nothing but a pain in the neck, thorn in the side."

The night drags on, the chant becoming background noise, like the hum of static on an old television screen. I am so weary that my body can no longer resist sleep. Finally, at six in the morning, I am given permission to stop.

The tortures never truly end—they just become the background hum to my existence. Bruises are measured, cataloged like statistics on a graph. They form the static patterns on the TV screen—the black-and-white dots endlessly at war. Each injury adds texture to the walls being built inside me, fortifying a twisted world inside my mind and heart. Yet even as these walls rise, the world remains formless and without order, a place of confusion.

It tells me I am worthless. It whispers that I am nothing more than a sacrifice thrown to the volcano gods, discarded by those who were supposed to love me. If this is what love looks like, then I must be worth nothing at all.

Chapter 8
From Torment to the Study

2nd Samuel 22:49 "God delights in rescuing the oppressed."

"Someday I will come back from the study to retrieve what I left behind."

Hatred flows through this house like dysentery, streaming from the mouths of those who live here. It's the blunt force trauma. It's the native language spoken within these walls. It's a war that won't break me overnight, but it's slowly, surely teaching me how to hate.

"Jack-a-puss, you make sure to tell them you got those bruises falling down the stairs," my aunt warns.

"I didn't fall down the stairs."

"Do you want to be taken away from your mom?" She fixes me with a look, a question heavy with consequences.

"No!"

"That's what'll happen." There's no remorse in her voice, no sign that the things causing these bruises will ever change.

I have no options. "Okay," I mutter, cornered and defeated.

"You don't know what would happen to her if you were taken."

Maybe it's a threat. Maybe it's just a warning that my absence would somehow affect my mom. Either way, the message is clear: I'm the man of the house. It's my responsibility to protect her.

She's so lost—adrift in a world she refuses to understand. How do you protect someone who won't take any accountability for their life? It's not just the fog of divorce clouding her mind. There's something deeper, a pattern woven into her being. She spills ignorance like an overflowing spring, attracting people who will control her, people who will make decisions for her—so she never has to. And somehow, I've become the one responsible for keeping everything together.

Icicles form as fast as her tears fall. Minnesota winters are brutal. Every step you take risks plunging into knee-deep snow—or slipping and landing flat on your back. But I keep moving, one foot in front of the other, escorting my mom to the bus stop. She stumbles beside me, her footing unsteady, so I stay close to keep her balanced. As we walk, she vents her troubles, pouring them out like steam into the frozen air. My troubles? They remain hidden, concealed behind the curtain, like actors waiting for a cue that never comes.

"I don't think I'm going to make it through the winter here," she sighs.

"It'll be okay, Mom. You can make it," I say, trying to sound encouraging. But deep down, I wouldn't mind leaving either.

"I don't want to stay. It's too damn cold."

"Me neither." My reasons are different, though, and my tone must've betrayed something—just enough for her to notice. If my mom ever manages to glimpse my feelings, it's a rare and fleeting moment. For once, she catches a hint.

Awkward Silence

"Why? Don't you like it here?"

I know better than to answer honestly. If I open that door, I'll never stop talking. It's safer to keep quiet. Any truth I share with her will only become ammunition later. Her loyalty doesn't shelter me—it just flies overhead, waiting to drop its mess on me.

She doesn't mean to betray me, I know that. But every time I tell her something in confidence, it circles back around—hovering, waiting—until it falls, splattering all over me.

"It's OK. I'm fine!"

This isn't true. I'm not fine. My sanity has sprung a slow, leaking drip, pooling beneath me. But do I even know what "fine" looks like? I am drowning in the disconnect between words and actions, caught in the grip of a world where evil holds sway. I need to find a place beyond this chaos—a place where I can simply exist. I can feel myself slipping away, seeking refuge in some undefined corner of my mind.

Look up, and all you'll see are books—towering higher than the heavens, forming the borders of my imagination. These shelves stretch endlessly upward, stacked with the knowledge of every pixel, granule, and particle of my existence. Every choice, every possibility—every future and its shadow—has been recorded here. Seraphim stand watch, some guarding access to these futures, others gently guiding choices that will close off certain roads forever.

This isn't just a library; it's an expansive, living study. Brass and glass frame the room's edges. Vats, condensers, and flasks sit among vibrating guitars, sheets of music, and tools that hum with quiet resonance. Lights flash, pulse, and dance—some static, some alive with motion. Mirrors hang throughout—some reflecting the soul's questions, others singing strange tunes. There is always a sense of something magical stirring. And still, the books stretch on and on. Yet, in an instant, this vast library can shrink to fit the confined space of my mind. This isn't just a sanctuary—it's the threshold into imagination.

Imagination has become essential. It's not just a game of fantasy—it's the gateway to the spirit world, and the spirit world is where I fight. This isn't to say that imagination isn't real. It's to say that imagination carries more power than it's given credit for. Without it, I'd have no fight left in me. I'd simply wither and die. Imagination sustains me. It's the gift God gave to keep me alive, and I will never underestimate it again. Through imagination, I've met the Wizard.

The Wizard is my guide—a presence between worlds, here to teach me. He fills the spaces in between—the gaps between lashings, the silence between insults, the brief pauses between tortures. In these moments, he gives me knowledge. And knowledge is power. He shows me stories, shares maps to hidden treasures, and teaches me the strength to survive.

"I'll be ready, Grandpa!" Nick's voice floats through the house—light and innocent. When he speaks with his grandparents, it feels like a glimpse of the real Nick. Maybe the other side of him—the side I know too well—is just a mask. Or maybe this version is the fake. I don't know the truth. I'm not even sure I could handle it.

It sounds like it's going to be a relatively peaceful weekend—Nick is staying with his grandparents. That leaves only Corine, but if I stay out of sight, she probably won't look for me. I'll take long walks with Dude, exploring the hidden places here in White Bear, mapping out new corners of the world I haven't yet seen.

Awkward Silence

I'm excited. So excited that I pinch myself to make sure it's real. Just to be sure, I peek in on Nick and see him packing his things. He slips a notebook into his bag, tucking it among his clothes. It's really happening.

"Come in here, Jack-a-puss."

It doesn't matter what he does now—I know I'll be free from him for the rest of the weekend.

"Get in there." He opens the door to the fruit room—a storage space lined with cinder block walls. The heavy door looks just like the kind you'd find on the walk-in refrigerators at restaurants.

But I don't care. The Wizard is waiting for me.

The Wizard fills the empty spaces with meaning. He exists to educate, to empower, to help me survive. He lives in the moments between—between blows, between names, between the suffocating waves of torment. In these gaps, he gives me something more valuable than safety: he gives me stories. Maps to treasure. Knowledge. And through knowledge, power.

I enter the cell, still holding onto the hope that in just a few minutes, Nick will be gone.

"I expect to find you right here when I get back. If you're not here, you're a dead man." He slams the door behind me.

Imagine—at the beginning of time, before time itself—there lived a great and mighty Wizard. If only I could be as I imagine him to be. If I were like him, I'd have the power to defend myself. The Wizard exists to get me through this. He teaches me with patience, guiding me until I outgrow those who claim to teach me. Plato's *Republic*, as explained by Socrates, becomes my playground of logic, tickling my feet—my "under-standing." Words and codes become the games I play to survive.

White is all frequency, I reason. Eight valence electrons are white. There's always a method to the madness and madness in the method, and it's through these mental acrobatics that I escape.

The fruit room is dark—pitch black. I could wait for Nick to leave and slip out quietly. But Corine might be behind this—or at least backing him up. No, I'm safer in here. I might as well remain in the safety of this dungeon-like cell, where demons can feast on my flesh, unseen. There is no light here.

"Why don't they love me?"

This is why it's good to have your own Wizard—to ask the tough questions.

"That's not just one question—it's many wrapped up in one," the Wizard says calmly. "Let's peel it apart and look deeply at what you're really asking."

My six-year-old brain tries to follow his logic.

"First, let's remove *you* from the equation. Now we're left with: *Why don't they love?*" The Wizard pauses, letting the words hang in the air. "The answer is simple: *They don't know love.*"

He continues. "Love is patient. They are not patient. Love is kind. They are not kind. Love isn't boastful or proud, but they are both. The truth is, they are too tangled in their own twisted souls to know love. The balance of Yin and Yang—separate forces that come together as one—does not exist within them. They are so top-heavy with ego that even the slightest breeze will knock them over. Love grows as a pure vine, untangled. But their souls are more twisted than a Rubik's cube."

Awkward Silence

The Wizard looks at me, his gaze steady. "And love," he adds quietly, "does not beat children for entertainment."

I stare at him with wide, unblinking eyes, absorbing his words.

"Now," he says, "let's answer the second part of your question. This time, we remove *love* from the equation and reinsert *you*. Again, the answer is the same: *They don't know you.* To them, you aren't a person. You are nothing more than the sum of the names they call you—the target of their animosity. Not one of them could tell you something as simple as your favorite color. To know love, they wouldn't need to know you. But without knowing love, they can't love you."

Time stops. Objects hang suspended in midair, frozen like statues. The room falls silent. The beams of light that once flickered now solidify into something tangible—whatever state of matter light is supposed to be.

"Aristotle says light is both a ripple and a wave," the Wizard remarks, his voice taking on a weight I've never heard before. "But this moment isn't about Aristotle's theory. No. This moment is about something much more important."

He leans in, and his voice drops to a whisper that resonates deep within me.

"I need you to listen—and *hear* me at the same time."

The lights throb with intensity, like a heartbeat.

"Since *you* know love, you are expected to love *them*. But—more importantly—you must discover who you are and learn to love *yourself.*"

Jack Taylor

The beam of light shatters into a million fragments, and the room snaps back into motion. Everything is as it was, but nothing feels the same. Though the fruit room isn't soundproof, it filters noise in a way that makes everything sound distant—like the faint chatter of children playing on a playground. The sounds are so subtle, it almost feels like they're all out there having fun, enjoying each other's company.

I hold on to one truth: whatever I face, I don't face it alone. I know I'm in the midst of a battlefield, though I can't quite place where that battlefield lies. They say the hardest realization is that the cages we live in are built from words, not steel. I feel hollow. Hungry. Lost. But my imagination carries the coordinates I need to find my way back home.

Home—what is home? It's supposed to be a place of comfort. A place where you can hang your hat without worrying that someone will fill it with chemicals or poop. Home is where sanity should reside. Yet I wonder: is it sanity I seek, or is it freedom that truly matters?

I glance beyond a tall shelf of books and notice something I hadn't seen before—a stained glass window glowing faintly in the study. Above it, there's a sign: **"Jack Taylor."** Below my name are rows of books, each titled after people I know—or will come to know. Their covers form part of a larger design that only makes sense when seen as a whole. It's no accident. It's as if to say that every person has a place and a purpose in your life. But some boundaries should never be crossed. A maid is not a wife and therefore, should never see you naked.

Here in the fruit room, I wrestle with thoughts that twist into unsolvable riddles. It's like reading a book where, between the printed words, faint shapes emerge—illegible words hidden in the white spaces. Sometimes these shapes blur and come together into pictures, and if I adjust my focus just right, the images seem to move, like the pages of a flipbook. Making sense of my world feels as impossible as decoding these phantom words.

The harmonious vibrations of Feng Shui hum through the study. Or at least, that's the closest word I can find to describe it. Everything here is mindful—every detail deliberate and complete. It's all in the details.

My mind, restless and frayed, keeps slipping back and forth—from the fruit room to the study and back again. Time has lost meaning. I've been locked in this fruit room for nearly forty-eight hours. Shelves of canned fruits and vegetables loom above me. The room is damp and dark. At night, the cold sinks into my bones, and by day, the air turns musty and suffocating. This place is just another chamber in the hell I've come to know. A child shouldn't live like this. No one should.

Thank God I have the comfort of the Wizard. Without him, I'd be stranded here. He is my escape—my doorway back into the study.

Solitude is better than the alternative, but it brings its own agonies. There's no bathroom here. Nothing to eat unless I break into the canned goods. It's a test of will—a game of mind over matter. Yet, even as my stomach twists with hunger and the cold gnaws at me, my mind begins to slip again. I drift—back to the study, back to the comfort of the Wizard.

Maybe this is just a dream. Or maybe the dream is a way for my mind to disconnect from the discomfort—an escape from a reality too heavy to bear.

"Here is another test of logic."

Behind him, a screen flickers to life, cycling through images—confrontation, war, destruction. Buildings crumble.

Lives unravel. Faces, broken and bloody, flash by, including one of me, taking a punch.

"These are the consequences of opposing ideas colliding," the Wizard says. "Lives lost over the smallest disagreements. But the truth is, conflict rarely begins in the present. The bitterness and anger of the past seep into every confrontation. Evil is evil— whether it's within you, around you, or woven into the world. The only difference is the scale on which it operates."

He shifts suddenly. "Here, in the study, we seek harmony. Pick up the guitar."

I blink, startled by the abrupt change. "Seriously. Pick it up."

Reluctantly, I reach for the guitar and strum a few chords.

"What's your name?"

"Jack," I reply, continuing to play.

"It's not Jack-a-puss?"

"No."

He doesn't smile. "What's the square root of five hundred sixty-four?"

I stop playing, my mind snagging on the question.

"That's the point," the Wizard says. "As long as you stay focused, you can keep the music going. But let distraction creep in, and the song unravels. This is life. When your environment supports you, distractions become mere ripples, and success follows. But if your surroundings pull you down, every step forward becomes an uphill battle."

Awkward Silence

I feel lost, as if I'm grasping at straws. This world, the study, the fruit room—it doesn't make sense. I think of lawmen trying to crawl inside the minds of serial killers. That can't be healthy.

The Wizard's words come back to me, simple yet pure. These conversations begin in innocence, like the way he teaches me chess—not just for the game but to understand strategy, to think beyond the immediate. But life isn't confined to a chessboard. It's a much larger game, one with vertical and horizontal moves that my mind can't quite grasp.

Our conversations evolve—or maybe they corrode—with logic that twists toward manipulation.

"If you sacrifice your queen," the Wizard murmurs, "you guarantee checkmate in two moves."

The lesson starts with strategy, but it plants a seed. The next steps lead down a path where outcomes are manipulated, and suddenly, I'm standing at the edge of the devil's playground.

The door to the fruit room creaks open. My aunt walks in, reaching for a large can of hominy. I sit there, unsure if I'm speaking aloud or lost in my thoughts. She doesn't acknowledge me. She doesn't even seem to see me, though I know that's impossible.

She turns off the light as she leaves, closing the door behind her.

The purpose of the study becomes clearer. It offers refuge—a way to escape the torment. But I can't help asking the question that gnaws at my soul: *Why am I treated this way? What am I doing that makes this okay?*

If I could find the answer—just one thing to change—would it realign the stars and restore my life? I want to go back to the happiness I was born into.

Music drifts down from the shed on the hill, where my cousin Mike's band is playing. The scent of burgers and hot dogs wafts through the air. Uncle Herb is at the grill, setting fire to the coals. He grins as I tease him, "Your head looks like a landing strip for flies."

He laughs and messes with me, showing me I am loved. The family gathers to fill their plates. I feel like the favorite child, though I know the other kids might say the same. These family gatherings are a ritual—a rhythm that repeats.

That was the life I knew. The life I want back.

Now, I sit here in the dark, trying to scramble for something solid to hold onto—anything that can make this world make sense again.

I begin to contemplate the idea that there is undeniable power in knowledge—power I must acquire to rise above this chaos. The power of love feels distant, but it remains my ultimate goal because love never fails. The power of suggestion could be invaluable. The power of psychology might help me understand my enemies more deeply. The power of science offers tools to confront the universal challenges I face. The power of philosophy invites me to stretch my mind. And then there's the power of hope and faith—unexplored, waiting to be proven.

The Wizard's voice cuts through my thoughts. "Fighting an uphill battle isn't the same as fighting a hopeless one. Climbing strengthens you, but if everything is uphill, eventually, even the strongest will wear out."

He pauses, then continues. "We are made up of three parts: spirit, soul, and body. Now imagine that all your thoughts are in harmony. There are no contradictions anywhere—nothing but clarity. Your mind is like a universe without conflict, with no dissonance in the vast space between your ears. That's mental clarity at its purest.

Now, picture your emotions balanced, perfectly aligned with your thoughts—no turbulence, no contradictions, only peace."

I try to grasp what the Wizard is suggesting, but it feels impossible. I believe that hurting others is wrong—unforgivable, even anti-Christ-like. Yet there's a deep-seated anger in me, an emotion that keeps circling my thoughts like a vulture. Depression lingers, prowling around the edges of my mind. I fight to keep it out, knowing that if it slips in, it will consume me.

Dark thoughts rise, unbidden. I imagine striking Nick or my aunt while they sleep—taking a wooden clog weighted with an anvil and ending them. It's a horrifying idea, yet these thoughts come because they feel like allies of my depression. The clarity the Wizard speaks of seems impossibly far away, like a destination I could only reach by circling the moon a few times.

The Wizard's voice remains calm, patient, as if he already knows the darkness I wrestle with. "So, let's say your thoughts and emotions are perfectly aligned. You've achieved this harmonious peace—an inner clarity that empowers you. But now your will steps into the picture. It enters the room, carrying all this peace and balance with it. What desires will you choose? What actions will keep this harmony intact?"

He pauses, watching me wrestle with the implications. "Now ask yourself: would dropping an anvil on your aunt's head maintain this harmony? Or would it shatter it?

And what if you reach this perfect congruence within your soul—only to light a cigarette? Suddenly, the peace is gone. Why? Because deep down, you know smoking is harmful. That knowledge disrupts the balance. Somewhere within you, a ripple forms—because part of you believes you don't deserve the greatness you're capable of.

Do you see it now? True congruence cannot exist when your actions betray your thoughts. Even the smallest inconsistency, the tiniest ripple, undermines everything. It's not just about others; it's about how you treat yourself."

The weight of his words settles over me, heavy and inescapable.

The door swings open. Nick stands there, grinning like a child who's discovered a secret.

"You're still in here? That's hilarious. Have you been in here the whole weekend?"

His laughter cuts through the room, sharp and unforgettable. It pierces through whatever fragile peace I was clinging to, and I know, without a doubt, that I'll never forget the sound of it.

Chapter 9
The Yellow Rose

1st Thessalonians 5:11 "Therefore encourage one another..."

"This will still bring a tear to my eyes. Thank you Golfview principal."

The boxes are stacked around me like a fortress of forgotten things. Some are labeled "Christmas decorations," while others bear ominous warnings: "Do not open." They surround the place where I sleep—a narrow bed space in the basement. The stairs creak overhead, broadcasting every movement from above like signals of incoming danger. Cobwebs hang thick in the corners, draping the room with neglect. The filth around me whispers that I have no worth.

This is where I rest.

"Crack!"

The sound hits before the pain. It's the unmistakable thud of a wooden clog colliding with my skull. I wake to it. The ache spreads, but I fight to contain it. Then comes the smell—foul and humiliating. Either I soiled myself in my sleep, or the blow to my head triggered my body to release.

"Crack!"

The clog strikes again, and warmth trickles from my scalp. Blood finds new paths to flow. I know what just happened: I've shit the bed. It's not the first time, and I have no explanation for why it's happening now—only that no one cares to offer one.

"Crack!"

This time, the blow lands harder as I try to block it with my hands. My bones absorb the force, but the clog still finds my head. There's no mercy. No end to this.

I've read somewhere that bowel issues like these are a common symptom of child abuse, but there are no therapists here. No one is coming to help.

"Crack!"

The impact echoes like the sound of a bat connecting with a fastball.

I scramble to clean myself, just in time to begin another day. It's not a life—it's survival. Every thought, every step is devoted to making it through the rituals of torment. These are the daily sacrifices I offer to demons: my peace, my dignity, my very existence. But somehow, I cling to the belief that God made me in His image and gave me strength—strength greater than anything these devils can throw at me.

Nick stands over me, smirking, a cruel puppet master.

"Stand against the wall with your hands to your side."

His fist slams into my chest—again, just like yesterday. He uses his whole body, channeling his weight into the punch. If only he put the same effort into ending hunger or bringing about peace. But no, his satisfaction comes from seeing me break.

The next challenge is the barbed-wire crawl up the stairs. He hurls things at me—anything within reach. The goal isn't to dodge them. The trick is to predict where they'll hit and shift my body to absorb the blow where it will hurt least. With my back turned to him, I read the shift in light and shadow to anticipate the trajectory. I have to think fast, or he'll throw harder next time.

When I finally make it upstairs, breakfast is waiting for me. A bowl of cereal—but not the kind anyone else would eat. The first bite sets my mouth on fire—Tabasco sauce scorches my tongue. Mustard follows, stinging and bitter. There's mayonnaise somewhere in the mix, turning the texture thick and slimy. And then, hidden in the mess, I taste the unmistakable foulness: dog poop. My stomach churns violently, but I force it down.

I move in stealth mode to pass my aunt, slumped on the couch in her half-asleep haze. As long as she's drifting in and out of sleep, she's not much of a threat—but my very existence disgusts her. I hold my breath, hoping to slip by unnoticed.

Then her voice cuts through the room, sharp and commanding:

"Get back in there and brush your teeth."

"I did," I say softly, feeling as small and defeated as a dog showing its belly in submission.

She scoffs, her disdain palpable.

"I didn't hear it."

I pull on my thin corduroy jacket to step into the brutal, twenty-below-zero weather. The cold slices through it like a scimitar through Jell-O, making me shiver before I even reach the sidewalk. Cherie walks beside me—my responsibility to escort to school. It wouldn't take much for me to sell her into slavery if it meant escaping my reality, but I know better than to say anything, let alone cry.

"Men don't cry, Jack-a-puss," echoes in my head.

Jack Taylor

I always feel like crying. There's not a minute of any day when the tears don't threaten to spill, but crying isn't an option. It never has been. Tears won't fix anything, and they'd only make it worse. Mornings are mechanical, part of the endless ritual of survival. I don't know who or what my aunt and Nick worship in these daily sacrifices, but there has to be something—it feels inhuman to treat a child this way.

As the school day crawls toward its end, the weight of dread settles deeper in my chest. The sorrow always swells in the afternoons, gnawing at me with sharp little premonitions. The ticking clock seems alive, its hands reaching out to strangle me. Then the door opens, and the teacher's aide steps in.

"Jack, the principal wants to see you in the lunchroom tomorrow before school."

Her words land like a death sentence. I search my mind, trying to remember what I could have done wrong, but nothing comes to mind. Whatever it is, it can't be good. I've never heard of a meeting with the principal that ends with smiles or kind words.

The dread clings to me for the rest of the day, winding itself tighter and tighter like a noose. That night, it weighs me down like a backpack full of lead. I'm already drowning under the burden of just existing, and if this school meeting gets me into trouble at home, I know what that means. I am as good as dead.

The moment I get home, the nightly ritual begins.

"Stand against the wall," Nick orders.

I obey. His fist finds my chest again, slamming into the same spot as always.

Awkward Silence

"Why aren't you walking the dog?" My aunt's voice echoes down the stairs, piercing and sharp. Her timing interrupts Nick's blows, but only because it takes his attention for a moment—not out of concern for me. Nick never stops until he's winded or bored.

"Nick, stop so he can walk the dog," she yells, not because she cares about my well-being, but because the dog needs to be dealt with.

I head outside, closing the gate behind me. The black lab, Dude, greets me with restless energy. He's a good boy—just wild. No one but me works with him, so he hasn't been trained properly. He's chained outside in the freezing cold, with nothing but a flimsy doghouse to shelter him. Our connection is undeniable. We are the same. When there's leftover grease from cooking, it gets dumped over his dry food. That's about the best care he ever gets. I'm certain if the ASPCA came here, they'd take him away without a second thought.

As I leave the driveway, my eyes drift to Kippy, Monica, Cherie and the neighborhood kids playing together. They're laughing, chasing each other, their joy rubbing salt into a wound that never heals. Every day, I pass by them, watching them laugh and belong while I live under this miserable regime. It stings in ways words can't describe. I am happy for them and yet, miserable in my own flesh. It feels like my heart isn't just breaking—it's being squished in my aunt's fist, the life oozing out between her fingers, but never enough to kill it entirely.

"Men don't cry."

That's what they tell me, so I don't cry. I tell myself it's fine. Someone has to do the chores. Maybe it wouldn't feel so unbearable if the injustice weren't so obvious. If it weren't so clear that I am worth less than everyone else. If there's a chore to be done, it's mine to do.

Jack Taylor

While I walk the dog in the cold, the other kids play street hockey, or tag, or whatever game they're into that day. It doesn't matter—I know they'll be done long before I return. By the time I get back, they'll have eaten dinner, taken their baths, and curled up in front of the TV. And I'll be left to squeeze myself back into the cracks of a life that feels less like living and more like surviving.

As unruly as Dude is, every squirrel, every cat—basically anything that moves—gives him an excuse to drag me down the street.

"Dude! Stop, Dude!" I can stay on my feet for a minute or two, but eventually, I go down hard. The thin corduroy jacket does nothing—it tears right through—and the gravel digs into my skin, leaving behind new patterns in my flesh almost every day. Each fall adds fresh texture to the ever-changing design of scars on my body.

When I get back to the house and clip Dude's chain, the call comes.

"Jack-a-puss, get in here!"

It's Nick, eager as always to start his nightly rituals.

"Put your hands to your side."

The first blow crushes into my chest. Air shoots out of me, but I keep standing.

"Sit down and don't move," he orders. The pennies come next—one after another—thrown directly at my face.

He kicks. He punches. He throws whatever he can grab. He makes me say things—things that make my stomach twist, but fighting him is useless. This night, though, he makes me do something new, something I've never experienced before.

Awkward Silence

"Go up the street like you're heading to school," he says. "On the side of the road, you'll see a small round container with a silver lid. Bring it back here."

I don't question him—I never do. I just go. I don't know what would happen if I came back empty-handed, but I don't plan to find out. Thankfully, I spot the container almost immediately. Its silver lid glints in the dim streetlight, and I scoop it up, relieved I didn't fail.

When I hand it to Nick, he opens it with a smirk. The pungent wintergreen smell slaps me in the face, thick and nauseating. I look at the stuff inside—it's dark and damp, a bit like wet dirt, but somehow worse.

"Eat it," he says.

There's no point in resisting. I pinch some of the brown substance between my fingers and put it in my mouth. It's bitter, sharp, and rancid. My stomach turns instantly. Before I even swallow, I feel my insides churn.

I try to hold it down, but the nausea builds, and soon I'm retching uncontrollably. I throw up again and again, the acrid bile burning my throat. Nick is doubled over with laughter, delighted at my misery. My body twists and heaves, spewing out things I didn't even remember eating—and some things I'm sure I never did. I catch sight of something shiny in the mess. A fish scale.

When I wake the next morning, I'm still groggy from the ordeal. My stomach feels like a hollow pit, and the memory of that wintergreen stench haunts me. But there's no time to recover—the morning ritual waits for no one.

"Stand against the wall."

Nick's fist drives into my chest again and again. Each hit knocks the air out of me, but I know better than to complain. I climb the stairs to get ready, my body still reeling from the previous night. The room spins, and before I can steady myself, a hockey puck flies through the air and slams into the back of my head.

Breakfast is another nightmare concoction—whatever Nick's demons threw together in the kitchen today. If last night's vomiting session hadn't emptied out everything inside me, this meal would have finished the job.

I manage to slip past my aunt without getting noticed, sneaking into the bathroom to brush my teeth. My mind races, trying to figure out what I could have done to earn a summons from the principal.

Did I accidentally kill someone? Could the janitor have slipped on a wet floor after I flushed the toilet, hit his head, and died? The absurdity of the thought almost makes me laugh—but it also terrifies me. The more I think about it, the more it feels possible. What else could it be? What am I being called in for?

The weight of anxiety crushes the wildflowers growing in my mind. I try to pace it out, to unravel the fear tangling inside me, but it's no use. The dread only grows stronger. Finally, I gather what little courage I have, thinking of David facing Goliath.

If David could face a giant with nothing but a slingshot, I can face the principal.

I don't have a slingshot, but I have my stones.

With shaky hands and a racing heart, I walk toward the lunchroom, where the principal waits. I spot him sitting at one of the small tables meant for kids like me, his hands folded neatly in front of him. This is it.

I steel myself, forcing my legs to move forward. Whatever happens next, I have to be ready. My fear follows me, heavy as ever, but I won't back down.

"You wanted to see me?"

The principal looks up from his seat and gestures to a chair across from him. "Yes, Jack. Take a seat."

In front of me is a vase with a single yellow rose in it. I don't know what to make of it, but I sit down like he asks. A moment later, one of the lunch ladies comes in carrying a tray and sets it down in front of me. Pancakes, eggs, and sausage.

The smell makes my stomach twist—half with hunger, half with disbelief.

"Jack, we can't control what you get for breakfast at home," the principal says, his voice soft. "But from now on, you come here every morning, and there will be breakfast waiting for you."

He offers me a warm smile. "When you're finished eating, the nurse wants to see you. Just stop by her office on your way back to class. But there's no rush—take your time and eat as much as you want."

I sit there, stunned, unable to respond. I can barely think. What am I supposed to say to this? My mouth is already full of pancakes and syrup—sweet, warm, and overwhelming. God is with me, I think suddenly, and I didn't even know it.

After breakfast, I make my way to the nurse's office, the warmth from the food still lingering in my belly. But that comfort fades the moment I step inside.

The nurse, a quiet woman with sharp, observant eyes, greets me with a kind smile, but I can feel the shift in the air. She isn't just here to patch up cuts and scrapes—she's here to measure something more dangerous.

She asks me to sit, pulls on gloves, and begins her examination. She runs her fingers gently over the bruises scattered across my body, each touch sending a ripple of shame through me.

She lifts a ruler, carefully measuring the dark marks. Bruises on my ribs, on my arms, and the ones across my cheeks—marks from when my aunt covered my mouth too hard.

"How did you get this bruise?" she asks, pointing to my cheek.

I swallow hard, my mind racing. I know what I'm supposed to say.

"I fell down the stairs."

I can feel the heat of my aunt's fury, even though she isn't here. Her eyes, in my mind, are blazing flames that will consume everything if I say the wrong thing.

The nurse studies me for a moment, her face unreadable. "I think we both know that this didn't happen from falling down the stairs, Jack."

Her words hit me like a stone. My heart pounds, and my breath catches in my throat. What do I say now? She can see it—the fear swelling in my eyes, the panic tightening around my chest.

Awkward Silence

After a long pause, she lets out a soft sigh and puts her ruler down. She doesn't ask any more questions. Instead, she quietly finishes charting my bruises on a graph, writing down things I can't fully understand.

When I return to the classroom, the usual hum of chatter feels louder than normal, buzzing in the air like static. I can tell something is going on before I even reach my desk.

There, sitting right on top of it, is an envelope.

I pick it up, and inside is a brightly colored card. "Happy Birthday, Todd! You're invited to his party! Saturday at 1 PM."

I stare at the invitation in my hands, feeling the weight of it press down on me. The rest of the class chatters excitedly, caught up in the joy of parties, presents, and normal childhood things that feel so far away from me, but I want to feel this. I don't envy them. In fact, they model for me what I aspire to have. I just want to find the joy for myself. The heaviness is the chains and shackles that must be broken in order that I may attend. I want to latch on to that joy, even as temporal as a party may be.

The laughter, the talking, the celebration—it all crashes over me, wave after wave, until I feel like I'm drowning in a sea of doubt.I don't remember the last time I laughed or the last time I felt like celebrating. I am in hell, and the only way out, at least for a momentary reprieve, is to attend the party and pretend like I belong there.

Chapter 10
Anatomy

Mark 10:14 "let the children come to me and do not hinder them."

"Forgiveness can be a difficult task but it is well worth it!"

A first-grader's social skills are awkward, and conversations about boogers and farts are the required certifications for membership. I don't belong. I could talk boogers with the best of them, but I have much meatier things on my plate. When I think back on some of the workplace conversations I've had as an adult, I don't think we've strayed too far from that same childish banter.

The condensed version of my daily challenges for survival is heavier than I should ever bring to the table. All of this is to say: I'm going to do my best to fit in at Todd's birthday party.

There have been other class functions—other birthday celebrations. There have been school carnivals and even spaghetti feeds, but this is different. This time, I'm determined to go. I never asked the right person before, but this time I ask my mom. Now, I just have to figure out how to fit in.

I've taken the time to study, and I can read my surroundings like no one else. I hone these skills every day, to the point of exhaustion. But awareness doesn't matter much if you can't change your environment. Still, if all I can do is evaluate my surroundings, then that is what I'll do.

I can look at a clock, set my internal metronome, and track time as if I control it. My sense of timing is precise, almost perfect.

Awkward Silence

When I walk into a room, I habitually examine every detail laid out before me. I don't have a photographic memory, but I connect with the shapes and how they blend together. If something is out of place, I notice.

For example, when I walked into Nick's room, I immediately sensed something new: a small box, smaller than a shoe box. I didn't see it right away, but it blocked my view of the linear line of the flag on the wall behind it. I also noticed that a hairbrush had been moved—the handle used to point directly at a sticker on the side of the table, but now it's off by just a bit.

Practicing this kind of awareness is more complicated than simply noticing your environment. You never really know if you're right until the object is smashed against your face—and by that point, it doesn't matter.

If your eyes are closed and you can't see into the next room—that is to say, if you can't see into the spiritual dimension— there is a carnal explanation for everything. But when you're on high alert, tuned to the smallest shifts in vibration, you notice the shadows that move and the subtle changes in reflected light. These flickering beams of light are the blue orbs—the little blue bastards.

Complete calmness, the kind of awareness that lets you notice everything without being noticed yourself, is a state few people ever achieve. When I lie still, I make sure even my breathing is quiet. If I breathe too loudly, it might annoy him. I lower my heart rate, slow my breath to barely anything—almost as if I'm breathing through my skin—and absorb every variation in light and vibration around me.

A mirror behind a poker table isn't ideal, but even if you remove the mirror, the light still takes the same path. Sure, the wall may absorb some of the light, and the angles of reflection may shift, but the overall behavior of light is consistent. This consistency is what I've learned to read.

It's not really a card trick—I just understand light and patterns in a way I can't fully explain. I can predict cards with about an 80 percent success rate. Sometimes it's about reading the angles of light, and sometimes it's more mathematical, like counting cards. The images of played cards seem to stay with me, burned into my mind as clues.

I've gotten good enough to make an impression. Madia, our neighbor, certainly thinks so. She can't stop talking about it at the party. "You have to see what Jack can do!" she tells everyone.

As one might expect, a call from my aunt is the hand that cuts the deck and slices my debut short. I will not have another chance for social interaction outside of school this year—certainly not one that puts me in the spotlight. The whole thing lasted twenty minutes, and within five, she was already there to pick me up. She told Todd's parents there was a family emergency.

I'm waiting out front when she pulls up. I get into the car, and wham! She hits me in the jaw so hard I see stars. As she drives down the road, her fists keep coming. The wooden clogs come off, and I am beaten into a bloody mess. Head wounds bleed, and this one is no exception—the blood pours down my face, and I have no clue why this is happening.

"I did what you said! I told them I fell down the stairs!" I plead with her as we enter the house. My mind races, scrambling for answers. "I wouldn't have gone to the party if I knew it would upset you!" I'm chasing shadows—trying to figure out what invisible mistake I made. I know the janitor didn't slip, so what could this be about?

Awkward Silence

My mom joins the chaos, and suddenly they are both beating me, taking turns. One holds my hands down while the other swings. Closed fists pound my face—my jaw breaks. I am bleeding, pleading, and begging for help, but the only one who could save me is the one holding me down.

From my cousin's bedroom, I hear the wet, gasping sobs of someone else being punished. My sister's cries mix in with the sounds. I see those stars again, dancing across my vision. The moments between blows are my only chance to think of a solution, but madness reigns. I can't make sense of anything.

"Stop! You're going to kill him!" Kippy, one of my cousins, cries out, trying to defend me.

But I am absolutely helpless. There is no action I can take that won't lead to more severe punishment. I am, in every sense of the word, stupefied. Bewildered by the idea that they can do this to me—a little boy who loves them, who tries to do everything they ask. I am that boy.

The pain is unbearable. This is nothing short of a bloodbath. I couldn't cry then, but I cry now—years later, remembering the pain and the exact moment my jaw started to click.

My mom and aunt continue beating me, tag-teaming their blows. The vines of trauma growing from these moments are tightening, twisting further around my mind. "Men don't cry," I whisper to myself.

"You could have gotten her pregnant!" my aunt screeches, delivering another crushing blow with her wooden clog.

"Men don't cry," I repeat silently, clinging to that mantra.

Pregnant? My thoughts reel. "I could have gotten who pregnant?" Is this what all of this is about? Six months have passed since whatever they're referring to, and I barely remember it—it was gone from my mind the moment it happened. But now, in this moment of agony, I know that memory will haunt me until the day I die.

If I could, I'd take a chainsaw to the branch this trauma grew from. This savage beating is embedding a lasting, distorted image of what women are like. That day—this day—will be one of the most impressionable of my life, at least until the moment when my whole world finally flies off the tracks.

In the back room at my grandparents' house—where it happened—there's no reason to even remember that incident. There must be more to this beating than that, something larger at play. None of this makes sense as a justification. But the truth is, I believe they came dangerously close to killing me that day.

The concussion they gave me is a gift I'll never be able to unwrap—I couldn't even touch my head, not with my entire body aching from head to toe. Something deeper, darker is at work here. Something much larger.

They must be demon-possessed. I can't see it any other way. The forces of evil are working through them—it has to be so. None of this is because of anything I've done. And this house? It is most assuredly a gateway to hell.

The torturous screams at night only add weight to my theory. Ghostly figures have been seen—first by my mom, then by Cherie. My mother's thoughts are twisted by the demon within her. Their minds are simple, easy prey for the dark forces that rule this place. This can't truly be them. What I'm enduring must be the work of something far more sinister.

Awkward Silence

The blood streaming from my nose, lips, and scalp is my grim reminder. Her words—*"You could have gotten her pregnant"*—still echo in my head, scrambled and senseless. That couldn't have been what she meant. The way she screeched those words—combined with the brutality—was not human. It was the voice of a devil. There is no way I could have gotten anyone pregnant, and yet this twisted accusation hammers into my mind. They aren't living in reality... but neither am I.

My innocence is slipping away, drifting further from reach. It is no longer intact—no longer a part of me. These are the challenges I now face. I keep muttering to myself, *"I was only six years old."* I cannot even fathom doing this to a child that young— yet they did.

I need to start fresh. *Wipe the chalkboard clean and begin again.* "Back to the drawing board," I whisper, retreating to the study. I dive into the books, one after the other, spending every possible moment away from the horrors of reality—a reality full of demons and devils. I am not ready to face a world where the supernatural lurks in every corner of my life.

"Exercise your spirit. Strengthen it to overcome the beasts before they can enter the passageway. Capture the demons before they infiltrate your mind. Slay the dragon before it materializes in the physical world."

All the trauma I've experienced here floods my thoughts. The static that always buzzed faintly in the background now sharpens into clarity. A new truth emerges—it must all be the work of demonic forces. Nothing else makes sense. People who love me could never be this cruel unless something dark and powerful were pulling the strings.

I begin to see a pattern—a strategy—woven into everything I've experienced since the day I descended these stairs into hell. There is a scheme at work, a purpose behind every act of torment. It all has one goal: to distort my reality. The purpose is corrupt, and each form of torture I endure serves the same design— to steal, kill, and destroy. Now that I see the pattern, I cannot unsee it.

I declare aloud, "God does not answer to the weather!"

One of the biggest lies they've planted in me is that God is a myth. Each time I cried out to Him in the middle of my suffering, and no relief came, it added weight to their lie. If they can convince me that God is a fantasy, I will seek myths in place of truth—a false belief system to imprison me further.

They've also tried to implant another toxic belief: *"Women are nothing but a pain in the neck, a thorn in the side."* If I accept this as truth, my hope for a healthy relationship is gone. If hope is stolen, then love is stolen. Through subtle brainwashing, they've planted this poisonous thought deep inside me.

I fear what will grow from these seeds. The weeds of bitterness are choking out the beauty of any flowers in my heart. I didn't even realize how deeply it had taken root until I noticed how much I struggle in relationships. My heart has hardened over the years, and I've buried my emotions beneath layers of coldness. These warped beliefs make it almost impossible to experience true intimacy.

On top of that is the contaminated soil of my self-worth. I believe no one could love me as I am, and if I cannot be honest, then intimacy becomes a lie. *Besides, women are nothing but trouble anyway...* Or so the lie says.

Out of all the darkness that followed me out of that hell, this one—the distortion about love and relationships—is the hardest to forgive. I've always longed for a family of my own. I can see it so clearly in my mind—what it would look like—and for a moment, I feel joy at the thought. But that joy is quickly replaced by sadness because reality tells me it may never happen.

Yet, even in the depths of this darkness, I hold on to one truth: With God, all things are possible. If God's will is that I forgive, then I will walk that path. Whatever it takes—no matter how long—I will do the work. I will forgive.

And I will not give up hope.

Chapter 11
Understanding the Damage

1st John 4:1 "Beloved, do not believe every spirit but test the spirit.."

"Once hope is gone self destruction has already begun."

One false belief connects seamlessly to the next, creating a chain that seems logical at first glance. If God answers to the weather, then He isn't ominous. If He isn't ominous, He can't save me from the storm. Without faith, it is impossible to please God. These thoughts weave into a deceptive narrative—one designed to separate me from the miracles God has for me. Every form of abuse has the same objective. It's an attack on how you think and feel, meant to shatter your faith. These distortions confuse your mind, cloud your emotions, and obstruct the clarity of your soul. The internal conflict that follows is a direct barrier to your connection with God.

Though my bones have healed, and the bruises, cuts, and scrapes are gone, the real injuries remain buried in my thoughts and emotions. Healing can't begin until you recognize that a problem exists. False beliefs and tangled emotions fester beneath the surface, hidden for so long that they erode hope. And when hope begins to slip away, the objective becomes clear: steal, kill, and destroy.

Once hope is lost, self-destruction has already begun. In the same way, a false belief—like *all women are the same*—can embed itself deep inside your heart. If every experience with women has been negative, this belief takes root, strangling any hope for a healthy relationship. But it's only a lie, another wall in the formation of the maze.

Awkward Silence

So how does a lie infiltrate the narrative of your life? It is invited in. It sneaks through cracks in your mind, disguised as truth. And once it finds its way in, it becomes an unwanted guest that lingers—long after the caterer has packed up and left. Lies make themselves comfortable, setting up camp in your thoughts until you begin to believe that they belong there.

If hope is still the tallest building, then the demolition isn't complete. There's still hope to rebuild. The first step is pouring the foundation—though right now, it feels like a tar-paved path encircling my heart. This road leads off into the unknown, with no clear destination in sight. All I can do is keep moving and avoid the potholes.

In just a year, they've erected so many false beliefs that I'll be digging through these skeletons in the closet for decades. Salvaging what remains untainted by their abuse will take nothing short of a miracle—and miracles aren't random; they're earned. It takes hard work to sift through bitterness and cling to the fragments of innocence that survive. This isn't a time to grow bitter. It's time to shine—to rebuild, to begin again. But casting out the demons that chained my heart is overwhelming. Tearing down the walls of deception is a task far too heavy for a seven-year-old boy, too young to even know how to weigh right against wrong.

Looking back on their misdeeds isn't pleasant, but it's the only way I know how to undo the damage. If I could erase the entire year, I would, because there's nothing of value left to salvage from it. A year at seven is enormous—one-seventh of my life, in fact. Take away the first three years of fleeting memories, and that leaves a full quarter of my life under the shadow of tyranny. These are supposed to be the most impressionable years, but instead, they were spent like loose change at a dollar store. Nothing valuable came from the investment.

What's left on the shore are the broken, fragmented pieces of who I used to be. Once, I felt loved and special. Once, I had hope. Now, all that lies shattered on the floor, and I'm left barefoot, navigating the wreckage with the constant fear that I'll slice myself open on the sharp edges. Every step forward feels like a careful negotiation with disaster.

The year has finally ended, and our time here has run out. It's time to leave, to move on, and continue the course of our lives. We're heading back toward Idaho. As we drive away, I feel an odd pull to look back—as if someone might be standing there, watching us leave. From this new angle, it all looks different. It's as if a dragon hovers overhead, its breath heavy and toxic, still lingering in the air. And somehow, I know the dragon will follow us. This isn't over yet.

But for now, there's victory to report: Minnesota is behind us, and I couldn't be happier.

Chapter 12
The Tyranny of Treachery

Malachi 2:16 "So take heed to your spirit, so that do not deal treacherously."

"From betrayal the walls of treachery are formed."

"Class, the Young Author's Contest is coming up, and I need you all to submit your entries," Miss Stanley announces.

Miss Stanley is my third-grade teacher. School has become my sanctuary. Though Minnesota is behind me, the tainted views still linger. I no longer live each day as if a bomb is hidden beneath my desk, but I can't shake the feeling that I now know evil—and that evil is still with me. It's likely that the evil is connected to me. It's the fear and anger that percolate inside, just beneath the surface, where they filter through and only emerge in my writing.

I really like Miss Stanley. She has a deep heart but, in some ways, a naive soul. She can see, yet she's blinded by her own senses. I've connected with her in thought. I know her mind. She's even caught me sneaking around in there.

"Jack, you are very gifted and talented, aren't you?"

"Is that really a question, Miss Stanley?"

"You can read me well, can't you?"

"Is that a question?"

"What I am wondering... This is ridiculous. Can you read my mind?"

97

"I'm aware of your thoughts. I don't know if that counts as reading your mind, though. The Wizard has taught me to be considerate. I wouldn't just jump into your head, but some thoughts are out there—you're just putting them into the universe." I answer the best way I know how.

"The Wizard?"

"He's just a part of me. He isn't real. I use the imaginary to fight the demons. He's the part of me that's all-knowing. He's the part that uses logic to form sound advice. I can't explain him very well."

"I am amazed by you. You're some type of prodigy, but I'm not sure what classification that would be."

"Here is my Young Author's entry."

"Thank you, Jack. Can we talk later after I think about a few things?"

"Sure."

The Spreading Infection

by Jack Taylor

East Side Elementary

Miss Stanley

3rd Grade

It began as a trickle, like ooze dripping from a leaky faucet. It seeped in as easily as the corrupted views of a fallen society. The first hideous creature crept through a small, unguarded opening. A distracting event had drawn full attention elsewhere. Who knows how long it skulked in the shadows, waiting in misery for its chance to encroach? It would have been held back by armed sentries at the primary gate—if they hadn't been called away to duty elsewhere.

This primary gate is immense. If I had to guess, I'd say a thousand people could walk shoulder to shoulder through it when fully open. The gate is bold and beautiful, even alluring. I might even call it tempting. Diamonds are sprinkled over platinum plates, and pearls are embedded in the ground as stepping stones. As the gate swings open, it does so in sections, each section hinged with gold pins. But for now, the gate is shut and locked.

On the other side of the gate lies the unknown. It is said that in that land, the air is like a vacuum, and darkness is created by sucking in the light. The ground is made of muddy clay that clings to your feet as you walk. Nothing can grow there that resembles life. Gravity presses down, heavier than the thickest thought. These are only stories, though, for anyone who ventures into that land has never returned.

It's possible, however, that this creature—the one that slipped through—is a human who has returned from that treacherous place. There is a legend about a brave explorer who ventured into the unknown. This could be him. In fact, it's believed he left a lifetime ago, though only a year has passed here. If this is that explorer, he's no longer recognizable as human. This creature has earned the name Torment.

Torment's head is grotesquely disfigured, as bumpy as a Bible written in Braille, and misshapen as if pressed in a vice. His skin is the color of ten thousand bruises, with boils and blisters oozing infection over half-formed scabs that cover old lacerations. His appearance is hideous, but what's more concerning is the way his mind has drifted from reality. It seems almost impossible for him to ever become human again, especially with the afflictions that now distort his perception of truth.

He slips in undetected, under the radar, so to speak. For the first time in a long while, Torment feels relief. A profound sense of freedom washes over him—he can finally breathe again. The vacuum-like air of that cursed land no longer chokes his lungs. He marvels at the sight of a dandelion seed drifting lazily toward the ground. A teardrop begins to form at the corner of his eye, but somehow, he sucks it back in. "Men don't cry," he tells himself. Living in that treacherous place would freeze any tear before it had the chance to fall.

Perhaps the time he spent with his companions in that treacherous land bonded them, much like soldiers are bonded during war. He begins to miss one in particular: Agony. In the strangest way, he yearns for Agony's presence. Torment tries to pull Agony through the gate with him by stirring conflict and turmoil within himself. He can't simply accept the freedom he's been granted. The tragic events he endured have altered him irrevocably. He knows he has changed—he's becoming painfully aware of who he once was compared to who he is now. The distance between those two selves is unbearable.

Every sensation is magnified. Every thought, every feeling, and every desire is sharply accentuated. If you had a dream last night of a million baby snakes slithering all over you—twisting and winding across your skin—the slightest touch today would make you react as if it were a snake.

A breeze shifts, causing a branch to brush against his shoulder. Torment loses control. Panic overwhelms him. The unexpected touch triggers a fear so visceral that he drops to the ground without resistance, as if gravity itself has pinned him there. He is surprised by his own surrender. Shaking and paralyzed with fear, he lies there, humiliated—but there is no one to see it. He is still hidden behind the gate. No one knows he is here, and if he has his way, they never will.

Where he came from, falling to the ground like this might mean never rising again. Gravity might hold him down, and the soft clay could begin to pull him in. If that happens, he could spend the rest of his life trapped in the mud. Others might walk over him, using his body as a mat to keep their feet dry. He would become prey to any predator that crosses his path.

Torment glances around to make sure no one is watching.

There is an equation here that just doesn't add up: the fact that there is no one around. No one saw him fall, and no one sees him rise again. The unsettling truth is that he hasn't seen a single soul since he slipped through the gate. He had been so consumed by the simple joy of breathing freely again that he overlooked the eerie absence surrounding him. Only now is it dawning on him— he is completely alone. There's no need to hide. He can roam the streets freely because, whatever drew their attention from the gate, it seems to have kept them occupied.

And with no one to join him, why not summon his old companions from Treachery? He calls for them, confident they will answer. After all, they had stuck tightly together through the horrors of the past year.

Misery arrives first, accompanied by the voice no one listens to—though it's not for lack of volume. If it could be given a name, it would be Bellow. This voice shouts from every rooftop and blasts through every loudspeaker. It cries out to be heard. But there is a paradox here—paying attention costs nothing, and yet no one gives it. Everything could be gained by hearing this voice, but with no one present to listen, it remains smothered in silence.

Soon after, Animosity strides boldly through the gate. While Misery slinks low, Animosity swells with defiance, thriving on rebellion. Though they are opposites in posture, they walk side by side—counterweights to each other. Misery hangs his head, burdened by gloom, while Animosity stands tall, feeding off anger. Yet, they need the others to balance them. When Animosity grows too headstrong, his rage becomes barbaric. And when Misery takes control, darkness floods the land like acid rain.

As the others appear one by one, they lose sight of the fact that they've been set free. The tyranny of Treachery is behind them, yet they stumble, unsure how to navigate this world of freedom. They feel adrift, disoriented, and lonely. Anxiety may be fading, but the sores remain—blisters still ooze, and infections still seep from half-healed wounds. They have lost their way. They have lost their purpose. And yet, they cannot simply vanish. They were born and fed—perhaps not by the nurturing we know, but by something that caused them to grow.

Now they must find a new purpose. Boredom creeps in, fed by their isolation. And boredom stokes the flames of chaos, a fire that grows hotter and more uncontrollable by the second.

They gather in the banquet hall, conspiring to reclaim control. Simply navigating life cannot be enough. They feel the presence of an opposition growing stronger, even though Happiness and his tribe are nowhere to be found. But the absence of Happiness lingers like a distant echo. It's a truth they know well: Misery cannot survive in the presence of Happiness. The two cannot coexist. If Happiness enters the room, Misery's reign would end.

At the long table, the scheming begins. Misery sits between Gluttony and Sloth. The two are kindred spirits, though their appearances couldn't be more different. Gluttony is massive—his rolls of fat consume the table in front of him. Each roll folds over another, like a cascade of flesh. Sloth, on the other hand, is barely functional, his body devoid of muscle or energy. It's a miracle he managed to drag himself to the table at all, though the importance of this meeting must have compelled him.

Pride and Greed enter together, hand in hand, as they always do. I've often wondered about these two—they seem inseparable. Meanwhile, Wrath sits at the table's head, simmering with unchecked rage, waiting to explode. Across from him, Envy and Lust take their seats, their eyes locked on Wrath, feeding off his anger.

At the center of it all sit Torment, Misery, Animosity, and Bellow, leading the discussion.

Misery clears his throat and addresses the room. "We all know what's coming if we don't hold on to our authority," he warns. "We will be ruled extinct. We cannot coexist with Happiness—it is an impossibility! Misery cannot survive alongside Joy!"

The room stirs, tension building as the others absorb Misery's words. "We must fight tooth and nail to keep those who oppose us outside the gate," he continues. "We guard the gate, and we destroy any hope that dares linger there."

Their plan is brutal but straightforward. Guard the gate. Crush hope. Keep Joy at bay.

They may have even taken a lesson from Sun Tzu's *The Art of War*—divide and conquer. And in many ways, they've already succeeded. They've sown division between Happiness and Joy, driven a wedge between Love and Tolerance, and fractured any sense of unity among their adversaries.

They are well-armed and determined. They believe they have the upper hand, with the best vantage point inside the gate. And for now, it seems they are winning.

But what they do not realize—what they *cannot* comprehend—is that hope is not so easily extinguished. It lingers, deep within, waiting. And while they may guard the gate and scheme against Joy, hope has a way of slipping through the smallest cracks.

The hope I speak of comes from a force far greater than what the eye can see. It is the power of the creator—of all things good and evil. It is the authority of the Source, the power of God Himself. To acknowledge God's provision is to surrender to the mindless antics of the dragon, now taking a transparent form in the uniting of these dark forces.

"Okay, class, the results are in from the Young Author's contest."

I know I'm a shoo-in, but I'm not even interested. Miss Stanley and I haven't talked since she confronted me about my heightened senses. I just need someone—*anyone*—who understands my gift, someone who believes me. I could try talking to my mom, but I don't feel like getting hit with her skepticism. If I told her, she'd just dismiss it as imagination. Miss Stanley, though—*she* was the one who started this conversation. She saw something in me. She understood the intuition, the spiritual connection I live with.

"Jack, I'd like to speak with you after class, if that's alright."

The bell rings, releasing chaos—giggling, running, the thudding of feet racing toward the door. I stay in my seat. I can feel her thoughts circling in confusion. She's not angry—there's no ill intent—but there's a cloud of hesitation in her. Something she hasn't figured out how to say.

She sits on the edge of her desk, facing me. "Jack, I've been thinking a lot about you."

"What about me?"

"Well, first, I need to tell you something. I didn't submit your story to the contest."

I blink, surprised. A pang of disappointment rises in my chest, and I know it shows a little. I thought she would understand the meaning behind my words. Out of all people, I thought Miss Stanley would *get it*. Maybe even relate, at least a little.

She continues carefully, "Your story is incredible, Jack. For a third grader to write something so powerful... it's astounding. I started to wonder if you had copied it from somewhere."

"I didn't. It's my story."

"I know." She nods, almost to herself. "As I read it, I started seeing trace elements of you—your mind, your experience— woven into every line. And that made me think... about what might be lurking beneath the surface of this story."

A shiver runs down my spine. "Don't dig too deep, Miss Stanley. Some bones need to stay buried."

Her expression softens, but I feel the invisible backhoe already digging, threatening to unearth graves I've worked hard to cover.

"I know." She exhales slowly, looking down at her hands. "Jack, I've thought a lot about what we discussed before. About your gift. And I've made a decision—I want to protect you, as much as I can."

Her words are sincere, but there's a naivety in them, too. She doesn't really know what she's up against.

"What do you mean?"

"Jack, people don't understand abilities like yours. Your story is so detailed, so beyond your years, that it might raise some questions. Questions you don't want anyone asking. Some people... they won't be curious for the right reasons. If they find out what you can do—if they see you the way I do—they might take you away from your family. They might try to study you."

She pauses, her concern evident, her voice dropping lower. "I don't want you to become someone's science experiment."

I meet her gaze steadily. "People aren't the ones I'm worried about, Miss Stanley. There are far worse enemies out there."

I wish she could see the creatures I've seen. If only I could make her understand. I need an ally I can trust.

"Jack, the people I'm talking about have power—the kind of power to take you away. If they realize what you can do, they could lock you in some military lab, experimenting on you day in and day out."

Her clueless passion is almost endearing. She doesn't understand the scope of what I face, though. Maybe she's genuinely stumped—or maybe she's just pretending, trying to throw the dragon off its scent. I can't be sure.

Awkward Silence

Miss Stanley shifts her tone, trying to brighten the conversation. "Anyway, I want you to know that your story *won*. Hands down, you won."

I tilt my head. "Then why didn't you submit it?"

She leans forward, smiling warmly. "Because some victories are best kept quiet."

I can't decide if that's wisdom or fear talking, but I let it pass.

Her smile softens. "I'd still like to celebrate with you. How about pizza? My treat."

I feel a grin forming, and I let it stay. "I love pizza."

"Great! Let's go then."

For now, I'll take the pizza. Maybe later, we can talk about the rest—the dragons, the gifts, and the dangers hiding just beyond sight. But for now, pizza is enough.

My third-grade year ended, and I said goodbye to the only person I thought truly understood me. I had learned more than I expected. Miss Stanley introduced me to science, especially electric circuits. I remember how she stressed that a circuit has to be closed for it to work. At the time, it felt like just another lesson, but now I see how that principle connects to so many parts of life. Everything needs connection to function—whether it's electrical current or people.

A Ryder truck sits outside the duplex where my family and I have been living. I know my world is about to crash. All day, I've sensed it coming—like the air just before a thunderstorm, heavy and electric, strangling my breath. Everything has felt off. Bugs swarmed me in unusual ways, the leaves twisted unnaturally in the breeze, and random noises jolted me. It's like the universe is conspiring against me.

"What's the truck for?"

Mom's voice rings out too cheerfully. "We're going back to Minnesota!"

The words hit me like a lightning strike. My whole body trembles, though I can't tell if it's from fear or anger. This can't be happening. I was just starting to feel okay again. With Miss Stanley's help—and Ruben's too—I was beginning to find hope. But the truck is proof that none of it matters. I need to escape, to step outside reality before it consumes me.

"The imagination is the threshold into the spirit realm."

The Wizard grabs me before I can say another word, pulling me into his study. He speaks in that hurried, jumbled way he gets when he knows he's running out of time to make me understand.

"You can test the health of your spirit by how your imagination responds. That's important, okay? Just stay with me here."

He paces, trying to fit the puzzle pieces of his thoughts into words. "It's like... let's look at your Young Author's submission. Your imagination, it's disturbed by Torment—that presence of darkness. I know, it's hard to explain to someone your age. The things you saw, the things you felt—they stayed with you, didn't they? It's like the dragon inside you heard everything you and Miss Stanley talked about, and now it feels threatened. And when a dragon feels threatened... it strikes."

He shakes his head, still tripping over his thoughts. "Okay, let's try something. Imagine you're older."

"Okay."

"How old are you?"

I think for a moment. "Fifty-six."

"Good. Now imagine that you have the understanding you'll have at fifty-six, looking back at the events that are haunting you. You remember your story, the one you submitted?"

"Yeah, I remember."

"That story came from your imagination, right?"

"Yes."

"And how many times have you heard people dismiss imagination? Saying, 'It's just your imagination'?"

"Too many."

The Wizard frowns. "That phrase makes it sound like imagination doesn't matter, but it does. God gave you your imagination for a reason. It's not just something to dismiss—it's a tool, a gift. Your imagination should be exercised, explored. It's a guide for your life. When you fill it with joyful things, your spirit grows strong. But if it's filled with the darkness you described in your story, that's where your spirit will live. And when that happens, hope starts to wither away."

I nod slowly, but something gnaws at me. "I get that, but... I didn't ask for the things that happened in Minnesota to happen to me. I didn't fill the world with darkness—it was already there. I was six. I had no control over anything."

The Wizard's gaze softens. "That's true. You didn't choose those circumstances. But listen—especially in the darkest hours, you have to turn on your light. You need to renew your mind. The road you travel with Torment at the wheel will wreck your desires. It'll strangle your happiness. You'll always feel like the world is out to get you, and if you keep walking that path, your relationships will either freeze, as cold as the Minnesota winters, or they'll burn to ash in a flash of rage."

He leans closer, his voice firm now. "You have to take your thoughts captive. Don't let them run wild in that darkness. You need to revive your spirit with imagination—flood it with life, power, and hope. You're not a victim of your circumstances, Jack. You're empowered *by* them."

I meet his gaze, but my eyes feel empty—like all the hope he's trying to give me has drained out long ago.

"Consider a topic like jealousy—it's vague by nature. Jealousy can take on many convoluted forms, each more subtle than the last. It can present itself in actions or in thoughts that simmer just below the surface. The Bible warns, *do not covet*— and coveting is a type of jealousy. At the heart of jealousy, though, lies a damaging message: that someone else possesses more value than you do. And when you believe that, you're telling yourself a story that only erodes your sense of worth."

There is healing in this time away, though I'm not sure how long it will last. Children are resilient, yes, but only to a point. They are also fragile, especially when love feels scarce. A child who doesn't feel loved is a child who feels unprotected. And now, just when I was beginning to feel a little safer, everything is about to change again.

I am returning to the pit—back to the lake of fire. Minnesota is known as the land of ten thousand lakes, but to me, there is always one more. It's the one I can't escape, a lake that churns beneath the surface of my mind, full of hidden monsters and memories I wish I could forget. Trying to wrestle my thoughts into submission feels like facing down a two-thousand-pound bull charging straight at me. Maybe I can do it. Maybe I can hold my ground—but I know it's going to leave me battered and bruised.

Chapter 13
Conforming to Cope

Romans 12:2 "Do not conform to the patterns of this world."

"Proposing an altered perception of reality"

Nick's thirst for destruction remains unquenched. It may never be. No matter how creative his methods, each act of cruelty only seems to stoke the fire, leaving him with an insatiable craving for more. I can see it in his demeanor—the way his demons still cling to him, taunting and pulling strings from the shadows. I didn't expect anything different. It's only been two years since the last time.

As I walk through the kitchen toward the stairs, the oppressive presence of unseen forces creeps over me. Obscenities whisper from realms beyond, scraping at the edges of my consciousness. But I am not as defenseless as I once was. I have learned the patterns, the methodologies they use. This is not a human attack—no, it's something deeper, something darker. The demons are using my family as hosts, hiding behind the faces of my cousin, my aunt, and others. I've spent time translating their actions into a language I now understand, though some things about these enemies remain beyond my comprehension—and perhaps always will.

Even with this newfound awareness, fear gnaws at me. If they pick up where they left off, I know I won't survive. I barely escaped the first time, and now it feels like I've been invited back for another helping of torment. Anxiety churns in my gut, relentless and overwhelming. The room feels heavy with it. This place has already tilted me to the edge—just one more step, and I may never find solid ground again. I can't tell if I'll ever truly be all right.

Yet something is changing. The field, once barren, now sprouts a small tree with delicate branches, growing ever so slowly. Figures that were once mere shadows have begun to take shape, like fog lifting just enough to reveal faint outlines. The silhouettes are still vague, but their presence is undeniable. They influence the landscape of my thoughts. Among them, my mother and Corine play leading roles, modeling what a woman is supposed to be. But other figures, like my grandmother and Miss Stanley, challenge those archetypes. The images are fluid, shifting like clouds in the sky. What looks like a horse at first glance becomes a mermaid as the winds change. One figure stands out—a woman who moves like a breeze, her presence delicate yet powerful. Her features flicker between clarity and dream: feathers sway from her earrings, her headband crowned with more feathers that ripple as if touched by an unseen wind. She carries herself with the grace of a Native American spirit, timeless and unyielding.

My thoughts are no longer easy to express. Saying *I'm sad, angry, or confused* feels like calling the Pacific Ocean a small pond or saying Mansa Musa had a few dollars tucked away—it's a gross understatement. Emotions refuse to fit into neat categories or be measured by any standard I know. It feels as though a fissure has opened beneath me, and from it flows a sluggish stream of molten lava, glowing red as it snakes through the cracks in the cobblestones. The walls around the courtyard reflect the fire's light, casting long shadows that flicker and dance. The flow is slow for now, just drops gathering to form larger pools. But with time, these drops could merge into a river so intense it carves a canyon deeper than the Grand Canyon itself. Each unwanted touch, insult, and provocation adds heat to the magma, building pressure. I am not numb—I can still feel, but the pain is now beyond words. It can't be summed up with simple phrases like *I hurt* or *I'm in pain.*

It has become something more—a slow, simmering transformation. This is how an apathetic heart is born.

Anger waits like a soldier at the gates, gathering strength with each new provocation. Pawns drift through the gates of treachery, filling the ranks, eager for battle. Day by day, their numbers swell, and war seems inevitable. But the timing is not yet right. I have to manage the intensity carefully, like light passing through a ruby held between mirrored ends, focusing until it explodes into a laser beam. Anger, when unleashed without strategy, is a wasted sacrifice—a reckless charge that leads nowhere. I can't afford to let it loose without purpose. Not yet.

A bubble rises from where the magma breaks through the cobblestone, swelling at the surface before bursting. The splash sends small spits of lava onto the bank, marking the beginning of the stream. This flow of lava—hot, seething emotion—spills forward with the liquidity of raw feeling, only to cool and harden into stone. It's the foundation of a mountain, gathering mass before the inevitable explosion. The air thickens with the acrid stench of sulfur, its vapor curling through unseen corridors of this mental maze. Somehow, it forms a bridge between two worlds, like an ionic bond pulling together two once-separate realms. As these bonds strengthen, I can feel the partition between them lifting, the walls dissolving.

I was walking down a familiar country road in the dead of night. I've taken this road a thousand times before, but tonight it feels different. The air is heavy with a mist—fog, smoke, or something far more sinister. It leaves a residue at the back of my throat, a bitter aftertaste that lingers like smoldering brimstone. This sulfurous scent must have drifted from another chamber of the maze, bleeding over from some dark corner I have yet to confront.

Awkward Silence

If my instincts are right, and this stench signals the partition between worlds coming undone, there may be hope for the rescue mission after all. But there's a chance the lava is burning through labyrinth after labyrinth, building toward a catastrophic eruption. If that's the case, then everything inside the maze—including me—will be consumed when it blows. And if it is going to blow, I'm racing a solid deadline.

"Stand against the wall with your hands at your sides." The fist slams into my chest.

"I have to do it again."

I stand still and take the hit, as if it means nothing. When he's satisfied, he shoves me into his room for the next stage.

"I am Iron Man." The grinding chords of Black Sabbath pulse through his stereo. The volume is just high enough to muffle any pained cries—but not high enough to raise suspicion from anyone downstairs.

"What do you know about God?" I ask, my voice light, as if I'm only curious.

"What?" He leans over to turn the music down a notch.

"I just wonder sometimes… about God. That's all. I just want to know what you think."

He hesitates, chewing over the question. "I know God exists, but I don't know much else for sure."

"Do you think it's possible that He's watching us right now?" I ask, my words deliberate, planting seeds that I hope will take root.

"I guess... all things are possible with God." His tone shifts, as if some old lesson from his Mormon upbringing is bubbling to the surface, cracking his certainty.

I watch the drop in his demeanor, sensing that something is shifting, however slightly. It's not a clean break—whatever holds him won't let go without a fight—but for now, it's a small victory. Even if only for tonight, I've planted doubt, made him think. It won't undo the demons that cling to him, but it's something. Misery may still reign, but for a moment, the battle tilts in my favor.

The host returns the next day, armed with a new strategy.

"Get down and give me fifty push-ups." His voice sharpens with the authority of a drill sergeant. Boot camp has begun.

A duffel bag sits in the corner, stuffed with concrete blocks, books, and other hard objects.

"Hit it until your knuckles bleed," he orders.

I throw jab after jab, unleashing combos until my hands throb and split.

"Five hundred sit-ups," he says, as if endurance alone will purge the demons.

This is still brutal, no doubt, but it's better than the tortures of Cameroon. The concrete floor wrecks me some nights, but I'm the only nine-year-old in my school who can do more than a thousand sit-ups. In a strange way, the things I endure here have opened something in me—a realization that maybe I *can* contend in this game after all.

Dude would have had icicles hanging from the eaves of his doghouse by now. His water bowl likely frozen solid, stuck in the snow just out of reach. I imagine his body had to be pried loose from the ice that anchored him to the ground. It's possible, though, that the ice was already melting in the first days of spring when they finally moved him. I don't know for sure, and there's no one I can ask. I only have my own conclusions, drawn from reason and guilt.

He only had me to care for him. Now, he's gone, replaced by another dog. When I was here, it was a battle just to keep him alive through the winters. Without me, I don't think he stood a chance.

Dude was an asshole. He dragged me down the street, gave me road rash, and slipped his leash more than once, leaving me wandering in a panic, searching for him for hours. I dreaded going back to the house without him—sometimes I'd rather stay out all night looking. But the truth was, he'd always wander back on his own. And if he made it home before I did, it was like he tattled on me, making it clear I'd failed to keep him in line. Either way, I paid for it. It was a lose-lose situation.

Yeah, Dude was an asshole. But maybe that's why I loved him. Maybe it was some twisted form of trauma bonding, forged through cold nights and scraped knees. He was my only friend. And thinking about how he was treated—how he probably froze to death without me—makes my stomach turn. If I wasn't there, who would have fed him? Some people shouldn't have kids—or pets.

Now there's a new dog at the house, a German Shorthaired Pointer. He's high-energy, bounding toward me the second I reach for his leash. His excitement is exhausting, but at least he's happy to get some attention.

The squirrel darts across the yard, and suddenly the dog takes off, jerking the leash. But I'm not six years old anymore—

I'm nine now, and tough as nails. If this dog thinks he's going to pull me around like Dude did, he's got another thing coming. Still, Coco-Mo—this new dog—sometimes gets the better of me.

We're out on the frozen lake now, and the steel blade of my hatchet sends chips of ice flying with every swing. Coco-Mo tugs against the leash as I hack through the thick ice, trying to keep control of both the leash and the hatchet. I swing it savagely, like a bushwhacker cutting through vines, until I break through.

With the hole cleared, I plunge my hand into the freezing water to check the traps I set a few days ago. These are muskrat traps, laid along the shoreline where the animals burrow into the embankment. Each pelt I pull earns Nick five or ten bucks. This is what I do—clearing paths through the ice, braving the cold water, all to catch muskrats so Nick can make a little money.

While Coco-Mo pulls against the leash, I reach deeper into the water, my fingers already going numb. I have to do this—check the traps, haul out the animals, skin them—before the nightly routines begin. There's no time to do my homework at home, so I get it done at school, whenever I can. And dinner? Most nights, that ship has already sailed.

All of this—the ice, the muskrats, the missed meals—it's all for Nick. It's his money, after all.

"Shut up Coke!"

Coke is doing handstands and somersaults, eager to get to the raccoon stuck in the trap. The trap is anchored to the ground with a chain and a stake, making it unlikely the raccoon can reach the log where I need to tie Coke up. This is one angry raccoon. We approach the log, and I spot a branch sticking up that I can easily slip the leash over.

Awkward Silence

"I have to deal with this. I have no choice," I mutter to myself.

I slowly and carefully inch closer to the coon. "You understand that Nick makes the rules, don't you?" I whisper, my heart racing as I creep a little nearer.

"It's either you or me. I'm sorry," I say, swinging the club and nailing the raccoon in the head. The cry it lets out is haunting, a sound so similar to an infant wailing. I strike again, and with each blow, I can almost feel the impact striking my own head. It cries like a baby, and it pierces my heart. But it's too late to just let it loose; once the animal is in the trap, it would devour me if it could. Its defense mechanisms are on high alert, and I have no choice.

"Even if I could set you free, Nick would take my head off if he found out."

Chapter 14
Men are Emotionless

Proverbs 15:19 "The way of a sluggard is like a hedge of thorns,"

"What is the training for? to become a monster? or to become a man?"

Cold water showers over my fingers, burning as if it were scalding hot. I have an inconsistent tremor that makes it impossible to unzip my jacket. My fingers are so cold that they shake and tremble with the intensity of a stretched rubber band just before it snaps. Fifteen more minutes of this water torture before I can even feel them. The sub-zero weather has wrecked me. I've been out in it, freezing my ass off, for more than two hours. Corduroy rags and holey mittens don't defend the front line very well. In fact, they don't prevent the frost's attack from any direction.

Again and again, I've reached my hands through the ice into the water. There are eighteen muskrat traps set—that's eighteen times chipping away at the ice, eighteen times plunging my hands into this freezing water. I feel as if my fingers are going to fall off.

I still can't unzip my jacket. I keep running this water over my hands for another fifteen minutes. I'd turn it just a little warmer if my fingers would cooperate. They say that's a bad idea, but I'd probably lick the wax ring of a toilet just to feel my fingers again.

My hands are shattered with bone cracks too numerous to count. The doctor can't even tell how many times my hands have been broken; he looks at the X-ray and still can't make out all the fractures. There have been multiple breaks, each with a different healing timeframe. Today, as my hands are frozen, they probably endure stress fractures anew. God made me tough as nails.

I hang the carcasses of these animals from the rafters in the garage, using small ropes around their feet. I have to hang them in such a way that the rope won't interfere with the incisions I have to make. I cut around their feet, then make a clean incision up to the anus. I slice around the tails of the muskrats, but with the coons, I handle the tail differently by dissecting it and peeling the fur around the tailbone. I peel back the fur from the incision, turning the skin inside out as I cut away where fat and connective tissue cling to the pelt. I have to be careful not to nick the pelt since that reduces what Nick will get for it. It's especially difficult to cut it free around the neck and face.

I hear the garage door open behind me as I trim away the fat. A few minutes later, Nick reaches over me and tries to force-feed me a piece of intestine from one of the carcasses I've already skinned. There's a struggle as he presses the rat's innards into my face. I drop the knife to the ground to avoid any potential stabbing. I press his hands away, and he finally stops. He hands me the intestine and commands me to eat it.

One might think they know what they would do, but there's a lot more here than meets the eye. There's a form of conditioning that broke me. I've been viciously beaten for disobedience more times than I can count. This threat hangs over me constantly. Yes, I ate that intestine with rat filth smeared on my face.

After skinning these animals, I go into the house to wash up and warm up. Sometimes I can have dinner before the day's closing rituals begin, but not often. I punch the duffel bag with the intent to kill it. It swings back and forth as my fists drive it one way and then the other. I do five hundred sit-ups, pretending to struggle as I approach six hundred so I can finally be done. Push-ups come next; he has me do multiple sets of a hundred, usually four or five. Then, of course, I stand against the wall to be punched in the chest. In the name of "making me a man," things get thrown, punches fly, objects swing; they say that to be a man, blood must be shed.

This isn't the type of man I want to become. I see nothing in these role models that I want to carry forward beyond this chapter of my life. Strength is a good quality to have as a man. Agility is valuable too. And having the mental fortitude to survive harsh conditions matters. In some ways, these experiences teach me things that help me reach these goals. But there are qualities that make a man far more important than what I see here. Where is integrity? I look for it and cannot find it. Where is truth, honor, courage? Yes, I'm taught a form of courage, but it's the kind that hides behind lies about "falling down the stairs." What difference does it make if I can protect a family if I can't love one?

Fear for my life and the monster I may become is what drives me to summon the Wizard. Today, it's clear to me that this "wizard" has always been a manifestation of dissociative identity disorder—a peculiar twist. I don't want to admit that my identity is shaped by these circumstances. Call it a coping mechanism, which it is, but if I use the psychological term—dissociative identity disorder—it's like I can hear the locks on the door to the rubber room clicking shut.

"Building rapport happens in just the first few seconds of a relationship," the Wizard's insight emerges from my mind. Maybe it's immature for a man to have an imaginary friend. I'm only nine, though, and it's not hurting anyone—besides, no one even knows what's going on in my head.

"A boy imitating his dad leaning against his car is one of the highest forms of communication. If you imitate Nick's gestures, you'll build rapport. It's a powerful thing because he'll almost see you as an extension of himself," the Wizard continues.

"Think of it as becoming a mirror that reflects his image back to him—his words, his gestures, even his emotions."

The world around me freezes as if time itself has stopped.

"You have to be strong. You can't take on his identity. You're just using this as a tool to keep yourself safe, but if you connect too deeply, you'll lose yourself. You'll lose compassion. You'll lose your morals. You'll lose the ability to love. You'll begin to take on his character. You'll become bitter and angry."

There is a heightened energy streaming through the classroom. It takes the form of excitement hidden by discomfort. There isn't a soul that would admit that it is an enjoyable discomfort, even though each and everyone of us are looking forward to it. We are beginning the highly controversial part of our curriculum. It isn't a controversial issue where the school board or parents are concerned but we, the students, shyly drag our feet like zombies as we walk toward this doom. We are passing the threshold and entering the world of dance.

"Nick, did you have to dance when you were in the fourth grade?" I ask him hoping to open up a conversation that gives me the smallest amount of insight as to what lies before me.

"Dancing is for faggots and pussies. Are you a little faggot? Jack-a-puss." His words stood erected in the empty field of understanding that I had on this subject. They resonated with vulgerity and hatred.

"Jack, we know that Nick is not the enemy but that the enemy is delivering his message through Nick. Ask yourself, what does the enemy have to gain from contaminating the soil of your understanding about dance?" The wizard begins to use his words to defend my innocence.

"Dance is liberating. Dance is used to make a connection, not only with your partner, but to the rhythms and sounds of nature. It can be a divine connection. Dance is a way into a portal of self expression. It is an art form that has to be experienced to truly understand it. If the enemy can discourage you from the experience he keeps you caged and destroys the possible connections that could form from it." The wizard persists with his analysis.

This memory is frozen in a time capsule that has been buried in shallow earth. I reach back through the pages that follow to lead the inner child out of this confusion. From this moment, I have avoided dance and the joy that can be experienced and expressed through it. I have missed the nearly spiritual connection of movements in synchronicity This is the perfect opportunity to demonstrate why I consider this a rescue mission.

The walls of the maze have been constructed of false beliefs just like this one. I have witnessed many masculine men that seem to enjoy dance but that is not enough to demolish the wall that was erected that day. At fifty-six years old I decide that it is time to advocate for this child. It is time to consider if it is something I would enjoy. I set an appointment for private dance lessons. The very first lesson the wrecking ball slammed into this wall. I felt like I had three feet. My coordination was still inhibited by echoing voices that established this false belief. I had to contend with the negative residue of this belief. But as the debris cleared there was a major sense of accomplishment. It wasn't the hustle or the salsa that fed the accomplished feeling. It was the opening of my eyes to the path of healing that it encouraged.

To see the open space where this wall was constructed was uplifting. The view that it blocked is beautiful. There were jewels unearthed in that lesson that had the power to heal.

The branches continue to grow. Each stroke of the pen shades the field a little more. My grandpa once said, "Jackie, this tree is about one hundred and fifty years old. Can you imagine the stories it might be able to tell?" I wonder what stories this tree is going to tell. If it were a fruit tree, would its fruit be bitter? I can feel hostility and bitterness growing in me. Will her image in the silhouette become disfigured from the chant of all women being a pain in the neck? It's too early to tell, but I hope that one day I'll meet a woman who contributes a good sense of moral character to add to the silhouette's picture.

The shape of the woman has become picturesque, leaving me pondering the symbolism of my desire for her. She isn't real. She is elusive. She is merely a silhouette in this dream, but the feelings are real. I can't quite understand her representation other than as inspiration.

Another figure seems to hover over her, but I still can't make out the image. It's fierce. It's powerful. But it's not defined well enough to tell if it's symbolic. It might be innocent; it might be the collective embodiment of all the evil in my world.

"Crash!" Gravel flies every which way, followed by the screech of tires.

"Hold on!" The orange Volkswagen Bug we're in slips into a ditch, and Quin steers the fishtailing car back onto the road. We're lucky not to have rolled in. Amazingly, he keeps it under control.

Quin is Madia's dad and an off-duty cop. He picks us up from the skating rink. Nick is at the cabin with his grandparents, and Corine is babysitting for some friends from church. With both hands that would strangle me not at home, I can move about freely, without fingers around my neck. I can go with Cherie and Madia to the skating rink. This is one of those nights when the demons reach beyond borders. I don't know how this works, but I know that nothing happens by chance. This whole thing is part of a larger scheme.

The station wagon that just collided with us speeds off as Quin brings the Bug under control. He reaches past my knee into the glove box and pulls out his pistol. There's a line of oncoming traffic, preventing Quin from discharging his weapon. The blasts of gunfire can still be heard. The chase is on. We're in hot pursuit, and bullets are flying. We tear through town as gunfire erupts around us. Cherie and Madia reach into the front seat to hold onto me. Now that the city limits are behind us, Quin can return fire. A blaze of gunfire echoes as he does. Cherie and Madia cling to me, their grip betraying their fear. I feel nothing—it's been a long time since I've felt anything. Today may be the day I realize most of my emotions have packed up and left. Each gunshot causes the girls to clutch me a little tighter.

When we catch up to him, the two vehicles nudge each other. Quin is trying to get this guy to stop. Each impact leaves fingernail marks in my skin. The girls are terrified, crying silently, their eyes pooling and streams running down their cheeks. I still don't know if I feel anything at all. Men don't get scared, and men certainly don't cry.

We chase him onto a country road in the Minnesota sticks by yet another one of those lakes. The life of that station wagon begins to seep away, steam rising from its hood. It finally comes to a complete stop. The motor likely seized from overheating—one of the bullets must have hit something vital. Quin swings open his door and, in a flash, is out of the car, holding the driver at gunpoint.

"Show me your hands." The driver fidgets.

"Show me your hands, or I will fire." The driver slowly raises his empty hands out the window.

"Now, open the door using the outside handle." The driver complies, opening the door.

"Step out of the car slowly." Quin backs up, keeping about fifteen to twenty feet between them. The driver steps out.

"Get down on your knees." The driver hesitates, reluctant to kneel. I can tell he's considering making a move on Quin, though he's unsure.

"Put that gun down!" A voice suddenly calls out from the woods by the lake. A man steps forward, seemingly appearing out of nowhere. He stops at roughly the same distance from Quin as the driver.

"Put that gun down!" the man repeats.

"I'm a cop!" Quin says, steadying his aim.

"I don't care who you are. Put that gun down!" The man moves closer to Quin. Beads of sweat start to form on Quin's forehead as he now has to keep two men at bay.

"Get down on your knees!" Quin commands the man from the lake, who continues approaching. "Get back, or I will shoot!" Quin's voice is sharp, and the man hesitates, taking a small step back, while the driver shifts slightly, leaning toward Quin. I can see it—he's preparing to charge.

"Get down on your knees!" Quin's gun moves back and forth between the two men, who refuse to comply. It's only a matter of time before one of them makes a move, or Quin fires. Tension thickens; this standoff can't last much longer.

Finally, I hear faint sirens in the distance. They're coming from town, but out here, the sound can travel miles. If these two are going to act, it will be soon. Quin's forehead glistens as the sirens grow louder.

Cherie and Madia are still latched onto me, their arms wrapped around mine so tightly I can't tell where one ends and the other begins. They feel like growths on my arm, but they're a reminder of the gravity of the moment.

The sirens are louder now, and flashing lights appear over the ridge. The police cars screech to a stop, officers jumping out with guns drawn.

I see the tension drain from Quin, his shoulders relaxing. It's almost as if he's free to start breathing again, maybe even growing hair again, as my grandpa would say. What we didn't know, but he did, is that he was holding those men back the entire time—with an empty gun.

Chapter 15
No One Gets In and No One Gets Out

Romans 5:12 "When Adam sinned, Sin entered the world."

"The snowball that is rolled downhill will get bigger."

Damaged thoughts breed insecurities, and from these insecurities, fear is born. The Wizard makes it clear: I am responsible for everything. If I weren't, then my actions wouldn't matter; the outcome would be the same. I am responsible. When I don't know what to do, yet do nothing, it only feeds my insecurity. Fear is now compartmentalized, locked away with Torment. Agony sits in serene silence, an unyielding constant within the walls of my mind. This defensive strategy demands a fortified perimeter—a minefield encircling the city's walls. It has to be impenetrable. No one can enter or leave. Even Cupid's arrows are barred. The armory is fortified, fully loaded to protect the heart. Misery, torment, and the others remain entrenched within, barring any possible intruder from infringing on the sanctity of this place.

A slow-moving stream of lava inches wider with each new assault. Damaged thoughts lead to isolation, further separating me from my heart. Still, it's no cause for alarm, though I worry that one day it might be.

I feel a tremor through my body, resonating from head to toe, pulling me back to consciousness. I've been convulsing. I've been seizing. I don't know how long I was out, but I'm on the cold concrete tile floor now, regaining my senses. I look up, eyes struggling to focus on the bed—the top bunk. I must have been sleeping.

"Oh shit, I thought I killed you," Nick laughs uncontrollably, the kind of laughter that would send milk out his nose if he had a glass in hand. *He thought he killed me, and it's funny?*

Apparently, he pulled me off the top bunk while I was asleep, dropping me straight onto my head. I was thrashing on the floor, unconscious. The ringing in my head drowns out my thoughts.

"You looked like a fish out of water," he cackles, laughter spilling out again.

As my mind begins to clear, I wonder how close I came to death this time. The reaper always seems to linger, lurking just beyond sight. The closer I get to death in this world, the more I can feel the Grim Reaper's influence within.

Treachery glows, bright and hot. The fire within has only grown, fed by recent events. I can almost see the Grim Reaper and the dragon, arguing over the terms of my demise. As I sit back and watch, the insanity becomes apparent—I feel no allegiance to either side. I don't care who wins the debate. I'm completely disinterested. The river of apathetic ash has risen higher than anyone could have foreseen, and I'm not sure the levee will hold much longer.

Fear remains locked tightly behind the minefield. I find myself growing indifferent. Death is neither the beginning nor the end. It may simply exist somewhere in the middle, unmoved by any shift in the world around it.

Sugar Lake is pretty sweet. While I am here, I get to eat, and there is reprieve from torture. Nick's grandparents have a cabin here. To say it is a cabin is like calling the Taj Mahal a house. That is an overdramatic statement, but Don Cardelli

once had a speakeasy where Al Capone hid out. It has been opened as a sort of museum of the underworld. I don't know his place in the food chain of mobsters, but I do know he is a great cook.

"Jack, tonight I'm gonna make you veal parmigiana. You need to pick the pasta."

In the back room, he keeps a tub full of every type of pasta you can imagine. I am very excited. Remember that most of my meals are still tampered with. Here, Don has a watchful eye over the meals he serves. Nick can't sabotage my plate if he wants to.

Gluttony— that big gross blob— churns behind the gate. Gluttony, in his creation, was denied basic human needs. Every meal feels like it could be his last. This feeling is valid. Demons ride the bronco of bucking thoughts, gouging their spurs into his flank. The words "you're a dead man" ring throughout the city gates as if it were on a loudspeaker. The implication is obvious. This lingering thought should be present in all things. Every thought should have death attached to it, so in every meal, there is that thought in the back of the mind: "It can be your last."

I would compare this to the idea of sales tax. As a store owner, I can't tell you I will pay your sales tax for you. I don't see a difference between whether you pay it or I do. The same amount of tax will be paid, but that lingering thought is omnipresent at this point. The government is in your every transaction. It is the forceful hand of subservience. "You're a dead man" is the same.

This sounds like the evaluation of the Wizard, but it exists within the gated community of emotion. It may be that the distinctive partitions of the maze are not holding back the line. The warlike evaluations may contain these emotions for now, but there will come a day when this changes. I have to wonder if these walls can support the weight. In this evaluation, it is not the altered ego.

It is bigger than this and reaching out into the world beyond the maze. It is shifting into a very complex social concept. It is easy to notice the similarity between greed and gluttony. From the inner workings of the maze, it is a short stone's throw to visualize the outside world becoming what is happening internally.

"Rigatoni!" And yes, the meals are amazing!

I know Don and Vera to be wonderful people. Going to the lake is a privilege that I do not have except to be there with Nick. Don and Vera go to bed early. They will place a peg in the hole if there are any real shenanigans. I mean, if Nick is to beat me, they will most likely hear it. Even if they do not hear it, Nick will not take that chance.

A chair smashes into the back of a big man who is sweating and spitting on everything within the ropes of the ring. Nick and I sit watching TV. He is watching that very old-school WWF wrestling. I just don't get into that, but I am not going to say one way or another. I zone out and pay no attention. I am off in the study, searching for ideas to win this chess game or to solve the riddles before me. I have been learning to play chess. I like the idea of expanding my logical strategies.

"Most of the game is played by getting into the head of your opponent, thinking about what his next move is likely to be. The most consistent approach to determine his future behavior is by analyzing his past actions," the Wizard begins to express an idea.

I don't know what to do with this information, but it makes sense.

"Another way to conceptualize this is to consider advertising. You may not be thinking about BK, but then a commercial comes on TV, and suddenly you know what your mission is for dinner. You can influence the outcome with the power of suggestion."

I understand his words. He is not speaking Greek. It all makes sense, but putting it into practice seems almost unrealistic. He is saying that I can win a game of chess by telling my opponent his moves. That is ridiculous. It doesn't work that way. It can't work that way. Or can it? I think about when I brought God up to Nick and how that changed the situation. It was just the power of suggestion.

"Imagine that Nick has the stats that deem him most likely to pair with you in the game three days from now. Start planting the seeds of suggestion. In three days' time, the crop should be ready for harvest. In order for this to be effective, you have to be willing to play the long game. You need to strategize beyond the game. Take your time. A single victory can change the entire course of the game."

"How do I determine which battle to win when I'm not sure what battles we will fight?"

"You take the offensive. You determine the battles," the Wizard suggests.

"He is too inconsistent unless I'm just going to start a fight." I reenter awareness of the room when Nick gets up to use the restroom.

"The fight can be anything you want it to be, and as long as you win, it will be your victory. The best part is that he doesn't even have to know he lost." A light turns on in my mind.

"I get it, but what?" These neurons firing back and forth between the Wizard and me are loose ideas, but they are imaginative and entertaining.

"Let's try this. If it works, we can start to imagine larger objectives. What can we say is pretty certain about this weekend?" We've got to start somewhere.

"I will be going out to set traps tomorrow and checking them on Sunday."

"We know, within reasonable doubt, that Don will want to stop for lunch on the way back to White Bear Lake." The Wizard is turning over the cards we are dealt.

"Yeah, he likes to do that." Usually, it's Nick's choice to go to Dairy Queen.

"Where would you like to eat?" I see the big question mark before me.

"BK," I respond.

"Funny you would choose BK. Didn't I mention it earlier?" He flips another card, allowing me to absorb the light of his perspective.

"Yeah, I guess you did." I chuckle to myself. This chuckle doesn't cross the stream into a physical cackle; it stays concealed in my imagination.

"Start advertising it to him, but do it very subtly. You'll have to advertise it to all of them, but remember to be subtle."

I think about how to be subtle, and the best way I can think of is to draw from the commercials. I mean, I can try to talk about a king eating a burger. I contemplate this and wonder about Nick's retribution if I'm caught in my words. I'm trying to influence him in a different way now, and I'm not sure how Nick will react if he grasps what I am doing. I have to be artful.

Awkward Silence

Anything other than this wrestling. I can't think when there is this level of ridiculousness. How can anyone consider this real—or for that matter, wrestling? It's sort of a depiction of modern-day politics.

"Do you want a Dr. Pepper?" I get up to fetch us some sodas because, as a habit, when Nick asks something like that, it's usually because he wants me to retrieve them.

"No, you wait here; I'll get them." I am bewildered. This is not normal. I instantly go on high alert.

After a few minutes, he returns to hand me a soda. I begin to drink it, and it tastes a little funny. I'm disgusted because I suspect he may have pissed in it. There is definitely something off about it. I sense the abnormality. Well, I guess I don't fully understand it. I start feeling strange. He watches me with anticipation, then starts laughing. I don't know what is happening. He laughs harder.

"Stand up." I stand up.

"Walk across the room." This sends him into hysterics. It's a few years later before I realize that I am drunk.

The next morning, I wake up groggy. I know I have to get up, but I don't want to. I can smell eggs and waffles cooking. I'm surely expected to be downstairs for breakfast.

"Wow, this is a whopper of a breakfast!" Here goes nothing.

Our plates are served, and forks are clanging. I don't want to push my agenda too hard, and I haven't naturally found another place to highlight during breakfast.

"Thank you for breakfast!"

"Jack, let's go!" Everything Nick says comes to me as a command; this is no exception, and the words should be interpreted as such.

In the woods outside the lake, there is brush. The terrain is rough and hard to walk through. A barbed wire fence separates us from the other side. That's where we are going, I guess.

Nick has a shotgun in his hand, and as he steps over the fence, the trigger gets jerked. The gun goes off next to my head. His eyes widen, and his face goes pale. He thought it was funny when he thought he had killed me before. He laughed while I lay shaking on the floor, but somehow this is different. The sound of the shot took him by surprise, and that's the only difference I can see, other than to say this was a near miss, while the other didn't miss at all.

"I almost took your head off." He is frantic. He is panicked. I edit the language in my mind.

"Yeah, you almost removed my crown." I press forward with my BK agenda.

"You can't tell anyone that this happened!" They wouldn't listen anyway. "If anyone asks what we did, you leave this part out, or you're a dead man!"

"I get it, I get it. Hold the pickles. I get it!" There is something growing in me—a sort of hope that I might be able to influence my life.

"Hold the pickles?" he questions.

"Yeah, leave that part out. I get it." I say this as if I am responding to another threat.

Awkward Silence

Is this another near-death experience? This wouldn't classify as a near-death experience to me, except for seeing and hearing his reaction. Maybe it was much closer than I thought. I still don't understand why this feels so much bigger than when I was actually physically affected. I was lying on the floor, flopping around, and somehow that made the news.

It's Sunday, and funny enough, we stop at Burger King for our lunch. This could be coincidental. It could be by happenstance, but it merits more exploration. I mean, advertisers use this methodology, and they pay millions of dollars for the opportunity to utilize it. If it keeps me alive, I would pay millions for it as well—even though I don't have millions, I can see a time when I will.

Chapter 16
Kissing the Devil's Ass

Psalms 1:1 "Blessed is the man that walks not in the counsel of the ungodly."

"When one sins for personal gain he may as well be kissing the devil's ass."

The way I process information has changed. It no longer clings to the innocent perceptions I once had. Now, it feels as if everything and everyone is against me, and my emotions follow the same path. Consequently, the decisions that shape my actions have also been altered. My thoughts, feelings, and will—the essence of my soul—no longer seem to belong to me. Peace and tranquility feel like remnants of the past. I carry with me the violent echoes of living alongside a murderer and those subjected to this hateful journey. Under this influence, my actions bring hatred into the physical world. I doubt they realized how they were unleashing their own demons on me, just as I was unaware of doing the same.

Footsteps pound the ground behind me, a loud percussive beat like war drums. The faster I run, the louder and closer those footsteps echo. The entire horizon is filled with people chasing after me, and the Grim Reaper himself is closing in. I thought the biggest puzzle of my life was deciphering the symbolism in this dream—until I embarked on this rescue mission. I have wandered seemingly endless trails, questioning at every turn if I am on the right path.

Death follows close behind, always near but barely missing. Then death claims its reward: Ted shot and killed a man with a .45 in the bar.

Awkward Silence

The man fell, and his life ended in a single, bold moment. I always knew my uncle had it in him. I wonder what sort of twisted narrative fills his mind. Does he hide behind layers of delusion, shielding himself from the accountability of taking another human life? Do voices whisper to him in his drunken depths, or is he resolute in believing it's either his life or another's? The man he killed posed no physical threat; it wasn't self-defense. He simply pulled the trigger and blew him away. This is the man I have been living with.

The stream of lava quickens. It's either a large stream or a small river, glowing red-hot. Once dim, it now burns brighter, illuminating a silhouetted figure in the tree. The figure is unmistakably a dragon, preparing its den. This dragon seems to crave dominion over both realms.

When I heard of the incident, my mind drifted through space and time, and I saw myself from an outside perspective, glimpsing what might be a memory. I am helping Ted push a rolled-up carpet from a boat into the lake. Am I an accessory to a crime? This can't be a real memory. But at times, it feels disturbingly real. The fact that I can even imagine this, let alone question its authenticity, is a tragedy in itself.

Smoke rises from the lava, and the light glows intensely. The dragon's insolent roars fill the air, overpowering the softened words of the Wizard. Lava floods from every pore of the city wall, bringing with it blasphemous declarations. I am left with feelings of worthlessness and torturous memories. Every bruise, cut, and wound seems to carry itself along the city walls. Memories of a time before this descent into hell have all but dissolved. The dragon feeds on every painful detail. Flames shoot from its mouth, scorching the earth.

The blue flame of the torch penetrates my flesh. It feels hopeless. The odds of having a normal life are stacked against me. There's no future—a family or marriage isn't in the cards.

"Women are nothing but a pain in the neck, a thorn in the side."

That mantra holds weight. My aunt hurts me because I remind her of her brother. I did it; it's my fault. My mom is oblivious to reality. I can't picture myself with a wife if she would be anything like my mom. With these women embodying womanhood for me, the repeated phrase plants seeds in the soil of my mind. And yet, I am responsible. I need to clear away the thorns and debris.

The flow of lava heats the city. It's the fire that burns within, misdirected. It oozes through the gates and seeps onto the walls of false beliefs, creating rock formations that seem like permanent structures—barriers that obscure truth. The child within me is still at large, but finding him feels as futile as searching for a needle in a haystack. Falling into this pit of lava would lead to a life of self-destruction.

The dragon devours confidence in one swift movement. Anything good leaves no trace. The loss is overwhelming, yet I can't cry because "men don't cry." The vines have begun to choke out any possibility of hope. The lava spreads across the ground of desolation where the dragon stands, covering up all life. Death crawls, seeping into the world beyond these walls.

"I can't hold on any longer."

The screams of emotional creatures dull my senses. A pasty residue of brimstone lingers in my mouth. Attempting to balance the numbness in my heart with logic has left moon-sized craters all over this landscape. There is no disguise to mask the infection or hide the leprosy. Depression fills every corridor, anxiety floods every hallway.

The fire from the dragon's mouth sets the nations ablaze. Built on lies, this infrastructure is somehow convincing. The incomprehensible truth is that the same doom shadows the natural world. It's a fate that fallen societies have always faced. Could this beast that has torn through me also be the beast manifesting in the world? Could it be the same force driving gender confusion, role reversals, and the dissonance plaguing our nation and beyond? Has this internal beast become external?

The ground beneath me trembles with fear. Ash blows out, covering the surface. Along the walls, a lava dome has formed. Creatures and their demons scurry across the dome and up the hillside, cloaked in ash and difficult to see. They climb through crevices along the new hillside. These are the demons within.

The debris left behind becomes the dragon's nesting place. Ash on the ground lies so thick that it conceals beings caught in the eruption. This eruption is no accident; it's a waging of war. It seeks to suck oxygen from the air and expand the kingdom of treachery. It's time to take up arms against this onslaught, but happiness and joy are not strong enough.

I must remember—this was supposed to be a rescue mission. I came here to find and save the child within me, to pull him out of the darkness. I can't believe how complicated this simple goal has become. Rescuing the child within has turned into a mission more complex than all of aeronautic engineering compressed into a single file. Emotions and thoughts have emerged from places I didn't even know existed.

If a single cell can hold bacteria or microorganisms, and a computer chip can contain millions of functioning transistors, then perhaps it isn't so hard to believe that bitterness, remorse, sorrow, guilt, and shame could unite to build a city within our souls. To protect our innocence from these negative emotions, we might summon Pride, Greed, Gluttony, Lust, Wrath, Envy, and Sloth— each a layer of defense. Together, they create a twisted version of truth, a miniature reflection of our society's structure. Each of these vices is a distortion of reality, a deception we use to spy on our enemies or to keep ourselves blissfully unaware of our true standing in the world.

Greed follows close behind this deception, as we hoard ideas and resources that could revolutionize society. Gluttony says, "As long as we are fat and happy, the rest of the world can fend for itself—unless, of course, they bring something to the table." Lust, at its core, is the desire for control, for the power to boast and conquer. Each of these impulses perverts the truth. If we dissect each vice, weigh it individually, and compare it to the ideals we believe in, we see the discord.

These seven "heads" gather to wage war against everything. They use the media to spread gossip and propaganda, governments to consolidate power, and religion as a veil to oppress under the guise of truth. Corporations and businesses become promotional tools for materialism; schools are used to shape and mold thought. Factories house prisoners in jobs that trap them, and money becomes the ultimate instrument of control.

In its purest form, money is innocent. But, like humanity itself, once separated from innocence, it becomes monstrous. Originally, money was not meant as a way of life but as a tool to balance trade. You might trade me a lamb for a cow, agreeing to pay the balance later. Yet this simple idea twisted into a game no one could have foreseen. Money became a commodity, not just a tool. Now it occupies the souls and imprisons the spirits of nearly everyone on the planet, its power reinforced by governments.

These vices conspire to feed a single body of misery, built from individual pieces of suffering, passed on through words and actions. Sin has a way of linking the victim to the act itself. This is why abuse survivors often become abusers, or why someone hurt by betrayal may become mistrustful. Sin captivates and enslaves as it marches across the battlefield. Satan, commander of a defeated army, enlists his captives to fight for him, while the seven-headed dragon—this body of misery—casts its shadow over the child within.

That child, the six-year-old who was wounded, is beginning to heal, though the sin remains inside him, boastful and unyielding. The lava crawling across the ground entices him, and the voices rising against his aggressors offer him a sense of solidarity. This shared ground of understanding is inches away from merging with him. Hell's celebration surrounds the child as its guest of honor. Enticed by the excitement, he nears that fateful connection.

Led Balloons float, singing praises to their dark master. The stairway that once led to heaven now winds down to hell, and queens revel, lost in their haze, while "another one bites the dust," tumbling into the abyss. The chants grow louder, and with each twisted anthem, the river of sin widens, a dark praise song for the beast.

It's time to move to a vantage point. I need a clear visual of this child—to pull him out before it's too late. A white snake can't hide well in the shadows; I watch it slither alone down the road. Slowly and quietly, I follow, reaching a ridge where I spot a small cave. It's just enough for shelter—a place to wait until the storm passes.

In the basement beyond a red-and-white checkered floor stood a bar—a cedar half-round with a granite top. Behind it, ordinary cabinets lined the wall, but one concealed a small hole in the wall's shielding. I was small enough to crawl in there, to vanish. It became my vantage point. No one could find me, and that was the point. Sometimes, hiding there was my only escape from the torment Nick would bring. And as I waited in that dark corner, I began to slip away.

In the heart of this mental landscape, Rage and Agony sit upon thrones by the lava river, united as if in marriage, casting judgment day and night. They sit as king and queen, ruling with relentless opinions.

"She doesn't love you. How could she? Your own family doesn't even love you. You are unlovable," Agony proclaims, as the court bows to her words.

Rage responds, "What do you think, Agony? Is there any chance he's lovable? Or should he just give up?"

"I think it's hopeless. He can't provide. He's unattractive, and he's certainly not smart, is he?"

"No," Agony sneers. "He might be the most pathetic of them all."

Their words grow stronger, feeding the brightness of the lava. It's as if the lava thrives on each negative thought, gaining strength from the relentless criticism. I realize that such dark opinions must be driven by a deeply distorted image—a twisted perception that fuels this self-destructive narrative. It's clear these views are planted from beyond, tainted by treachery. I see some of this in my own experiences, in the fragments of family dynamics from back in Minnesota.

This is more than just negative self-talk; it's a false belief system taking root. Every critical thought feels like a screen, shielding me from an uncomfortable reality, one that drives people to desperate measures. This darkness breeds resentment, the kind that fuels conflict, even wars. Coveting a different life stirs this poisonous ooze. The same desperation that compels a thief drives an alcoholic to escape reality, and a person haunted by shame to avoid confronting the truth.

And yet, here I am, sharing this story. Am I, in a sense, spreading this infection? I want to lead others out of it, not trap them in it. I never meant to treat anyone with ill intent—yet I have. I don't see myself as evil, yet I've allowed that river of lava to flow through my veins. My struggle has been against a self-worth I've never fully known, a love I could never hold onto because I had no source of it.

Suicide, tragically, has become an epidemic. There's a profound imbalance in society, a rift that has led to this crisis. To ignore it is to ignore every path forward, every branch that may grow through the next few chapters. And as this journey continues, it's clear I'm not alone in this fight—just as the child within isn't alone, either. Together, we'll take these steps toward finding a way out.

It is the beast on the throne, the dragon spewing fire that creates smoke thick enough to obscure the truth. The flames devour the pages formed from the tree of life—my life. The demons that once warned me of approaching dangers now run wild, rampaging within. They've taken control of my mind, my city, my study, and my maze. They are in my decisions, tangled in my emotions. They are the all-encompassing reality that binds me. And I don't know this—I don't even suspect it. I am captured, yet unaware of my captivity.

From this vantage point, I see the desolation beneath the foundation he walks on. The one I speak of holds the child hostage. But the child isn't alone; there are too many captives to count. A line of prisoners stretches through the treacherous city, each holding a whip. Just as confusion begins to rise, a sharp "CRACK" cuts through my thoughts.

"Strike the one in front of you," comes the command.

The sound of the whip echoes, each crack followed by the same command, "Strike the one in front of you." It is the rhythm of treachery, the beat that drives this city. The whip's strike, the flash of flame on flesh, the muted screams—it's all drowned out by the blaring speakers that drown out agony, only letting faint cries slip through. It's the hollow wail of a little boy, trapped in a maze of wizard's thoughts, his heart encased in stone. It's the subdued cries of a public, led blindly by a capitalist beast, from a carnal world toward spiritual ruin.

Watching it turns my stomach. I can't imagine any reasoning, any thought that could justify being in this line, whipping the one before me. I wonder what force would feed on people's minds to turn them against each other this way. I never understood how Hitler rallied his followers. It seems the same— like following a warped, broken system. Some will follow it all the way to the depths of hell, while others will break away as if pulled by a force beyond them. And here's the truth that unsettles me: capitalism, as a concept, is an earth-bound currency that won't pass through heaven's gates. So why do we continue to hold on to it here?

The flames leap from the lava bed with fierce intensity, illuminating the growing crowd of demonic presences. An army, vast and formidable. I see that the one at the front of the line is somehow promoted—or, perhaps, he's forced to start again. The structure is unclear, but it has the feel of a twisted hierarchy, a "foreman" of sorts at each level. Here, advancement is earned by stepping over the fallen, using them as rungs on a ladder. But no matter how high you climb, no matter how many you step over, you're only lifted just high enough to kiss the devil's feet.

Awkward Silence

The price for following this piper is rarely disclosed until it's time to pay. Prison is part of the cost, though sometimes it comes with a discount. My uncle went to prison for five years— five years for ending another man's life. The eyes that look down from heaven surely see it differently. And though I think there's no deeper point of degradation than taking a life, I realize that's only one perspective. A single lie, whispered and repeated, can cascade through lives like fire, causing more damage than we might ever know.

Scripture offers me hope for my uncle's eternal fate, and I cling to that hope. I am not the judge, and I'm grateful for that mercy. When he squeezed the trigger and the man fell, it seemed as though I was, in some strange way, delivered from my own hell. Perhaps that sacrifice had a purpose from a heavenly perspective. Yet, darkness and fire remained within me because that was all I had to offer.

The survival instincts, like those of a wizard, etched themselves deeply into my mind. But these thoughts have shifted from desperate pleas of a litigator advocating for my life to become the cold, unyielding walls of my internal maze. The relentless fire of treachery scorches my emotions, leaving a legacy of flames that, if not extinguished, could burn for eternity. There was a deeply rooted anger within me, glowing among the embers surrounding this inner city. I didn't even recognize the anger—it was but a faint light, casting shadows on the demons within. Yet, when unleashed, it flared into full-blown rage, ignited by the fuel of painful memories.

There's a sense of urgency rising from the ruins, urging me toward the twisted morality of this town. I need a clearer view, a better understanding. And as I search, I find myself surrounded by empty, dark eyes. I wonder—are these the eyes of captives beaten down into submission, or am I staring into the eyes of the enemy itself? A deep sorrow binds these gazes together, reflecting no light and no hope. They are easy to overlook at a glance. How many times have I, as a father, become a stranger to my own daughter's eyes? Her eyes, so beautiful and crystal blue, mirror my own. I look into them, admiring their brightness, but how often do I look beyond the surface to see her emotions, her racing thoughts? Only when you truly look through the windows of the soul do you notice what lies within—fear, sadness, perhaps anger. If you've looked away for too long, you may only see a storm of emotions, speaking of chaos. And if chaos is visible, chances are choices and circumstances are already cluttering the room. In my own eyes, I see a hard-won victory. Though tired from years of battle, they still shine with life.

The enemy is ruthless. His purpose is to steal, kill, and destroy everything he touches. Though his ultimate goal may be death, he takes pleasure in inflicting suffering along the way. He knows that your agony inevitably becomes the agony of others. Viewed through a spiritual lens, this is the very image of hell.

I move past those thoroughly stained in the acidic grime of treachery, creeping along the harsh textures of my surroundings, cloaked in silence. Each breath is measured to ensure no sound. I can't afford to be seen. Waking the dragon would be a certain, terrifying end.

The molten red glow of lava provides the only light here. The earth trembles slightly, the crack of whips echoing in the distance. The scent of death, decay, and obsolescence fills the air, and the taste of sulfur clings stubbornly at the back of my throat, as bitter and acrid as ever.

Creatures of all kinds are arranged like game pieces on a red-and-white checkered floor, an unsettling assembly beneath the looming shadows. I need to reach the boy. I let myself move with the natural ebb and flow of the environment, blending into the shadows cast by the structures around me. I proceed with quiet faith, willing even my thoughts to harmonize with the dissonant atmosphere. I am as subtle as a ninja.

Once again, I see him—huddled beneath the dragon's ominous underbelly. A bead of sweat forms on my forehead as I edge closer, moving at the slow, unhurried pace of lava. Each step is deliberate, as I don't want to startle the boy; any sudden movement or quickened heartbeat could awaken the beast with no weapon to defend ourselves but a stick from the ground.

A rogue thought crosses my mind, threatening to disrupt the delicate harmony of the place, and I see the dragon stir slightly. I focus on regulating my own heartbeat, forcing even my eyes to stay perfectly still, fearing the slightest movement will betray me. The precarious calm shivers, like a tension momentarily disturbed before settling back into place.

With the grace of a tiny ballerina, I edge closer, as though shape-shifting into the surroundings to avoid the creature's field of vision. Now, there is only the dragon between the boy and me. This dragon is a nightmare made real—a manifestation born of a child's most profound pain and torment. Its appearance is beyond fierce: a monstrous red with seven heads crowned in twisted diadems, ten horns jutting from its neck like spears aimed in every direction. Words fail to capture the visceral horror of its face, but its features feel like a culmination of every form of torment—bones breaking, flesh burning, unending violence. All the agony of abuse distilled into a single, grotesque being.

I'm almost upon the boy when he senses me and startles, awakening the dragon within him. Fire blasts from the creature's nostrils, searing my hip. Ignoring the pain, I rush forward, scoop the boy up like a football, shielding him as best I can. He wriggles and protests slightly, but nothing matters now except our escape.

I had mapped an escape route when I entered this hell, but now everything was crumbling. The walls shook and fell, the riverbed shifted, and the ground quaked with eruptions. Hope slipped away with each tremor. The once-subtle red glow burst into blinding light, signaling what would surely be the largest eruption since time began. Debris showered down, hurtling toward us.

In the darkest shadow of my existence, I recognized the truth—this city, this beast, this maze—all of it was woven from the trauma within this child. I slowed myself, willing my heartbeat and breath to quiet into a soft whisper. The calm soothed the chaos around us, but I realized that this wasn't just a simple rescue.

Nick wasn't my enemy. Corine wasn't my enemy. They were caught in their own inner demons, tortured from within, much like I had been. I should have stared down those demons and laughed at them, something like this:

"Men don't cry, Jack-a-puss," they'd taunt. "No, but they do laugh," I'd say, laughing hysterically. "What's so funny?" "You're comparing me to a man, and I'm only six years old," I'd respond, laughter uncontained.

I should have laughed like a crazy boy, at the absurdity of their insults. Laughed with the understanding that the real enemy was on its way to an eternity of fire—a fire that once smoldered in me but would not consume me. I hadn't known that then.

"Let my people go so that they may worship me." The imagery felt too familiar to ignore. The Pharaoh, clinging to his hold on the Israelites, seemed a perfect physical embodiment of this beast. He held them in bondage, just as I had been held all my life—until now.

Chapter 17
The Writing on The Wall

1st Samuel 31:4-5 "Saul took his own sword and fell on it."

"From the earth a carrot grew."

Bear with me as I try to make sense of what I have encountered so far. I have heard it said by men much smarter than I that our thoughts, feelings, and will are all legitimate and eloquent parts of us that can be invisible to the outside world, yet are the essence of our lives. They constitute our soul. Each part of our soul impacts the other two. If you are truly in the battle, your thoughts can partition your other thoughts, your feelings can conflict with your other feelings, and your will can seem to act spontaneously, stumbling and tripping all over itself. Your will appears to neither agree with your thoughts nor your emotions. This is the rubbish left behind by each contradiction and every deception that you have faced. The confusion of truth is the walls of a labyrinth that can leave you searching for hidden gems of truth in the brash scree for a long time. It becomes a house of mirrors filled with disfigured reflections. The bent and drooping mirrors of insult are the lies you bump into as you try to find your way through the maze. I could literally bump into myself on the way out of the house and not recognize any familiarity.

The walls of the maze follow me out of treachery. Yes, I have been brought out of the city of treachery; I have been delivered from the physical realm of this bondage. I am no longer in Minnesota. I am no longer standing defenseless next to the wall while a fist is implanted into my chest. I am no longer forced to eat the morning concoctions. I no longer spend days alone, locked in a fruit cellar, but I am probably just as much of a prisoner as I have

151

ever been. It is my inability to escape the memories that cause me to respond as if it is still happening.

The turmoil stirring within my soul might only be visible from a look inside, but my intolerance of peace should be a big, bold billboard sign across my forehead. Scrapes, bruises, cuts, and blood testify beyond doubt to physical injuries, but injuries to the soul are only identifiable through actions or the inconsistent acts of the will. Chaos and disruptive behavior are the cuts and bruises.

It isn't a conscious decision to kill myself that somehow, supernaturally, overpowers my will. I have ingested the darkness, and it is poisoning my soul. That shadow was cast beginning in my thoughts. It drained from my mind, shading every cell on its way to my heart. It purged outwardly into my limbs, where the will is acted out. The vipers are coiled, preparing to strike. They are striking, but I am not dying. It is an attempted murder. It is the collective events that have directed my path: the false beliefs, the caged thoughts, the bottled emotions, and the bound spirit. The attempt on my life may have initiated in Minnesota, but who's to say I won't bleed out slowly?

Shame is a prison that will put its fences up around you no matter where you are. It will close in the fields between you and freedom. The mere opinion of others, if left unchallenged, can be those fences closing in. It appalls me that I stepped into this trap. God has given me stewardship over what will happen to this little man that He created—this precious being, His most favored—and I couldn't seem to keep him safe. I am that little man.

Self-loathing has positioned itself on this battlefield. It is the extended version of guilt and shame. It takes responsibility for everything maladjusted in the universe. It tries to take on the role of God and then implodes when it can't meet those self-perpetuated expectations. It is here to stomp out hope.

Awkward Silence

One might say that I had nothing to be ashamed of, and that is true. It's not my fault, but when those who are supposed to love you tell you that it is your fault, how can you argue with that? If I were to take a closer look, I might find that love often casts blame on the weakest link. I was six, so I was the least able to defend myself. This definition of love, as it has been acted out through actions, needs some tweaking.

Some logic still prevails. I mean, if Ted were to be my role model of a man, then I would have shot and killed his wife. I would have shot and killed his son. And dare I say, I would have shot and killed my mom. Some might have said Ted was a "man's man." He smoked Lucky Strike non-filter cigarettes. He would likely chew up barbed wire and spit out nails. The hate in his heart was also non-filtered. Everyone was a "pussy," "spic," "nigger," or "faggot" (please forgive me for these words). If you showed any compassion, or for that matter any human decency toward another human being, then you qualified as a "pussy" or "faggot." And God forbid you apologize or take responsibility for an action, because that would qualify you as weak—otherwise known as a "pussy."

This is what I was in training for. This is what I was meant to become. It took a long time to wipe that hate stain off of me. This is not just a crimson stain; this is pitch black and raw evil. In fact, I absolutely despise that language, but every once in a while, in an unguarded moment, one of those words will cross swords in my mind. That is the strength and depth of the mental conditioning. I can take a punch. I can deliver a punch. I can endure torture, but I will never deliver it. No matter how you slant your eyes, the picture emerges that he was not a model of a man.

If I had stayed in the hands of this enemy any longer, I would have learned to cast the blame, and Ted would not have been guilty of murder. I might have defended his demons and the demons of my own choices. It would have been the fault of the unarmed man. It may have been the fault of the gun manufacturer. It may have been the fault of the bartender who served the drinks. I agree with those who would say it was the fault of the demons inside him. Those demons have taken refuge in sin since the opening chapters of the Bible. It would have been his duty to seek deliverance, but his male pride would have been far too magnified for that. That is one thing that Ted and the Pharaoh in Egypt, during the time of Moses, had in common: both of their hearts were solid stone.

Guilt and shame are the dirt shoveled on top of my casket. The lack of love is the hand that holds the weapon, but the weapon is yet to be identified. I argue against this constituent of shame, but it is shameful what happened to me when the music level was turned up. You can't just leave a room, pull up your big boy pants, and forget how you've been violated. Self-loathing digs the grave. It is my inability to move forward. It's as if there is a right-turn-only sign at every corner. In the moments between the signs, it feels like forward movement. It feels like you are making progress, but a few turns later, you find that you have only been around the block.

I am still connected and bound by the way I have learned to think. In this regard, the wizard did me no favors. He taught me survival skills, strategic defense, and even a gentle offense. Wrapped up in this self-preserving cognition are deception, manipulation, and a lack of congruence.

From the dammed-up river of emotions, the city of treachery was formed. The discipline it takes to completely contain strong emotions is self-defeating. With every new feeling that ends up on the riverbed, a new structure is built to house the vagrant emotion. Each structure restricts the ebb and flow and, in the end, will lead to an eruption that makes the threats of Yellowstone volcanic activity seem insignificant.

Awkward Silence

Without thought or emotion to assist in the decisions of the will, everything feels meaningless. Every decision becomes selfish as I try to make sense of the world and fill the void left inside of me. The will used to be fed with thoughts of encouragement and feelings of hope, but since the thoughts can't be trusted and the feelings are mere illusions, the will can only do the best it can. The will seeks instant gratification because it is all that it can feel. It seeks mindless opportunities that don't use up too much hope, because once all hope is lost, the grave is filled.

I was in the desert, and my spirit was darkened by my soul. Those three figures ruled over my body and my spirit, confining it in darkness. With each instantly gratifying move of the will, my spirit was pulled further into the depths of that darkness. The extreme desire for instant gratification would percolate as a thought of escape from the elements of life that had entangled my emotions. To be set free from the constraints of life is the internal conflict of the will.

This struggle is consistent with what the Israelite people endured during their forty years of wandering in the desert. I, too, wandered. I could not see that the promised land was in front of me. All I could see were the remnants of days past, and no matter how hard I tried, I just couldn't seem to escape these modified renditions of truth.

Chapter 18
Deranged thoughts Captains Suicide

Exodus 14:14 "The Lord will fight for you, and you only need be silent."

"If you can believe this, I could not see all that I had to be grateful for. I was blind."

The absence of light is a bit different from darkness. Darkness surrounds me, where the cold concrete floor meets the shelves filled with canned goods. The absence of light is what I keep hoping you will see, but you don't see me. I am invisible. The light that once shone out is gone. The roar that pours out of me does not cross my lips but instead manifests in this note of suicide. The words are not written; they cascade from actions that a blind person can monitor. Are you not aware that I no longer beam? Ignorance has you trapped in a world where only one opinion matters. Selfishness is the décor that closes the windows and pulls the drapes shut.

"There's still a gallon of vodka in the boat from the camping trip." As quickly as the thought poured into my mind, the bottle was bone dry. As the alcohol flowed through my veins, it became a river that separated me from pain. I could see pain on the other side, sitting on the shore with a bonfire burning, waiting for my return. But for now, I was free to flirt with disaster. I was no longer attached to this pain. The paperwork had been filed; the marriage was annulled. As long as I lived on this side of the river and she stayed over there, I was good. The question becomes: how is it that the things I carried out of Minnesota have become whispers of suicidal tendencies? Nick never once said, "Go kill yourself." It is strange that what was planted grew into this. Those weeds strangled the flowers in the bed of hope. It is hope that protects life.

A 1970 Pontiac GTO is arguably one of the most desired muscle cars. I stand on the hood of this car, diving into the street. I am so drunk that I am convinced I cannot be hurt. I dive off the hood of the car onto the pavement. A drunken thirteen-year-old has no understanding of conscience. My behavior is irrational and, in this case, bizarre. In what mindset, drunk or not, would it seem like a good idea to dive headfirst onto the pavement? When the stars clear from my mind, I will do it again. It isn't until after the third or fourth time that I begin the blackout phase of this drunken fiasco.

"Sleep it off," my stepbrother Steve says as he leads me to the backyard. Steve is trying to shield me from the consequences of my actions. As I lay there with the stars above spinning uncontrollably, I drift into blackness. Hushka, my dad's malamute, roars with a howl to wake the dead. Hushka pulls on my hair and wails. Hushka saved my life. My dad got up in time to save me. The ambulance arrived quickly enough to save my life. The doctors and hospital staff responded swiftly to save me. I should have been grateful, but I wasn't. I would have preferred death to what I was living.

The unruliness began to take over. I began to understand, perhaps learned from my drunken state, that I could escape the prison of hatred, guilt, and shame, even if only for a little while. Shame seemed to be pronounced, accented, and defined by those two letters that begin the word: sh, shush—keep it quiet. Never share your feelings because that is weak. It makes you sound like a pussy.

The program of silence keeps your violators safe. When you're backed into a corner, protect your family. I am the man of the house. When the school nurse asks those inevitable, difficult questions, lie. Nobody really wants to hear the truth anyway. The truth just opens a door of responsibility that few are eager to face. In that regard, the truth falls upon deaf ears. I communicate the truth in many ways. I convey that something is wrong without actually speaking those words, but no one is listening.

It has been some time since my parents' divorce, and it has been three years since Minnesota was nothing more than a whisper in the wind. However, the demons just couldn't leave well enough alone. They had to agitate the formula in the pot. Mom, in what seemed to be the next step in a streak of questionable decisions, decided to wear Danny's ring.

My skin exuded rage. There was no way I could let this man come into my life, knowing nothing about anything, and take control of it as if he were getting behind the wheel of an automobile. I had ridden in the passenger seat before, and it hadn't served me well.

A few months ago—three months ago—I was in a car accident that totaled the car and threw me into the windshield. My sister's boyfriend, Tom, was driving. We were on Fairview, heading home. The intersections along this road are uncontrolled. As we approached the corner of Shoshone and Fairview, a car speeding up to the corner T-boned us. We had the right of way, but that didn't seem to matter to the driver of the other car. It was a solid hit that sent me crashing into the windshield, hard enough to crack it. The car that struck us pushed us into a telephone pole. Both cars were totaled. I was a man about it—I wasn't hurt.

Now, Danny is driving my mom's car, and we are on the same path toward home. As we near the intersection of Shoshone, I say, "Hey, be careful of this intersection." Danny's arrogant demeanor begins to toy with me as he presses the accelerator.

"I'm serious—be careful of this intersection!"

Awkward Silence

The memories of the accident with Tom swirl in my mind like snowflakes in a freshly shaken snow globe. I can see the shattered glass and the wreckage. This is the premonition of what is coming. I feel an intense release of adrenaline as I see the expression on the driver's face in the approaching car. I can read his lips and hear the curse words that follow. That's when the words spill out of my mouth: "I fucking told you to be careful of this intersection, but no, you have to be an asshole!"

Danny's playing with the accelerator diminishes the sincerity of calling it an accident. I know it's not intentional from his standpoint, but there's something else pulling his strings. I know nothing of the spiritual war I'm embroiled in at this point in my life. The calamity is simply endorsed by hate-filled people. The entire world appears to be evil, and I am stuck in it. The likelihood of experiencing this same collision at the same corner within three months is astronomical. It's hard to make sense of what just happened.

Truly, I would be blind to arrogance. After all, it is the splinter in my own eye that makes it invisible to me. But I knew one thing: Danny was like fingernails on a chalkboard to me. His every action seemed to declare his dominance over me.

He barked orders and commands as if he were the chief mechanic, while I made every attempt to avoid him. I grew ever darker, coated by the pitch upon my heart. I wouldn't have been content with anyone Mom brought around; that goes without saying. However, this man may have been carrying demons heavier than mine.

A young man can only internalize something that feels like a nuclear attack for so long. An inescapable atomic explosion is looming. As the buttons are pushed, he can choose to ignore the impending strife, throw himself over the blast, or strike back. This is not yet a war of flesh and blood, but it is escalating. Every collision is meant to assert control in the spiritual realm. It is an aggression intended to press me to my knees in humble, unquestioning obedience to him. Danny pushes the buttons that threaten to breach the walls holding back the inevitable. Those walls are solid, but a small charge placed in just the right spot can initiate a chain reaction that continues indefinitely. He seems constantly intent on exchanging blows that aim to confine my spirit to a space no bigger than a bread box. His goal appears to be deflating my spirit and shoving it into a dark hole where it can never shine. Perhaps he is trying to deflate my ego, but his tactics are all wrong.

There is no doubt that my ego has been high-flown. It makes perfect sense that after being subdued in hell and stripped of all humanity by demonic powers and principalities, I would compensate where I could once set loose in the natural world. My ego may be enlarged, but it is fragile. It is not meant to be toyed with. A pin can be inserted carefully into a balloon, causing it to leak air, or it can be pricked, resulting in a "pop."

"Keep him away from me today. I swear, Mom, I will beat him beyond recognition." I warn her to keep Danny at bay. He had just taken a pry bar to the deck lid of my car. It wasn't anything special, but I did a lot of dishes to save for it.

"You'll do what?" he says as he enters the room and pushes toward me.

"Get back, or I will hurt you!" I warn again.

He pays no heed to my warning and pushes forward. I'm not sure what happens next, other than that he is suddenly bleeding from the path my fist made across his face, beginning at his chin and ending above his eye. It takes me a moment to process what just occurred. Blood streams from him like water from a hose.

"Pop!" There it is—the detonation of the charge that triggers a chain reaction.

"Mom, I didn't mean to do that." His blood is flowing from several points of origin.

"Mom, I really didn't mean to do that!" Shock overwhelms my ability to comprehend the situation.

Losing self-control is the scariest feeling in the world for me. If I am not in control of myself, I can only speculate what is. I can't see that emotions are controlling me; I live in apathy. I don't have emotions. The kickback from emotions I'm not aware of feels like someone else is riding this bull. Shock is a way to describe living with dissociative disorders. It's like a constant state of shock. Speaking to someone in this state may bypass the conscious mind and go straight to the subconscious, where there is less awareness. In this manner, reality becomes a shattered illusion.

The idea that I am dissociated and live all my hours in a state of shock is a fact, but I have to wonder what it is I am experiencing now. Is it panic from seeing the blood? If I understand that bullets flying by my head won't disrupt the "peace" in my cognition, then why don't I understand the sheer panic of this situation?

Out of the corner of my eye, I see the barrel of his pistol coming around the corner. I can make out the sight on the barrel, the cylinder, and a finger on the trigger. Time slows as I bolt out the back sliding door, my knees nearly hitting my chin to avoid the junk littering the yard that he seems to accumulate. I hear the sliding glass door open behind me as I round the corner of the house, picking up speed as I sprint across the street.

I had such a crush on the neighbor girl, and now this is going to expose just how white trash we are. Knocking on her door in fear for my life isn't the picture of strength I want her to see. There's nowhere else for me to go, and holding my composure feels impossible. The embarrassment of this exposure weighs heavily on me.

This is the day my mom chooses him over me. He is clearly in the wrong, having damaged my property, yet he instigates the conflict and won't stop invading my space. He refuses to back off and let me process my anger. I warn him several times, but he keeps antagonizing me. This is the day, as a teenager in high school, that I realize I have to fend for myself.

Miracles never cease. I'm staring down the barrel of a gun, but I also see my diploma in the distance. Looking back, it's miraculous that I made it to graduation. I walked across the stage to be handed my diploma, but it was a struggle. I had to rely on the goodwill of some of my wonderful teachers to help me. I was a mess. My system had been poisoned with arrogance and bravado, and my pride was placed in all the wrong things. It weighs me down, making me sad to think this is who I was as a teenage boy.

In the apartment, she scrambles to find her clothes in a full-on panic. Her name slips from my grasp the moment I hear it. She was the one dancing provocatively, keeping eye contact with me as I played my sets. I performed three sets, and each time a lyric mentioned a drink, I took a shot. It's a wonder I remember my own name.

Our clothes are scattered illogically from the kitchen to the bedroom and throughout the entire apartment. It's unlikely she'll be covered before the door swings open. It won't be long before the guys show up as my backup alarm.

"Good luck with that. I'd just go in the bathroom until they leave," I say to her just as the door swings wide open.

Awkward Silence

"Jack, Mr. Flowers sent us to make sure you're awake for fourth hour." It's a similar story every morning. I wonder if they're disgusted by my behavior or just there to gawk at the nakedness of my guests. She, whoever she is, closes her eyes and covers her face, frozen like a possum.

"Yeah, there you go, babe. If you can't see them, maybe they can't see you either." I understand her embarrassment, and there's likely a bit of fear or shame, too, because when she brought me out of the bar, she couldn't have known I was still in high school.

"Guys, get out of here so we can get dressed," I urge.

It's a good thing I found an apartment just a block from the high school. My fourth-period class is critical for me; I won't graduate without it, and I'm dangerously close to failing due to my attendance. Ironically, it's a writing class that might rob me of my scroll, cap, and gown. There's ink in the chamber splattering the disorderly words that describe my struggle to succeed in my education to become a writer.

I have Mr. Flowers for my first three periods, and he's aware of my situation. He's an amazing man, enabling me despite knowing the risks. He's taken the big picture into consideration and agreed to help me in spite of myself. The boys he sends over return with the same stories every time.

Back then, rent was cheaper than a can of tuna in today's market. My apartment cost three hundred fifty dollars. Compared to today's prices, it might sound like I lived in a dump, but it wasn't. The thing is, I earned three dollars and fifty cents an hour, so I had to soak up every hour I could. I worked seven days a week after school and on weekends as a dishwasher at the Shang Hai restaurant. I was only a dishwasher until one of my high school crushes walked through the door; that's when the apron came off, and I became the assistant manager. From Monday to Thursday, it was just a three-hour shift. Friday to Sunday, I worked six hours, give or take. After work, I played guitar at bars to earn a few more dollars, plus I received a child support check of seventy-five dollars a month from my dad. I could eat one meal a day at the restaurant. If I had been financially responsible, I could have set a budget that was tight but doable.

Financial irresponsibility crept in around the time my mom married Danny. Before that, I had a paper route and was trying to save money for college. Each month, after collecting subscription rates, I would stash the cash under my mattress, but it always seemed to disappear. I never had the chance to set a budget or even sleep on a lumpy mattress. Sometimes, I was short on my payment to the paper. The lack of control I had over my finances gnawed at me. I was the man of the house, but ultimately, my mom's financial recklessness wore me down.

Playing guitar in bars was where the women came from. I'm serious; it felt like they were manufactured right there. It's like a mist would fill the room, and out of it, a woman would appear. That's why I never seem to wake up before Mr. Flowers sends the boys to check on me. The peep shows and guitar gigs became my identity in high school, and I carried that with a sense of arrogance. It sickens me that I'm allowed to live like this. I brought women home to avoid being alone. I don't like my life, and without companionship, I'm not sure I would have made it this far.

The decisions I make leading up to graduation are influenced by the demons of treachery still slithering through my soul. The shadows have taken over nearly everything that resembles my humanity. I can't see the resurrection from where I am; I can't look beyond the very literal perspective before me. As sad and pathetic as my life has become, I never dripped a drop. As long as I had booze, sex, and drugs to hide behind, I couldn't feel the agonizing pain.

Chapter 19
Prophetic Dream

Acts 2:17 "I will pour out my spirit on all people. Your men will have visions and dreams."

"The beast speaks words of blaspheme but the saints and angels speak words of praise."

It is April 28, 1981, when I have this dream. This dream will define my life forever. It is this dream that has me seeking the key to flight. It is this dream that drives me to find my inspiration. It is this dream that sets off the chain of events leading me to the still waters. The key found in this dream will unlock doors that have been hidden from my sight.

I am walking down a country road in the pitch of night. The moon is big, but there is no light. For a moment, there is nothing before me and nothing behind me. I am guided only by the coordinates of direction, with no expectation of a destination. There seems to be nothing illuminating my path; every step should be taken carefully, yet my carelessness dominates. Remnants of the past try to sneak up on me, serving as a defining point. I've walked this road a thousand times before, but this time, it is different. There is a mystical quality to the air, a dense smog that I can both smell and taste, like the smoldering of brimstone. It is eerie and uncertain, as though it's a path through darkness where evil dwells.

At the crossroads, I find a field. In my waking life, this field is empty and barren, but here in my dream, I am surprised to see a tree. The tree is surreal; it isn't present in my waking life, yet here in this dream, it stands tall. Its branches are undefined, carrying a purpose for all humanity. The tree itself feels purposeful, breathing life and possibilities into the air. Its leaves rustle in the breeze, although I can't tell if the breeze is cool or warm; it is simply

166

refreshing. I wonder if this is the tree of good and evil or the tree of life that has remained out of my view. For the purpose of this dream, it is *the* tree—one that carries a message.

I pause to consider this. I hope that whatever it signifies breathes life. I hope it develops into a story that inspires and gives hope. The tree seems to encourage me, filling me with hope that will, in turn, be passed along. I believe that hope can spark more hope, encouraging others to grow.

Lining the horizon behind the tree, like a backdrop, are smoking factories with bright lights shining through the tree, creating the illusion of a woman with fiery hair wearing a pendant. I am captivated, as if by love at first sight, but I reason with myself that this is just a dream—that she is only a silhouette. As I continue walking, I utter words to express my wonder at what this dream might be telling me. The allegorical complexities of the dream feel important. I begin to analyze it, exploring its meaning even as I dream.

On the surface, the backdrop of smoking factories feels like a cry of destruction. It's as if these factories are smoldering due to war or bombings. The unsettling sense of a man-made cataclysmic disaster is inherently conflicting, reminiscent of the nature of war itself. This scene speaks to the carelessness of humankind, as if we are bent on destroying the very creation of God. I sense an energy here—the destructive spirit of Satan—attempting to annihilate what God loves most: man. And in doing so, it also aims to destroy the habitat that God created for humanity. If Satan is waging war against God, this feels like a strong message of hatred towards the Creator. That he would have man destroy his own environment carries an even stronger message: "This creature you love so deeply is itself the enemy, damaging the home you built for him." It's a mockery.

Jack Taylor

In my dream, these images of smoking factories or scenes of destruction feel deeply personal, as if I am the factories. If that's the case, then I, too, am under attack. The smoking factories, as if on fire, serve as a warning, and the light that shines from this distant chaos produces translucent images within the tree. Each of these images, at every stage, offers inspiration and hope.

The woman with fiery hair represents, in dream language, a dialogue between my conscious and subconscious mind, according to Layne Dalphen. This holds true in this dream. I'm meant to consciously analyze each element within the dream itself. Yet her impressionistic details may be deceptive, suggesting a hidden identity. If she represents the church, there's a hint of the church's deceptive allure. I spend valuable time contemplating this. Since Satan is the father of lies, leading his followers through deception, this detail in the dream carries weight. She is significant to me. She means the world to me.

As I walk on, I feel a strong urge to look back, sensing that someone may be watching. From this new perspective, I see the leaves flutter in the wind, forming the image of another woman. She appears as a Native American woman with striking emerald eyes. Leaves, resembling feathers, dangle from her ears and adorn her headband. I wonder if this could be the same woman.

Also, from this angle, I glimpse a dragon hovering above her. I want to save her, but I reason that neither she nor the dragon is real. Ultimately, what they represent is real, but here, they are merely silhouettes within a dream—a visual transcript of communication. I ponder their symbolism and how they might correlate with my life outside this dream. Their images are evasive, not even fully defined.

Because women are often seen as nurturers, I consider this woman's nurturing nature as a key to unraveling the dream's meaning. If she remains elusive and undefined, it may mean that I

168

don't fully grasp the concept of nurture or love. For now, I'll catalog this piece of the puzzle. To me, she represents a powerful argument for love and relationship. Perhaps women are not merely a source of pain or challenge but embody a love that intoxicates the spirit, unbounded by mere emotions. Where true love exists, it touches every loving relationship. It becomes a universal parallel, spanning from the highest connection to the simplest bond. The ultimate expression may be Christ's love for the church.

This woman may reflect any of these connections, but most central to my soul is my relationship with Christ. This dream seems to draw me closer to that divine relationship, the highest and most profound love I know.

The Native American culture places substantial importance on the environment. Many indigenous people view the earth as their mother and other living beings as kin. Biblically, this resonates with me because we are created by God and birthed from the dust of the earth. The breath that gives life comes from God. The earth is a creation to be respected, not worshiped, as it is the handiwork of a sovereign God. To honor the Great Spirit, one must show respect for His creations.

The dancing feathers that hang from her ears and adorn her headband are captivating to me. They carry the weight of American history, moving gracefully as symbols of freedom. These feathers speak of liberty, like the flight of a bird, representing an unburdened spirit. They are markers of bravery, respect, and blessing. They symbolize spirituality and spiritual growth. War bonnets made of feathers often carry prayers for victory through courage, but this headband indicates her single status. The feathers are both alluring and seductive with their dance, mesmerizing and captivating in their movement.

I feel an intense need to learn everything there is to know about this woman. I position my thoughts in such a way that I can truly understand her. My search is not just for who she appears to be but for what she signifies to me. I am more interested in her purpose than in her identity. To me, she is raw inspiration placed here by God. She is the driving force behind my actions, standing beside this growing tree of creativity. She means everything to me because, without her influence, my words would just be disjointed phrases. Where would I be without this inspiration? I understand that it is not solely her but God who is the true source, using this vision of a woman to inspire my hand. There is nothing more nurturing than a mother, and being born from the soil embodies the very essence of nurture: to nourish, to feed, and to protect. I have no desire to resist the awakening of this emotional masterpiece— emotions that were once locked away, but now I hold the key.

For now, she remains intangible, merely a vision— beautiful, yet still just a vision.

Emerald eyes are often seen as a connection to the spiritual world. This rare eye color implies a deeper perception beyond the ordinary. In contrast, my crystal blue eyes shift to green depending on what I wear. Crystal blue suggests a soulful insight, and I am drawn into a vision of spiritual gains through the piercing gaze of those emerald eyes. These spiritual gains refer to insights into a world on a catastrophic path, where battles rage all around us, and our ignorance is to blame.

It takes a moment, but realization comes swiftly, like a Prime delivery. She exists within me because this is a dream. A dream is not filled with others but is instead the dreamer's perception of them. This brings me back to the idea that learning about her is really about understanding what she means to me, which, in turn, means learning more about myself and my elusive identity. The circle of thought is vast, yet it leads me back to the truth that she is a divine gift in my dream, placed there by God because He knows what will inspire me to take action. She may not be real, or perhaps she is, but certainly, she is an idea that propels me forward on my mission of passion.

And so, I come full circle to acknowledge that she is inspiration itself, and I choose to call her Inspire.

The dragon, too, is an inside job. I contemplate what outward symbols define a dragon for me. I must think in the language of dreams, where this dragon holds powerful meaning. With an inside view, I can discover its deeper significance. In Chinese culture, the dragon is a symbol of luck, and this connects for me with the etymology of "luck," derived from "Lucifer." This association is consistent with attributing God's blessings to chance, or to Lucifer, rather than to divine intention. This aligns with the dragon's representation of evil in the book of Revelation.

The hard truth is that, since this is my dream and my perception, the dragon may represent something within me. It may symbolize a threat to innocence, the accumulation of pain, hurt, and past injuries that have become potent within my psyche. This dragon has had a profound influence over my soul. My will has been shaped by distortions in my sense of self. Accepting that she, the woman in my vision, symbolizes inspiration, and that the dragon represents a threat to her, reveals my underlying fear that my inspiration could be taken from me—a worry rooted in a lack of faith.

Looking from a higher vantage, outside of my dream, the dragon's threat appears to extend beyond my personal world to the broader world, as she, my inspiration, represents the world to me. Communities today are responding to such fears with faithless measures. The dragon, an evil hovering over the world, only lurks within the fragmented compartments of this maze. My inspiration, in this view, is being misrepresented by the dragon's shadow. Though the dragon wields great power in every sense of the imagination, his influence is ultimately an illusion based on deception. His true strength lies in his ability to mislead, nesting within those who seek power for personal glory.

Satisfied with the insights these symbols offer, I continue into town. I am taken aback by the scene before me: everything is chaotic, almost upside-down. Trash litters the ground, and people move about in disorder. It's as if a circus has come to town, but without the sweet scent of candy apples or corn dogs. People everywhere are behaving in the oddest ways. Today, I might compare it to downtown Portland, but in 1981, I had no frame of reference for this. I only knew one thing—I had to find Inspire.

A man approaches, looking lost. But if I had to guess, I might say I'm the one who seems out of place in this chaotic setting. I approach him and ask, "Have you seen the woman who represents my deepest desire? She's elusive and fleeting."

"The dragon is not evil!" he exclaims. I'm startled; I hadn't even mentioned the dragon. Instantly, I envision Inspire taken by the dragon, trapped by its influence. I realize I must wield words to slay the dragon and free the world from its deceptions.

After all, "The pen is mightier than the sword."

I approach the next person I see and ask, "Have you seen the woman wearing the pendant?"

"The dragon is not evil!" she responds. It feels as if there's a scripted dialogue, a shared mantra. A form of brainwashing seems to be at play, forcing people into a confined way of thinking, like hamsters in a wheel.

"Oh, my friend, the dragon is indeed evil. To understand this, we must first recognize that the dragon seeks a position of power, so it inevitably entangles itself with those in influential arenas. In the letter to Pergamum, Jesus warns that the church is becoming entangled, even intertwined, with the world. Governmental entities and divisions hold the very power that can seat a dragon. These divisions represent the mystery of the dragon's multiple heads, all feeding the same beastly body—a body seducing God's bride and leading her astray. This evil lures the world off its path, much like Balaam and Balak, who placed a stumbling block before the Israelites, leading them into sin and immorality. It is this dragon that causes people to fall, driving them into darkness and depravity.

Now, let's examine the current state of our economic system. Like most systems, capitalism inherently leads to imbalance and corruption. It may begin innocently enough, but as the dragon grows, its true nature is revealed. Its deeds become apparent only when society reaches a tipping point. Adam Smith, the father of capitalism, argued that a person could serve the community by focusing on self-interest. But this self-focus is the downfall of society, and the church has become entangled in this ideology. Yet, 1 Corinthians 13 teaches that love is not self-centered. We do not operate within a system of love. Perhaps that seems acceptable for now, but the day will come when the objectives of others conflict with your own. You will fight but be overtaken. Then, they will decide that everything you cherish should belong to them. When a man's worth is measured by selfish gains, he will fall. Where there is power, you will find the dragon, its roots tracing back to the church of Pergamum. In 312 AD, Constantine had a vision that led to the church's entanglement with worldly power.

Now, let's look at the justice system. It is rife with imbalance. We often call it a broken system, but in reality, we place Satan on the throne. The injustice we see is but a symptom of the deeper malady of unforgiveness. Revenge has become synonymous with justice. But true justice is found only through dying to self and taking up your cross. Hostility spreads like a disease, hidden under the guise of justice. A system that exalts punishment over teaching, that denies the healing of the heart, is one where the dragon reigns. By aligning ourselves with such an ungodly system, we place the dragon in authority. God alone should be on the throne; it was His principles that we once upheld in the creation of this nation."

As I speak, I notice a crowd gathering, their eyes fixed on me. But to my surprise, anger begins to simmer among them. Though they listen, they refuse to comprehend my words. They are looking for a scapegoat, a sacrifice to appease their rage—like worshipers of a forgotten volcano god. They fail to understand that Jesus has already become the sacrificial lamb. Sin does not need to spread further than the cross.

Suddenly, as if to save me from their growing hostility, a small, blonde woman steps forward and says, "My dear man, you must be tired. Why don't you come with me? You can rest and relax, and begin your quest again tomorrow." Seeing the anger of the crowd, I decide to follow her.

After a brief period of rest, I reach for the door handle to leave.

"My dear man, you mustn't go until you've had some of my delicious cheesecake," she insists.

"I love cheesecake," I reply, "but I fear what it may cost me in the end." As with every temptation, there comes that moment of decision. You can weigh the pros and cons, but sometimes, the moment slips away before you can act.

"Don't leave until you've met my brother and his wife," she says. I turn to see a woman with fiery red hair.

"This can't be," I think to myself. "She can't be married…
that makes no sense! She is certainly not the silhouette in the tree."
I feel the unmistakable pull of love at first sight, yet knowing she
is married, it would be against my moral code to pursue her.

Confused, I realize I must continue my search. I need to
find the woman I have been seeking. The image in the tree remains
undefined, and though this woman bears a striking resemblance to
the first one, there is still something unexplained. The second
woman's emerald eyes are vivid in my mind, yet they only deepen
the mystery.

I find myself, once again, preaching the message to the
church of Pergamum. I passionately share my views on the
separation of church and state:

"Matthew 6:24 says, 'You cannot serve two masters; you
will either love one and hate the other. You cannot worship both
God and mammon.' Mammon is not just money—it is the spirit
that attaches itself to greed, lust, power, and idolatry. Some of you
may think you have mastered this balance, that you can navigate
the system without being consumed by it. I won't argue with you.
Perhaps it's possible. But let me challenge you with this question:
What about your brother who does not have it under control? He
lusts after greed. Will you lead him into temptation? And if he
succumbs, will his infection ripple through the entire system?

Everything is backward in our world. If a product were
made to last forever, there would be no incentive to repurchase it,
and the manufacturer would go out of business. The system thrives
on planned obsolescence, keeping our eyes fixed on worldly
distractions rather than on God. As for work, it should be
motivated by love—not just the love of providing for one's family,
but the love of God. It is a love that drives you to labor tirelessly
for the sake of your neighbors, your community, and other
believers. It is no coincidence that the very next verse, Matthew

6:25, tells us not to worry about what we will eat or drink, for God will provide."

Once again, I can see that my words are stirring the crowd to anger. I have so much more to say to cut away the tangled vines that have bound the church to the state, but I sense that they might kill me for it. The church is so deeply entangled with the world that it may be nearly impossible to sever the cords of deceit that bind it. Ironically, it is not the governmental leaders who seek to silence me—it is the very church that I seek to edify.

I remind myself that this is just a dream. Otherwise, I might go into cardiac arrest from the adrenaline coursing through me.

I begin to run. The mob is close behind me, filled with those who have wielded power and their loyal followers. I hear the walls of their treacherous stronghold collapsing, feel the vibrations of their pursuit. Ahead, the trail opens up from a mountain pass, revealing a valley that expands into a meadow. I stumble twice but manage to keep my balance. As I look up from the ground, I see a sea of people rushing toward me. Those behind me are gaining ground, but the crowd ahead seems just as relentless.

I continue running, but I see no destination. The situation feels hopeless.

Then, off in the distance, I catch a glimmer of light. It is the figure of a woman running toward me, the light reflecting off a pendant around her neck. A theory forms in my mind: perhaps we are being driven together by the forces of collapsing emotions, drawn by a mutual desire to be free from tyranny. Jesus is the light, our beacon of hope. If the pendant symbolizes hope, then running toward it is an act of faith.

Those chasing me seem similar to those pursuing her. We both race through the meadow until, finally, we meet in each other's arms—a moment symbolizing love. Hope, faith, and love endure. We drop to our knees and surrender. At that moment, the earth trembles and shifts, turning 180 degrees off its axis. Those who had been chasing us are shaken loose from the surface. They scream and wail as they are torn away—the merchants, the kings, the powerful ones who had clung so tightly to the world.

When the shaking stops, a profound peace settles over the land. She and I stand together, amazed at what has transpired. But then, another tremor strikes, and we cling to each other once more, fearing that this time, we too might be shaken free from the earth. Suddenly, a brook springs forth in the meadow where we stand, a symbol of new life.

I awaken, exclaiming, "That was a prophetic dream."

Yet fear grips me. The people chasing me in my dream— they are all going to die! If only I could keep my mouth shut, I wouldn't provoke them. They wouldn't chase me, and I wouldn't be responsible for the world tipping off its axis. At that time, I believed prophecy to be literal—as if this dream was a prediction of actual events. I couldn't see the symbolic language, even though it was so clearly presented within the dream itself.

Chapter 20
The Factory Backdrop

Daniel 4:33 "Immediately what had been said about Nebuchadnezzar was fulfilled. He was driven from people and ate grass like the ox."

"Shame is useless! Useless is not encouraging, comforting, or edifying! It prohibits others from learning from your experience"

The sway in her walk could cause angels to fall. There's more hip motion than I ever thought humanly possible, yet here it is, right before my eyes. I'd heard whispers about the new hottie working with us, but no rumor could've captured the vision now striding through this grimy factory. She has it all—or so it seems.

Today, I'm fortunate. I get to spend my breaks ogling her, lost in a haze of admiration and desire. I follow behind her, my eyes glued and dilated, until she disappears into the restroom, leaving behind a lingering trace of perfume that's both erotic and intoxicating.

I toss my lunch onto a table and slump into a chair, hoping—praying—that she'll choose to sit beside me rather than vanish into the ladies' locker area. I've never been in there, but if it's anything like the men's, it's equipped with a full break setup. Luck is on my side. Her eyes sweep the room, searching, until our gazes lock. In that instant, there's a silent understanding: she's already decided to sit with me. She saunters over, her presence commanding every ounce of my attention. Her eyes, her smile— they tell me she's shopping, and today, I'm the most appealing product on the shelf.

Awkward Silence

This place, a glass bottle factory, is your run-of-the-mill industrial grind: dirty, grimy, filled with workers who've barely scraped by the minimal requirements. To survive here, you have to join the ranks of the walking dead. The relentless shifts demand a friendship with amphetamines; there's no other way to endure. The deafening roar of machinery drowns out any semblance of joy or, for that matter, sanity.

"Hi, I'm Jack," I manage, leaning in with a half-grin.

"Well, hi, Jack," she replies, her voice smooth as honey. "I'm Lacey."

She's like a manifestation of every adolescent fantasy I've ever had, as if all those Playboy centerfolds came to life in the form of this woman. The sexual tension in the air is electric, a storm gathering strength as I watch her lips wrap around a popsicle. She knows exactly what she's doing. Every flick of her tongue, every glance she throws my way, is designed to drive me mad. And she's succeeding.

Our conversation is nothing more than flirty small talk, but it's enough to catch the attention of the factory's other phantoms. Gossip spreads like wildfire, engulfing every department before we even get started.

Lacey awakens something ravenous in me, an insatiable hunger that no amount of indulgence can satisfy. She's tethered to the very heart of lust, and I'm drawn to her like a moth to a flame. Desire and passion can masquerade as love, especially when viewed through the distorted lens of narcotics. In this life, it's all too easy to numb the pain of a broken heart when you're already drowning in misery. Every inch of her screams danger, yet she navigates the treacherous waters of her life with the ease of someone who's forgotten what it means to care. Together, we're just two wounded souls, self-medicating our cuts and bruises, unaware of how deep the wounds truly go.

Her family's connections run deep into the underworld—a shared thread that binds us together. My own family danced around the edges of that abyss, though I was never directly involved. Unless, of course, tossing that carpet into the lake is a real memory. But for her, it's not just history—it's her present. By proxy, it's now mine too. The tendrils of the South American cartels extend to her family, though several layers of intermediaries stand between them. One of those intermediaries was a 25-year-old kid. He ended up dead, his body dumped on the steps of the police station with roses clutched in his lifeless hand.

The drugs become my escape from the relentless torment of my thoughts, just another step further down a dark road that shows no sign of turning back. With every hit, I descend deeper, edging closer to a crossroad that feels inevitable.

For a time, I have someone beside me on this unlit trail. I believe I'm in love, but never having known love, it's impossible for me to discern the difference. I can't possibly comprehend the darkness of the spirit that guides her, except to assume it's probably the same one guiding me. The spirit that clings to bitterness and anger is compelled to attract others with equally troubled souls, destined for destructive tendencies. This is the foundation of dysfunctional relationships.

Oh no, no one would see our bitterness. We don't take it out on others—except, of course, when you consider that our hearts are hardened. We won't let anyone close, and if they get too close, we run, leaving them in the dust. I suppose, when you look at it head-on, we do hurt others. But mostly, we take it out on ourselves. Both of us have this unconscious attraction to self-destruction.

Awkward Silence

Yet, it doesn't feel like this is the core of who we are. We're having fun. We're exploring possibilities together. We're on a mission to outrun the wretched past. It should be easy with the assistance of speed and coke. The race is on, and we're taking every shortcut along the way. We only stop long enough to pick up our clothes off the floor after our marathon sex.

We arrive in Lake Tahoe just before Christmas, 1986. It's a quick getaway. We check into the hotel, then take the elevator up. Our room is on the eleventh floor, but I want her right now. I push the doors open slightly to stop the elevator. Not a word is spoken. I bend her over and begin to slowly penetrate her. We're lost in the moment, completely oblivious to the fact that the elevator has rebooted. The doors open on an unknown floor, but we don't care. The moment reconciles any and all other details.

As the elevator begins to move again, we straighten ourselves up. When the doors open once more, I carry her to our room. No sooner do we step past the threshold than we continue what we had begun. It's amazing. And in that moment, I'm certain she conceived. Lacey drifts off to sleep, but I'm brimming with energy.

A couple of hours later, I find myself sitting at the blackjack tables, a pile of chips stacked in front of me. I think I've won about $13,000. But then, a man approaches, disrupting my flow, and I'm certain he's working for the casino. He plays into my youthful vanity with expert precision, placing bets of $1,200 per hand. There's something in his gestures, the subtle posturing, that lures me to do the same. I can't pinpoint his strategy, but they're acutely aware of the psychology of a young man who's ahead in the game—and they know exactly how to cunningly destroy him. That pile of chips shrinks quickly. I do manage to leave before I go into the hole. In fact, I'm still a couple hundred ahead, but it feels like

I just lost my new Harley. If I had left with that $13,000, that's probably what I would've bought.

I make my way back to the room, aching from the realization that they beat me because of my own arrogance. As I step out of the shower, Lacey is just waking up. She has no idea that I've been down at the blackjack tables. She has no concept of the fact that I had just won and lost so big. She thinks I was asleep beside her the entire time, and I'm not about to ruin her day with the truth.

"Let's go down and get some breakfast, then maybe gamble a little?" she suggests.

"Let's do it!"

The weekend has been wonderful, but it's time to leave. It was filled with entertainment and sex—I feel like a new man. We stand at the counter, waiting to check out of the hotel. My wallet is a tight fit in my pocket, but I manage to retrieve it. Lacey is fidgeting with the car keys while the clerk speaks on the phone.

"Your room has been comped," the clerk announces.

No sooner than the words leave her mouth, Lacey looks at me as if I've just killed an endangered species. I haven't even processed that it's likely been comped for my blackjack escapades. The simple relief of not having to pay for the room is all I've thought about. I had no clue I might have to defend myself.

"Taylor, what did you do?" Her eyes reflect a mix of confusion and maybe a little anger.

The clerk quickly smooths over the situation. I'm sure she's dealt with something like this before.

"Oh no, your room was comped as a promotion," she explains with a wink. "It's just in hopes of seeing you here again."

She smiles, adding, "Oh, but next time, we would appreciate it if you took the stairs." Lacey's face turns a shade of crimson I didn't know she was capable of.

***

Christmas is here. I know it comes every year, but with it, the usual traditions take their toll. It becomes less exciting, just another hoop to jump through in our commercialized world. But this year feels different. I'm as excited as I've ever been because Lacey and I are sharing it together. And, well, I've done something a little sneaky.

We're at her family's place, opening gifts. I hand Lacey a wrapped box that she thinks she helped me pick out. After we got back from Tahoe, we wandered the shopping mall, scaling every aisle, squeezing through crowds, trying on clothes, and playing with random items. She's confident she knows what's inside. The smug look on her face tells me so.

"I wonder what this could be..." she says playfully, shaking the box.

She wants everyone's attention, anticipating the beautiful necklace she thinks I bought her. She's made sure everyone knows she's in on the secret and is eager for the grand reveal. As she unwraps it, her expression shifts. She's expecting the necklace she chose, and technically, it *is* a necklace—but not the one she picked out. This one is the dream piece she eyed if money weren't an object. For a split second, her jaw drops. I see emotions flicker across her eyes. Then, just as quickly, she explodes. I've never seen a switch flip so fast. She's furious.

"Taylor, what did you do?" she snarls, fire practically shooting from her nostrils. It's actually intimidating. Her mom reaches out, holding her back as if to stop her from striking me. I'm completely bewildered. I didn't see this coming. I feel foolish for trying to give her what I thought she wanted.

Her entire family crowds around, gawking at the necklace. The women and girls take turns trying it on, while the men subtly hint at wanting to know how much it cost. Lacey gradually regains her composure.

"Jack, that's too much," she says, her voice softer now. "You shouldn't have done that. I'm sorry for how I reacted. The necklace is beautiful. I absolutely love it, but it costs more than my car. You can't do that. It's absolutely gorgeous! But still, you shouldn't have."

"Lacey, if I knew it would piss you off, I wouldn't have done it. I was hoping for a slightly different reaction," I reply.

"You are the kindest, most generous man I've ever met. I'm sorry again for my reaction. I really love it! Thank you! I love you."

"It's okay. I just won't try to surprise you anymore."

"Jack, I like surprises. This one was just... a little too much."

"Do you really like surprises? Because, well... I'm a little scared to introduce you to my next one."

"Taylor, what else did you do?" she asks, eyes narrowing.

"Lacey," I begin, taking a deep breath, "I love you. I want to be with you in the elevator of life, through all the ups and downs. Will you marry me?"

Awkward Silence

The room goes silent as I drop to one knee.

There's no immediate response. Lacey's eyes well up, and her family is on pins and needles. As tears begin to pool, I reach into my pocket and pull out a ring I had bought when exchanging the necklace. She had pointed to this ring, dazzled by its glamour, while we were Christmas shopping.

"Yes, yes, Taylor, I will marry you!" she exclaims.

And that's the answer her family had been waiting for. Cheers erupt, and champagne and good liquor make their way into the room. It feels like they're happier about this marriage than even I am. I know they've been hoping to see Lacey settle down; she's been wild for far too long.

Over the next few days, the celebrations continue. We're on top of the world. Lacey is so thrilled that she starts making wedding plans before our impromptu engagement party even winds down. Her mom is on the phone, calling every friend and relative. The excitement builds, swelling with each conversation.

A couple of weeks pass, and we're still caught up in the whirlwind. I haven't even had a chance to tell my own family about our plans.

"Taylor, things can't always be this good," she says one day, her voice heavy with something I can't quite place.

My heart plummets. It's like falling from the top floor with no warning. Intuition is tricky—sometimes, emotions can cloud its signals. But this time, there's no mistaking it. That sinking feeling settles deep, like a weight in my chest. Lacey is supposed to be here, but she isn't. Maybe that's why my mind is searching for answers, why my intuition is urging me to investigate. Without consciously deciding, I find myself driving to her ex-boyfriend's place. I'm not exactly looking for proof of betrayal, but... deep down, I'm expecting it.

I turn the corner, and there it is: her car, parked in his driveway. My future, the one filled with wedding plans and Hawaiian honeymoons, seems to evaporate in that instant. There's no ink on the invitations yet, no set date. But I've already bought the honeymoon package—two weeks in Hawaii, complete with dreams of mai tais on the beach, parasailing, and seeing her walk toward me in white. Now, that vision is shattered, replaced by the cruel reality before me.

The joy that filled my heart just moments ago is gone, replaced by an overwhelming sense of sorrow. I'm paralyzed. The bitterness spreads like sulfur, hardening every chamber of my heart. I move through rage so quickly that I end up in a catatonic state. Numbly, I lift the arm of her windshield wiper and slide a deposit slip beneath it. I can't face this. I can't face *her*. I could confront him, but what would that solve? Revenge is tempting, but I know better. He only did what I would've expected if given the chance. As for Lacey, I know she's responding to her own fears. But in the end, it's on me. I wanted to trust her, but I didn't. I wanted that perfect life with her, even though I was never blind to the risks. I just chose to ignore them, willing to sacrifice myself for the dream. But that doesn't lessen the pain.

I drive aimlessly, without a destination or plan. The only thing I'm certain of is that I don't want to feel anything. Her words echo in my mind: *"Things can't always be this good."* I scoff bitterly. "No, Lacey, you made sure of that," I mutter under my breath as I pull up to her sister and brother-in-law's house. I don't want to be alone. I'm desperate for comfort, for someone to tell me it's going to be okay.

As soon as I start talking, it all comes pouring out. It's like the incoherent sobbing of a child—you can't make sense of the words because they're choked by tears. My accusations against Lacey spill from me like venom from a beaten dog, one that doesn't know whether to bite or roll over and expose its belly. But somehow, through it all, Lacey's sister understands. It's almost like she's heard this all before.

"If it's any consolation, I think she's making a huge mistake! And don't you dare take her back! I mean it, Jack, because I'm certain she thinks you will." Her voice is firm, and I can feel the sincerity behind her words.

I can feel my eyes start to well up. "I'm going to use your restroom if that's okay," I mumble.

"Of course."

In the bathroom, I stare into the mirror, unsure where to even begin looking for my composure if I lose it here. The reflection staring back is a tormented young man, raw and broken. Whenever there's turbulence in my life, it's like every demon from Minnesota finds a way to crawl out of the shadows to crush me all over again. They're cloaked behind the current pain, nearly indistinguishable, but they're here. And they're not here to comfort me.

"You're worthless, Jack, a waste of oxygen," the thoughts taunt. *"Lacey just confirmed it—you're unlovable. Her sister and brother-in-law would agree if they knew you any longer. Do everyone a favor and end this charade. Look, there's a razor blade on the counter."*

These thoughts don't even feel like my own, yet they're disturbingly persuasive. I catch myself considering them for a split second, but then I shake my head. No. I can't disrespect their home like that. I splash some water on my face and leave the bathroom, desperately trying to scrub the dark thoughts from my mind.

Jack Taylor

"Jack, stay here tonight," her sister insists, handing me a blanket and pillow. "It'll do Lacey good to wonder why you didn't come home."

Grateful but exhausted, I lay the pillow on the floor and pull the blanket over me. I cover my face with it, trying to hide the tears that are now flowing freely. The ticking of the clock is the only thing grounding me, a metronome in the silence. Above me circle the relentless reruns of Lacey and our relationship, her words haunting me: *"Things can't always be this good."* They're followed by desperate cries from the suicidal thoughts that chased me out of the bathroom. Eventually, even those fade, leaving me alone with the raw, aching emptiness.

"That's it! I've had enough of this life!" The words scream inside my head with a terrifying clarity. I know exactly what I'm going to do. The decision feels final. The razor blade is still on the bathroom counter. But just as I steel myself to get up, I feel a light touch on my chest.

It's gentle, almost like a cat landing softly on me, but they don't have any cats. I try to sit up, but I can't move. The pressure doesn't increase; it just holds me there, firm and unyielding, as if it's pinning me to the floor. I struggle, but my body won't respond. The weight holds me there until, eventually, exhaustion pulls me into sleep.

When I wake up, Lacey is gone. She's disappeared, and I learn later that she's pregnant. I didn't know—I might have suspected when it happened, but I didn't really know. Her words, *"Things can't always be this good,"* echo endlessly in my mind, a relentless loop that I can't quiet. They're like ash from a volcanic eruption, burying everything I thought I knew. And with all this ash, I can't see anything anymore. I can't see a future, can't see

188

any path forward, can't even imagine building a life here without her.

I'm not ready to acknowledge that the shadows I've been grappling with are my own. That maybe it's the darkness inside me that keeps tearing everything apart.

The pain isn't confined to a single chamber of my heart. It's not just about her or what we might have had together. It's the carryover from a lifetime of rejection, a legacy I can't seem to outrun. The truth is, I know we aren't ready to settle down—but I need a win. I need someone to choose me, to want me above another option. But like a gambler addicted to the rush, it's not the winning that consumes me. It's the self-destruction. This addiction flows through me, every fiber of my being as it moves like molten magma. The idea of fixing our relationship has become tangled in my mind, poisoned by my corrupted thoughts.

Lacey's heart seems to hold an elevated view of the gangster lifestyle, a code of conduct that I'm trying to infiltrate. It's my immature perspective on why we're apart. In my mind, bonding with her means aligning with that world. It's this warped force driving me into a canyon that cracks open in the earth beneath me. The fall could be bottomless. All I see is darkness as I peer over the edge.

To dive headfirst into this crack feels like a monumental decision, one I can't reverse. The distortions of reality take hold. The only thing I know is that I want to reconnect with her, and I think I can do that by building a dynasty. Gaining the world, losing my soul—that's the price, but I can't see it through the flashing swords of cherubim guarding the fire I'm walking into.

I've placed my intellect in the highest of places, and it's here that I craft my plan to build the dynasty. Selling the powder creates small piles, but manufacturing and distributing it—that's what makes big piles. I don't know how to make these concoctions, but I convince myself I can learn. It can't be that hard.

One night, sitting passenger in a car driven by Lacey's cousin, we stumble upon a massive drug deal. There's more money in front of me than I've ever seen. A suitcase full. A river runs through this small town, a smugglers' dream. It's not large enough to attract attention, so the drugs come in and the money goes out with the rising tide. This is the first step. I can sell these vapors that roll in, but masking my pain—numbing it—seems to matter more than anything else.

The fantasy of building this empire, this dynasty, is smothered by the pillow of my dreams. Once again, I find myself directionless. The emptiness inside tries to reach for Lacey's hand, but that's the rising evil in my soul. If I take her hand, I have nowhere to lead her. I'm in no condition to lead anyone, least of all her. We'd just keep wandering through the same desolation. This land stretches further than my eyes can see. My conscience is barely a whisper now, and there's nothing left to fill the void.

Building an empire from scratch is impossible for me. The land is too barren. The grains of sand are too loosely woven to gain any real footing. There's no inspiration. It's clear that she isn't inspired, either. Every thought of winning her love is a deception. If I built this empire, she'd still be Lacey, and I'd still be me. In my desperate search for love, I've taken the hand of the devil—and I can feel the intensity of the flames. My kingdom is divided. I'm at war with myself, and every battle is bloody.

The poisonous fumes of the drugs feed my descent further. They have become the masters of my mind. The internal changes they've wrought feel like stardust and lollipops, but my outward reality is grim. The empire I seek isn't real. Chasing it is like chasing the pot of gold at the end of a rainbow. The leprechaun

I've been chasing hides where there's no light. There's no clover or lucky charm in these dark places.

The motion of her hips swaying side to side drops a bomb on my life the day I meet her. The explosion reverberates through everything, becoming the backdrop that stands behind the tree in my dreams. The blast lights up the sky, casting a silhouette through the branches, and the percussion of it is felt for years to come. The smoke fills the air, thick with the stench of brimstone. The force of the explosion throws me clear from the factory, and I chase after the false hope of love.

When the bomb goes off, it blows the shoes right off my feet. I get high and skip work, staying out running amok for weeks with no sleep. The aftershock of the fallout is the loss of my home. I don't need a bed to sleep in if I can't sleep. I don't need a place to cook food if I can't bring myself to eat.

Eventually, sleep comes—though not in a peaceful way. Sleep deprivation warps my reality. The shadows of my mind begin to take form, and I live like King Nebuchadnezzar, a man turned animal. I climb trees like a monkey, seeking a place to sleep off the cold ground and finding a vantage point for a lookout. Soon, I don't need drugs to escape; I exist as a ghost, unseen and unnoticed, for months at a time. I'm hurting, and no one can help me.

Then, one day, I emerge from hiding. There's still a tiny spark inside me that wants to live. I walk the streets barefoot, disconnected from everything. It's then that I catch a glimpse of Lacey, looking as if she's thirteen months pregnant. I hide from her, retreating into the shadows. From my hiding spot between the entrance of a business, I catch a glimpse of my own reflection. That's when I make the call to my brother-in-law for help. I've left the world behind to live in a cloud, and now I need to leave California.

Chapter 21
The Shell Cracks Open

Mathew 11:28 "Come to me all you who are weary and burdened, and I will give you rest."

"The yoke is scrambled."

In the shade of the dragon's underbelly rests the child within. He is lost, alone, and overwhelmed by all that he is harboring. In a way, it's almost laughable to think of the child first learning to retrieve a toy that has fallen beneath the coffee table. He bends over to pick it up. He rises and strikes his head, causing him to drop the toy again. He bends over to retrieve it, stands, and once more bumps his head, repeating the cycle. This feels familiar, as if I too am caught in an endless loop—I can't seem to make it through the fog. I have been down this road a thousand times, and the answer seems so surreal that it defies belief.

Reliving this tale is difficult. Tears begin to steal my breath, yet they open a pathway directly back to the child in the lair. "Men don't cry," I was taught. But as I watch the dragon surrounding the child, I speak gently, "It's okay to cry." I feel the emotional layers unfolding, revealing thoughts that drift beyond the shallow waters of reality and into something deeper.

The lair is heating up. The walls seem to adjust, compensating for the rising temperature. Something is happening. Something is changing, altering the natural world. It's becoming clear that what I once perceived as the natural world may not be natural at all. As I consider the dragon's lair and its conceptualized value system, it seems to manifest in the world around me. On a collective level, the land of treachery appears to be expanding into our reality. Yet, just a few tears and a few gentle words seem to shrink the internal boundaries of that treacherous land.

"Hey, you be careful. I don't want to read about you in the paper." These words echo in my head every time I wake up.

It's early afternoon, and I have a pan on the stove with a bit of butter melting. Watching the butter form little streams as it runs from the heat feels symbolic. It's like me—melting in the frying pan of life.

I love to cook. I learned it out of necessity. I started making crepes for my brother and me once we moved away from hell for the final time. Our mom would come home late in the evening from work. She got off at five, but she liked to drive around, window shopping. She was probably reminiscing about her glory days, thinking about what she would be doing under different circumstances. My mom had her own demons, ones that likely took root in the hell of Minnesota too. I remember her biting at her forefinger, making the oddest sound, and saying, "I wish I were dead." Later, they called it anxiety—go figure.

So, I would cook. I've been told I'm pretty good at it, but this isn't a gourmet dinner I'm working on here.

A gentle knock on the door lifts my gaze from the liquid butter. I remove the pan from the burner to answer it. One of Lori's friends is standing there.

"Lori's not here," I say. Lori is my roommate and the best wing-girl you could ask for. It wouldn't be beyond her to send a friend over to get acquainted with me in her absence. She might not be back for a while.

"If it's okay, I'll wait for her," the friend responds.

The popping of the skillet draws me back to the kitchen. She follows directly behind me.

Awkward Silence

"Would you like a fried egg sandwich?" I ask. Hey, I told you this wasn't going to be a gourmet meal.

"No, thank you." She replied.

I crack the eggs open and plop them into the pan. With the swift movement of a samurai, I wield my spatula, and the festive cooking is underway.

"Danny gets back tomorrow! I can't wait," I say, excitement bubbling up.

Danny left a week ago on his motorcycle. He had a sheet of acid and a destination, but not much else. Some high school friends of ours lived in Phoenix, Arizona, and he craved adventure. That's about a thousand miles on what I remember as a Honda CB500—a brutal, uncomfortable ride.

"Danny's dead," she says nonchalantly, as if the words mean nothing.

"What?" I feel the blood drain from my body, as if a valve has just burst open at my feet. What she said can't be true—but why would she lie?

"Lori's friend Danny? He died in a motorcycle accident."

"Lori's friend? Danny is my best friend." Anger rises within me like a tidal wave.

"Get out of my house!" I shout, my voice thundering.

She stumbles back, moving clumsily toward the door. As I repeat myself, she panics, colliding with every piece of furniture between the chair and the back door. The stairs prove too much for her to handle upright, but she doesn't slow down, sliding down on her backside.

No one wants to hear about the death of a loved one, and there's no good way to break that news—but this feels like the worst. I don't want to believe it. I can't believe it. She doesn't know, but as much as I reject her words, I feel the truth of them deep in my bones. I turn off the burner and collapse into a chair. I remember nothing after turning off the stove.

She couldn't understand the bond Danny and I shared, and it isn't her fault—but the way I received the news was devastating. I don't want to believe her, but there's an unshakeable certainty that it's true. If only she hadn't spoken those words, maybe it wouldn't have happened.

I lost my best friend. He ran his motorcycle into a motorhome. It's not just heartbreaking—it's beyond that. I would have screamed in agony, pure and unblemished agony. But it's not unblemished. It's agony marred with pain, anger, and perhaps a hint of rage. I can't show emotion, especially not sorrow, but it takes over my body. It consumes my soul and spirit.

I wake up hours later with no recollection of falling asleep. I don't know where my mind had wandered, but there, clenched in my hand, is his obituary.

I haven't let go of a single burden I've been carrying. The weight has become unbearable. I am a mess. I am broken. There's a possibility I have a daughter I can't claim—I don't even know if she's mine, yet she haunts my thoughts. Now, I've lost my best friend. Suicide has been on my mind since childhood. I am self-medicating. I am on drugs, and reality is no longer my ally. Now, that death wish I've always harbored feels all too real. If I want to live, I have to fight back.

I look around and realize all my friends are trapped in the same courtyard of treachery. Of course, that's where I met them. We are all burning in our own hell. We are young and clueless about life. We are prey, wild game hunted by Lucifer himself. We're not just hunted; we're influenced, filled with despair. Sin is our affliction, whether as victims or aggressors. The result is always the same: pain or death. Each of us carries our own afflictions, but it's the one thing we have in common.

I want out! I want to help bring them out too! But I don't know how. The only thing I can think of is that drugs are the common link binding us together. Drugs are the enemy. It's the war on drugs that triggers these thoughts, but I am blind to the moral decay around me. I am oblivious to the world collapsing beneath my feet. Somehow, I missed the lesson on the crumbling of our society. I know the cornerstone is still intact, but decay is spreading as society drifts away from its foundation.

Even though I have immense life experience, it exists mostly in solitude. My experiences are not to be shared. I do have a social circle, but that's only because they're in no position to judge my lack of social skills. After all, who cares if you say something stupid when you're all high? But with people who are well-adjusted, I can't hold a conversation. I am exposed to torture, stuck in an otherwise empty box. Any social connection I have feels counterfeit because I can't be authentic—and I assume everyone else is just as fake. I have to be careful not to reveal the secrets of the house, while also hiding any sources of hope I might have. This lack of social grace, born from my isolation, is expressed as naivety.

Naivety is simply poor choices laid bare. My reasoning isn't tainted by greed, lust, or vengeance. I genuinely want to help. But my perception of help has been distorted by my warped worldview. I think in simplistic terms: if drugs are causing all these issues with my friends, and the government has declared a war on drugs, then that puts me close to the front lines. I decide to become an agent of drug enforcement, but I'm blind. I'm naive. I'm not stupid, but sometimes it feels like stupid is as stupid does. I quickly learn that the enemy exists just as much within the system as it does outside it.

On my first mission, I'm sent to enter a drug house and make a purchase. It sounds easy enough. They fit me with a wire and send me in. There's intel that a meth manufacturer will be dropping off a delivery there. The information comes from the local task force, who are backing me up. I've already spent some time getting to know Sean, the dealer who owns the house they want to bust. It's on this flimsy foundation of trust that my betrayal is built. But I justify it to myself, thinking it's for the greater good.

Sean answers the door and lets me in. As I start to maneuver toward buying some dope, the sound of a police radio crackles through the house, loud enough for everyone to hear. It definitely seems deliberate. Panic floods Sean's eyes, overtaking any trust he had in me.

"There's nothing here," Sean says, contradicting his own words just moments earlier.

I leave his place feeling like the task force has betrayed me. I can't see it as anything but an intentional mishap. I don't understand their purpose, but this incident feels like a pebble lodged in my shoe—a constant irritation.

"Jack, you need to attend a court hearing tomorrow," they tell me. "The defendants are part of a large ring. You won't have any part to play in the case, but I want you to get your feet wet in the operations of the federal court system."

I read over the case history and understand that the men on trial were tempted by the potential profits of their venture. None of them have a history of violence; they simply fell into the arms of temptation.

Awkward Silence

I look into the beast's eyes—the judge's eyes—as he slams down his gavel, sentencing them to 25 years to life. This is not justice. This is not what I signed up for. These men need help. I'm naive, still trying to grasp where true help can come from. The war was supposed to be against drugs, not the men enslaved by them. But the war is something far more profound. It's a war of powers and principalities. It's a war that involves every soul on this planet. It's a spiritual war.

I chose this path with the intention of doing good, but it's impossible to please God without faith. My decision had no correspondence with faith. Hope is dim, and love—true love—is something I desire, but I don't know him. I wasn't a part of that case, but what I witnessed in that courtroom was a tragedy far deeper than I could have imagined.

Guilt begins to gnaw at me. I might be partying side by side with people who consider me a friend, but all the while, I'm supposed to be finding the source of the party favors. Befriending people who are just as broken as I am is hard, and it makes me feel like a hypocrite. The guilt weighs on me like a crushing burden. While mingling among addicts, I start talking to them about treatment. But as I learn that treatment is just a revolving door for so many of them, I feel lost.

I remember a day, shortly after I returned from California. A good friend of mine drove me to the steps of a treatment center. She insisted that I get out and commit to recovery. But I didn't get out. I didn't recover. Instead, I find myself here, bound by some sense of moral obligation to "fix" the problems associated with drugs. Eventually, Annette gave up trying to get me to commit to that treatment center, but I still consider it one of the kindest, most thoughtful things anyone has ever done for me.

It's truly inspiring when someone shows just a little bit of love. Her act of consideration led me to start exploring other options. I felt I needed to stay involved because I was convinced that drugs were the enemy. Maybe it was the drugs that drove Lacey away, or that took Danny's life. But deep down, I know the answer isn't to imprison those afflicted. The solution doesn't lie in the devil's deeds. Lying about who you are to go undercover is still a lie, and that's the work of Satan. And this barely scratches the surface of the corruption involved in this so-called war on drugs. I've come to realize that I want no part in the evil that lies at the core of this twisted idea of justice. My new mission becomes doing for others what Annette did for me—offering a way out, a chance to heal.

But that ever-present cloud, that fog, that thick brimstone smoke keeps burning, obstructing my view of just how broken I really am. This haze only feeds my self-righteousness, making it harder to see my own flaws.

The spirit of Judas taunts me, corrupting my soul. I never felt sympathy for Judas. To me, he was always the one who betrayed his teacher and friend—the one who committed treason. He deserved to die. I still think he did. But if I were to judge, I'd say the same thing about myself. The difference between him and me? It's in our motivations. Judas did it for money. I did it because I truly wanted a world free from the heartbreak of addiction.

I wonder if Judas ever had those blackouts, those moments where you come to consciousness mid-sentence, unaware of what you've said, only to see people staring at you as if you've confessed to something unthinkable. I wonder if he, too, was embodied by demons, because I feel that darkness within me.

I see horrific things. I see a child in a wheelchair, withering away from malnutrition. I see extreme neglect. I see men passed out in children's rooms, and I can't begin to fathom what they're doing there in the first place. These children have no guidance, no protection. There are teenagers sharing needles with their parents as if it's the equivalent of sitting down for a family dinner. And I see teenage girls selling their bodies just so they and their families can share another bag.

I rage against these men. I hurt many of them, even the parents who should have protected their children. I made calls for wellness checks, hoping someone would intervene. But what I've seen sickens me. And that sickness begins to infect my soul. It starts to build a deceptive wall inside me. This wall tells me that these parents and others are trash, that they're no good, that they're the filth of the earth. But as much as I want to believe that, I can't form that complete judgment because I can see that these kids, now damaged, may one day grow into adults just as broken. If they aren't helped, they might become exactly like their parents.

It's not rage we need. The horrifying realization that these innocent children could become their parents shocks me into clarity.

This nightmare unfolds into a hellish scheme. From the streets of poverty and despair, through the hands of money men exploiting the vulnerable, to a justice system rife with corruption, the cycle ends in a graveyard of shattered lives. Once people fall into this abyss, they're unlikely to escape. And here I am, stuck in the middle of it again. I can smell the sulfur burning. I can feel the heat of magma radiating against my skin. I am here, held in this place, driven to make a difference—but I don't know how.

Her heart cries out to me in the stillness of the night, when all is quiet. The silence around me is so profound that it feels like her breath rustles the leaves on the trees. This little girl, born on November ninth, is all I can think about. I hope she is well. I pray that addiction hasn't stolen anything from her, that the enemy hasn't reached her. I've learned her name is Faith.

The chaotic, unmanageable clanging of swords striking together in the spiritual battlefield ignites the strife within. Here in this realm, trust lies deeply wounded, severed from the natural world. It no longer exists in the soul or the body and clings only faintly to the spirit. The war relentlessly wages on, eroding the very attributes of love. Without love, there is no hope of defeating the enemy. The dragon and all his minions occupy the soul, slipping into the physical realm by crossing the threshold of an open door. Trust, faith, and hope—those once-mighty barriers—are absent, having been called away to fight, leaving the gates wide open. And that's how the darkness came in, to take over the territory we now call treachery.

They invaded the mind first, twisting and contorting thoughts until they turned completely upside down. These corrupted thoughts seeped into the emotional core, seizing control. The wizardry of these thoughts masqueraded as reason, but in truth, they were the vines of deceit that entangled innocence. From this entanglement, the dragon was conceived, and the fruit of that vine was poison—a poison that seeped into the soul.

Yet, the roots of this tree grew ever stronger, even as the poison coursed through its veins. But then, an idea—a possibility—brought a shift: the thought that Faith might be my daughter. This possibility stirred something in me, loosening some of the sludge I've been wading through. The shoreline of my despair still bears the claw marks where I tried to escape my self-pity. But now, I'm moving back, determined to find Lacey. I will have the paternity test done. I will stand on my own two feet. I will conquer my fears.

I am not afraid of death; I've spent most of my life wanting it, hoping for a do-over. But I do have fears. I fear those final moments before death, when my life flashes before my eyes, and I realize it was all in vain. I fear that I have endured the torments of hell only to find that it was for nothing. I fear that I will never escape the sludge and that all I'll ever know is misery. I fear that all my efforts to save others from their addictions will amount to nothing. I fear that, in the end, I will stand alone on the grounds of my convictions.

But my most immediate fear? I fear that Faith is not my child. I fear that all the emotional energy I've invested in the hope that she is mine will crumble into another reason to despise my life. And if she is mine, I fear fatherhood itself. I fear that my mess of a life will spill over into hers, making it her mess to clean up.

"If you're certain this is what you want," he says, his eyes betraying a deep concern, "I'll authorize it. But you'll need to report to the local task force once you arrive. Under no circumstances are you to go into the Oakland field office."

In that moment, I realize he's genuinely worried. He knows where I'm headed. He's been in drug enforcement for years; he knows the hot spots. He knows exactly what awaits me in Antioch.

"I'll make them aware you're coming," he adds.

The local narcotics team is backing me up for what will be my second mission in drug enforcement. This time, I'm supposed to infiltrate a motel room where cartel distributors are operating. The task force has set up a perimeter around the motel, and one of the detectives drops me off in the parking lot.

I enter the room, and three Hispanic men are waiting inside.

"Hey, you want a beer?" one of the men sitting on the bed asks, casually tossing me a can.

I catch it and tap the top—something I've heard prevents it from spewing if shaken. As I do this, the man on the bed answers his phone. The conversation is brief but sharp, and I watch as his demeanor shifts, his eyes darkening with anger. He reaches behind an open case on the bed. My instincts scream that it's time to leave.

I make a snap decision, grabbing the man standing by the door. Wrapping my arm around his neck, I drag him backward out of the room, using him as a human shield because I know bullets are about to fly.

It was a gun the other man reached for—I glimpsed it just before he fumbled with it. The moment I'm through the door, a shot rings out. I drop the man I was holding and run, my heart pounding as if the bullets are chasing me. I sprint around the corner of the motel office just as a patrol car cuts me off.

"Are you Jack?" the officer asks as I'm doubled over, gasping for breath.

"Yes," I manage to say between breaths.

"Why didn't anyone come in?" The words spill out before I can stop them, my mind racing, paranoia thrumming in my veins. This is only my second time in the field, and already, I'm wondering what the hell is going on.

"I don't know, man. I'm just supposed to pick you up and take you back to the station," he replies, almost too casually, as if this is just another day on the job. But it sure as hell doesn't feel that way to me.

Back at the station, I storm in, still trying to steady my breath. The detective in charge is lounging behind his desk, feet kicked up like he's on vacation.

"What the hell was that?" I demand, my voice a mix of anger and disbelief. "I could have been killed, and there was no one there to back me up!"

The detective lowers his feet and leans forward. "Jack, after I dropped you off, some car started tailing me," he explains. "I tried to shake him, went all through downtown. I... I got spooked. I bailed and came back here."

His words leave me reeling, my anger morphing into something colder. Fear? Betrayal? I'm not sure, but confusion is settling heavily on my shoulders. If nothing else, we could've at least intercepted the drugs and flushed them. Even that would've been a step toward fighting this so-called war. Instead, they just let these guys keep pushing their product. I have no idea what kind of war they're fighting, but it sure as hell isn't the one I signed up for.

The realization hits me like a gut punch: the war they're fighting is not the same as mine. Sure, there's some overlap, but the cracks between our agendas are becoming too clear to ignore. I try to use the system to push my own mission forward—getting help for the people caught in the crossfire—but I need access to their resources to do it. Without that, I'm just another guy trying to take down giants with a slingshot.

Yet here I am, about to make a move I never thought I would: going back to work at the glass factory. The thought fills me with a kind of dread I haven't felt in years. The image of that blazing factory, the orange glow against the night sky, haunts my memories. Those factories got bombed to the ground, and if history has its way, it could happen again.

Going back to that place is the last thing I want. It's where I still see Lacey's ghost in the hallways, where the air is thick with memories I'd rather forget. But it's also a goldmine of information about the drug world—a place where whispers turn into leads. And

I need a job to maintain my cover. Factory work gives me a shield, a plausible cover story. Nobody expects a factory worker to be working undercover for the DEA. And as an agent, the latitude I have is... generous, to say the least. The rules I operate under are defined by the agreement I signed—a simple contract, unless I decide to dig deeper and go off-script.

But stepping back into that world feels like stepping into a minefield. Every choice, every conversation, could lead to another betrayal, another blind corner where I could end up alone again, outgunned, with no backup in sight.

Chapter 22
Turn Back the Hour

Isaiah 38:8 "The sun's shadow went back ten steps on the stairway."

"Don't overthink it."

I know that somewhere within the clandestine operations of these streets, I will find Lacey. Somewhere in the whispers, I will detect the call of her voice. As connected as she is, she may already know that I'm in town. It's been three years—three very long, difficult years. I wonder if the spark would still exist. But I can't afford to think that way. I have one objective: to find out about paternity.

That whisper of her voice in the wind carries me to a neighboring town. It's been almost a year since I arrived and began searching. Faith is going to be four in a couple of months, and I haven't seen so much as a picture. I wouldn't recognize her by sight, but I wonder if I'd be able to spot her on some deeper, instinctual level.

I walk toward the door, and it feels as if every step is in slow motion. I can feel anticipation accumulating in the left side of every cell in my body. Then, in that same slow motion, I take another step, and anxiety builds on the right side of every cell. I'm not entirely aware of what I'm doing. Maybe I'm poking the devil with a stick.

A flashback hits me—I'm eight years old, just walking out of a movie we watched in church. I didn't believe in the Mormon views, but this film crawled beneath my skin. It showed a boy being beaten at home, which led to social isolation from his classmates. He was taunted for being different, bullied relentlessly.

His tragic end came when, as a cruel prank, the other kids tied his shoelaces together. He tripped as he stepped off the bus, unable to regain his balance. He never got up again. That day, I raised a stick as my sword and declared my vengeance on Satan.

"Can I help you?" a man asks, his voice coming through the screen door.

"Yes. Is Lacey here?" I respond.

"No, she's out picking cherries. Can I tell her who stopped by?"

"Jack."

I barely make it back home when there's a knock at my door. My jaw hits the floor so hard it practically bounces back into place. Before I can react, Lacey latches onto me in a big hug. I don't even have time to notice she's wearing the necklace I got her for Christmas. There was a time when I dreamed of this—when I wanted this kind of response so badly that I would've given anything for it. But now? I don't know what I expected, but this isn't it.

I pull her into the entryway and shut the door. Yes, it's Lacey. Her appearance still does it for me, but there's something different about how I feel. Maybe it's self-preservation. I can't afford to get entangled in her web again.

"Taylor, I have missed you so much," she says, her voice soft.

"Lacey, I came to see you because I want a paternity test." I half-expect her to laugh, to say something that contradicts everything I've been thinking.

"Yeah, you have the right to know," she replies, almost too calmly. "She could be yours, but I'm not sure. I can't be sure."

A heavy silence fills the room, painting the walls with the weight of what was just revealed. I don't know what to say. She's just admitted, in so many words, that she cheated on me. Still, there's something to be said for honesty, even if it comes out like a cat let loose from a bag.

After a few moments, I look at her and say, "You look fantastic." I can feel the bitterness melting away from my heart, just a little.

"You do too, Taylor." She always grins seductively when she calls me by my last name. There's a subtle bite to her lower lip, a slight tilt of her head, and a light in her eyes. But I can't let that in. I have a single objective, and I have to remind myself of it four or five times over the next five minutes.

"I need to go, but we'll need to get together to discuss the paternity testing further," she says, standing up.

"When will work for you?" I ask.

"Thursday. You can pick me up at my house at five."

"I'll be there!" I call out as she reaches for the door handle. She abruptly turns, hugging me and pressing a quick kiss to my lips.

"And Taylor..." There's a pause, that seductive look washing over her again. "It's wonderful to see you."

I can't do this. I have to keep reminding myself that the only thing that matters is the paternity test. I repeat it to myself every time a stray thought pushes through the chambers of my mind. I remind myself over and over again until Thursday finally arrives.

Jack Taylor

As I pull up to Lacey's house, a man slams the door behind him. He glares at me, and I wonder if he's the same guy I spoke to through the screen door. He climbs onto his Harley, revving the engine excessively before speeding off. It's almost laughable how much of an ass he looks, but my instincts are sharp. I have a pretty good idea of what just happened. I can even feel a twinge of empathy for the guy. Lacey must have just told him it was over, and then I showed up. That would explain the look he gave me.

"I have to keep the focus on Faith," I remind myself yet again.

Lacey and I are just going to dinner to talk about paternity. That's it. I don't want to rekindle anything. In fact, I plan to pick the least romantic place possible. I can't take her to McDonald's, but pizza seems neutral enough.

But even as I tell myself this, I know I'm lying. I don't want to feel this way, yet I can't help it. She tore my heart out of my chest and ground it into the dirt with those six-inch stilettos. And still, I want her so badly that I can recall the moisture of her lips, the sound of every moan. I can vividly picture myself tugging gently on her hair just as the elevator doors opened.

This is a battle raging in my soul—my head versus my heart. But in the end, it's my will that will carry out whatever the triumphant side decides.

It's obvious which side will win. Anyone listening to my inner dialogue would know. I already admitted I'm lying to myself, which means my head has already surrendered to my heart. There's really no point in pretending to fight it. It's a mistake. I know that. But maybe if I stick to my plan—take her out for pizza—there won't be an opportunity for anything else. I won't have to be strong.

Awkward Silence

But when she opens the door, looking like an "Oh my God" moment come to life, I know I'm toast. I'm clearly walking off a cliff with no escape route, narrow or wide. I try to play it cool, but it's impossible. She's taken the time to separate each eyelash perfectly, with more precision than goes into building a computer chip. I'm finished. And she knows it.

I manage to hold out all the way through the pizza arriving at our table, but the full spectrum of light soon shines on what I know will be my bad decision. Her shoe slips off under the table, her foot sliding slowly up my calf, then my knee, and finally resting on my thigh, inches away from igniting the fire I'm desperately trying to keep under control.

"Let's get out of here," she says in that sultry tone that pulls me to my feet like a puppet on strings. Without a second thought, I follow her out the door.

The rhythm of our hearts matched beat for beat. Each breath I took felt synced with hers. The sounds around us became musical notes, spoken in unison. For that brief time, we were one being. The arch of her back was perfectly poised with each thrust, each movement in perfect harmony. Somehow, the night slipped away, and when morning arrived, reality seeped back in. It was amazing but, perhaps, shameful. I suppose it's what comes next that will determine that.

"Taylor, if you can make an appointment for the paternity test, we'll get it done," she says softly, breaking the fragile silence.

"Can I meet her?" I ask, my voice hesitant.

"She may not be yours. You know that, right?"

"Yes," I reply, the words tasting like ash. "I've pounded that into my head for nearly four years. But still, she's a part of

211

you, and I'd love to meet her. I don't want to confuse her, though. In fact, Lacey, I'm just Jack—an old friend of yours."

"I don't know when Jeff will let me have her. He has custody right now, and he's keeping her from me," Lacey says, her voice wavering. A tear almost forms, but I know better. She never lets them fall. She'll become emotional, maybe even kick and scream, but cry? Not a chance. That would mean admitting vulnerability, and that's something she's never allowed herself.

We're together now, and it's nice, but there's always this lingering fear. I have to make a conscious effort to trust, to combat the thoughts that swarm my mind like a relentless army. This internal conflict means that the war is being fought in my soul. My thoughts are turning against my feelings, affecting my will. It's a true fight for the territory of my heart.

"You know one day you'll wake up, and she'll just be gone," whispers that cynical, demonic voice in my mind. It strikes like clockwork every few minutes.

"You're out of your mind if you think you're going to live happily ever after."

This voice is relentless, antagonizing me, feeding me a spirit of fear. I feel helpless, defenseless against these attacks. I have no weapon, and this enemy shows no mercy.

The thoughts are unyielding. They scatter my focus, blurring the lines between past wounds and present fears. I hear the cries of the wounded echoing from the battlefield in my mind. Trauma from the past is charging at me, trying to advance from my thoughts into my emotions. I need to set up a perimeter, a mental concentration camp, to keep these thoughts locked away.

Awkward Silence

"She was supposed to be here at five." We've been together for about six months now, and this is the first time she's ever been late. All those old feelings of abandonment come storming back, battering the gates of my fragile trust. I remember the way she left before—how she was just gone without a trace.

"It's seven o'clock. Go to her house," I tell myself. The keys are in my hand, but fear roots me in place. I'm terrified of what I might find when I get there.

"If she has a guy there, ask no questions," I think, steeling myself for what could be another betrayal. "Just prepare for battle."

The war that began in my mind is now manifesting through my will. Soon, it could spill over into the physical world, into actions I might regret. I can feel the line between rational thought and raw emotion blurring. I'm standing on the edge, and one wrong move could tip me over.

No, if there's a guy there, it doesn't mean that she's with him. It could be anyone. No, she would've called to let me know. She would've called to invite me out.

I rap on the door, then take a few steps back. With my knuckles clenched into a fist, I prepare myself. A few moments pass, and my adrenaline has stretched time to its limits. Just as I'm about to knock again, the most adorable little girl answers the door.

"Well, don't just stand there, come in," she says, and my heart melts.

"I've been waiting a long time for you to get here," she adds, nearly bringing me to tears.

"You've been waiting for me?" I ask, kneeling down to her level.

"You're Jack, right?"

"Yes, I am."

"Then yes, I've been waiting for you!" She looks up at me with eyes that melt all the rock and debris around my heart.

"Wait here. I have a surprise for you."

One look at her, and all my pain ceases to exist. Not a single thought runs through my mind. I am completely and utterly captivated. I am in awe.

Suddenly, the song from Cher begins to play, *"If I Could Turn Back Time."* And that's when Faith comes out into the hallway. She's wearing high heels and a pink feather boa, flinging it around as she sings to me.

I am speechless. She obviously rehearsed this. She waited for me to arrive to perform. I'm caught in her spell—her willing prisoner. I can't take my eyes off of her. I am so overwhelmed with joy that I can't even put it into words. As I write this, I'm still filled with gratitude for that moment. Thank you, God, for that gift! It seems to make everything in my life up to this point worth it. If I could turn back time, I would watch this moment over and over again. Every time I feel dislocated, I'll rewind this scene and play it again! If there's ever a reason to conquer the beast inside me, this is it.

"She made me promise to stay in my room until her performance was done," Lacey says, entering the room.

"What took you so long to get here? She's been waiting," I ask, still in awe.

Lacey wraps her arms around my neck. "You were supposed to be at my place at five."

"I know, but now you know why," I reply, unable to control the tears that start to flow. I'm overwhelmed with emotion. I've waited so long for this moment, but I never expected anything like this.

"I have dinner ready. She insisted that we wait for you," Lacey adds with a shrug.

"Oh my! She is AMAZING!" I say, wiping away my tears. "You know it will crush me if she's not my daughter, but nothing can take away how amazing she is!"

This may be the first time in my life—at least since I was six—that I'm truly grateful. This experience may be the moment I turn full circle in my understanding of life. Not only does God exist, but He actually loves me. He actually cares about me. That realization is beyond words. The understanding that the God who created the universe loves me is more powerful than any of the hardships I've faced. He is beyond anything I could ever confront. He is the Alpha and the Omega. He is the beginning and the end.

A couple of months pass. My heart is connected to this beautiful child. She has an identity full of compassion and care. She is truly an amazing creation of God.

"Okay, Lacey, I've scheduled the appointment for the paternity testing. I thought it was DNA testing, but it's actually HLA red cell testing. Anyway, we need to be in Sacramento Monday." It's not far to Sacramento, and we can make a day of it, have some fun while we're at it.

"Okay, that works. I'm excited for the results. She's so much like you," Lacey says.

A couple more days go by.

"Tomorrow's the big day," I remind Lacey, though I'm sure she doesn't need reminding.

Faith and I are playing games and having fun. I am beside myself. We're playing the game where the puzzle pieces are on a timer, and when your time is up, the pieces all pop up at you. There's a startled look in Faith's eyes when the pieces pop.

"My name is Faith."

"I know. Don't you think I've been paying attention?" I tease her.

"Yes, but it's Faith Marie."

"Of course it is," I respond.

"But I don't know what my last name is yet."

The puzzle pieces pop in my mind. I'm genuinely puzzled by her statement.

"Lacey, you haven't said anything to her, have you?"

"No! Of course not."

Okay, maybe I'm reading into something I shouldn't.

Now Faith and I are playing hide and seek. I have to count while she hides. She's so cute the way she tells me it's my turn to count, every single time. She's in the shower, hiding behind the curtain. I play it up, but in truth, there aren't many places to hide at my place.

"Hmm. Let's see. Is she in the closet?" I throw open the door.

"Nope, not in there."

"Is she under the bed?" I get on my knees.

"Nope, not there either."

I sneak into the bathroom and pull back the curtain quickly. She shrieks and giggles, then says, "Daddy!" Oh my God, it's wonderful!

"I have to go to my sister's tonight, but I'll be back first thing in the morning to head to Sacramento." I haven't seen her sister since we've been back together, but I trust her. I know as long as she's with her sister, everything's okay. Her sister likes me. I have no reason to doubt what she's saying—well, not without digging into ancient history. But Monday came and went. Tuesday flew by, and I sat in disbelief. Wednesday, I was in the same position on the couch. Thursday, I decided I better call in to work. I kept replaying the scene of pulling back the shower curtain.

"Daddy!"

Some say she's pregnant again. My heart doesn't know what to feel, and my mind is broken. I'm living in a time loop, circling over and over again with zero understanding. I'm not among the living anymore. I feel like I literally died that day. Death wasn't what I expected. It wasn't paradise—it was filled with monsters of corruption. If I were to say that I died that day, then I was in Hell. I embarked upon a journey that had no end. I had to make this world a better place, a place where Faith could grow up and never know the toils of this bitterness. But I turned, and she was no longer there. She was no longer in my line of vision. She was gone.

Faith may not be my daughter. She looks so much like her mother that breaking down physical attributes for comparison is impossible. For my sanity, I'd like to just accept that she's not mine, but I can't. The not knowing eats away at me. It's the maggots feasting upon my cells. It's the synapse making that final connection, an infinite loop of thought that never ends.

Chapter 23
Blessing in Disguise

Mathew 5:10 "Persecution for the sake of Christ is a blessing in disguise."

"I was an abomination. I am a changed man."

I know that God makes no mistakes. If any error is to be made, it will be made by me. Right now, I'm soaking in alcohol, trying to numb the pain, when Tonya appears.

She and I had a one-night stand a couple of months before I found Lacey. Since then, Tonya became obsessed with me, though I gave her no reason to. Perhaps it was because she harbored a deep disdain for herself. I made it clear that I didn't want to be with her—in fact, I was quite rude.

"Can we talk?" she asks me.

"Tonya, yes, I think we should." From my seated position, I pull out the chair beside me.

"Hold on a minute." She walks over to the barmaid and whispers something to her before returning. Once she's seated next to me, I begin to speak.

"You know, Tonya, what happened between us before—it should never have happened. We should just be friends."

Before she can reply, the barmaid brings over a couple of shots and drinks.

"We can be just friends," Tonya says, leaning in, "but I want some of this on the side." She reaches over and grabs me, holding onto my cock.

"Listen, Tonya, I'm not in a place where this could be good at all. I shouldn't be making any decisions right now." I scoot back in my seat.

"What decision? I'm taking all the guesswork out of it—no commitment," she insists.

"I'm doing everything I can just to avoid feeling anything. I don't want to feel. I'm trying my best to cope with losing Lacey and Faith. I can't handle any complications right now."

"Jack, I don't want anything from you except light conversation and sex." She rubs me again, more insistently.

The drinks keep coming, as if drawn from a freshly drilled well.

"Saluti," we toast, clinking glasses. One shot after another, we down them.

"I let it happen again," I mutter, starting to regret how much I've been drinking.

"You let what happen again?" Tonya asks, her eyes narrowing.

"I found Lacey," I say, my words beginning to slur. "I told you about her before."

"Yeah, she's the one you may or may not have a daughter with, right? So, did you ever find out?" she presses.

"Nope. She left me again before we could get the testing done," I reply, feeling the sadness hit me like a wave.

"Never mind. I think I'm getting drunk," I admit, my words now fully slurred.

"So," Tonya says, her tone shifting, "you want to be my blow-up doll? My sex toy?"

I shake my head, unable to picture Tonya fitting into that role. "You mean you just want a no-strings-attached sexual relationship?"

"Exactly," she says, clarifying. "Just friends. No expectations."

"Just friends?" I ask again, needing reassurance.

"Just friends," she confirms, a sly smile playing on her lips.

That "just friends" thing? Well, it faded away over the course of the next nine months. It was supposed to be one night—just that one night. We drank the drinks she ordered, which kept coming until she knew she had me. We made it to her car, and that's where we conceived my Katie. Good God, I couldn't live without my Katie now. However, I didn't always feel that way.

"I'm pregnant," she told me.

"You have got to be kidding me."

"No, I'm pregnant," she reiterated, more firmly.

"Well, what are you going to do?" I asked, seeing the disappointment flash in her eyes. She clearly wanted, maybe even expected, a different response.

"Get an abortion!" I snapped. God, what a cruel thing for me to suggest. I was not okay. This was more than I could handle, but I brought it on myself with reckless choices, decisions that were never rooted in any kind of sound mind. Twisted thoughts lead to twisted actions. I was unwell, grieving the loss of Faith, yet faced with a new opportunity to raise a beautiful child. And perhaps, therein lay the problem.

No, Tonya and I would never have worked out in any kind of relationship. I detested the kind of woman she was—bossy, controlling, manipulative. She was deceitful, both in her dealings with others and with me. She wouldn't have liked me either if it weren't for the fact that, to her, I was just a contest to win. Maybe, with effort, we could learn to co-parent. That was the best I could hope for.

But the stress pulls me right back into the center of my turmoil. Emotionally, I never grew beyond the age of six. I've been living in a world filled with dragons and demons, completely detached from what others might consider reality. There is absolutely nothing in me that resembles the figure of a man—a father. I can't even begin to fantasize about stepping into that role; it feels so far removed from who I am.

If someone asked me to audition for the part of a father, I'd probably show up wearing a necktie, simply because Ward Cleaver wore one on *Leave It to Beaver*. That's the closest vision I have of what a father is supposed to be. But in my mind, the waters are murky, unclear, and likely filled with the beasts of my childhood nightmares. Fear seeps in when I think about the kind of dad I might become.

The only certainty I have about fatherhood is that I will not be like the role models I had growing up. If I even suspect that those old demons might rise from the depths, I would rather swim to an island so remote, so desolate, that not even the thinnest whisper of emotion could reach me.

Chapter 24
Confused as the Philistines

1st Samuel 14:20 "Then Saul and all his men went to battle. They found the Philistines in total confusion, striking each other with their swords."

"Bones under the sand "

I try to continue my life as if none of this had ever happened. I'm back in the mindset that I have to change the world—now, if for no other reason than that Faith and Katie need to grow up in a better world than I did. I feel the need to redefine my life, to be a force for change. I would become a sacrificial lamb if that's what it takes. I don't care if I die in the process; I have to create a place where the enemy cannot bind my daughters.

All things considered, there really is no logic in my thinking. I've snapped. My primary objective is a death wish, maybe even to be a martyr.

If there is any one human being who embodies the wizard in this carnal world, it would be Chuck. He speaks to me using the tactics of conversational hypnosis and neuro-linguistic programming. I recognize this from my studies. He seems to have good intentions—perhaps even playing a part in saving my life. Then again, it could be him who set the wheels in motion to take my life. I can't be sure; his language has so many twists and turns, it slithers like a snake in its deceptions. When I say "deceptions," I mean the unspoken truths, the hidden meanings, that lurk beneath his words.

Chuck is a Vietnam vet with two Purple Hearts. I imagine he's been through some things, but I never ask him about it, and he never offers. The only reason I know about his medals is because I've seen them in his war case.

He was extradited from Costa Rica in 2004. By that time, I had committed myself to healing. I was writing—much like I am now—when the U.S. Department of Justice contacted me. They wanted me to be a witness in a case they were building against him as a kingpin. At that point, I hadn't seen Chuck in eleven years.

"You want me to be a trial witness against a man I haven't seen in eleven years?" I asked.

"Yes, we believe that you have pertinent information for this case," they replied.

"Let me get this straight. You're reaching back eleven years to charge a man for crimes that allegedly happened back then? And you want me to bear witness to events that will determine a man's fate, based on things that happened over a decade ago?"

"That is correct," they confirmed.

"I can't even remember what shampoo I have in my shower. I will not testify to events that happened eleven years ago."

The sophisticated shifting of the sands—they're trying to unbury bones left in the desert. As I said, I'm here in my music store, sifting through this wreckage, and I can't think of a single reason those old bones should surface now, unless it's through the efforts of Satan himself. I'm struggling to make sense of the very things they want me to testify about.

I would love to skip over this part of my life entirely. Honestly, if you've seen *Breaking Bad*, then you would have a pretty good picture of the context surrounding me back then—but you wouldn't see me in that picture.

Awkward Silence

I was the one who thought I was invisible. I was the rat that everyone knew was a rat, except for me. I was wearing the jacket that said I was working drug enforcement, but I no longer cared, and so I got swept up in the great escape.

I don't know if I was very courageous or just very dumb. God did make me courageous, and He gave me a strong moral conviction—one that I distorted and confused with the help of the demons that had been shadowing me. In retrospect, I realize I was both very brave and incredibly naive.

"Hey, Jack, there's a guy in Bethel Island who wants to meet you." This is Chuck's initial summoning. The message came through a guy I work with at the glass plant.

When I arrive at the place, the first thing I notice is a pair of boots sticking out of a fifty-five-gallon barrel. There's a DEA jacket lying on the ground next to the barrel. I can't tell if there are feet inside those boots, and I have no clear idea why I'm here. God has my blinders up for a reason. Sometimes, ignorance truly is bliss.

As much as I would like to remain uninformed, I can't ignore the fact that I'm here because, at some point, I signed up with drug enforcement. I hadn't been active in that world for a while, though—it's devils fighting devils. Nothing good comes from hiding behind fictitious names. In fact, all the lying is just one of Satan's tactics on display within the system. If something can't be done with integrity and by God's rules, then it isn't worth doing. But nobody knows this is how I feel. If my name has been leaked into the underworld, it wouldn't be part of an official file; it would be scrawled on a piece of paper, passed hand-to-hand in the shadows.

To some, manufacturing methamphetamine is an art. To others, it's a science, and to a few, it's pure magic. I could stretch that further and say it's driven by greed, exploiting society's weaknesses. In my mind, the weaknesses I speak of are those carried by people who've endured the kind of pain and trauma familiar to me. In this mystical, clandestine world of drugs, there isn't a single person I've met who hasn't been broken by tragedy long before they boarded the train to this underworld.

The pharmaceutical industry, when you look closely, isn't much different. It's just legal, with enormous profits because it's a protected field. I once knew a doctor who would prescribe Klonopin to attractive women and then schedule follow-up appointments after the drug had taken hold in their systems. Klonopin has a side effect—it makes women horny. He would capitalize on this to his advantage.

In the underworld, this is the mindset of many so-called "magical-thinking" cooks. There are countless ways to create a similar substance. They ionize ephedrine to turn it into meth or use phenylacetic acid combined with potassium acetate to make the street drug. This isn't a tutorial, but rather an acknowledgment that this darkness exists, born from the twisted thought processes of those like the "wizard" I encountered in Minnesota. In this world, the escape from reality is what rules.

Ah, the journey I've had with this wizard. He came to me as a means of coping, and he's led me to the very edge of the world. But looking over that edge, the view is not what one might imagine. Symbolically, it feels like the end of my life, teetering on the brink.

I've heard stories of elaborate labs hidden deep in the sloughs. Some say there's even an underground lab with an entrance through a shaft hidden beneath a car. I can't say whether Chuck owns these labs, nor can I truthfully gauge his level of involvement. For all I know, he might just be a pawn in a much larger scheme.

Awkward Silence

But what I do find curious is the way some products are packaged to interact in unique ways. I don't believe that's mere coincidence; I suspect it's by the design of a cunning creature deeply connected to big industry. For the sake of names, let's call that creature Beelzebub.

Chuck is sitting with a big guy, someone I'd simply describe as "unmade." That's the best way to sum him up. They're in the middle of a conversation when I walk in and interrupt.

"Come on in, Jack," Chuck says, gesturing me forward.

We exchange a bit of small talk before he hands me a piece of paper. "Now, *that* is how you do it, right there," he says with a grin.

It's a formula of sorts—a method for adding that elusive hydrogen atom to ephedrine. But there's something more to it. Scribbled on the paper is an incantation tied to the process. Yet, try as I might, I can't read it. The words are in English, clear as day, but I cannot comprehend them. It's as if God Himself has shielded my eyes. I'm dead serious—I see the letters, but they might as well be hieroglyphs.

Now, the conspirators who sit at the table with Greed, Sloth, Gluttony, and the rest of their sinful entourage suddenly have faces. These people have infiltrated positions of power. It's as though I've ascended to a position where I have a bird's-eye view of Satan's very ass. I don't belong here—I know that deep in my soul—yet here I am, and it feels like there's a reason for it.

Chuck summons me often. I feel trapped, as though I can't just get up and leave, even though every fiber of my being wants to. Despite knowing I don't belong here, there's a gnawing feeling that there's a larger purpose for my presence. I can't quite identify it yet, but somehow, God has placed me here. I just don't fully realize it's His doing.

From this moment on, I begin to realize I can't go anywhere in public without someone tailing me. I start to suspect my house is bugged. I can't even use the men's room in a restaurant without one of them shadowing me. I'm seeing the same faces over and over. They've been with me all along, following me. Some of these people I've spotted at Chuck's place. Over the past two years, they've been a constant presence. I haven't been alone—not for a single moment. Running isn't an option; that would make me look guilty.

Then, a familiar face walks in. She knows me—I can see it in her eyes. And suddenly, a lot of things start clicking into place. She works with the local task force. They've dragged me through this hell to monitor the flow of information. Maybe it's a blessing in disguise that I lost my mind when Lacey took Faith away; it means no information has leaked from my side. That was nearly two years ago now. But with my radio silence, they might see me as disposable. Either way, I'm in a tight spot if this woman, who I once knew as Robin but now goes by Gina, is truly a conspirator.

There are quite a few people in this room, most of them affiliated with cartels and gangs. The atmosphere is almost relaxed, but I have to blend in—I definitely don't want to stand out. I understand why I'm here, but I'm not ready to give up the ghost just yet.

"Jack, you have gorgeous eyes," Gina purrs, beginning her seduction.

"Thank you! You're pretty hot yourself," I reply, playing along. I think I understand what she's doing.

"You think I'm hot?" she teases, her tone playful. At this point, I'm no longer worried that she might say something that would get me killed. There's a trust here, albeit a fragile one. It's no small thing to trust someone to this degree in a place like this. And I'm not about to betray that trust, either.

We slip into a kind of role play, an act that could be exciting in another context. But they say all the world's a stage, and this one feels like an off-Broadway production with life-or-death stakes. The vibe in the room is shifting, and I can sense that the others are closing in. I'm watching their movements carefully. It's no accident that we're all here.

The walls are closing in, and I can't shake the feeling that the performance isn't over yet.

"Where are you from?" she asks, her eyes studying me intently.

"I was born right here in Antioch," I reply. "But I've spent most of my life in a little town in Idaho called Nampa." At this point, I'm not going to come up with a cover story. My intuition is screaming that they already know everything about me. Besides, I have no desire to lie. The words of the Antioch police chief echo in my mind: *"If the end justifies the means."* But I don't agree with that mentality. That's exactly where you end up staring into the flames, searching for redemption.

"And you, Gina? Where are you from?" I ask, trying to maintain a casual tone while staying hyper-aware of my surroundings.

"I've lived all over," she responds with a small smile. "My dad was in the Air Force, so we traveled a lot." Her cover story doesn't convince me. Call it a hunch, intuition, or just a gut feeling—I'm certain we're not here by coincidence.

She's standing close now, holding a pool cue upright in front of her. Our playful banter has drawn the attention of others in the room, and she's as aware of it as I am.

"I don't want to stand anymore. Can I sit on your lap?" she asks, not waiting for a response before settling onto me. I place my hands on her waist, playing into the role of desire. It's not a hard part to play—she's stunning. In another world, I'd love to lose myself in her, but right now, our priority is to get out of here.

Her position on my lap gives us both a clear view of the room. She wraps her arms around my neck, bringing her face close to mine. Her lips brush against mine, and for a while, we just touch and giggle, playing our parts as if we're a couple lost in the heat of attraction. It's a convincing performance. Then, her hand slides down to subtly stroke me, all while pretending not to notice the eyes watching us. She leans into my ear and whispers, "Do you want to take me home?"

Before I can respond, Harry's voice cuts through the tension. "Jack isn't going anywhere!" he barks. "We have business to attend to."

That's her cue to leave. She gives me one last lingering kiss, her eyes filled with a concern that almost makes my heart falter. She knows the stakes. We both do. Without another word, she slips out, likely heading straight back to the task force. I can only hope they've got their eyes on this place tonight, although I know these outlaws are well aware of who she really is. They're not stupid—none of them would have survived this long if they were.

Now, I have no reasonable choice but to go along with Harry's plan. He wants me to go to Idaho with him. Could I say no? Maybe. But with my head metaphorically (and possibly literally) on the chopping block, there doesn't seem to be much I can do. I keep telling myself this is all in my head, just paranoia. Yet, a part of me is so tired. Maybe I'm ready for it to be over. I'm not afraid to die, but lately, I've been sensing the presence of something greater—perhaps God trying to reach me.

We drive deep into the desert, far away from any sign of civilization. Miles and miles of nothing stretch before us when Harry decides to pull over.

"Let's get out and stretch our legs," he says, almost too casually.

I step out, noticing him tucking a pistol into his waistband. For a moment, everything slows down. I've been living with the guilt of betrayal for so long that this feels almost like a fitting end. Even though I haven't betrayed anyone outright, living this double life feels like a betrayal of everything I once believed in. And maybe that's enough.

I've long since lost faith in the system. I saw the devil himself when that gavel came down. I tried so hard to bypass the red tape to get people help, to get them into addiction programs. But somewhere along the way, I lost myself. Maybe this desert, under the hot, unforgiving sun, is where it all ends for me.

Yet, I haven't completely given up. Not yet. I might not have a gun, but if I stay close enough to Harry, I have more than a fighting chance. For now, I play ignorant. I'm supposed to be clueless, just another pawn on a mission to transport drugs to Idaho. That's the role I'm supposed to play—the one I've played for so long. And maybe, just maybe, that will be enough to keep me alive for another day.

"This would be a good place to leave a body," Harry says, his voice heavy with intent.

For a moment, his words hang in the dry desert air. I'm staring into a reality that I've been avoiding for so long. The truth is, I don't know what my endgame looks like anymore. I'm trapped between two worlds—one of corrupt law enforcement and another of ruthless cartels. I don't want to work for drug enforcement because I see it for what it is: corrupt, self-serving, and evil. But aligning myself with the cartels and gangs, knowing I'd be helping to poison people, is equally damning. No matter which way I turn, there's no clean escape. I made the choices that brought me here. I got tangled up in this mess. I lost friends. I lost hope.

I close my eyes for a second and take a deep breath, letting the hot desert air fill my lungs. The landscape stretches out endlessly, a vast, desolate horizon. And as I stare at it, a thought strikes me: *If the God who created all of this wants me to die today, then I will die today. But if He wants me to live, there's nothing Harry or anyone else can do to change that.*

"Yeah, I bet you could dig down six inches anywhere around here and you'd find bones," I respond, trying to play off Harry's grim statement, matching his tone.

Something shifts within me at that moment. A strange calmness washes over me, a peace I can't quite explain. It feels like I've taken my first breath in years. Slowly, I step back, just out of arm's reach, my eyes locked on Harry. I watch as his bravado falters. His knees begin to shake, his confidence crumbling. His face is pale, and his hands tremble so badly they look like they might fall off at the wrist. He tries to speak, but what comes out is just incoherent babble, his words tangled and meaningless.

I don't know what he's seeing, but whatever it is, it's breaking him down in real time. He looks like a man who's come face to face with something far beyond his understanding, something that shakes him to his core.

232

Awkward Silence

And there, in the heart of that desert, with Harry trembling before me, I take my first step toward surrender. For the first time, I acknowledge God's power over my circumstances. I'm reminded of Rahab in Jericho, how she declared the God of Israel to be the true God, and how that act of faith spared her life.

It's only a small step, but it's the first one I've taken in a long, long time. And I know there will be many more to come.

Chapter 25
Saved by Grace

John 3:18 "Whoever believes in Him is not condemned."

"Where is your treasure?"

She stood before me like a candle, her eyes glowing, her face dripping away like melting wax. She was unidentifiable—I couldn't see a thing with clarity. Moments ago, she had handed me a glass of tea, and now...

"I don't feel well," I muttered.

"Feel your pulse," she instructed, her words reaching me as if spoken through a garden hose.

I placed my fingers on my wrist just in time to feel two very distant and faint pulses—and then I was out. I could feel them dragging my limp body into the back room of the house. I was aware of the movement, but there was nothing I could do to stop it. I didn't know who they were or why they were taking me back there.

"Am I going to die?" I managed to ask, my words surfacing as if I had spoken them from the bottom of a swimming pool.

"It's up to you," the voice responded. "You have to be honest with us. Someone hired me to kill you, but I like you. So, I want to know why someone wants you dead. What did you do?"

"You'll live if you're honest," the voice continued, still unrecognizable.

"I... I worked for drug enforcement," I confessed. It was hard to get the words out, but I wanted to live. I wasn't sure when I decided that, but I knew for certain that I didn't want to die.

"No, we know that, and that's not why," the voice replied, dismissing my admission.

"Then why does someone want you dead?" they asked again.

"I don't know... if that's not the reason," I said, struggling to speak. Despite my immobility, I was still surprised that revealing the darkest secret of my life had garnered no reaction.

"I told Tonya to get an abortion," I confessed next, thinking that might be the reason.

"That's pretty bad," they said, "but that isn't it either."

I realized I had problems, but these were the worst of my actions—surely one of them had to be it. I could hear them talking among themselves, but I couldn't discern what they were saying.

"I... I stole some wheels off Mike Mitchell's car," I admitted. It was a stupid, impulsive thing from my youth. I'd never stolen anything before, but those wheels were just so shiny. In truth, I didn't have a clue why I did it. It troubled me that I couldn't recall even thinking about it before acting. This could be the reason, I thought—Mike's brother, Dino, was indicted and took a plea for murder. I didn't know the full story, but maybe this was the mistake that would get me killed.

"No," they replied. "Mike forgave you for that when you apologized to him."

"I was connected to people who manufactured drugs," I said, starting to rethink who these people might be. If they didn't care about my past in drug enforcement, maybe they were the kind who would kill drug dealers instead.

"No, keep going," they urged.

I emptied out my guilt bucket, one confession at a time. Each time I revealed another sin, it was never the one they were holding me accountable for. I was thoroughly searching my soul, but every detestable thing I spewed out wasn't the answer.

It got to the point where I even confessed to throwing a golf ball that hit a kid in the shin back in third grade.

And that's when I heard another voice—a voice that hadn't spoken until now.

"What do you know about Jesus?"

"He was the brother of Satan." The words slipped out, a remnant of the Mormon influence I grew up with. It was odd to me that I used Satan as a reference point for Jesus, but that was what I had been taught.

"No, that's not who Jesus is," he chuckled softly, "but we'll get to that later. Do you accept Jesus as your savior?"

If anyone in the history of the world needs a savior, it's me.

"Yes," I whispered.

The moment I said it, my eyes opened just long enough to see men walking single file out the door. I heard them leave, the door closing behind them. Then, suddenly, an eruption took place—not outside, but within me.

Inside, I was trying to soothe the child—my inner child. I cradled him like a football, trying to calm him. As I did, we grew together, both of us equally wounded, bearing the same memories, the same pain, and the same desperate desire to escape it all. There was a decision to be made. The question arose from somewhere outside me: **Do you need a savior?**

Yes. Yes, I do.

In that moment, the child and I merged. We were no longer separate; the divisions of my life blurred, and I was whole again. But now, I was running, the walls crumbling around me. I tried desperately to hold them up, terrified of what lay beyond. I couldn't keep it together—the walls were coming down. But the allies had arrived. The angels were here under the authority of the King.

The ground of desolation quaked as foot soldiers marched. A mighty force shook the entire city. In the physical world, I felt my body tremble as the darkness fled. This was something beyond my comprehension. Gravity began to lose its grip; debris was being sucked into an abyss. I heard someone say, "Wow, this is unreal. He's floating—he's levitating."

The rivers of magma erupted, spitting balls of fire onto the shore. These fiery orbs were the demons that had been submerged, tortured in the flames. Now they were landing, forming the devil's foot soldiers—the manifestation of my tortured soul. The intensity of it all forced the flow of that river out of me, a supernatural purge into a bucket beside me.

The conflict became a methodical military operation, surreal in its strategy. I stood in the center, watching. I was in the eye of the storm, bullets whizzing by, just as I had been when I sat in that Volkswagen with Quin. But now, I wasn't just numb to it. For the first time, I felt a deep, overwhelming sense of safety in my decision to accept Jesus.

I could see the angels forming a perimeter around the city's boundaries. Anxiety mounted as they began to close in, drawing the circle tighter. The walls of deception crumbled with each new confession.

"I threw a golf ball that hit Timmy in the shin," I confessed, and another wall fell.

The maze of false beliefs collapsed as I lifted up the Word of God: *"Though I speak in the tongues of men and of angels, if I have not love..."*

"Love is patient." They had never shown me patience. That was not love, and another wall crumbled.

"Love is kind." What they showed me was not kindness. Another block of deception fell away.

"Love is not jealous." I realized I could not truly love while being consumed with jealousy.

I heard the echo of an old, tormenting thought: *"God doesn't love me. If He did, I wouldn't be here in Minnesota."* But the Word countered it: *"For God so loved the world that He gave His only begotten Son, that whoever believes in Him shall not perish but have everlasting life."* Another block crumbled.

"The wizard is here to bring me comfort, encouragement, and edification," I had once believed. But then, scripture arose: *"Beware of false prophets who come to you in sheep's clothing, but inwardly are ravenous wolves."* A thin line of blocks fell.

"Jack-a-puss," came another whisper from the past. But then: *"I have been given the power to trample on snakes and scorpions."* Another block fell.

Awkward Silence

"You are worthless," they had told me. But the truth was: *"I find my worth in Jesus, in the One who created me. He deemed me worth more than His own life."* With that, the blocks crumbled and fell, each lie dismantled by the light of scripture.

"Whose report shall you believe—man's or God's?" I asked myself. Every input from my past was now in question. Absolutely everything I thought I knew was up for grabs. If it didn't align with God's Word, it was false. And with that, the walls shook violently.

"By His stripes, we are healed."

"He made the pillars of silver, the bottom of gold, the covering of purple, and the midst paved with love." There is a major transformation happening within me. The King of Kings is not merely ripping out what was there but is rebuilding it in His glory!

I still stand in amazement as I watch the joy that the angels take in their work. They are rejoicing for me! *"I raise a hallelujah in the presence of my enemy!"* Songs of praise and worship clear the smog and the smoldering brimstone flavor.

Those who once held whips, intending to "whip the one in front of you," are now disarmed. Guilt is confessed with each answer to the question: *Why would someone hire me to kill you?* Sin is forgiven by the price paid at the cross. Shame no longer holds me in prison. There is no longer any reason for self-sabotage or punishment. They are never to pick up their whips again.

The table of the conspirators is broken up. Greed tries to run but stops to pick up the pennies. Neither gluttony nor sloth can flee. Gluttony breaks his seat trying to rise. Pride is too proud to run. Envy, lust, and wrath are all cast out with the flow of the river.

They had to know this day was coming. No one knows the day or the hour except the Father, yet there have been wars and rumors of wars. These wars have been consistent for twenty years. I am now twenty-six years old, and there has not been a peaceful moment for two decades. I have seen more hatred than brotherly love. Yes, they had to know this day was coming. Corporate greed has made its way to the top. Gluttony and sloth ignore the unjust dealings of others as long as they are unaffected. Pride will watch the self-destruction unfold before it admits it was wrong. Then, Pride parades, carrying an old symbol of covenant. Not since Sodom has there been such a bold statement leading to such a loss. Envy and lust have invaded the media, causing greed to flourish. Yes, all heads feed the same body.

The dragon has now been slain in the spirit. It is only a matter of time before he dies off in the soul. His thoughts have less impact, for there is no longer any shock factor to his ridiculousness. If he continues to seek that shock factor, I don't know where it will lead—perhaps to public beheadings on every street corner. That may not be far off. We are just now seeing same-sex scenes on every program. We are just now reaching the point where society says it is okay to abandon our moral values, adopting the values pushed in our drunken state. We are just now getting to the page that suggests theft is acceptable up to a certain dollar amount. Yes, we can read that this day is coming with no doubt. We all know it is near. We can feel the heat of the fire of hell radiating on our skin if we pay attention.

For a long time, I believed I was responsible for the condition of the world. I could barely take responsibility for the muck of my own life. The demons cast out this day were far more effective than I had given them credit for. I would have continued to carry the burden of the world's condition, left in their hands. Eventually, and probably today, I would have been defeated. This may have been the day I ceased to exist in the natural world. I would no longer have been able to influence either good or evil in this realm.

The volcano erupts, throwing ash everywhere. A depth of ash spreads throughout the entirety of treachery. There is so much ash that I am covered from head to toe. It is volatile—gasping, the last breath of treachery. It is Pharaoh releasing his hold on the Israelite slaves. It is the beast letting go of his grip on me. It is the devil's future last breath before he enters the gates of hell.

Chapter 26
Out from The Ashes

Isaiah 61:3 "To bestow upon them a crown of beauty instead of ashes."

"The angel showed me where it was hiding."

As I rise from the ash, a new hope arises within me. It is the rebirth of my spirit and a new perspective on life. Still covered in ash, there is a period of edification that follows. It brings me back to the carnal world, but now, instead of my thoughts and emotions controlling my will, my spirit is in charge. Though my spirit is still in its infancy, it needs nurturing.

"Jack, there are some essential elements of self-care that you've been deprived of." She has an angelic glow that seems to accentuate her speech.

"I don't want you to become embarrassed or defensive. I know it's not your fault. Can you promise me you won't be embarrassed?" She looks at me earnestly, concern in her eyes.

"I don't think I will be embarrassed." Suddenly, I feel like I am six years old—innocent and peacefully attentive.

"Would you mind if I bathed you?" she asks.

"I'm not apprehensive at all," I say, as though I've been waiting for the opportunity to use a big word.

"That's a big word, 'apprehensive.' Did you learn that in school?" She must have brought out my age regression purposefully, to teach me what could be a sensitive lesson. It must be rare that a grown man in his twenties has never been taught general self-care.

"No, I learned it in the future." I smile broadly.

"Well, that makes sense." She smiles back at me, equally amused.

She pulls back the shower curtain, then ties her hair up in a scrunchie. She begins running the water and rinsing the tub.

"How is the temperature of the water?" she asks, gesturing for me to come feel it.

"It's a little cool." She makes the necessary adjustments.

"Jack, you're not going to take a bath in your clothes. Take them off." I'm overtaken by shyness.

"I thought you weren't going to be embarrassed. Be a big boy," she says with such nurturing encouragement that I can only respond by dropping my clothes.

I stand there, almost like I'm waiting to be admired.

"Go ahead, get in the tub," she says.

I step into the tub and sit down. She uses a container to pour water over my head.

"Remember everything we do here today, and I want you to do this every time you bathe. When the water is poured over your head, I want you to think about how God gives water to the thirsty," she says.

"Like when He causes it to rain to water the plants?" I ask with childlike sincerity.

"Yes, and more," she exclaims.

"Then, as you lather the shampoo in your hair, I want you to think about God's love for you. I want you to feel that love move through your fingertips as you caress your scalp."

"My aunt used to wash my hair, and she would dig her fingernails into my scalp. I know she was trying to hurt me, but I pretended like it felt good. She would dig in harder, and I would still pretend it felt good," I reminisce.

"You don't need to be afraid of her anymore."

"After it's lathered up, it's time to rinse it out. As you rinse it, think about how God is cleaning you—inside as well as outside. Don't miss the opportunity to feel every speck of His love." I could feel the love move through her fingers, all the way through my body, soul, and spirit—a chill that rushes through me.

"Did anything happen today that was unusual?" she asks.

"I saw a cloud that spelled my name! You may think I'm crazy, but it was clear—it said 'Jack.' It wasn't like one of those where you see a bear, or a dog, or a sailboat. No, it was clear—it said 'Jack.'"

"I know, Jack. God was telling you He loves you." I smile wide, filled with so much joy. It's overflowing.

"Jack, we started with your head, and now we're going down to your toes. I don't want you to scrub. I want you to be gentle and caress your skin. Use a washcloth, but gently. Be nice to yourself. Show yourself the deep love that God is showing you."

I am gleaming with so much affection. This is certainly not how I've been taught.

"Don't miss a single cell of your body. It all needs this affection—every cell and every fiber, inside and out. The inside you will cleanse with your thoughts of love and compassion. The outside with the gentle caressing. I want to watch you do it now."

I begin to move the washcloth over my body, just as she said. It still isn't like when she does it. I suppose practice makes perfect.

"Don't forget under the elephant's ears," she says. I think she's making a joke, and I blush. I've completely washed myself from head to toe, and it feels better than any bath or shower I've ever taken. I feel so much love for myself—it's something I've never experienced before.

"Jack, you've accepted Jesus as your Savior. You've chosen to become part of God's family. All authority in heaven and earth has been given to me to invite you in. In a moment, I will baptize you in the name of the Father, the Son, and the Holy Spirit. When Jesus sacrificed Himself on the cross, He made atonement for all your sins—past, present, and future. Jack, all of your sins— past, present, and future. His love for you transcends time. This water is symbolic of washing you clean, spirit, soul, and body."

She submerges me under the water, and when she brings me back up, I see the image of heaven, with angels celebrating. I feel amazing.

"On this day, all of the angels of heaven rejoice and celebrate," I hear. The celebration rings in my ears.

As I stand to my feet, she takes a towel and gently pats me dry.

"I want you to show yourself love, even as you dry off. You are worth more than all the diamonds and jewels of the entire earth. Begin to show yourself that. Communicate that to yourself. Make it an everyday gesture." She looks at me with eyes that seem to penetrate into my soul. In this moment, I understand that I have not been very kind to myself. In not being kind, I've failed to show God the appreciation He deserves.

"Jack, it's time to brush your teeth. Again, I want you to do it slowly and with self-love."

"My aunt used to sit out in the living room, and if she didn't hear the toothbrush scrubbing my teeth, she would make me do it again and again."

"Jack, I told you, you don't have to fear her anymore."

I gently begin to brush my teeth, massaging my gums as I go. I take my time, making sure each tooth is cleaned, and that my gums and tongue are satisfied.

"Everything you do—brush your hair, eat, drink— whatever you do, should be done with the knowledge of God's love for you." She lights up brightly.

"Why is this such a new experience?" I ask.

"Isn't it wonderful?" she replies, shutting down my question. That's to keep my focus on God's love. The past doesn't matter anymore. What's important is that I've learned to embrace a fresh beginning.

"What does the guitar do when you push up on the strings like that?" she asks.

I would love to tell you who she is, but I have no idea. I think she's an angel.

"It's called bending the string. It raises the pitch," I answer in a vulnerable voice, as if I were just a child.

"It makes it sound like it's stressing out. It almost sounds like it's going to start to cry."

The angel continues, "Will it sound differently if you think about it that way?"

I play a few licks with bends. I consider how the guitar might feel if it were human. I string some licks together, and I notice that they sound different. The licks are more life-like.

"Yeah, that's what I'm talking about! Do you hear the difference?" I can objectively hear what I just played as if it's been recorded and played back to me.

"Yes!" she exclaims.

"Jack, you're already an amazing guitarist, but you're playing too much in your head. It makes it sound mechanical. You'll be even more amazing once you make this simple transition."

The angel continues, her voice shifting slightly as she brings up a new thought. "What are these?"

"They're the tuning machines," I answer.

"What do they do?" she asks.

"They're used to raise and lower the pitch to tune the guitar," I reply.

"So, each string is tuned to a singular pitch?" she questions.

"They're tuned in many different ways. Standard tuning is E-B-G-D-A-E, from the highest to the lowest string. But we can tune them to anything we want—like open tunings too," I explain.

"Can you tune all the strings to a single pitch?" The angel's question seems more like an invitation to explore a new way of thinking.

"I don't think I've ever done that, but I'll try it." A few minutes later, I have all the strings tuned to a B note. I start playing around with it mindlessly.

"Oh, wow, I really like that!" she says, as if she's been recording me. For just a second, I'm swept away in the clouds by this revelation. Then, like a whisper, I'm suddenly back in the moment.

"Have you ever tried to write?" the angelic woman asks.

"I like to write, but I'm really not very good at it. I did write something in third grade that my teacher thought was really good, but I'm not sure she understood what I was trying to say." I could swear I was speaking like I was still in third grade.

"Do you like to write songs or stories?" she asks, gently probing.

"I don't know, maybe both," I reply.

"Can you write me a story?" she requests.

"Sure," I say, enjoying the attention. But as I think about it, I realize how much my perspective has changed. I had a heart of stone before. Everything I did was dictated by my thoughts, and I never explored my emotions—something she seems to be guiding me toward.

I begin:

"Imagine in the beginning, before there was time, when all things were still, and there was no motion. There lived a great and mighty wizard who defied the principles of time and motion. He had powers beyond belief."

"Stop for a minute, Jack," the angelic woman commands.

"Don't you like my story?" I think it started pretty well.

"I like it fine, but I wonder… do you like me?"

"Yes, I think you're pretty," I respond, surprised by the turn of conversation.

"Don't you think I might like a story that tells me you like me? Maybe a romantic story."

"Okay, I can do that," I say, thinking hard. You see, my idea of romance has always been skewed. I thought it was just about buying gifts and flowers. Maybe it's just something I've never fully understood. I'm stuck.

"What's wrong?" the angel asks.

"I'm pretty sure I can write erotica, but is that the same as romance?" I ask, uncertain.

"Erotica is not a story without sex. Sex is the purpose of erotica. Romance, on the other hand, centers around the love story. It doesn't even have to have sex to be a story," she explains without hesitation. Her tone almost sounds scripted, but in a way that feels comforting.

"Oh, okay. I'll try a romance. But I don't know if I even really understand what romance is, except maybe giving gifts and flowers. I want to know—like, is it a feeling? An action? What is it?" I feel confused. Is romance more than I thought?

"Jack, romance is just a love story. Haven't you ever been in love?" The angel's look is inquisitive, as if she's asking something obvious.

"I thought so, but maybe not. Maybe I felt love for Lacey, but it was superficial when it came to the test of time. We weren't meant for each other, but the sex was good. I believe love has the power and authority to break through to depths that cause real change. I know people say they don't want someone who will try to change them, and I believe that. But if someone inspires me to want to change, that's different. I mean, entering into a relationship is a change. You were single, and now you're not. That alone is a shift." I pause, trying to make sense of my own thoughts.

"What if you can just imagine what it might feel like in the future if you're inspired to want to change?" The angel's wings begin to spread, revealing she really is an angel.

"Okay, I think I can do that," I say, quietly taking in the moment.

Chapter 27
The Future in The Pen

Revelation 14:13 "And I heard a voice from heaven telling me to write."

"The words are prophetically etched in my heart."

Jack must look like a crazy man to anyone passing him on the road. He has been laughing and singing to himself for the past half hour. With no radio reception and no song lyrics readily coming to mind, he scrambles for words to pair with melodies. It's like reaching out for a glass in the dark—awkward and uncertain. His singing voice isn't much to boast about either; in fact, it's probably better suited for a talk show host. This clumsy, fumbling attempt at making music is the source of his laughter.

He is trying to shake off the day's events. It's been one of *those* days—where the pressure was on, and he just wasn't in the mood to lead his crew. Days like this aren't common, but when they come, he can't help shutting out the world and wondering why he still puts himself through it all. He could change things, take a new path, and do something different.

Jack glances around, trying to regain his bearings, and realizes he isn't where he thought he should be. Somewhere along this drive, he lost track of his navigation. But that's okay. He's not in a hurry to get anywhere, and this detour might even give him a chance to explore something new.

He starts circling around, searching for a scenic route, and finds himself led to a small town nestled next to a river. There doesn't seem to be much to this place. With nearly a full tank of gas, he considers stopping but then decides to press on to the next town. His eyes wander, taking in the quiet charm of the community. Again, he debates stopping but sees no signs of activity.

As Jack pulls his focus back to the road, he reaches for his water bottle. It slips from his hand, tumbles out of the cup holder, and lands on the floorboard.

"Ugh, figures," he mutters. "I guess I'll stop here after all."

He pulls into the parking lot of a convenience store—probably the only one in town—and parks just as he decides to stop. It's a small gas station with a modest sign reading *Stinker Station*. Only two cars are in the lot, which is just as well, since there are only three striped spaces.

Jack turns off the engine, rolls up the window, and steps out of the truck. As he enters the store, his eyes meet hers. In an instant, he is captivated. It's as if he had been searching for those emerald eyes all his life. They are familiar, beckoning to him in a way he can't explain. A deep yearning stirs within him, something ancient and inexplicable, as if tied to a time before his very existence. He knows, without a doubt, that he must meet her.

"I'm not good at this, but I just have to meet you. Are you single?"

"I am, but maybe you should start with, *Hi, I'm… what's your name?*"

"Jack."

"Hi, Jack. And now you say, *I really want to spend the rest of my life with you.* Just kidding. Hi, Jack, I'm Candy." She holds up a Payday candy bar with a playful grin.

"You're funny. But seriously, what's your real name?" I gesture toward the candy bar.

"It's Candice. And for the record, I rarely let anyone call me Candy. I just thought I'd try it on for size."

"Well, I think it's sweet." I grin, hoping my attempt at wit matches her energy. She's sharp and playful. I could really like this woman.

"Do you live in town?" I ask.

"Yes, I do."

"How do you like it?" I'm suddenly eager to know everything about her.

"I love it. I moved here about ten years ago. It's a wonderful place to raise my kids. I have two boys—they're my whole world." Her face lights up at the mention of her sons.

"I live in Nampa. Thanks for asking."

"I was getting there," she says with a teasing smile.

"I know. I could tell by your body language that you wanted to know. I wasn't being sarcastic—I genuinely appreciate your interest." I smile back, feeling a connection building.

"How do you like Nampa?" she asks, her smile lingering.

"I like it a little less than I did ten minutes ago."

"Why's that?" she asks, tilting her head slightly, her curiosity piqued. She's clearly expecting me to say something charming like, *Because now my heart is here with you* or *Because you're not there.*

Instead, I shrug. "Just because." I figure I'll let her fill in the cheesy line herself.

She laughs softly. "I absolutely love your smile."

Jack, don't say the word 'love' in any context right now, I scold myself silently.

"Thank you," she says, biting her bottom lip. That's a good sign, right?

"What brings you to town?" she asks, tucking a strand of hair behind her ear.

"Honestly? Divine intervention. I was trying to clear my head after a rough day at work. My mind wandered to music, and, well, I was singing and having a full-on conversation with myself when I realized I had no idea where I was. Then I spilled my water, and gravity—or fate—pulled me here. To this moment."

"So, you believe in destiny?" She tilts her head slightly, her curiosity piqued.

"Not exactly in the *everything is pre-written* sense," I reply. "But I do think there are supernatural events—maybe even a spirit guide—that steer us toward the important moments in life."

"So, you think this is an important moment?"

"It feels like the most important moment I've had all day." My response catches her off guard. A subtle laugh escapes her, accompanied by a snort.

"All day? Really, all day?" she teases.

"If I'm being completely honest, it might be the most important moment of my entire life." My serious expression takes over. "I've had a pretty rough life."

She laughs again, another soft snort escaping her.

"That's two," she says, smiling.

"Two?"

"Yeah, two snorts."

"Well, I think it's adorable." I can't help but grin, and it's not going anywhere.

"Okay, riddle me this," Jack says, his tone playful. "If you were crowned Miss America, what world problem would you solve? What's your passion?"

"Jack, that isn't really a riddle." she says trying to bust his chops.

"I know that it isn't a conventional riddle. Your answer is just a piece of the puzzle. You have become my riddle, a riddle that I hope to understand but never resolve." Jack says filled with a confidence that he has drawn from a supernatural well of thought.

"I'd focus on empowering women," she replies, her voice steady. For a moment, something flickers in her expression— something vulnerable. She's been hurt, I can feel it. And I understand; I know what it's like to feel powerless.

"That's truly commendable," Jack says, his tone sincere. "The votes are in, and Candice—you are Miss America."

"Well, thank you! Thank you all! Y'all are just wonderful!" She waves dramatically, playing along.

"Y'all? Where did that accent come from? I hadn't heard it until now."

"Oh yeah," she says, laughing. "I'm originally from Texas."

"You didn't move here to this little Idaho town to evade the law or anything, did you? No Texas Rangers looking for you?"

"Ha! No, darn it. I *do* like a man in uniform, though."

"You keep talking like that, and I'll end up joining every law enforcement, fire department, and military branch just to show up in every uniform for your approval."

"Ah, role play—how fun!" she quips, her eyes twinkling.

In the background, Bryan Adams' *(Everything I Do) I Do It For You* starts playing.

"I love this song right now," I say softly, the moment feeling perfect.

But something shifts. Her demeanor changes in an instant, and I can't pinpoint why. It's like I've hit a nerve, triggered something buried deep. I don't know what it is, but the connection we had just moments ago feels like it's slipping away.

"Jack, it was really great talking to you," she says, her tone kind but distant. "I need to get home and feed my boys. Maybe we'll see each other again."

Jack wants to ask for her number, but the subtle brush-off vibe stops him. He knows better than to push.

"I would absolutely love that," I reply, meaning every word.

From the moment Jack watched her walk away, his life changed. If he wasn't praising God for the miracle of that encounter, he was thinking about her. When he wasn't expressing gratitude for the revelation of God's will, he was reflecting on how to become a better man, one who could live up to what she deserved. In his heart, he was preparing a place for her, just as Jesus prepares a place for us. If Jack wasn't strengthening his relationship with Jesus, striving to embody the virtues of love, he was thinking about how he could share those virtues with her.

Jack saw her as a tangible symbol of God's love—a gift, not the entirety of His love but a manifestation of it in the physical world. Meeting her was transformative. A fire ignited within him, unlike anything he had ever experienced. It refined and redefined him, burning away the old and purifying the new. Suddenly, every intention he had was for the good of mankind, and every thought was motivated by a higher purpose.

His perspective shifted dramatically. He no longer desired to work in the electrical field. He was done. Jack had found his purpose, and it began with confronting himself.

He began to face the demons of his past—battles he had avoided for too long. Jack carried the weight of trauma, which had given rise to maladaptive behaviors and responses. Diagnosed with Complex PTSD, he often experienced triggers that elicited unnatural reactions to ordinary situations. These demons—lurking in the shadows—waited for opportunities to cause the most harm. They were spiritual battles, and for the first time, Jack felt the will to fight back.

Before meeting her, Jack had accepted these battles with resignation. But now, he had something worth living for. He couldn't let the darkness win. He drew strength from thoughts of her, encouragement from her memory, and hope from the pendant she wore. These thoughts inspired him to take steps of faith toward healing and hope.

Though he felt lost without her, he was more driven than ever. Each door he opened in his journey of self-healing revealed a new way to express his love and devotion. This path of self-discovery awakened a desire to share his healing journey with others. He realized she, too, had suffered trauma. With her in mind, he opened facilities to provide comfort, encouragement, and healing to trauma victims.

Through his healing, Jack learned a profound truth: recovery requires proactive engagement. A person can remain a victim, adapting to a life of coping with pain. They can settle into the conditions of their trauma and accept their circumstances. But healing demands more—it requires fighting like hell to overcome.

Living in surrender to trauma is not true healing. It is merely survival. Surrender keeps a person trapped, unable to see beyond their pain, stuck in the belief that their worth is defined by their suffering. This mindset prevents them from realizing their full potential, locking them into a cycle of coping rather than thriving. True healing, Jack realized, comes from shifting focus—from the pain and its effects to the source of hope and restoration.

Jack's journey became a mission to help others move beyond surrender, empowering them to reclaim their lives and discover the purpose that pain had once obscured.

When people remain trapped in their trauma, it's tragic. They become tethered to the demons that rule their lives, flipping through the pages of their story without truly understanding. Even when they think they've moved forward, the same narrative reappears on the next page, just with different faces or settings. It's all part of the same unrelenting cycle—a new branch of the same old tree.

Jack poured everything he had into creating facilities dedicated to treating CPTSD and PTSD. His first project was a ten-acre property where horses were integrated into therapy, providing a unique and healing experience for patients. He began speaking at churches, rallying communities to join his mission. "If we allow these demonic coping mechanisms to spread unchecked, society will crumble," he warned. "We must shift from mere coping to true healing."

Jack's speaking engagements bore fruit, and the reach of his labor of love began to expand. Facilities started opening across the state and into neighboring regions. Evidence of their effectiveness grew, and the difference he was making brought attention to his ministry. However, this success also drew the attention of a darker force. The traumas he fought against weren't just personal struggles—they were a calculated strategy by the enemy of life to separate humanity from love and goodness. Coping, Jack realized, was the enemy's greatest weapon.

This realization became his life's work: to counteract the enemy's strategies, to educate communities, and to expand the Kingdom of Heaven. He spoke wherever he could—churches, community centers, and even casual gatherings—spreading the message of healing and redemption.

"There's a grim misconception in society," he often began. "We are told to simply accept people as they are. Logic tells us to place limits on what they can overcome. But growth comes through challenges, and challenges are often misunderstood. They don't come to crush us into submission; they come gently, urging us to grow. The Laodiceans were scolded for their complacency in the seventh letter to the churches in Revelation. And today, we face a similar danger."

He continued, "Traumatized people develop coping mechanisms, but coping is not healing. In fact, coping feeds the demons within. When we accept maladaptive coping mechanisms, we're essentially saying, 'You're not worth the effort to help heal.' Let me be clear: tolerating destructive behaviors is not love—it's fear. Fear of change, fear of the unknown, fear of being exposed. When we allow someone to remain stuck in their pain, we are saying, 'I don't want you to heal because your healing will reveal truths about me, and I'm not ready to face them.'"

Jack shared a prophetic dream he had: "In the dream, I saw a dragon hovering over her, and it was only when my perspective shifted that I could see it clearly. Trauma clouds our perspective, and healing demands a shift in how we see ourselves and others."

He concluded with a call to action. "We can dress up maladaptive behaviors however we like. We may excuse rudeness as just 'part of who they are.' But if we do that, we give the demons inside free rein to feast on them. Instead, we must support healing and cast those demons out into the abyss. Join me in this mission. Support Divine Fortress Ministries as we heal society, one individual at a time."

After each speech, Jack moved on to the next, refusing to waste a second in his mission. In moments of stillness, he conversed with God, drawing strength and energy to continue. These moments weren't idle—they were part of his joy. Jack delighted in the work, knowing he was partnering with the King on this sacred mission. To Jack, it was an honor to work side by side with his Hero.

That fateful encounter at the convenience store had been the first stroke of a baton conducting a great symphony. The first movement was the greatest expression of love Jack had ever experienced—God's love, revealed through a story written in eternity, thirty years before. Jack knew what God meant, even if others might not fully understand it. That love became the driving force behind everything he did.

The second movement began with the next stroke of the baton. Every facility Jack opened, every speech he delivered, every demon he slayed, and every word he wrote—including this story—was inspired by that brief but life-changing encounter with

Candice. Through her, Jack found the duality of purpose: to heal himself and to heal the world.

Chapter 28
Peanuts and Caramel

Job 23:13 "God controls destiny."

"It is an amazing story of love."

"Wow, Jack. That is really good. You can write romance," the angel said.

"Thank you, but is that really romance?" I questioned my vision.

"What do you mean? It's a story of a man who, upon meeting a woman for the first time, burns with a passion so deep that he changes his entire life. It's a story of a woman so special and gifted that she ignites the flame of desire, and she does so in such a way that she corners him, leaving him no choice but to look to the heavens for help. It's a story of God's love being so bountiful and amazing that it is the air around, between, and inside all things."

"It felt real, almost like I was just writing what I was seeing."

"Yes, Jack, you were writing a prophetic insight," she said, as her wings lowered again.

"That's wild!" I quietly shouted. By that, I mean the intensity was a shout, but I held it back so as not to alert the world.

"Does that mean these are things still to come?" I asked.

"It will come in its own way. Prophecy is designed to reach the depths of all levels of your being. In other words, it is meant to reach you at the level of your spirit, soul, and body. To reach the depths, it speaks all truths, but sometimes the symbolic nature is difficult to see when you are covering your eyes."

"I had a prophetic dream once." Again, I was like a little boy, filled with excitement and amazement.

"You've had many more prophetic encounters than you know. Do you remember when you were young and the old lady walked up to you and handed you something?"

"Um, yes. She handed me a cassette." I couldn't have been more than eleven years old, but there was something about that moment that has stayed with me. I was walking home from school when she approached me with the cassette. It was a cassette entitled Backmasking. This is something the music industry did to introduce subliminal messages.

"When she handed it to you, you saw something." The angel was bringing out my recollection in such a way that it felt as if it were happening again, at least in my mind.

"Yeah, I saw myself playing on a stage in front of thousands of people. Then I saw that it was me, but it wasn't. I changed my mind. I didn't want to be on stage. I would have been a rock star, but it would have killed me."

"Yes, that was never the life meant for you, but that vision was a prophetic one that will save your life," the angel said, standing.

"That was you? Were you the one who handed me the cassette?" I asked, amazed.

"Yes, I am a messenger of YHWH."

"Oh my, yes, I can see it now. Thank you!" I declared with a sincerity that came from deep within me.

Jack Taylor

"Thank me no more than you would thank a postal worker, but give all the glory to God!" the angel expressed.

"If the words that I wrote become prophetic, what happens if I alter the words that I write? Does that change the meaning of the prophecy?"

"Jack, that is a dangerous way to think."

"Why?"

"If you've been given a gift to encourage others with what you see, but instead you consider how you can manipulate it to achieve your desired outcome, it becomes a misdirected path. It's a selfish mindset, and it does nothing to affect reality, but it will distort your view of reality. It's like you place your own obstacles in the way, blocking your own view."

"Is the desire that I feel then just a carrot dangling from a string? I mean, I don't see the outcome. Jack has this deep desire that motivates his life. It encourages him to fight the demons of this world. It drives him to build places that help others overcome the effects of trauma-based illnesses, but does he ever reap from what he sows? Why can't I just write the Disney ending, where she acknowledges the efforts of his love, runs to him, and they live happily ever after?"

"Can you draw?" the angel asked me.

"My grandma was an artist, and my brother is good at it, but I'm not."

"Maybe you should try again," the angel insisted.

I gripped the pencil as if it were a handle at the edge of a cliff, holding it firmly. As I began to push it across the paper, I did so with angry force. The scene I tried to draw was dark, gloomy, corrupted, and ugly. It was influenced by a dark force still within me. There were words written in block letters that formed the contour of a rock cliff. The name Corine was written, disguised in the storm of graphite hitting the page. Corine is my aunt's name, but she's also a woman who is with a friend. She and I had some electricity, but her boyfriend was a friend. Yet I had lust-filled eyes when I looked at her. I could feel every tense muscle contract as I shaded every shadow cast upon the side of the black mountain of graphite.

"Try again, but this time, be gentle with the pencil."

I drew a wavy line, and then another. I tilted the pencil and followed the lines. I began to see a vine. As it continued to take shape, I saw the beginnings of a rose. The petals of this flower opened in bloom. A dew drop fell from a leaf on the vine. I moved the pencil, and now the vines were numerous, not entangled but growing with shapely distinction. More flowers developed in different stages of bloom, from completely closed to fully open, and everywhere in between. Some thorns were sprinkled about the drawing, with no rhyme or reason for their placement. The rose petals were shaded and highlighted according to the direction of the sun. I felt as though this rose bush was exiting my body and appearing on the paper. A sense of satisfaction began to wash over me.

"That's where it is hiding," the angel said.

I looked at what I had drawn, unsure of where something could be hiding in this picture. It was simply roses and vines. The vines weren't thick brushstrokes that could conceal anything, and the roses were pretty simple as well.

"What is hiding, and where?"

"If you look closely at your drawing, you can see the unique shapes of women."

"Oh. Oh. And there are tears."

"Yes, Jack, you see it. They are the thorns in the side. Do you see that?" the angel said.

"Yes, I see it hiding, but what does that mean?" I asked the angel.

"It's a depiction of guilt and shame. When something is hiding, it's like Adam and Eve hiding from God; it's from shame. The red roses indicate that it is associated with romance. The different unique bodies show that you have been promiscuous. The tears are..."

"The tears are mine," I interrupted her.

"Yes, Jack, but you are not meant to be bathed in or baptized into guilt. You are not meant to live in guilt. Guilt is supposed to be just a signal to tell you that something isn't right, so you can go the other way. It's not meant to be anything more than an indicator light that tells you to change your behavior or direction." Her words made so much sense, but I had been feeling guilty for things I hadn't even done, packing it around like a giant suitcase.

"Haven't you ever wanted to have a family?" she asked.

"Yes, probably more than anything."

"When you were hurt as a child, you fell into the shame of it. It was not your shame to bear. Then, when they beat you for the childhood curiosity that wasn't even your curiosity, they solidified the shame. And the thorns in the side are relevant too, aren't they?"

Awkward Silence

This made me pause. It troubled my heart to think with the purity I felt now, in contradiction to the way I had been living. Memories stepped forward from the graveyard of my mind. I could see all the one-night stands illuminated, as if they were being poured into a blender. There were many I didn't even remember. Only a few differentiated one from the other. I realized I had never really felt love.

"Jack, you must understand that this is the scheme of Satan. He wants you to feel this shame so that you will hide from God, from love."

I feel grave remorse as the blender shifts and shuffles these memories. Then, a prideful moment steps up to the edge of the blender.

"Did you get some?" my dad asks me. I was behind the pool with the neighbor girl. We were kissing and exploring the features of our anatomy. I must have been eleven or twelve.

"You've grown so connected to shame, and scoring is now something to be proud of, that healthy love seems impossible. The thought of being married and raising children is so far from any thought of reality that you gave up on God."

I feel emotions surfacing like they never had before. A wave of discomfort, almost to the point of pain, came over me. It was like a pebble dropped into water. The waves rolled out from that center point in my heart and then back in again.

"You are afraid to love. You are afraid to raise kids. You are afraid that you will become the monsters that raised you."

As much as I won't admit to fear, I cannot deny that she is correct. Again, real men are not afraid of anything, at least that is the perspective I grew up with. And if women are nothing but a pain in the neck, a thorn in the side, then it is better not to get involved. A real man doesn't go for that mushy love stuff anyway.

"Tears are trudging through the muck. There will come a moment when these tears will pour out, and no dam will be able to hold them back."

"God intended sex as a beautiful thing. It is meant to be the purest form of intimacy, and yet it became shameful and dirty."

I can feel these words in my heart. They nudged one of those tears out from the muck and nearly caused it to fall. I think of all that I have missed by not understanding how to heal. I think of the message she is bringing me, and though I hear her and understand her, I don't know how to get there from here. I'm grabbing on to the heartbreak, but I'm oblivious to the change I need to make. I know that sounds impossible, but I'm oblivious to the change I need to make, I know that sounds impossible but it's true completely oblivious. I may have been taking this as a scolding instead of a loving helpful instruction.

"It is this that is hiding within you that prevents you from being able to just write the happily ever after story that you were considering. This muck would destroy the outcome."

"Then I have the vision and the desire, but it's doomed for failure."

"No! Do you remember your prophetic dream?"

"Yes!"

"What happens at the end to cause the world to turn upside down?"

"We drop to our knees and surrender."

"That's right. You don't try to write your own ending; you surrender to what God has already designed for the fulfillment of perfection."

"How do I know that she will surrender with me?"

"You don't know unless you trust. Love always trusts (1 Corinthians 13). Remember the pendant that flickered with reflected light? That is hope. And as you run toward the hope, you are responding with faith. When you surrender, it is the ultimate act of love. You surrender your entirety to the possibilities of love. Jack, the end has been written with margins bigger than you are capable of even fantasizing about right now. Trust God to do His part. He does His part better than you could ever do. Trust Him. He loves you. Remember that Lucifer thought he could write it better than God, and you know what happened there. Trust God and do your part. He will guide you to clarity. He will guide you to prepare your heart. He will lead you with love."

"Jack, do you know what Jacob's ladder is?" the angel asks.

"Yeah, it's like those two antennas with the arc that climbs up between them."

"Yes, that is right, but that is not the type of Jacob's ladder I'm asking about. The Jacob's ladder I'm talking about was in a dream."

"I don't remember that dream."

"It's a dream written in the Bible. Jacob saw in his dream angels ascending and descending to earth from heaven, and from earth to heaven. It was the stairwell that bridged the gap between heaven and earth. It is Jesus who fills this gap."

It feels like she is trying very hard to get to a point, and I am waiting for her to get to that point. There have been some very interesting things that have unfolded from this conversation, and she hasn't seemed to struggle with it at all, but this—she is.

"This, us talking, this is a transcendental realm. We are not in the physical realm. We are in the realm where the soul and the spirit communicate. Above this is the spiritual realm."

There is certainly a reason for this, but I can't hold onto it forever. Her words are almost like getting poor reception or hesitation. I really am not sure, but I focus in longer.

"There is a reason for the poor reception. Much of the conversations we've had are going to be very fragmented in your conscious mind. Your memories of this will be, at best, spotty. There is a condition that you are unable to let go of for the moment, and because of that, you will cycle through a while longer."

"A condition? What do you mean?"

"You are replacing barriers that will block your view of Jacob's ladder. You are hiding yourself just as in the picture you drew, and that will prevent you from entering the transcendental state. You are unwilling to let go of immoral sexual behavior. The shame is overpowering your physical being, and there is nothing to be done until you choose to let go of this stronghold. Once you are able, then the healing can continue."

"I am willing."

"Jack, you are willing, but this unwilling entity, this unwilling part of you, wills to continue sabotaging you from every angle."

"What got me here? I mean, was I given a drug?"

"There are many who believe that drugs will get them here, but if that were true, then Jacob's ladder would be a drug. What would happen if you can't find that substance? No, it is not a drug."

"Then how do I find my way?"

"Do you remember the tale of Hansel and Gretel?"

"Yes."

"You are deep within the forest of your mind, and in order to find your way, you may have to search for the breadcrumbs. These breadcrumbs are more like gems that you will have to unearth from a combination of plowing the fields of your mind and fertilizing it with scripture. These gems will lead you back to the beginning. It is all in that you accepted Christ as your savior."

"I don't understand."

"They will lead you back to authenticity. They will lead you to who you were meant to be and to whom you were meant to be with."

"How do I get there from here? And what about my current situation? There are people who want me dead."

"When you open your eyes, all of that will have fallen away. 'The battle belongs to the Lord' is a statement that should give you comfort, but it is also a command not to engage in strategic military-type thinking. That strategic thinking detours you into rough roads of anticipation and worry. It will deplete your rest. That, for you, was wizard thinking. Let that go! You will have a power that you should become familiar with. There are great things in your future. Trust in God!"

Chapter 29
Before My Eyes

Psalm 119:18 "Open my eyes that I may see wondrous things out of your law."

"Everything is more vibrant!"

It is only conjecture how long I have been away on this trip. The images fade quickly as I open my eyes. I've never slept like that before. I feel refreshed, free from the taunting guilt and shame, though I'm unaware such feelings ever existed. I can't even explain the incredible power that has come over me. It's as though I could walk on water.

Vague impressions surface, unclear glimpses of things that might have happened while I was away. Were they dreams? I remember someone saying, "He's levitating." My thoughts and memories are scrambled, fragments colliding in my mind. There is the crashing thunder of falling beliefs. Yes, this must all assuredly be a dream. I recall holding my guitar and having a conversation that gave me a fresh perspective on playing music. I remember words pouring from my mouth that were not my own. Whatever happened, it leaves me longing to remain in this feel-good state. I have absolutely no fear. It's as if the tortures and treachery I once knew never existed. Somehow, I know biblical themes I don't ever remember reading. All of this is mysteriously unexplainable.

I had been shattered, my pieces scattered across the continent. All this time, I thought I was trying to save the universe from peril, completely unaware that it was I who needed saving. Jesus stepped in and saved me in a mighty way. He gave me hope. He brought me comfort. He removed the dragon from my heart. He showed me a love so unparalleled that I could never have imagined it. He spent time with me. He opened the gates of heaven and allowed me a glimpse inside. He entrusted me with power—real power. The power to say to a mountain, "Move," and it would. All I have to do is trust in Him.

Taco Bell is on the right-hand side of the street from this direction. Across the street is the unemployment office, and Cavallo Road lies ahead. There's a Quick Stop where the homeless and beggars congregate. This overwhelming sense of peace and joy flowing through me is amazing. The stench of those living in cardboard shelters, tortured by life's harsh circumstances, paints a visual image of the valley of the shadow of death. That shadow hovers over each of these people. I wonder how much closer a person can come to death and still remain in its shadow. Yet, my head remains lifted above the mess before me. These are the big, white, puffy clouds that accentuate the beauty of the day. I feel bigger than life—not in comparison to my surroundings but in spite of them.

I am experiencing a true connection with the Creator of the universe. Through His creation, I am learning to praise Him. He lifts me and praises me through every act. That sunrise was undoubtedly meant for me—and for anyone else willing to claim it. If that isn't a statement of praise, nothing is. I am beginning to understand the simplicity of it all: He is not some arrogant master who craves my praise. Instead, as I praise Him, intimacy grows between us. I consciously avoid the thoughts that might corrupt the relationship we are building. Negative self-talk constructs a path of destruction, but speaking praise brings light and life. Just as speaking well of a spouse exalts the positive, the color of the water is determined by the dye poured into it. Keep pouring in the positive because even a small amount of negativity can corrupt the whole. I could never praise God as vibrantly as He praises me. God is good!

Out of the corner of my eye, I notice a little boy approaching me with a snarl on his face. He can't be more than four years old, yet he has the boldness of a terrier challenging a Great Dane. Surely, his demeanor reflects the tragedy of his environment. I can't help but wonder if Child Protective Services even knows he exists.

"Get out of my world," he hisses at me.

I smile and continue on my way. The implication is clear: this little demon, rooted in the boy, believes it has some kind of authority over me and the spirit traveling with me. It's genuinely humorous—a Chihuahua trying to drop its voice as if channeling André the Giant.

I consider making the effort to cast out the demon, but I know that without changing the boy's circumstances, it would return straight away.

A short time later, just around the corner, another man repeats the same message as the child. "Get out of my world!" It could have been the same voice.

Once again, I smile. I'm not familiar enough with the spirit world to claim absolute understanding. I feel empowered and fearless in the face of the underworld, yet I'm not here to judge or command. I'm simply an observer.

"If that was my kid, I'd lock him in the fruit cellar," someone mutters from a nearby table. The voices coming from around me feel like echoes of the dead—words long buried in deep graves.

"I looked at him lying there, and I laughed," comes from the next table.

"It could be worse... You could have gotten her pregnant," says another.

"I've got a pain in my neck and a thorn in my side."

"I thought I killed you—and I laughed."

For the first time, I truly take stock of the world around me. I wonder: just last week, would I have even noticed these taunting spirits? Or would they have remained invisible, along with other ghosts in unseen realms? Would these words have affected me subconsciously? Would I have heard them at all?

This is the same place that once held me as its prisoner. The difference now is that I can see the keepers. I see how they taunt those who are oblivious to their existence, forcing deeper levels of submission. That should fill me with dismay, but I realize—it was me, just days ago. These demons taunted me day and night, and I was completely unaware.

Now, I see it happening. I see the taunting, the harassment. As long as I remain in the spiritual realm, I'm aware of these antagonistic forces and remain untouched by their effects.

A thought forms in my mind: *How many times have I been the one sitting at the other table?*

I know these people are not evil. They aren't the problem. Yet, in a world dimmed by distraction, their hearts speak words that neither comfort, encourage, nor edify. They let words flow through them as though they are ventriloquist dummies with the devil pulling the strings. Unknowingly and unwillingly, they taunt and torture.

God continues to show me amazing miracles. Sometimes it's hard to believe my own eyes. I feel like the servant who suddenly saw the chariots of fire. When you witness time stop and a jet frozen in midair, it's awe-inspiring—but so extraordinary that it makes you question your sanity. This is where the enemy wedges doubt.

Let your words be straight. Let them have purpose and intent. Let them comfort, encourage, and edify.

Twisted words are like a snake scurrying away. Contradictory words neither comfort, encourage, nor edify. The windier the trail, the longer the road.

"You surely can't say you saw time cease," the voice of doubt whispers. "Everyone will think you're crazy. There's a rational explanation for everything you've experienced. It wasn't divine."

"God, am I going crazy?"

There's a knock at the door. I answer and let my cousin Chrome in.

"Jack, you're not crazy. I'd tell you if you were," Chrome says with a cheesy chuckle.

And just like that, I ask, and God answers.

Through it all, the tree continues to grow. Its branches stretch north, south, east, and west. Branches grow from branches, with vines tangling among them, emphasizing confusion. The wizard thoughts twist and cannot be trusted. The heart of stone pumps rivers of lava. Torment builds the land and gates of treachery. Conspirators gather around a table. The maze stretches endlessly, while the dragon holds its captives. The meek observer stands at the center, trying to make sense of it all. There's the inspiration of emeralds, the promise of a woman, the hope of the pendant, the faith of steady feet, and the love that surrenders—so powerful it causes the world to shift on its axis.

And this is just in the spirit realm.

In the soul, thoughts are manipulative, deceptive, and strategic, fueled by maladaptive survival traits. Manipulative thoughts take over, steering me. Deceptive thoughts mislead me. Strategic plans are crafted against me as I struggle to take them captive. It's exhausting. Emotions are barricaded and locked away.

As for the will? It has disassociated from the thoughts and emotions—it simply cannot trust them. Some thoughts may be genuine, and some emotions that slip through the barricades may be authentic, but the will cannot authenticate them. It does what it can: minimizing collateral damage. Often, it seeks to halt forward motion entirely, fearful of leading into treachery again. It doubts everything. It acts only to maintain the status quo.

And so, there is no one to lead the body.

The body, disconnected from the will, acts on its own. It seeks instant gratification. I've found myself saying things like, "Yeah, I didn't see my choices leading me here," as if my decisions somehow unraveled into outcomes vastly different from their apparent sum.

This may feel inconsequential now, but over time, these patterns work to weaken the commitment I've made to Jesus. Despite the challenges to my faith, I cannot deny the mysteries that have been unveiled.

Reasoning... Reasoning tries to find rational explanations for the endless questions arising on this journey. Yet, there is sufficient evidence that many answers can only be found in faith. I feel like I'm trying to cram infinite ideas into a finite space, a hoarder of knowledge. Rodents scurry through boxes and files, collecting data as it's called upon. Boxes stack atop file cabinets, whose drawers are crammed full. Somewhere in this vast collection are files labeled *All-Knowing*.

I reason that everything I've seen could be man-made. No, jets don't freeze in midair.

But then there are the animals. They seem to lie down, ready to take commands from me. This can't be manipulated, can it? Unless... these are trained animals placed deliberately in my path. That thought feels crazy—yet is it any crazier than believing that God, the Creator of the universe, loves me so deeply that He would cause animals to submit to me?

Even a possum on the telephone wires stops in front of me. It pauses there, watching me for what feels like fifteen minutes. It's almost as if it's waiting for instruction. Then, without a sound, it turns around and retreats, heading back the way it came.

And Adam had dominion over all the fish of the sea, the fowl of the air, and the beasts of the field. This authority was given to him in the Garden of Eden, and he maintained it until the fall. When Jesus bridged the gap, did He restore that dominion to us? It would certainly seem so. All these animals, eager to submit, appear to recognize that original authority.

Filled with an excitement and energy I've likely never felt before, I begin to clean out the shed. It's a typical garden shed, crammed with more junk than useful items. The birds are singing their version of *King of the Road*. There's a profound sense of completeness washing over me, as though I've stumbled out of a dark corridor into brilliance.

I know my thoughts can't be trusted, yet there's such stillness in my mind. If it's possible to have no thoughts at all, that's where I am now. All that flows outward from me is a radiant sense of love and compassion for everything around me.

Awkward Silence

Mindlessly, I start removing objects from the shed. With each item I clear away, my cognition feels more vacant, and I become increasingly aware of the radiant love pouring through me. It's as though the boxes of irrelevant junk represent the clutter in my mind, preventing me from accessing what I truly need—the valuable, tucked-away articles at the back.

Among the items I remove are cobwebs dotted with the bodies of trapped insects—residual self-defeating convictions fluttering feebly, caught in the mental snares we build for ourselves.

Nearly everything has been removed from the shed when I hear the sliding glass door open on the other side of the deck. My awareness sharpens to a level I've never experienced before. It's bizarre—I feel hyper-aware of everything around me, yet my mind is completely clear. The spaces where nagging, haunting thoughts once resided are free of rubble and detritus, replaced with an incredible clarity.

"How in the hell are you doing that?" Corine asks.

There have been two Corines in my life—my mother's sister and this one, who is decidedly not her.

I glance back and realize what she's referring to. Boxes are balanced precariously on shovels, which are pivoting on a rake used as a fulcrum. Other boxes are balanced on their corners, as perfectly as a coin standing on its edge. Everything moves slightly in the summer breeze, creating the illusion of a slow, graceful dance, much like the rustling leaves in the trees.

The choreography of it all feels both surreal and strangely harmonious.

"How am I doing what?" I ask, knowing full well what Corine is talking about. But I want her to explain it in her own words, to put her mind in the right space.

"The boxes and the rakes—all of this! How are you doing it?"

I smile. "I'm over here. The boxes, rakes, and shovels are over there. All I've done is set them down. What they choose to do from there is on them." I joke, hoping to lighten the mood.

"Jack, you're freaking me out. How are you *actually* doing that?"

"I'm trying to tell you, Corine, I'm not doing it. When I put them down, I was filled with joy. I was free of everything that tries to weigh me down. I was singing and praising God, just loving Him. That's all."

"So, you're saying God is doing this?" she asks, her voice tinged with sarcasm.

"Yes! Don't you see? I've always said that love is a word of balance. Look at the letters: *L* is the twelfth letter of the alphabet. *O* is the twelfth from the back. *V* is the fifth from the back, and *E* is the fifth from the front. Love is balanced.

"If love is seated on the throne of your heart, you'll see favor. This? This is just God sharing balance with me. He's showing me love by speaking to me in my own understanding of it. Isn't that amazing?"

"I don't believe in God. This is something *you're* doing," she says, crossing her arms.

"That's too bad, Corine, because He believes in you. And let me ask you something—why is it easier for you to believe that

I somehow have the power to make boxes dance than to believe in God?"

"Because you're Jack! I can see you. I can hear you. I can feel you. And you're amazing, so it makes sense you could do this."

"Everything good in me is God living in me. By the way— God is love. They're inseparable. So, as He shows me love, He's revealing Himself to me! Isn't that incredible? He just showed *you* His existence. You, who doesn't even believe in Him. He showed you!"

Corine's expression darkens, uncertainty flickering in her eyes. It's clear she doesn't know what to think. Sensing that she needs time to process, I step away from the conversation, letting her wrestle with her thoughts.

I turn back to my task, continuing to clear out the shed. I thank God for the opportunity to share this moment with Corine and for the floating boxes that made it possible.

In the corner of the shed, a massive spider has built its web. My attention is drawn to it in wonder. A foot from my face, the black widow seems to gaze back at me. Its distinctive red marking catches the light.

A thought, sharp and clear as a slide from a PowerPoint presentation, fades in: *In the Garden of Eden, there were spiders. All things were created for Adam to have dominion over. That includes the spider.*

The thought resonates within me as an *if-then* statement: *If the spider was created for Adam to have dominion over, then it is a gift from God.*

As the thought fades out, I feel a deep peace settle over me.

Troy sneaks up behind me, grabbing at my ribs and shouting to startle me. But I don't flinch. Not a single nerve is out of place. I've just made peace with the black widow—and every other spider—with that simple idea: they are gifts from God.

I refuse to be at war with any gift from God. To reject such a declaration of love would be unthinkable. I'd rather burn in the pits of hell than despise something God has given me in love.

"Wow, you have nerves of steel," Troy says in amazement. "I would've jumped out of my skin," he adds with a laugh.

I turn to face him, my smile wide and unwavering. "How are you?" I extend my hand for a shake, but as he reaches out, I pull him in for a friendly hug.

"I'm doing well. What's going on with you?" he asks, though his tone carries a hint of concern, almost theatrically so.

"Life is amazing for me. I can't even begin to scratch the surface of all I've been experiencing," I reply, my joy radiating through every word.

"Corine called me. She told me about this magic trick you're doing. I had to see it for myself. Jack, this is... well, it's a little freaky."

"I'm not doing it, Troy. It's a message of love from God."

"She said that's what you told her, but come on—I had to see it with my own eyes."

"Yeah, it's so cool! I was just clearing stuff out of the shed, setting things down like normal. I didn't even realize what was happening until Corine asked me how I was doing it."

Awkward Silence

"I don't believe you. How are you doing it?"

"Troy, it's not me. It's Him."

He crosses his arms, skeptical. "You're serious? You're saying God is doing this?"

I nod. "When my grandma was alive, she once told me, *'The word is love.'* She loved speaking in riddles, and this felt like just another one of her puzzles. She had some impossibly hard riddles over the years, but I vowed to solve this one.

"I started with the dictionary, but most definitions were about affection, and that seemed too shallow for the depth of her meaning. Then I noticed something interesting: *love* is the middle word in the unabridged dictionary, which felt symbolic. I thought about the letters. *L* is the twelfth letter of the alphabet, *O* is the twelfth from the back, *V* is the fifth from the back, and *E* is the fifth from the front. The letters are balanced, front to back.

"That's when I began to see love as a word of balance. But even that wasn't enough to crack her riddle. I turned to the Bible, looking at passages like 1 Corinthians 13, trying to connect it all. Still, I couldn't quite figure it out. Then my grandma passed away, and I thought I'd never solve it.

"I didn't solve it. But today, I'm satisfied that the answer has been revealed to me. It's God's love. That's what she meant—it's His love that satisfies."

Troy's smile is thin, but I can sense his unease. "Jack, that's a little deeper than I'm ready to go."

I soften my tone. "Troy, do you believe in God?" I gesture toward the boxes, still floating in their surreal dance.

He hesitates, then answers, "I was raised Southern Baptist. I don't know what I believe anymore. If I were still in that world, though, we'd probably call this witchcraft. Boxes don't float, Jack. They just don't."

"Well, it's not something I know how to do," I reply. "I can't even think my way out of a paper sack. This isn't some mental power. It's Him, Troy. This is a statement from God, and because I believe that love is balance, I see this as an intimate expression of His love."

I pause, watching Troy wrestle with his thoughts.

The shed, cluttered with its dusty relics and cobwebs, seems to mirror the inner shed of my mind. The webs stretch across both spaces—sticky traps of partial truths and exaggerated fears. When I swipe at them, they cling stubbornly to my shirt and hair, just as lingering doubts and fears refuse to let go of my thoughts.

A large part of the mess in my head comes from avoiding spiritual truths, bending reality to sidestep topics that might make me seem crazy. But now, I've bowed to the truth. I've stopped worrying about what others believe.

The Bible is full of stories that defy earthly logic—stories of invisible armies, dry bones rising, and miracles that shatter the boundaries of the natural world. Those miracles didn't stop with the pages of Scripture. They still happen. They're happening now.

Chapter 30
Chimes at the Beach

Romans 9:19 "Doesn't the potter have the right to mold the pottery for his use."

"The messages washed up on shore is becoming evident."

I feel a prompting to take a walk. It's not a thought or an image, nor is it something I hear—it's just a knowing, deep and unshakable. Without hesitation, I set off, guided by this invisible pull.

I pass an elderly woman by her car, struggling with her keys while trying to reach for a bag of groceries.

"Would you like some help?" I ask, smiling as she glances up at me.

"That would be wonderful!"

I carry her groceries inside, exchanging kind words, and leave her with a wave, resuming my mission.

About a quarter of a mile later, I see a man wrestling with the stubborn roots of a shrub he's trying to remove. The sight fills me with joy, the kind that bubbles up from the soul.

"Let me give you a hand with that?" I offer.

"Sure," he says, slightly surprised but grateful.

"Do you have a small garden shovel and something like a pry bar?"

"Yep, give me just a second."

He returns with a spade and a sturdy pipe.

"Thank you," I say, taking the tools.

A bit of digging, some careful prying, and soon the shrub is free from the earth. As I prepare to leave, a hummingbird appears.

It hovers near my shoulder, darting back and forth, almost playful. Then it flies directly in front of me, meeting my gaze. For a moment, it seems to study me, its tiny wings a blur. After a moment, it darts above my shoulder again and flits away, leaving me with a curious warmth.

Not far ahead, I notice a woman struggling to push an old mower through her yard.

"Would you mind if I finished that for you?" I ask.

She wipes the sweat from her brow, clearly exhausted. "How much will you charge me?"

"Nothing. You've done most of it already," I reply with a grin.

"Well, that's a price I can afford," she says with a tired laugh.

I finish mowing her yard, exchange pleasantries, and continue on my way.

The path winds unpredictably, and soon I find myself by the San Joaquin River. Its waters are wide and steady here, flowing with a quiet power. I follow the riverbank for a while until I come to a small sandy beach.

Awkward Silence

The sight stops me in my tracks.

The beach is littered with broken glass, shattered beer bottles, and other debris. The chaos of it feels like an affront to the serene beauty of the river. I sit on a rock, my heart heavy with an undefinable sadness.

As I gaze at the broken glass, a memory surfaces—a bicycle my dad once sent me for Christmas in Minnesota. I remember the joy it brought me, but now, inexplicably, I recall it being destroyed. I didn't remember this before. The memory is hazy, like it's been buried for years.

Tears well up, and I let them fall, flowing as steadily as the river.

"It's about time," a familiar voice says.

I glance to my side and see her—the angel who washed me, the one whose presence feels like coming home. She sits beside me, her expression gentle yet firm.

"How can people be so disrespectful?" I ask, my voice breaking. I don't even know if I'm crying over the beach, the memory, or something deeper. It all feels connected.

"Don't you dare hush those tears," she says, her voice laced with authority.

"We've been waiting for these tears for a long time."

"But men don't cry," I say, trying to stifle my sobs, a pitiful attempt to hold onto some sense of composure.

"They most certainly do. Did you know that even God cries? He has cried for you many times."

Her words pierce through my resistance, and when she reaches out to embrace me, I let go completely.

I hold her tightly, tears streaming unchecked. The moments stretch, unmeasured, as if time itself pauses to witness the release of my pain. The silence is profound; only the sound of my tears pattering against the ground fills the air.

Yet, gradually, another sound emerges. A soft tinkling, subtle and rhythmic. It's the broken pieces of glass on the shore, gently stirred by the waves. The shards sing together like wind chimes, a delicate harmony born from chaos. The symbolism isn't lost on me: the shattered fragments of my life—my identity—are beginning to find a way back together.

"What is happening to me?" I ask, turning to the angel.

"It's amazing, isn't it?" she says, her wings now visible, glowing faintly in the dimming light.

"Yes, it's wonderful, but also confusing—maybe even a little frightening," I admit.

She gazes at me, her expression one of deep compassion. "Let me ask you this: Will you accept the free gift of God?"

"What does it mean for me to accept it?" I ask, hesitant. My past weighs heavily on me, a worldly burden I'm unsure I can release.

"It means that when you believe upon Him and accept His gift, you will have eternal life," she explains.

"That sounds great, but... how will it change my life?" I ask, wary of the cost hidden behind the promise.

"Jack, it is His desire that *everything* in your life changes. Your life has been marked by pain and turmoil because sin has been exalted over you. He wants you to live in abundance and joy—that is the spirit He intends for your life."

"It sounds like the 'free gift' will cost me everything," I say, my voice tinged with doubt.

"Think about where you'd be today if He hadn't intervened," she says gently. Her words hit me hard. She's right—without Him, I'd almost certainly be dead.

Still, uncertainty lingers. "I have a pattern of making rash decisions," I confess. "I don't want to make one now that ends in eternal regret. Can I take some time to think about it?"

"He says you can take as long as you want to decide. You've already allowed Him to save you. From here, it's about seeking the depth of commitment you're ready for."

Her words reassure me, but part of me still holds back. If I'm honest, I want the best of both worlds—to keep my old life while embracing this new one. Maybe that's what's holding me back: my fear of fully letting go.

"Jack," she says, her voice full of energy and certainty, "you have been born again. Your spirit is alive! The God of Abraham, Isaac, and Jacob wants you to *know* Him. He's reaching out to you. Isn't that amazing?"

"God wants to know *me*?" I ask, my voice breaking with disbelief.

"God already knows you. He wants *you* to know Him! That's the only way you'll truly be able to make an informed decision." Her enthusiasm is contagious, but my mind struggles to comprehend the magnitude of it all.

"How can I know Him?" I ask, feeling the vastness of the Creator against the smallness of my understanding.

"Ask Him," she says simply.

"Ask Him what?" I reply, unsure where to even begin.

"Anything you'd like to know about Him," she says, her words inviting me into intimacy.

Hesitant but curious, I look toward the sunset and ask, "God, what is Your favorite color?"

The answer comes not in words but in the highlighted shade of blue painted across the sky. It's vivid and alive, filling me with wonder. A laugh bubbles out of me, unbidden and pure.

Encouraged, I keep asking. Question after question, like a child discovering a new friend. And with each answer, a connection deepens. This isn't a distant deity—it's a God who listens, who speaks, who reveals Himself in ways both profound and personal.

But as the conversation flows, doubt creeps in. *This can't be real.* The thought plants itself firmly in my mind. *Am I losing my mind?*

The angel notices my hesitation. "What's wrong?" she asks gently.

"I don't know if I'm sane," I admit. "If I doubt this is real, then I'm not really believing in Him, am I? That doubt—it's like a wall between me and the truth."

Awkward Silence

She places her hand on my shoulder. "Walls can be torn down, Jack. And He'll help you tear them down, one by one, if you let Him."

Her words resonate deeply. I sit there, the river flowing beside me, the shattered glass still singing their soft tune. The moment stretches into eternity, a quiet invitation to continue breaking down the walls within my heart.

Chapter 31
Sold My Soul

1st Kings 21:20 "Elijah answered, I have found you, because you have sold yourself to do what is evil in the sight of the Lord."

"You can't sell what you don't own!"

In the following months, I am walking on air. The fine line separating me from heaven is very subtle, but it begins to get wider and more pronounced with each cunning attack from the enemy. In the spiritual realm, I am a baby fighting giants.

The first attack is an argument between two young ladies. They are jealous of me. The argument escalates into a chaotic situation. One of the girls, in fact, drove her car into the other girl's car. It's obvious to me that the enemy is simply trying to steal my peace.

As if that weren't enough, the girl who caused the accident ended up being committed to a psychiatric ward. She acted out with self-destructive behavior in a tantrum meant for a three-year-old. With a three-year-old, you can understand the rage—they haven't learned to use words to communicate their feelings yet. But this girl is in her 20s and certainly has an adequate vocabulary.

I have to admit, it's a slow descent, but with each continuous strike against my peace, I begin to lose ground. That fine line grows wider and wider. I sin. I compromise my heavenly place for sin. I engage in frivolous, meaningless sex and put everything I had been experiencing in jeopardy. I risk everything—absolutely everything—on a whim. But I don't give it another thought; what I fail to recognize is that I hurt God. I hurt the one who had poured so much into me. I've never heard anyone's testimony that was so evident of His love, and yet I turned and ran. My memories are shattered and fading into darkness.

I remember drinking the tea. I remember being pulled into the back room. I summon up my fear that I was going to be killed. I do remember accepting Christ. I have a faint recollection of holding a guitar while a woman spoke. I remember cleaning out the shed. I even remember the boxes balancing. But I couldn't make sense of why they were balancing. I'm fuzzy on the distortions of reality. There are just a lot of pieces to this puzzle that remain censored from my consciousness. With the little information I carry, I begin to piece together unholy truths. I start to think of the whole experience as an initiation into some secret society. I suppose this notion came from the similarity I saw to the movie *The Skulls*.

I sit in a parked car, trying to regain my peace. I am contemplating the vast uncertainty of this thing called life. I'm not even sure how to go about getting this peace back. It shouldn't be missing. These disruptions have nothing to do with me. As I sit in the car, a train of limousines circles around me. They enter, pointed directly toward my body, toward the driver's side door, and then exit after going around and passing by the front of my car. As they drive away, I can see their license plates, and each one references a corporate giant—most of which have been accused of being Satanic or belonging to the Illuminati. This just steers my mind further from the truth. It makes me consider that I may have been arbitrarily selected to join a secret society.

As much as my memories are fragmented, I can't comprehend what has been happening. In this case, the more complex the explanation, the more valid it seems. If the explanation were to take form completely in the physical world, then I would have no other choice but to surrender to a psychiatric hospital. But I still remember my cousin appearing from nowhere, with no other mission than to tell me I'm not crazy.

Most of the time, I would not consider Chrome, my cousin, an authority on mental health, but in this scenario, it is not him that I was listening to. This evaluation was above what I recognized as Chrome's diagnosis. As perplexing as this all is, I cannot allow my mind to keep spinning on the topic.

Oh, what a tangled web we weave. The webs in the shed stretch across the entire width of the shed. I'm speaking of the shed above my neck as well. There are partial truths, held in like flies, and exaggerations, held in like moths. These webs are sticky and stubborn. I wipe one away from the wall, and it ends up attaching itself to my shirt. I wipe them away from my shirt, and they wind up in my hair. No matter what you do, these webs make you feel dirty.

The practice of deception can be the most socially acceptable sin of all. It is a tool used in sales, and we are all aware of that. It is used in undercover work in law enforcement; it hardly seems right to lie and deceive in an attempt to do good. There's an oxymoron in there somewhere. It is used to puff up your résumé, which is another level of depleting your self-worth. You might tell yourself instead, *I am capable and worthy of this job on my own merits, because of who I am.* I venture to say that if you have to puff up your résumé, there may be deeper issues that merit repentance.

Deception is rampant. It is the infectious discharge that oozes from a mouth and forms those stringy, sticky, and stubborn webs. It fences off the entrance to protect the grounds of intimacy. In essence, when you lie to me, I must consider: Have I created a safe place for your truth?

Awkward Silence

The most intimate scene I can imagine would have existed in the Garden of Eden. There, man and woman were naked and unashamed. They would have been playful in their frolicking. Trust would have been the sky above them and the ground below them. Distrust would not have existed. Truth would not have been hidden behind walls of deception. Everything would have been open and honest. It would have been more scenic than the Amazon, more beautiful than the accumulation of all the sunsets and sunrises in a century's time.

Then trust was broken when they listened to the serpent, and that opened the floodgates of evil. All they had known was good. Now, their innocence had been stolen. They now knew evil, entering as shame. It is breaking trust that destroys intimacy. It is the evil coming through the broken trust that alienates them from God. And it is the truth that has risen from that grave to resurrect and restore trust.

Truth can be found safely tucked away behind walls of trust, guarded by cherubim in the land of intimacy. Intimacy is more precious than gold or silver. The truth is the way and the path to the book of life. Jesus is the truth, the way, and the life!

It can be said that I had no safe haven in which to develop trust. I sought intimacy, but if I am absent of trust, I am still connected to sin. I am not trustworthy because trust does not live inside of me. The bond of trust is broken all around me. I can't trust, and therefore, I cannot be trusted.

Chapter 32
High Heels and Powder

1st Corinthians 10:13 He will not allow you to be tempted more than you can withstand."

"When you are aware and your mind knows the spirit resisting is easy."

High heels that go up to shapely legs covered in stockings—those must have come from Victoria's Secret. Those legs continue up to a figure to drool over. The dress she was wearing made me want to roll out the red carpet. Her facial features were those of a fantasy. Her hair was dark and held perfectly in place. If I have a type when it comes to physical appearance, she is it. She's standing at my doorstep, the image I see when I open the door.

"Is Jack here?"

"Yes, I am he!" I answer with the enthusiasm of a schoolboy. I'm just happy to be here and to be the one she's seeking.

She makes a hand gesture behind her, and I watch a limousine drive away.

"Can you drive me to the bank?" she asks.

"I suppose so. What, does the limo driver have an aversion to banks?" I tease.

"No, he's indifferent to them, but it's not his check that we'll be depositing." I'm deeply puzzled by her statement, but I can't think of anything else I'd rather be doing right now than being locked in the cab of my truck with such a delectable woman.

"We've got to hurry, though, or the bank's going to close," she says insightfully.

"Well, let's go then." I reach for my keys, open the door for her, and get in the truck.

"What bank are we heading to?" I ask.

"You bank at Bank of America, don't you?" she asks, obviously having done her homework.

"Yes, I do."

It's a very short ride, and not much time for flirting. I pull into the parking lot as she writes a check to me from Yure Yeka Records. At the bottom of this check, in the memo section, it says "advance." The amount on the check isn't life-changing—it's about $500—but how can I complain? I'm the payee, and it's $500 I didn't have before. I haven't signed any agreement for consideration. In other words, this is just free money at this point.

"Go ahead and deposit this into your account," she says. Now, I see nothing wrong with doing that, as long as I don't spend it before I know what it's for. And like she said, the bank is about to close, and if this is something that needs to be dealt with today, now is the time.

I deposit the check, but of course, I have reservations. I can't think of a single thing that couldn't be reversed. If it's a bad check, I'm not spending any money. If it's a stolen check, I'm still not spending any money. So, I don't see the harm, and yet I am eager to find out what all this is about.

"Let me take you to dinner," she says as I get back into the truck.

This, I have no reservations about.

"Where would you like to go?"

"I'm not real familiar with the area. You suggest a place, but I want dancing with my dinner." Dinner and dancing sounds like a romantic theme but a little too good to be true. It's not that I haven't taken someone I've just met for dinner and dancing; it's that she has initiated this whole thing. She has sought me out, and I still don't even know her name.

"Before I can make such a commitment, I need to at least know your name."

"My name is Marty. I apologize for not introducing myself. It's just that I know so much about you that I feel like we've known each other."

"Okay, Marty. There's a great place called Humphries. I'll take you there."

"This is on the company's dime, so spare no expense. Is there a nicer place, or is that it?" she explains.

"That's the nicest place in town. It's where I would take a beautiful woman like you on a date if I wanted to impress you." I put an emphasis on "date" to gauge her reaction.

"That sounds perfect."

While we were seated, having a cocktail, I was looking at the dance floor. Though I'm no dancer, I still enjoy the intimacy of moving together to the music. Just as I worked up the nerve to ask her onto the dance floor, her phone rang. This was a time before cell phones became widely popular. You had to be rich or well-connected to have one. I had actually never seen a cell phone before this, other than the big box known as a car phone.

"Hello."

"No, he hasn't signed yet. I just got here, and I'm sure the negotiations are going to take a while." I was only hearing one side of the conversation, and of course, it piqued my interest.

"It's like I told you before, he's not a dumb man. He's going to want what he's worth, and that's going to be a lot." I shouldn't assume she's talking about me, but somehow I feel flattered.

"I'll be sure to let you know how things go." With a quick goodbye, she hangs up.

I look at her with curious eyes.

"Jack, I've been doing this a long time, and I'm going to advocate for you, but you're gonna have to trust me." She looked at me with sincerity—or at least the appearance of sincerity.

"Right now, all I want to do is dance."

My imagination wanders, but the reality is, I still have no clue what's going on. The tidbits of information, the very attractive woman, and the promise of money... It has to be a set-up, but I'm willing to wait it out for the punchline.

The evening is delightful. I was the envy of every man in the place. On the dance floor, she toyed with me. She picked food off my plate as if to form an intimate bond.

At the end of the evening, I take her back to her hotel. It's an extravagant hotel in a neighboring city. I pull up to the doors as if I were going to drop her off and leave. A valet steps out to take my keys.

"Come up, I want to show you what I bought for you," she says, excited.

The elevator takes us to a plush suite on the top floor. I'm amazed and quickly go to the windows.

"What a gorgeous view."

"Yeah, the view is why I got this place." She stands very close behind me. I can feel her breath on my neck for just a moment, and then she steps away.

"Come here, look at what I got you." It was a very beautiful and reasonably expensive acoustic guitar. I can't help but pick it up and begin to serenade her.

"Would you like a nightcap?"

"Sure, what do you have?"

"Anything you want." There's a slight pause of enticement, then she continues, "There's a full bar."

Everything about the tone of our conversation, the body language, and the subject matter is seductive. My mind makes a natural leap, but then…

"Jack, will you pick me up in the morning?"

"Marty, what's all this about?"

"I told you that you're going to have to trust me. I will get you the most from this deal."

"But I don't even know what this deal is."

"It's best if you don't know. That encourages me to advocate for you more strongly. I know you may feel lost right now, but trust me."

I'd like to think it was something in the way she said, "Trust me," that gave me confidence, but I know that's not the case. Truth be told, it had nothing to do with what she said and everything to do with her method of seduction. I am putty in her hands.

"Let's get some breakfast," she says to me as I enter the lobby of her hotel the following morning. She looks fantastic and ready to conquer the day. I'm aware that the hotel clerk is captivated by her essence. The drool is a dead giveaway.

"Sounds good." I did put a little extra effort into fixing myself this morning. I'm not sure she noticed. She didn't say anything to boost my confidence, yet I did catch her checking me out. Maybe that's just wishful thinking, but if I find myself in the same place tonight as I was last night, I'll try to crack that code. I thought about her all night. It would be controversial to say my thoughts were purely lustful. The word *pure* and *lustful*, in and of themselves, contradict each other.

"Coffee, coffee, coffee," she giggles, emphasizing her desire.

"Do you like lattes and mochas, or are you more of a straight coffee kind of girl?"

"I like just fresh-brewed black coffee, found only in small-town cafés," she says matter-of-factly.

"I know just the place. Don't be put off by its name. It's called Roadkill Diner."

"Now, there's a marketing strategy. Who the hell would name their diner Roadkill?" She crinkles her nose, and though it's meant as an expression of disgust, it makes her look even more adorable.

"I'm certain their marketing strategy is only meant to attract the locals and is totally dependent upon word of mouth."

"Yeah, but seriously, who does that?"

"They do, and I'm sure you'll be impressed with their country-style breakfast."

"I'll trust you. I mean, you did well last night. That restaurant was amazing. But your credibility is on the line here. And I'm only trusting you because I'm asking you to trust me."

"Speaking of that, are you ready to let me in on any further clues about this riddle?"

"No, not yet. Let's just enjoy each other's company. I've got some things planned for today that I think you'll enjoy."

After breakfast, we went to the bank. She wrote me another check to deposit in my account. It was exactly ten percent more than the first check.

"Go ahead and deposit this, would you?"

Again, I evaluate the circumstances. I feel a little turbulence in my mind, but I decide that I can't get in trouble just by depositing checks. I'm acting in good faith, assuming that the memo, "advance," is a declaration of a potential agreement. As of now, I haven't invested anything into the outcome.

"Let's go to your favorite music store."

Awkward Silence

I steer the truck in the direction of Gil's Music.

"While we're in here, I want you to show off some of that God-given talent of yours. I want you to play as many guitars as you want to get your hands on! Oh, and most importantly, I want you to have fun doing it."

There's a guy playing a simple riff. I listen for a moment and decide I can make that riff come alive. I join in with him, playing a third above what he's doing. Then, I place my notes a third and a fifth above his. He begins to smile. That's my cue. I take it to another level, soloing over the top, working my way up and down the neck. He's loving it.

I take my focus off him, continuing by syncopating the riff. It's then that I notice people are starting to surround us. I hear her telling everyone to make sure to come see me play live at the amphitheater next spring. She's busy marketing me before we even have an agreement. She's just that confident we'll strike one.

Another man starts playing a chord progression that I can't help but join in on. I take the progression into a harmonic minor scale. I can tell he's never thought to do that, even though he seems reasonably seasoned. Changing up the voicings of the chords, I can see he's enjoying himself.

There's a young lady with some skill who starts playing. I sit in with her. She's playing some metal ideas, which inspires a new approach. I play purely from the Phrygian minor mode, incorporating some sweep harmonic techniques that move her to ask me, "What are you doing there?"

I take a few minutes to explain it to her.

"When you use your palm to gently touch the string at the fifth, seventh, or twelfth frets, depending on where you're fingering your chord, you get your harmonic. Then, if you move your right wrist to follow that shape, you get your sweep."

I place the guitar on the wall hanger where I grabbed it from. People are clapping and cheering. One of the cashiers comes and fetches the guitar.

Upon exiting the store, I look in the back of my truck. It's filled with gear.

"Did a little shopping, did ya?" I playfully ask.

"You were amazing. You earned this gear," she smiles.

"There must be $20,000 worth of gear here." I take a better look at what she got.

"$25,600, to be nearly exact." A big, beautiful smile lights up her face.

"I can't afford this! And I can't accept it if I don't know what this is about."

"Jack, I thought you were going to trust me. This is just a drop in the shallow end of the deep pool you're swimming in."

"I don't know, Marty. It feels like a dream coming to life, but I'm afraid of what it'll cost me in the end." Just then, the recollection of my dream and the cheesecake march to center stage in my mind.

I haven't thought about that dream much for a long time. If the dream were time-linear, then I'm at the intermission point. I'm resting up for the next big surge, based entirely on that thought of what it'll cost me in the end. I haven't been preaching, but I've been pissing people off. And yes, there are those who wanted to kill me. The dream didn't play out the way I expected. In the dream, as perplexing as all the symbolism was, it seemed as if I was on a high horse preaching. The words I spoke in the dream were good; I mean, we've certainly fallen from the righteous path. The words I spoke then still resonate today.

We have unorthodox compliance among governments, media, big business, organized crime, and certain religious interpretations, all under the same roof, sharing the same table. That light shines brighter as Epstein's island story breaks loose. People are always concerned about the "one-world order," but my friends, it has already come. While we've had our eyes on governments, big business has crept in and now rules globally.

But I have to explore the idea that the dream wasn't chronological, because the theme of people wanting me dead didn't seem related to my preaching.

When I was a child, my course had been diverted. I watched a movie where a man sold his soul to the devil for fame and fortune in music. After seeing that, I said, "I want fame and fortune. I'd sell my soul for rock 'n' roll." I was a naïve, innocent child. How naïve I was. Is that the decision I'm facing now? The tactics from a higher standpoint could be the devil's way of capturing me. I mean, sending a beautiful woman to engage me in this venture is a scheme of genius.

"Jack, what could it possibly cost you? I mean, really, you don't have much. It seems to me you just have everything to gain."

Chapter 33
The Dance of Business

Revelation 18:11 "The merchants mourn the fall of Babylon."

"There is nothing outside of heaven that is holding business to integrity.'

Day in and day out, she continues the dance she began. She buys me groceries. She buys my friends groceries. She buys more gear. And each day, she gives me a check ten percent larger than the one before.

This morning, when I arrived to pick her up at her hotel, she was not ready.

"Go on up," the doorman relayed her message to me.

I hear the shower running as I enter the suite. I grab the guitar I left there and begin to play as the water shuts off. A few minutes later, she peeks her head out from behind the restroom door.

"Jack, call the bank and ask for your account balance."

It's a reasonable request, since the money in there isn't mine. As I pick up the phone, there's an overwhelming feedback that resonates throughout the room. She darts out of the bathroom, completely naked.

"What was that?" she asks.

"It was feedback," I answer, trying not to get slobber on my words. Her unclothed body was superior to Cleopatra's, surpassing anyone I could think of, historically or presently.

"What would cause that?" she asks.

"Recording equipment is my best guess. When I picked up the phone, it created a loop for feedback, like a microphone in front of a speaker." I sound intelligent, but am I sure that's what happened? I'm only reasonably sure.

"Try it again."

I pick up the phone, and this time, there's no feedback. Before I dial, I rest my eyes upon her body again. Lust has taken over my mind, but I am prevented from acting on any physical desire. It is difficult to imagine myself in this room with this gorgeous woman, and I really don't want to have sex with her. I think it surprises her as well.

She returns to the restroom to continue getting ready. I make the phone call.

"Thirty-six thousand, seven hundred and eighty-four dollars."

She is disappointed that I didn't throw her down and ravage her. I can see it in her demeanor, feel it in her tone. And I just want to avoid the subject because I don't understand it either.

"If it's OK with you, we're going to the recording studio today," she says with pouty lips.

"Cool, let's do this." I don't know what this is, but let's do it anyway. The recording studio sounds fun.

On the way out of the hotel, I see a van with a sign that reads, "Yure Yeka Mobile Recording Studio."

"That explains the feedback," I point at the van.

She didn't hear me or pretended not to hear me. We got in the pickup and left.

This studio, from the outside, clearly screams high-end. The building is in an expensive real estate area. The doors to the monitored and secured entry are massive, and as soon as we approach, I hear the electronic lock disengage.

In the reception area, there was a couch with a coffee table, and literally, a mound of cocaine. My eyes were open. I understood the objective. I wondered how many of these artists had been exploited by the corporations through the enticement of drugs. I knew that I wasn't going to be one of them. In my teens, I would have been easily manipulated. But just a few pages back in this tree of my life, you can see that I accepted Jesus as my Savior. Yes, I can see this no other way than as a conspiracy for the devil's objective. A few pages of this script may have been singed, but my soul belongs to Jesus.

How does one act as if they don't see the heaping pile of dope on a coffee table? That's exactly what I did. It was nonexistent in my room. I moved forward to explore the otherwise amazing studio. There were panels on the walls that were electronically activated to switch from a side with a cushion to a hard panel. This, you might comprehend, was for the sound in the artist's room.

"Jack, we're going to send something through the monitors, and we just want you to play whatever you feel to the music."

I could see the sound engineer messing with the sliders. I could see Marty standing next to him. The music began to play. The first piece was a basic 1-4-5 progression accenting only the power chords. This type of progression is kind of fun to play with because there's nothing that says it has to be major or minor. The third of the chord is what determines major or minor, and the third is not played in a power chord.

As a soloist, the notes you lay down are what define what is felt. I like to go back and forth from a blues or minor pentatonic scale to a major scale. Speaking emotionally, this can bring out everything from sadness to happiness.

The second piece they played for me, I jumped right in with arpeggios and very few passing tones. It was fun, but not really my style.

The third one—now, this one spoke to me. I used subtle chromatic lines by adding the flat fifth and flat ninth. I teetered from low-end to high-end taps. That created a sort of unique contrary motion.

Just like that, I had been in the studio for seven hours. I listened to the playbacks and chose to retake a few. Overall, I was having a blast. I set down the guitar to let them know I was finished.

"Jack, come sit by me." She was on the couch with that pile in front of her.

"That was amazing," she said.

"Yeah, thank you. I had fun."

"Jack, you are very talented. Ron couldn't believe how you can just jump in, no matter what style we throw at you." She scraped out a line from the pile.

"Do you want one?" she gestured to the dope.

With a flash, I could see what the future would hold if I said yes. I had known far too many good people who had given their lives to drugs. I was one of those people, in large regard. I saw this as a tool that the corporate studio would use to exploit my work or obtain my soul for the devil, whichever way you look at it. So the temptation wasn't the coke. I had no hesitation or reservation about the dope. She, however, was a seductive temptress that could manipulate the spots on a leopard. I avoided the hurdle once, but that didn't mean that the next one I wouldn't trip and fall on my face.

An impression comes over me as if I am seeing her in revelation. The light dims. The shading on her face accents the highlights of the crimson flames. The fires of hell rise up in and around her. She sits upon the beasts back on a throne that is surrounded by minions in worship. She wears a crown that she believes gives her power. In this light the skin on her face begins to wrinkle and sink. Her beautiful features fall away and her darkened heart becomes the image that I see. I would like to warn her of the snare that she is caught in but the power of her position squeezes until she has no more vision of reality. She wears a facade of power draped over her by men like me, men that she mnipulates. It is only a brief peep, only a glance into the spirit and then her beauty returns.

Getting gacked out of our minds to shack up and shag for a few days sounds tempting. That body, her body, still resides in a picture in my mind but it has been tainted by the awareness of her heart. I would love to have a little coke to numb it up and then go eat. I would love to put an uncontrollable arch in her back as she climaxes in multiples, but she is the same tool. She will be used up and washed away as soon as the next ambitious young lady wants to sell her soul to seduce and manipulate the men the devil sends her to. There is a high cost to wearing this crown. The trap that she is entangled in is not very different from my own. It is a similar trap- the money, dope, and power over her situation is the bait. She probably rose to this level of control by the similar vow, "I will never again be so vulnerable that I lose control.".". I won't be one of these men.

"No, thank you." I think my response stuns her. I think that both of my responses have shocked her. She is just not carrying herself with the confidence that she once had. Her crown is now tilted.

"Let's get out of here and get some dinner." She walks away from the line that she made for herself.

I am now viewing Marty through different lenses. As beautiful as she looks on the outside, I can see the worms and maggots that feast upon her insides. She no longer has any appeal as far as I'm concerned.

We have shrimp scampi, and a truly beautiful view of the river, but it has no effect on me romantically.

"Won't you come up for a nightcap?"

"Marty, I am exhausted. I think I'd better just go home and get some sleep. I'll see you in the morning?"

"You can sleep here!" There is a distinguishable desperate tone seeping into her words. I don't know what she stands to lose if she doesn't reel me in all the way into the boat, but I do know that she is aware she is losing her ability to easily manipulate me. The tools aren't working as she thought they would.

"I'd better not, Marty. I'll see you in the morning."

"Yeah, we'll try this again tomorrow." She walks off with a bit of a huff.

Oh, something must've occurred during the night that restored some of that lost confidence. Her posture and demeanor are lifted. She is wearing her crown high upon her head with pride again.

"Jack, I heard about a cafe called The Buzz Inn. Do you mind if we go there?"

"I don't mind at all. I love that place." It's in Oakley, one town over, and their biscuits and gravy are fantastic.

"I heard about The Buzz Inn from one of the maids at the hotel," she informs me.

"I hope you're hungry because they serve a good portion." I smile.

"Yes, I'm famished."

This sunrise is meant for me in its totality. It must be, because it is unbelievable. It's in front of us all the way to the diner, and she says not a word about it. She's preoccupied with other thoughts, and I can tell she's oblivious to it. It is breathtaking.

Breakfast is wonderful, and the conversation is good, but I can't help it—I feel as though she knows everyone in the restaurant. It isn't that she is being sociable with these people; it is the eye contact and the subtle gestures. I don't know why it matters that she knows everyone there. It's just another layer in this confused riddle.

"Are we ever going to discuss the terms by which I earn the money in my account?"

"Yes, Jack, I think we'll clear it all up for you today!"

I open the door for her to let her into the truck, then I get in. I put it in reverse and begin to back out. Just then, an old sedan delivery blocks my path. It's forest green, looking like a fresh paint job. On the side, there is a message painted in sort of a calligraphy-style writing. It reads: "I've got your girl." The delivery wagon sits in front of me long enough to ensure that I've read the message.

"Where is Lacey, anyway?" Marty amplifies the message.

I feel a chill run through my entire body. Lacey and I haven't seen each other for quite some time now, but that doesn't mean that I don't care about her. She was my first love. I'm receiving this message as a threat to Lacey, but maybe I'm just being paranoid.

"How do you know about Lacey?" I can't filter the concern in my voice.

"I did my homework, but I was just wondering," Marty says.

"I'm going to stop at the quick stop. Do you want anything?" I'm trying to let go of this, just in case it's paranoia.

"No, I'm good, thanks."

Anxiety has reached out its shriveled hand to take hold of me. I haven't smoked in some time, but I feel the need for a cigarette. I purchase a pack and light one as soon as I exit the store. I signal to Marty that I'll be just a minute.

"I almost forgot you smoked."

I put the truck in reverse again, and there's that delivery wagon blocking my path once more. I read the message again: "I've got your girl."

"Where is Faith?" Marty's question follows the sedan once again.

I'm fuming inside. I don't believe in coincidence. I'm still trying to give her the benefit of the doubt, but I'm not sure what to do about this. If this keeps growing, what am I supposed to do? I can't report it. It would easily be played off as if I'm some paranoid psychopath. There are other people involved, the driver of the delivery wagon for one and I am sure there are others. How far will they go?

"I have no idea where Faith is."

"Oh, I'm sorry. Hey, there's a music store in Pittsburgh I want to go to. Will you take me there?" She goes on like nothing happened and expects me to do the same.

"Sure."

I've gotten quite used to the promotional theme of our music store visits, but today she wasn't promoting. Yeah, she purchased a few items: a guitar, strings, a tuner, and a notepad. Yes, everything has changed for me. I feel it in my bones.

Pittsburgh is two towns over from where we encountered the sedan delivery wagon. I put the truck in reverse, and once again, here's that sedan delivery. Now, if that's not a message, I don't know what is. I waited for her to say something. I truly thought she was going to. This time, she elected not to say a thing. Even if this was just happenstance, she would've had to notice this too. No, I denied the devil, and now he's come after me.

"I'm not feeling so well. I think I'll take you back to your hotel."

"That's OK, Jack. I'm sure you have a lot to think about."

To me, that was a smooth confession that I couldn't prove.

Awkward Silence

"Just because I can't see who's in that wagon doesn't keep you safe. You better watch your words because it is you and you alone that is within reach."

"Relax, everything is going to be fine. You'll see."

That reminded me of something I once read about assuming positive intent in every conversation. Then a thought materializes in my head: Before Adam and Eve ate from the tree of knowledge of good and evil, we would have had no knowledge of good or evil. Good and evil would have been undivided. Our cognitions would have been undivided. There would have been a wholeness that was neither good nor evil.

This situation may seem like an evil plot, but what if I continue to presume good intent? I know that God is over both good and evil. This should not bother me. My God is bigger than any circumstance. It is not my battle!

Thoughts can become entangled very easily. When they do, it becomes difficult to release the knots. I'm pacing my driveway, sorting through what has happened since I met Marty. The clarity of my thoughts has shifted substantially, but it happened a little at a time.

I return a call from a number left on my pager.

"Antioch Ambulance, can I help you?"

Just then, my pager goes off again, so I hang up and return the call.

"Delta Memorial Hospital, can I help you?"

The beeper goes off again.

"Flayhiff Mortuary."

315

There seems to be another pattern, a possible message being sent to me. Start off with the ambulance that takes me to the hospital, but I don't make it, and then end up in the mortuary. I guess it could be read another way, but I don't know what that would be. Then, my pager goes off one last time. It literally went crazy in my hand, and then all of a sudden, the liquid crystal display blew up.

That's a good trick. I have no idea how this is done. I can only picture a van with a transmitter, like some kind of disc, sending the signal from nearby. I do not know how these things work.

I get in my truck and start driving around, pursuing something that will make sense. I take a right-hand turn, and all of a sudden, there are flashing lights behind me. I pull over. Before I can even consider telling him the type of day I've had, he hands me a ticket that has already been written. He hasn't even asked me for my license, and he already has the ticket in his hand.

"We can do these things the hard way if you'd like, but maybe you just don't know what you're up against." He hands me the ticket and walks away.

I circle back around to the house and down the street in front of Big O Tires. I see that sedan delivery. I walk down there and stand beside it. I read those words one more time: "I've got your girl."

A man walks out and asks me, "Can I help you with something?"

"What is the meaning of this paint job?"

"Nothing really. Me and the boys, we were just having fun and sprayed it last night. It'll probably be painted differently tomorrow."

"So, no significant meaning?"

"Nothing to speak of."

I have been studying every curve of his facial features. If anything happens, I want to be able to describe him. As I begin to walk away, though...

"We'll catch you later, Jack."

"OK, so do I know you?"

"No, but I know you."

Before I can get back to him and pull his scrawny ass out of that delivery wagon, he's gone.

The world is filled with obstacles, some big and some small. If you can't see over, under, or around them, you must go through them. If you don't and you allow them to continue to block you, then you will never know what's on the other side.

Chapter 34
Lit'l Mama's Music

1st Corinthians 10:13 "No temptation has overtaken you except what is common to man."

"I love Cheesecake but I am afraid of what it will cost me in the end."

There are entirely too many pieces missing. The impressions are nothing more than a rough draft. The elusive memories and the lack of understanding are synonymous with putting together an all-white jigsaw puzzle. Pieces emerge, and I take them, turning them every which way, trying to make them fit. But no matter how I turn them, they just don't completely slip into place. I could use a mallet and force them, but that would trigger a chain reaction of rubbish—and that's what I printed: rubbish. The storyline became the important thing to me. I wrote with the intention of making sense of the clutter, but again, it was important to me that others could understand and believe the obscurity of my story. It wasn't about healing, although it began with the inspiration for healing.

Inspiration comes fast and furious. It may take a minute for your thoughts to catch up to your emotions, but it's like a predetermined destination that you can't find. Then, in an instant, you blink, and you're there—or at least now you're aware of its existence. That is what it is like to me. I am now aware that it is on the map, but I can't get there from here.

I left California to replant my roots in Idaho. I have missed it here. My nephews and I are having lunch, and somehow—I don't even know how—I fall into leasing a storefront and opening a music store. It all happened on a whim. One minute, I'm dabbing my Mandarin chicken into my fried rice, and the next, I'm purchasing musical equipment for the store. I didn't have any money to speak of. I had saved about eight grand, that's all. All the money from Yure Yeka Records had vanished out of my bank accounts the day of the delivery wagon. I have no idea how that happened, but it wasn't mine, so no harm, no foul.

Lit'l Mama's Music is a safe place. It is the calm between the storms. It is the intermission where I can rest. "My dear man, you must be exhausted. Why don't you come back to my place? There you can rest and begin your quest again tomorrow." The dialogue of this portion of my dream is so spot on with this part of my life.

I had guitar students of all ages. There was a man, eighty-eight years old, who was amazing. He told me stories of WWII. He was captured and held as a POW in Osaka. We traded some of the events that tore us apart and some of the glue that held us together. At the end of his journey, he said to me, "Jack, the same demons that attacked me as a POW attacked you as a child. You are strong, to be that young and survive. I wouldn't have made it through your camp. I had the other prisoners and a couple of humane guards to help me get through."

"There's no way you can compare your apples to my oranges. You are amazing. You survived the big one."

"If it were not for God, there is no way I would have," he exclaimed.

"In that way, we are the same, I am sure." It seems to be a bonding point for those who survive, that is, after the anger and bitterness have diminished.

Carry is a server at the restaurant next door. It's convenient to be right next to the Hong Kong. The food is suitable, and they usually have an attractive staff. Carry fits the bill, but she has a very bubbly personality that exasperates me. It's like she's trying to work the "dumb blonde" angle. In this persona, she locks up her authentic self behind walls of superficiality. She's not stupid. In fact, she's very perceptive, but somewhere along the line, she's learned that this behavior works for her.

In the same breath, I'll also admit that I have adapted to learned behaviors of my own—ones that lure me into a sinful pattern of lust and fleeting physical connections. I'm nothing more than a marauder looking to get laid. If I'm more than that, I might delve into the psychology that keeps her authenticity caged. I might try to develop trust through intimacy, and in doing so, set her free from the false belief that this persona works for her.

But I am a ravenous animal. I have nothing good to say about that. I've lived my life seeking the shelter of instant gratification, and just like so many before me, I have no intention of pursuing anything more than a sexual relationship with her. It's an unfulfilling addendum. There's an emptiness that makes the act itself nothing more than another notch in the bedpost.

This is another point of avoidance in my writing. I reach for a smoke. The smoke isn't going to make me feel better about myself. I have to push through this. The lurking devil is covertly concealed in my shame. The devil's mission is to kill, steal, and destroy, and the fact that I'm reaching for such a self-destructive tool of avoidance is tantamount to the self-loathing brought on by this shame.

This confession, in regards to Carry, opens Pandora's box. Every ghost of my past starts marching outward, carrying with them haunting attachments.

I've always wanted a family. It has always seemed like an impossibility. I tend to gravitate toward the unhealthy, thinking that it adds strength to my resolve. I don't know how to heal, or if I'm even able to take the time to heal. At times, even now, it feels overwhelming. It whispers to me in these corrupted thoughts, "It's too late. Even if you can heal from being the monster you were created to be, you'll never find someone who can love you. Especially once they see the rapacious agreement you've made with your demons."

It doesn't matter if this confession destroys any chance of intimacy. I have zero tolerance for the things that will keep me bound and chained to the basement walls. I have to heal at all costs.

"There's a concert tomorrow night. Do you want to go?"

"Let me check my calendar... um... yeah, I'll go with you, Jack." There's an excitement she doesn't try to hide. She's not actually looking at a calendar—it's just her playful way of interacting.

A light swirls around the room. I barely notice it as it flits like Tinkerbell, too preoccupied with Carry to care.

It is the morning after the concert. Carry had called her brother's wife while I slept. She told her about the night, and now she's come to meet me. She's mirthfully trying to get our attention by reflecting a mirror under the bedroom door, teasing, "I know what you guys are doing in there."

I don't know if that means "stop what you're doing" or "hurry and finish up." My best guess is to finish up. The objective is clearly to embarrass us, and it works. The humor in this, though, is a reflection of Tinker Bell's personality. Grant me this—many of the things Jim Carrey does would not be funny if anyone else were doing it. In fact, if I were to act the way he does, you'd just call me an idiot. But I laugh every time I see him do those things.

Carry soon heads out to talk with the peeping Tinkerbell. Once I've collected myself and become willing to face the music, I leave the bedroom as well.

"Jack, this is my brother's wife, Jennifer."

I'm stunned. It can't be her. She's married. Yet, I'm suddenly pulled into a dream that seems like it happened so long ago. She's a fiery redhead, and I'm captivated, as if it were love at first sight.

"What were you guys doing in there?" Her voice is playful and delightful, and I can feel my cheeks flush with embarrassment.

"Hi, Jennifer, I'm Jack."

"I know who you are. I've seen some of your work," she says, referring to the mirror reflection. Once again, I'm overtaken by embarrassment.

There are more playful antics, leading to heavy laughter. Jennifer is witty, funny, and beautiful. And, of course, she's married.

"Jennifer, it's been a pleasure to meet you, but I really have to go open the store."

"Jack, are you going to come by tonight?" Carry asks.

"I really need to do my laundry," I answer.

"I can do it today," Carry says. "I have to do laundry anyway, so it wouldn't be a big deal. Then tonight, you can come by. I'll have Jennifer and Steve come over, and we can watch a movie or play games."

Awkward Silence

The way Carry says "Jennifer" makes me imagine her impersonating the determined and frantic maiden, using Jennifer as bait for the trap. Carry's perceptive—she sees the connection between Jennifer and me. These types of connections are hard to understand. It turns out we have a lot in common. She grew up in dysfunction as well, and we share a similar way of viewing the world around us. Of course, I don't know this yet.

"If you're sure... I mean, it's a lot to ask of you to do my laundry." I crinkle my nose.

"Yes, really, it's no big deal at all. Like I said, I have to do laundry anyway," Carry insists.

"I guess... okay." I take the bait. I have to see Jennifer again. I have to meet her husband and see how they interact. She's married, and I won't cross that line, but just being in her presence fills me with purpose. It's a curious reflection.

"I'll be by in about an hour to pick up your laundry," Carry says.

That day, I am inspired. I begin to write out the story of my life, sitting in the backroom of Lit'l Mama's Music. The words are flowing, but the connections are missing. There are gaps between the fragments of my past that I just can't seem to fill. An outline of a tremendous story exists, but there's no end in sight. Writing is therapeutic, but healing takes second place to the story itself. At this moment, the most important part of the story is the ending. The fragments buried in the blind spots of my mind might provide a fitting conclusion, but those are graves I'm not yet ready to excavate. There is a prophetic dream unfolding right before my eyes, and I want to share it with the world.

Carry comes to meet me with a kiss and a hug. She looks at me longingly, which, if everything were right in my world, would be amazing. It would be the sense of security you long for in a relationship. But cracking the code of the mutant distortions embedded within CPTSD doesn't happen all at once. First, the awareness of the problem has to rise to the surface. I don't feel comfortable with her affection. Apathy has taken root in my emotions, aside from anger. Affectionately angry doesn't really exist.

"Jack, this is my brother, Steve," Carry introduces us.

"Hi, Steve." I extend my hand to shake.

"We got the movie *White Chicks*," Carry informs me.

"We'll start it when Jen gets here," she continues.

They're trying to make me feel comfortable, but it's somewhat lost on me. I don't feel at ease in the nuances of social graces. It always feels so contrived. I'd rather discuss the relationship between your thoughts and your home decor than talk about the weather, unless you're going to tell me how the weather affects your desire to play racquetball. Honestly, I think what I'm looking for is authenticity, and these two aren't really able to exist in such a small box. They're not dumb people, but the conversation, so far, is labored.

Then Jennifer walks in, and all tensions lift. She brings an elaborate sense of familiarity with her, a feeling of comfort that's hard to describe. We get to venture into the deep end of the pool. I guarantee I'll be wearing my safety vest, but still, she feels authentic.

After the movie, we talk for a bit, but the hour grows late. Steve and Jennifer head home, and I'm thinking about leaving.

"Were you able to get to my laundry today?" I ask.

"Of course! I told you I would," Carry says, her voice playful.

"Where are you hiding it?" I respond, trying to be playful in return.

"Where else would it be? I cleared a little space for you. It's hanging in my closet, of course," she says matter-of-factly.

The way she says it makes me wonder if that's just a normal thing to do. At the time, I thought this might be a classic case of a "stage four clinger," but looking back on it now, through different lenses, I realize that maybe I should be willing to pay the price for the muffin I eat. I think that's just part of being a man. If I had thought this way in the past, I'd be a whole lot thinner.

The next morning, I'm about to slip out to open the shop when I see Carry in the kitchen. I'm standing there, trying to decide whether to take my clothes with me or not. Do I slowly peel back the bandage, or do I just rip it off? I already know that Carry has more invested in this, and I really don't want to hurt her. My conscience is starting to tear at my mind. I decide I'll get them later, and I step toward the door.

"Oh, Jack, don't leave until you've had some of my delicious cheesecake."

In that moment, the entirety of my prophetic dream slams into my consciousness. It's as though a pause button has been pushed while I reach for the handle. I'm living in what I've always called the "intermission" portion of my dream. And yet, in the back of my mind, I still retain the image of Jennifer and me running toward one another through a meadow. It's what I wrote about in *Prophetic Dream*. It's the mallet trying to force a piece into the puzzle. The dream had been clear on this point: I was leaving to find the real woman who had been taken by the dragon.

But this is too far out of my comfort zone. I want a genuine relationship, but I don't know how to define genuine here. The persona Carry wears shields her from being completely authentic, but there's the possibility that she would be loyal. She would fulfill "wifely duties." The problem is, that's just not how I'm trained. To be faithful to me isn't about loyalty. It's about a belief in your partner that transcends normal expectations. It's about a partner who is willing to take on the devil with you because she believes you can. I don't want to surrender to the scraps that fall from the table; I want to surrender to the abundant life that God promises. But maybe it's just that she's nice, and I'm not used to a woman who's not full of sassy spunk—or even a mean streak.

I haven't seen Carry in so many years that I probably wouldn't recognize her if I passed her on the sidewalk. But Jennifer? We've just celebrated twenty years of friendship. There's never been anyone in my life more thought-provoking than Jennifer. I love her deeply.

Chapter 35
Poking the Bear

1st Peter 5:8 "Be sober, be vigilant, because your adversary the devil walks about as a roaring lion, seeking whom he may devour."

"If you are dumb enough to poke the bear you get what you deserve"

The devils within me antagonized the beast within Tonya the day I told her to get an abortion. It was a shrill shriek of fear that scorned the woman and unleashed that beast. Flames shot out from her nostrils—bursts of fire that would target and scorch me countless times in the decades to come. A shriek rang out, reverberating through all matter and antimatter. The echo of that implosion became the hardened bitterness of an unforgiving heart. Torment had expanded the borders of Treachery to annex her heart and the surrounding real estate.

Most events in my life can be written in chronological order—but not this chapter. The cards would be lost in the shuffle. Katie, my daughter, was born in the middle of the "breaking bad" part of my life. Bringing this chapter into chronological order would open the floodgates to story after story of chaotic disruption. I choose my stories carefully, not because I'm here for the story itself, but for the healing. The stories I select to share reflect God's great mercy and love. Most of them could be summarized as the same tale repeated: different days, different people, but the same broken patterns.

Case in point: my daughter was born on a day I was at a gathering. I was so disconnected from reality that I failed to recognize the prestige of the underworld figures in attendance. If you've ever stepped onto your porch, you might recognize some of their names. Reputation and gossip are dangerous games, but if you can spin the story in your favor, you might just deter unwanted attention. Anonymity can be guarded with tales fierce enough to intimidate the spots off a leopard.

At the gathering, a man sat in a chair flanked by two young women, kneeling as though worshiping him. They fawned over him, rubbing and loving on him. I introduced myself and started a conversation. I could tell he knew who I was.

Two burly men began walking toward us, and I assumed they had an issue with me speaking to the man. He raised his hand, and they immediately turned away. I finished our conversation and began to leave.

"Good talking with you, Jack. By the way, I'm Sonny," he said.
"Nice to meet you, Sonny," I replied.

I stepped outside to enjoy the night air, only to realize my car was gone. "Where's my car?" I muttered, scrambling around as though it had moved itself.

I had given a ride to a guy named Robert Cameron, and I knew in my gut he had stolen it. It was a 1977 Corvette. Just as I was about to lose it, a beautiful 1938 coupe pulled up, and Robert stepped out of the passenger seat.

"Where's my car?" I demanded.

"It's right where you parked it," Robert replied.

"No, it's not. Where is my car?"

"He wrecked it about half a mile up the road," the driver interjected.

I felt my blood boil. Rage consumed me as I paced toward Robert, ready to tear him apart with my bare hands. Every sound around me became amplified, and the pounding of my heart reverberated through my veins. For a moment, I reconnected with reality—or at least the reality that demanded his blood.

Robert pulled a pistol from his pocket. The weapon spoke to me for only a split second before I pressed on toward him. Suddenly, two men appeared, one grabbing each of his arms, and hauled him away. It was the same two men that were headed toward me when I was speaking to Sonny. I inherited the two body guards. They moved so quickly I hadn't noticed them approach, even though I thought I was aware of my surroundings. A small crowd stood about fifteen feet away; I assumed they'd come from there.

I never saw Robert again.

In every story, there is the dominant presence of God. The fact that I'm still alive is evidence of that, as far as I'm concerned. Each story, all the way back to when Quinn held off those men with his empty pistol, shares one thing in common: I was numb and disconnected. I can see now the signs of dissociative disorder. I can't tell you exactly how it started, but I know this much: I stepped out, and the demons stepped in.

I've often described dissociation as living in a constant state of shock, where a person becomes highly susceptible to suggestion. It's like a hypnotic trance, with every encounter serving as the hypnotist commanding their suggestion. Just a couple of years after living in this state, I was saved and delivered from this dark, creepy condition.

There's no healing in these stories save to face the enemy. I am relatively unaffected by the individuality of each event, much like I'm unaffected by the specific instances when Nick stood me against the wall to be punched. It wasn't as if each time was more traumatic than the last. It's hard to pinpoint when I became apathetic or disconnected. Perhaps it was somewhere in the midst of all the moving parts.

As for the non-linear presentation of this chapter, it has less to do with the reckless things I did to get myself killed and more to do with the guilt, shame, and resentment surrounding the birth of my child. The resentment may even stem from the twisted realization that I now had a reason to live. I was still apathetic and disconnected—but that's exactly what Jesus was delivering me from.

My child was only two weeks old when the infection spread into the courtroom. The man seated on the elevated bench held tightly to his gavel. This monster had no real concept of justice. His only goal was to fuel her anger with vengeance.

My lack of maturity wouldn't have helped. If I were in his shoes, I likely would have taken her side too, instead of trying to reconcile the differences and create unity for the sake of the child. The goal should've been to focus on the child, but in my mess of a state, I likely wouldn't have allowed for that. It's fair to say that none of us, in this situation, were walking in righteousness.

Sparks showered the courtroom when the gavel slammed down. That day, a decree for child support was issued. I had already accumulated significant arrears. Now, I understand the costs of prenatal care, doctors' bills, and transportation to appointments. I won't complain—I lacked the means to take accountability.

Awkward Silence

Financially, I was scraping by on $12.72 an hour. Mentally, I lived in a distant land. I lacked the capacity to take full accountability, and emotionally, I hadn't grown beyond six years old—except in apathy. Paying $900 a month was an unfathomable demand, yet that's what they required.

To call it a "request" undermines the authority the courts believe they hold. It was a demand, laced with threats and accusations. The dehumanizing name-calling—branding me a "deadbeat"—was a declaration of war, as Sun Tzu would say. Stripping me of humanity was their opening strike.

You would think that a government "of the people, for the people" might approach this differently, asking, "What can we do to help?" But the world outside has taken on the conditioning of the beastly system within. Instead of compassion, they come at you spitting fire and throwing stones. It's a sharp descent from the Protestant principles this country was founded on.

I fly that stick high in the air. It is my sword, and with it, I will take Satan's head off. I may be an innocent child, oblivious to the weight of my words, but I have been made with intent and purpose. I may not yet know how to use my shield or wear my armor, but I carry the authority of the King!

By His authority, I have begun this quest. Jesus has chased off the demons and lit up the shadows. That malicious crowd has been evicted, but I remember what they look like. When I see them reflected in the external world, it seems they need to be dealt with in the same way.

This country, too, needs to rediscover its inner child. It must search through this *Dragon's Lair* until it finds the innocence it once had. Just as in my own healing, this nation must take accountability. When we become accountable, we can change the direction we are traveling. It's long overdue for us to leave this dark, winding country road we've stumbled down too many times.

History shows us over and over the destruction we're heading toward. If I can call myself a successful prototype of healing, then it's time to build the full-scale model.

As of today's eclipse, I believe God has spelled out His warning in all capital letters. His patience, we must admit, has been long-suffering as He's watched wickedness prevail in our hearts. Through our actions, we've shown that money, power, and control have competed with understanding, compassion, and love. In the end, though, understanding, compassion, and love will prevail, and money, power, and control will be cast into the lake of fire. I don't want to be tethered to any of those things when that happens.

In the meantime, there are no two ways about it. I see only one choice before me. The threats rain down like projectiles, tearing up the ground around me. I have to make more money, because only more money will satisfy this perpetually starving beast. Yet, the truth is, nothing can satisfy this beast. It isn't truly about the dead Presidents. No, it runs far deeper than that.

This is about control—keeping the population in check. Look closely at the objective, and you'll see that the system is designed to be complex and confusing, obscuring the fact that it's only two feet per dollar from slavery. It may feel like free choice until something disrupts the flow, and then you see it for what it is.

I begin my electrical apprenticeship with the hope that someday I'll make enough money to survive. But the real challenge is getting to that point. Each night after work, I climb into my "home." Often, I sleep with the gearshift digging into my ribs, my feet hanging out the window so I can stretch out.

Awkward Silence

Three nights out of four, I'm woken by a cop knocking on the window. I'm required to prove I have at least a $20 bill. Without it, I'm deemed a vagrant and locked up. Now, tell me that bill isn't their god. There's more emphasis placed on that piece of paper than on the human being it's keeping in a place of discomfort—a place designed by none other than Satan himself.

Don't get me wrong—the system isn't pure evil. There are still good ingredients in the mix. But more and more, it slips away from the narrow gate and veers toward the wide passage. You might not notice it as you go about your day—until it affects you. And when it does, it becomes all you see.

I can't say it's the expense of child support that put me in this predicament. That would be an excuse I can't justify. There are too many contributing factors. The hardness of my heart and the barricades in my mind have undoubtedly become the treatable conditions.

I begin to conjure up a diabolical dissertation, born of my fragmented   memories: "Ask not what God can do for you, but ask what you can do for Him instead. Ask Him to lead you in your calling. We all know that Mark 16 tells us what we are called to do: spread the gospel, cast out demons, and heal the sick. If we do this in order—spreading the gospel first—we can then cast out demons. It's crucial that a person first accepts Christ before we cast out their demons. And in most cases, once the demon is gone, so is the illness. So, ask not what God can do for you; ask what you can do for God!" The pastor was very animated with his words and gestures during this sermon.

The sermon, in its entirety, is a rendition of the Kennedy speech. It weaves in patriotic ideas but focuses on taking hold of your identity in Christ. It moves me to ask the hard question: "What is Your will for my life?"

Over the next eight months, I ask this question daily. I'm working on a project in Chico, California, and every weekend, I return to Antioch. I have no pressing reason to go back—it's simply the comfort of familiarity. Whether I stay in Chico or return to Antioch, I'm sleeping in my truck.

The routine is wearing on me. My hope is fading. At first, I convinced myself this was just camping—and I love camping. But this isn't the kind with campfires and s'mores. Instead, I feel judgment radiating from every person who passes by. Over time, my mind starts whispering that society has cast me aside. I fight these thoughts for as long as I can, but I don't have much fight left. My hope has dwindled, warped by the distortions of my fragmented memory. My faith grows thin, like a single thread straining against the pull of a swirling cesspool.

Yet, even with all I've lost, two things remain—two things that cost nothing: hope and faith. They're the only lifelines I have to keep me from being pulled under with the wastewater.

"God, what is Your will for my life?" My question now carries the weight of a meager surrender.

"Come to Me, all you who are weary and heavily burdened, and I will give you rest."

I need rest, and I finally acknowledge His authority.

The nickname "preacher" became mine to own, a gift from my co-workers. I suppose it was on account of while they were drinking shots and smoking Sativa, I was reading scripture. I wasn't pitching anything to them but they still liked to tease. They had nicknames for everybody and practical jokes were passed around the crew daily.

Awkward Silence

On the last day of the job in Chico, I sink the final nail. As I drive away from the job site, I hear it clearly: "Preacher."

I assume my coworkers have found a way to mess with me. I pull over to the side of the road and begin searching my truck. Surely, I'll find a speaker or some device planted to trick me. I tear through the entire vehicle but come up empty.

The fragmented memories that could've helped me understand—yes, this is God speaking—are hidden behind walls of deception. I had chosen to return to the sin of promiscuity, a decision rooted in my refusal to forgive my offender. That choice rendered my memories useless, clouded by my own rebellion.

For miles, the word *preacher* churns inside me, unraveling my thoughts. I recall my dream, and more importantly, its outcome—a world turned upside down. In the dream, God shook the planet, and millions fell away. The dark forces pursuing me were ripped from the earth, shredded by His power.

"If I say nothing, if I preach nothing, maybe it won't happen."

I grasp at this hope, telling myself, *God doesn't need me to preach. He could make that rock preach if He <u>wanted</u> to.* My ego is laughable.

Maybe there's a way to comply without stepping fully into the prophetic. If I stay silent, the shrills of the renegades who've chased me need never curse my ears. I tell myself I can still deliver God's message without speaking it.

I'll write it instead. Methodically. Carefully. I'll craft my challenge to the enemy with the precision of a duel, crossing swords without ever opening my mouth.

Chapter 36
Sprung

Philippians 3:19 "Set your affections on things above."

"A spring that is wound too tight will eventually be sprung."

My fear still sits higher on the throne of my heart than He does. I'm not ready to address this yet. I have to start making sense of the dream. It should be blatantly obvious. The dark road most certainly represents the sinful life I've been living. The tree that exists only in the dream, not in waking life, must symbolize the passage of time. How much time do I have? How many more times will I travel this dark country road?

I lack the understanding to fully decipher the symbolism of the dream, though it has consumed my focus. I try to examine the world around me for clues, forcing square pegs into round holes. I invent situational connections to the dream, constructing belief systems to explain its meaning. Each understanding I think I've achieved eventually crashes and burns.

I crawl through the apprenticeship program, surviving on sheer will. I am no longer without shelter. The hardness of my heart has softened, though it hasn't fully healed. The lair where the dragon once resided seems empty, but there are still shadows and critters lurking. Complete surrender remains elusive, just as in the dream. That surrender doesn't happen until I meet the woman in the meadow, running from our enemies. I'm clearly not ready for it yet.

That molten lava—the barrier between my heart and the outside world—has returned. Then, I see her, and I'm mesmerized. Katie. My daughter.

I don't want to admit that Tonya and I coming together could have created something so beautiful. For years, bitterness clouded my view. I imagined flaws in Katie before even meeting her, as though she might have one arm longer than the other or some physical imperfection. Yet here she is, perfect in every way. Her eyes sparkle—she got the best of both Tonya's and mine. I stare at her in disbelief.

"Dad's awe supost to live with moms," she says, her little lisp and Maine accent melting my heart completely. She's freaking adorable.

Tonya moved to Maine shortly after Katie was born, and I interpreted it as her way of getting as far from me as possible. The court granted me "liberal" visitation rights, but Katie is now four, and this is the first time we've met.

"Watch her head," someone says as I lift Katie above my head, oblivious to the spinning ceiling fan.

Thump, th-thump, th-thump.

I win Dad of the Year for that one. The shocked expression on Katie's face is unforgettable—her eyes and mouth switch places like they're playing musical chairs, and her little nose anchors it all in the middle of the merry-go-round.

"Oh my, I am so sorry. Are you okay?" I set her down gently.

"Ya, I'm okay. Just don't do it again," she replies matter-of-factly.

Awkward Silence

This child has stolen my heart. For so long, I believed God hated me. Just last week, and for two years prior, I spent nearly every non-working hour staring through the grimy window of my pickup truck, gazing into the void of my life, inspecting the uninhabited soul within me.

Today, though, something is different. A room is being built within me. The long-vacant control center now has Katie at the helm, filling it with life and purpose.

"Jack, you can stay here at my dad's house. He's leaving, so you and Katie can have space to bond." I can feel the manipulation in her words, but I don't care. I just want to be near my daughter.

My hands move so fast, they seem to break the sound barrier as they reach from her hands to her feet, and then from her feet to her waist. Katie's body is flipping and twirling around me like I'm a jungle gym. There are many unexpected swivels in her movements, and I'm amazed she doesn't hit the ground. Unlike the ceiling fan incident, I'm a ninja in this moment, moving with precision and grace.

Tonya had a son when we met. Her marriage didn't last, but she and her ex share in raising a well-mannered, energetic boy. When Tonya moved to Maine, she met a man, and they co-parent a sweet little girl. It seems I'm the one who defies the gravitational pull, the one who's gone against the grain.

Katie's brother tries to use me as his personal jungle gym. Up he goes, down he comes, around and around. But Katie wants her turn again, and so the cycle continues.

My emotional maturity is on par with her brother's. To anyone with a reasonable sense of emotional intelligence, it's obvious that Katie loves her siblings. A mature man would embrace all three of them for the sake of his daughter, and I do. But it's not out of emotional maturity; it's a demand from Tonya. In order to spend time with Katie, her and her other children must be there, too.

I play in order to be near Katie, but I resent it. It's like a resounding gong or clanging cymbal—actions devoid of love. These children have no real understanding of who I am or what my role is. I suppose they know I'm Katie's father, and in their minds, that might make us related.

"Jack, there's something you should know," Tonya begins, fumbling with her words. "After we spent the night together the first time, I asked you what you'd do if I got pregnant."

"Yeah, I remember. I know I told you I'd do the right thing, but I haven't," I reply, overwhelmed by the emotions of finally meeting Katie.

"This isn't about you," she continues, still struggling with her words. "I need to tell you something."

There's a long pause before she adds, "When I came to the bar, it was on purpose."

I wait, unsure of where this is heading, but she continues.

"I wasn't on birth control because I wanted to get pregnant."

I take a breath, looking down at Katie, who's now tucked into bed. How do I even respond to that?

"I'm on birth control now," she adds quietly.

I want to reject this invitation, but the weight of the past chapters we've written together—these fragmented pieces of our story—seem to boil within me like a witches' brew. A concoction made of mismatched thoughts and emotions: the eye of newt representing the knowledge that Tonya and I would never work, the fillet of fenny snake symbolizing the slithering manipulation on a quest for control, the wool of bat signifying the blind leading the blind, and the tongue of a Komodo dragon representing the split speech of hostility.

No, Tonya and I are a contradiction—our relationship would only lead to destruction. She is controlling, manipulative, and deceitful, and I am, in many ways, the same. For a brief moment, it might feel like a game to see who would conquer and prevail. But it's clear she would win, because I'm not out to hurt anyone. I won't defend myself in a battle that isn't mine. If she were to win, it would mean a complete surrender to her. But when I surrender, it'll be to love, not to control.

The complication is that because I don't surrender, she is still at war. That makes me the unwilling victim in her game. I'm no stranger to being a victim; I've played that role all my life. In the process, I just lie on my back, letting her scratch my belly. I don't participate in the name-calling or the war efforts. Being a victim is like wearing an old sock—it gets so uncomfortable that eventually, you have to do something about it. But Tonya, she's vindictive, and I don't think I've said that enough. Vindictive.

Now, as the clock ticks and the bewitching hour arrives, I find myself lying there with her. Naked, I feel shame. I feel like I've given her false hope. I have no intention of continuing this. We'll probably keep going through the motions until her visit ends, but I can't see a scenario where this benefits either of us. We don't agree on anything, and she would even deny that statement. The tension between us is toxic, and it's damaging to Katie's development.

That little girl, my daughter, has stolen my heart. And in the quiet of my mind, I wonder if we could somehow make it work. But the truth is, I'm the one holding onto false hope. I'd entertain any situation that didn't involve surrendering to her control, but I'm not ready to speak those thoughts aloud.

A couple of weeks have passed, and then everything gets strange. I start receiving calls from Tonya, slurring her words in a drunken stupor.

"Why don't you love me?" Her words are hard to understand, tangled with the familiar Maine accent. But I'm too educated to get tangled in this.

"Tonya, I don't even know who this is," I respond, trying to end it before it spirals.

"It's me, Tonya."

"Call me back when you're sober." I insist, hanging up. The conversation is over.

But there's nothing quite like a persistent drunk. The slurred speech writhes like a snake. It's a weird thing to think about, but alcohol seems to turn people into something serpent-like—language twisting and slithering, their movement erratic, not graceful like a snake, but far from a straight line.

"It's me, Tonya," she says, calling again.

"Call me when you're sober." I hang up again. But almost immediately, the phone rings once more.

"What in the world is this?" I show Kristine the phone.

Kristine and I are friends. We met at a local music store. She worked there when Marty bought all that gear for me. When I came back to the store after the whole Marty incident, Kristine remembered me. We've gone on a few dates—nothing serious, but we spend a lot of time together.

Kristine has the voice of an angel. I've attended a few of her opera performances, and I never thought I'd enjoy opera, but it's been incredibly powerful. And she's amazing. Tomorrow, we're headed to Lake Tahoe, where her opera company will perform. I'm excited about it. She asked me to go after she booked the room.

"Um… it looks like a map." She unfolds a paper, revealing what looks like an architectural drawing of a house. It's hard to take it seriously as a true design, though, because it's drawn with wavy lines in colored pencil.

"Where did it come from?" I ask.

"The envelope says Maine."

I take a deep breath, letting out a sigh—because a shallow breath just wouldn't do the trick.

"It's from Tonya."

"You could sleep here," Kristine reads the bubble in the drawing. "You wouldn't have to sleep here with me. Your office could be next to Katie's room." The drawing is odd but the included bubble text and arrows pushes it completely over into loony.

Kristine starts reading the map, and my cheeks flush with embarrassment.

"This has to be the strangest thing I've ever encountered," she says.

"You must have really rocked her world, hitting every crazy button along the way."

"She's not crazy. She's probably just drunk." I defend her, though I'm not sure why. Maybe I empathize with her, knowing she's probably feeling out of control.

"You can't fool me. That woman is sprung."

We're driving, crossing the San Joaquin River, and Kristine is behind the wheel. Finally, we're leaving Antioch for this operatic weekend. It's going to be a great getaway, just a short trip, but the energy feels good.

Then my phone rings, and I recognize the tone of Tonya calling.

"Hello?"

"Jack."

"Yes, Tonya. What's up?" I can tell she's been drinking. I don't want Kristine to know. I'm a little embarrassed by it, honestly.

"Did you get the diagram I sent?"

"Can we talk about this later? I'm on my way to Tahoe, and it would be rude to talk about it now. I'll call you when I get there."

"Okay."

I hang up, but before I can even put the phone down, it rings again. I expected some delay, just because the call is coming from Maine, but no, it rings immediately.

"Tonya, I'll call you back when I get to Tahoe."

"Oh, okay."

Kristine's energy shifts slightly. There's a faint disappointment in her voice, like a subtle shift in the atmosphere.

Then the phone rings again. Not even ten minutes later. A pit forms in my stomach.

"Tonya, what part of 'I'll call you when I get to Tahoe' didn't you understand? I really have to go!"

"Sprung! She is SPRUNG!" Kristine says, waving her hands in front of her dramatically.

"I'm sorry," I murmur.

"You shouldn't be sorry," Kristine insists. "She's the one acting crazy."

"I know, but what do I do?" I shrug, feeling lost.

"Are you still thinking about possibly going to Maine?"

"No, this behavior is exactly why it wouldn't work. I can't imagine it being good for Katie."

"Well, if she calls back before we get to Tahoe, just tell her you and I are going to Tahoe to get married," Kristine suggests with a mischievous smile.

I would never have thought of that, but she's got a point. If I did that, it would certainly get her off my back. Kristine wouldn't have made that suggestion unless something was floating around in her mind, but I wasn't prepared to stand before an Elvis impersonator to say my vows—not this weekend, at least. The idea of Kristine and I as anything more than friends hasn't crossed my mind. I've accepted that we're friends, and whenever there's any hint of something more, it seems to create a different dynamic, especially on her side.

"Nothing good can come from a lie." I reluctantly throw off Kristine's suggestion.

"Yeah, but by the time you tell her it's a lie, we'll have had a wonderful weekend." A naughty look lights up her face.

I know I can't do this. I'm at my wit's end. Everything I come up with just feels like manipulation. I can't let that back into my life. It's a demon I can do without.

The phone rings.

"Tonya, I didn't want you to find out like this, but Kristine and I are going to Tahoe to get married."

"Oh... congratulations. I don't think I feel comfortable with you talking to Katie anymore."

And then the phone went dead.

"That backfired!"

"What did she say?"

"She congratulated you on your marriage." I'm still chuckling at the absurdity of it. Maybe it's because it relieves the tension I've been carrying, caught in this emotional mess. Laughter fills the cab.

"She then said she doesn't feel comfortable with me talking to Katie anymore."

I laugh even harder. She pulled the rug out from underneath me, and all I can do is laugh. Truth be told, this simplifies things in a way. She holds all the power, and I don't have the means to fight back. Lawyers cost money that I don't have. As much as that little girl got under my skin, wormed her way into my heart, life will go on. As for my heart, stone will surround it again.

"That's awful. Why are you laughing?"

"I don't know what else to do. I will not let Tonya intimidate me or exploit Katie. What if you and I really were here to get married? Can I actually give her that control?"

In those few words—"I don't feel comfortable with you talking to Katie anymore"—I lost all empathy for Tonya. She struck like a viper, no compassion for me, and that lack of compassion turned into hate. The hate grew and grew. It consumed every ounce of humanity she had left. That hatred spread across the distance between us. It was my own sin, reflected back at me through her actions. And with each new connection, that sin seemed to magnify.

Chapter 37
Oil and Water

2nd Corinthians 6:14 "Do not be unequally yoked with unbelievers."

"The divisions and separations posts rivers between the heart and feelings."

I attempt to reach out to Katie whenever the moment feels right. The repeated response of the phone slamming down in my ear becomes increasingly annoying. This went on for months, maybe longer. The frustration building inside me was more than I could bear. I can't linger in defeat forever. This is a travesty; it feels as though I've been plunged into a river of muck. It's my fault— when my tongue moved and produced those words, "Kristine and I are here to get married," I signed my death warrant.

Her jealousy is dark and sadistic. It seeps through every avenue afforded to her by the corrupt, vengeful system. She even stretches the limits beyond the law. Justice is not the prime objective. It isn't even the secondary objective. From the world's system, its main function is to feed the beast. The wheels spin to advance the equitable profit of the economy.

Tonya accepted a position with the child support collections division of Health and Welfare for the state of Maine. I suspect she uses that authority to stalk me, and it turns out I'm not wrong. I receive threatening letters every other day, even when I'm current on my payments. This is not just a black cloud hovering over me.

Tonya, unaware of what she's doing, begins taking her frustrations out on Katie. It may seem like a subtle thing, but when she tells Katie that I am a no-good piece of dirt, and then, out of the side of her neck, says, "You're just like your dad," the message is clear: Katie is a no-good piece of dirt. She forces her to her room, saying, "I've had enough of your dad's attitude for one day." I haven't even spoken with Tonya in years.

The shards of shattered memories are like a jigsaw puzzle I have to reassemble. The heaviness that was once lifted from me now carries the added weight of the recording industry, homelessness, the electrical apprenticeship, and fatherhood.

Granted, it is unfair to all the good men who are fathers to call what I'm doing "fatherhood." The weight I'm feeling is less about fatherhood and more about guilt and shame. It is incontestable that I spawned a doomed destination when I found Tonya. Despite everything, I have to put the pieces back together.

In an effort to multitask, I open a music store to generate an income that will give me the opportunity to work on this puzzle.

Little Mama's Music is the first step in healing the distance that has developed between my mom and me. The name itself serves that purpose. It's a gesture of love that I hope will spark a bond. The departed memories didn't include the demonic, residual sadness etched into my soul, but if I hope to heal, I have to forgive.

Everything I'm doing has therapeutic value. I exercise in the morning, play music in the afternoon, and spend my evenings writing. I have no idea what it takes to heal. I petition a memory, hold it in my hand, turn it sideways, and then put it back. I do this time and again, building the book called *Prophetic Dreams*. I see the book taking shape as the story of my life, and I taste the dog shit all over again. It contains all the elements of a good story, except for the ending.

The ending of a story is the most important part. Without a good ending that sums everything up, it's nothing more than fragmented memories. Just so happens, that's what I wrote. There was no resolution. There was no healing. The end did, however, offer a prophetic word for my future. Arrogance stood with pride and others to seal the pathway for the fractured particles of memory that remain unresolved.

I must've smelled the stagnation in the air. The words of Lacey, "Things can't always be this good," became transparent. I pretended it wasn't all slipping away.

In 2007, I had to close the store. It's what they call the 2008 recession, but it hurt me early, considering that musical instruments are not a priority during recessions. However, booze sales drive the economy. I never understood why. We had the same workforce, the same needs, and the same materials that we had when it was thriving. Someone put the decimal point in the wrong place. There was nothing that should've hindered the economic flow.

Skip a page, and the story's ruined. I spoke of pride and arrogance, but you may not get the full photographic image.

"You need to do something about your daughter," Tonya says, her voice cracking.

"I've been waiting 11 years to hear this. What's going on?" With concern, I still can't hold back a developing smile.

"She's a runaway!" Tonya blurts out, her words tumbling out without pause.

"We have to find her!" Somehow, I still understood.

"I know where she's at. She's living in a trailer with no power or water," she exerts.

"How long has she been living like that?" Concern wiped away my smile.

"It's been a while now. I kept hoping she would come home. She's talking about quitting school. You have to do something with your daughter." There's a moment of silence.

"This is unacceptable, Tonya." I'm stunned.

"Well, then, do something." If there was ever a time to wear men's clothing, this was it.

"First, we have to agree on one point. This is my relationship with Katie. This is not your relationship with Katie through me." I had to set this condition as a solid base.

"You have to keep me informed. Even if it's your relationship with her, we need to try to co-parent." She made it sound like everything was my fault. She made it sound like I was why the Middle East is not at peace.

"Agreed. I will keep you informed unless doing so will break the bonds of her trust."

The smoke is still clearing from all the bombs and smoke grenades that Tonya has launched at me when I decide to grow beyond the confines of guilt. Nothing she has to say is going to keep me from entering that burning building to pull my daughter out. I know that's a strong metaphor, and I have no right to use it, but it's what I was feeling inside. My baby is in trouble, and I have to be there to build her up. No opinion of me matters. It doesn't matter to me what you think or what Tonya thinks. The only thing that matters is that Katie is in trouble. It must be pretty bad because Tonya wouldn't have set aside her pride—and, for that matter, her animosity—to reach out to me. And yet, she knew she could, which is a controversial message written in Morse code. I hope you understand what that means.

"Hello, child, this is your dad." By genetics, this is true.

"Daddy Jack?" There is excitement in her voice.

"Yes, Katie, it's me." I take a deep breath.

"Don't believe Mom. It's not as bad as it sounds. What did she tell you anyway?"

"Well, for starters, that you're talking about quitting school. You know that having a diploma is important, right?" I hope this is an agreeable statement.

"I suppose so." Okay, so maybe we're not in complete agreement, but there's enough there to work with.

"What's the problem? Is it too difficult?"

"No, it's easy." I know it isn't because of difficulty. There's nothing that can convince me of that. It's not the academic portion. It's the rebellion. She's entitled to buck a little. She has a dad she knows very little about, and what she does know is through the persnickety flight of her mother's chatter. She has cause to rebel, but it's now my job to make sure she doesn't get hurt while she's vaulting.

"Then what is it?" I listen carefully for her tone.

"All the girls are bitches." And there it is. It's the classic casting of stones. A glance into the vernacular is a peek into the disturbances.

"I can understand that. I wouldn't want to go to school in a hostile environment either."

"You get it." She connects with me.

"Yeah, I do, but there have to be other options. Let's brainstorm for a second."

I give it a few seconds before I wave the baton to signal the choir. I'm not trying to dominate her with my concerns. I'm trying to invite her into a dialogue of solutions to the problem of the hostility at school.

"You could do night school." I start with my favorite option.

"You could even do online classes. Or, at the very least, you could just go for your GED."

"Yeah, huh. I never thought of night school. I'll check into that!"

"Katie, I don't want you living in a trailer, period—especially not one without power or water." School isn't important at all in the bigger picture. It's my first approach, but not my highest objective.

"Yeah, it kind of sucks." She's been roughing it out for nothing more than to make her point. I just have to find out what her point is.

"Okay then, I think you should come live with me." I'm excited by the notion. I'll understand if she doesn't want to, but here's an opportunity I don't want to slip by. It's an occasion that can relieve the hardships she's enduring, living in a boneless structure during a Maine winter. There's a chance for healing and bonding.

"Can I come visit first to see if I even like it? I mean, we haven't seen each other since I was four." She's an intelligent young lady.

"Absolutely, Katie. In truth, I wouldn't want it any other way. I just got excited about the prospect of seeing you. Hell, in my head, I already had your name added to the mailbox. Katie, I understand what you might be thinking. And I'm pretty sure that everything you ever thought you knew is up for a challenge. Knowing your mother as little as I do, I speculate on what she may have told you. She is impossible. But I'm sure there are truths sprinkled on top of those lies. I should have screamed at the top of my lungs. I should have fought with everyone who got in between you and me, but I felt as if I was beat up. I couldn't afford a good attorney. None of that really matters. What does matter is that you know I love you."

"Yeah, Mom is impossible! I can understand your dilemma. She works at Health and Welfare Child Support Collections. I've seen her stalking you on the computer at work."

She just confirmed my presumption, but it really doesn't matter now. All that matters is that my daughter is coming to see me.

The funny part about meeting your daughter, whom you haven't seen in 11 years, at the airport is that if you don't recognize each other, you may end up standing right next to one another while you explain where you are to the other on the cell phone. She walked right by me. I didn't recognize her, and she didn't recognize me. I called her phone to find out where she was, and this beautiful young lady was standing right in front of me. I should've known her. She is flesh of my flesh. She looks enough like my sister, but I was still expecting that four-year-old girl. I reached out to give her a hug, and she did the whole side-hug thing.

Awkward Silence

It seemed strange to me, but I have to give her space and time to warm up to me.

Over the next few days, we talked and talked. She had brought me some things from her elementary school years. It's impossible to make up for this time lost, but I'm going to do my best to bring about a great future.

I was in my room, lying on my bed with my shirt off. I was watching TV, getting ready for bed when she opened the door. I quickly got up and put on my shirt.

"I just wanted to say good night again."

"What do you want for breakfast?" I like to cook, and this was a good opportunity to bond.

"French toast!" She didn't have to think for a second. That answer sprinted out.

"Done! Good night, sweetheart!" I kissed her forehead and walked her to her room.

There were a few more times when I would be lying in my bed with my shirt off, and she would barge in. I would simply rise and put my shirt on. I know it's uncomfortable seeing your parents half-dressed, so I was trying to be respectful.

Then there was a day when I was lying there shirtless. She barged in as usual, but before I could get up to put on my shirt, she grabbed me. She pulled me back down to the bed and laid with her head on my chest.

"I know I've been acting a little funny, but you should know. Mom told me you were a pedophile." There is a scream that wants to be released, but I held my cool.

Jack Taylor

"I am a lot of things, but that is not one of them," I said.

There isn't a cell in my body that isn't disrupted by those words. I want to scream, but I have to keep composure. I can't believe she would say that. Out of breath, I said,

"You know your mother better than I know your mother, but I know she will stop at nothing to wreak havoc on my life. I am not a pedophile. I have never even been to a Catholic church." I threw that in there to lighten up the mood.

"I know, Dad! I've been watching you. She did have me a little freaked out, but I know now." I can't help but spin this in my head to see it from Katie's point of view.

"Didn't she even consider how you would feel coming to a strange place? That was a thousand times more malicious to you than it is to me." The dragon's lair once again is disturbed. I don't know if I can hold back the volcanic eruption.

"I know the truth, so her slanderous statements can only hurt me superficially. You don't know that she's fabricating a vicious lie. She's your mom; you're supposed to be able to trust her. So, as far as you know, it's the truth. Then she allows for you to be brought out here. If it was true, or even if, in some twisted way, she believed it as the truth, she delivered you into the hands of a predator." It isn't my intention to turn her against her mom. I just spoke without thinking.

"Yeah, she's been very strange. When she answers the phone when you call, she acts like you're the cool kid calling for the nerd. She acts so weird. I don't know how else to explain it." She speaks like a student, but I can completely understand her point.

Awkward Silence

"Katie, you should know the truth. I am not the same man that your mom thought she knew. Actually, she never knew me at all. We worked together for a very brief period. She was the assistant manager at Round Table Pizza. I needed to make some extra money. I was still working at the glass plant, but delivering pizza was a part-time gig that helped me earn a little more. That's where I met your mom. Often, after I finished my shift, I would stick around to drink a pitcher or two of beer. I shouldn't say this, but you want the whole truth, right?"

"Yeah, keep going."

"Well, I didn't like your mom. She was a control freak, and I wasn't attracted to her. She didn't have good things to say about anybody, and I figured that was just because she didn't fit in. I mean, she was so controlling that she couldn't just chill with the other employees."

"Yeah, some things never change. She is still a control freak." She rolls her eyes.

"Anyway, one of those nights when I had a couple of pitchers of beer, she caught me while I was drunk. I don't know that I would have said no if I wasn't drunk, but it was sort of like liquid courage working in reverse. The drunker I got, the easier it was for her to say what was on her mind."

"I can see that." She nods her head.

"Anyway, that was our first one-night stand. I felt terrible, and to compensate, I was a chicken shit and just avoided her. She didn't want to be avoided, and it was obvious that I sprung something inside of her. But that's when Lacey and I got back together."

"Remind me of who Lacey is?" She asked, since I hadn't spoken of Lacey yet.

I brought Katie up to speed on Lacey and told her how I thought we might have a child together. I told her how we agreed to get paternity testing done, and the night before she left me for the second time, I explained how it might be possible that she had a couple of sisters.

"Katie, when your mom wanted to talk, I had just had my insides ripped out. I was a mess. Your mom had been appearing nearly everywhere I went."

"Was she stalking you?" She made that assumption, which gave it validity.

"I'll let that be your best guess." I shrugged my shoulders and lifted my hands.

"She was." She drew the dots together.

"That night, I told her that we should have never crossed the line from friendship. She got me drunk, and you were conceived. I knew that your mom and I would never be able to be a couple. I didn't want that at all. We would have killed each other. Could you imagine your mother and I being together?" I wondered.

"No, you're right, it wouldn't have lasted." She confirmed my belief.

"I just wanted to escape. I didn't want this. I was selfish. It was about me. I am so sorry, but I told your mom to get an abortion. I am so happy that she didn't listen to me. And it didn't have anything to do with you. It was all about me. I was a bigger mess than you could possibly have imagined. Some things that led me to that I'll tell you later, but I thought I should tell you that so you will know that your mom's anger toward me comes with good cause."

"So, you never wanted me?" Sadness filled the room in an instant.

"Katie, I love you! I was just a messed-up kid. When you were four, I nearly asked your mom for her hand, but it would have been entirely for you, and it would have ended up making things worse for you. I'm telling you this because I want to have an honest relationship with you. I have never really had an honest relationship with anyone in my life. Can you forgive me?"

"Well, at least you're not a pedophile." She laughs a little. "Yes, dad, I forgive you. I can even understand it more than you think. I already knew that. Mom told me, but she also told me some things that happened to you when you were young."

"I don't know how she would know anything about when I was young," I questioned.

"Aunt Kristi told her. They wrote to each other." I had no idea about that.

"It doesn't excuse anything, but you should be respectful of your mom. I wasn't a good man." I want Katie to be peaceful and not always feeling like she needs to pick a side.

My shame overwhelmed me for a while, but holding onto it isn't going to be productive in healing the torment that has reached out from me to attach itself to Katie. She needs someone who is going to be strong—someone who will guide her with honesty and integrity.

"Dad, I don't respect her though. Do you know how many times she told me to go to my room because I remind her of you?" That turns my stomach.

"That was not right for her to do that. There is no excuse for that, but maybe this will help you understand—she was hurt, and often times, hurt people hurt others."

The idea that she would treat Katie poorly on my account is not something that is easy to hear. I've always assumed that Tonya, at the very least, is a good mother. That set my mind at ease during these 11 years. I never thought to infer the possibility that my daughter might be in brutal hands. In my opinion, this is mental brutality. The things Katie must've been going through, if this is any insight into her normal behavior, would be excruciating. I choose not to believe that this would be typical.

By not accepting this cruelty as the norm, I can remain in my bubble. I can envision Katie growing up with stability, which was more than I could offer. If I allow this pinprick to burst my bubble, all that hope is gone, and my accountability reaches new limits. As my shield of self-preservation disputes this single act of barbarity, it takes me outside of myself and unlocks the vault to questions.

"Why did you run away from your mom's?" My child is not unruly. She is polite. She is helpful. She is amazing. So, the first tier answer forms: she is not happy.

"I just can't put up with my mom's shit anymore." Her response might be a little manipulative because she knows the dynamics of the relationship between her mother and me. If she ignites the shrubs of blame upon her mom, I am likely to declare an alliance to feed the fire. This can be common ground, the foundation of relating. But a common enemy cannot be the bedrock of a relationship with my daughter. The structure built upon such will fail.

Chapter 38
The mysteries of Valentines and Family

Mark 4:11 "The mystery of the Kingdom of God has been given to you."

"The riddles and the puzzles are the mysteries of God, once solved the world opens up."

"Happy Valentine's Day!" I've been up cooking breakfast when Katie walks out.

"Ugh. I hate Valentine's," she declares.

"Get dressed. We've got some things to do today!" No daughter of mine is going to disregard any day. I don't have strong feelings for the holiday, but I'm going to make this a wonderful day. I'm setting a new tone. I want her to build a monument based on this day. Like I said, it isn't about the celebration the world sees. In future relationships, I want her to have certain expectations of the man she's with—expectations that yes, there will be days marked as monuments for remembrance of how God works in our lives. I'm going to be a father.

"We begin our journey by going out the front door and down the street. Come on, keep up."

"Dad, you're being weird." She smiles ear to ear.

"I know, I know, but do try to keep up!" I might be accentuating my weirdness, but again, this is for memory's sake. I'm not great at speaking with accents, and you wouldn't know my British from my Japanese, but weird and crazy is the target to make it memorable.

Boise isn't a big city. It's an awesome city. We can walk and be anywhere we want in no time. Since I didn't have a plan, there's no specific direction we're going.

"I want to draw your attention to the store on the left, but this is where we turn right."

"Dad, are you back on drugs?"

"Child, I love you, but you're going to have to stop lollygagging around. We've got things to do." I overemphasize the gestures of my hands.

"Dad, stop being so weird." Don't. Stop. Don't stop, is what I hear through her giggles.

"Hey, child, this is a store with my name on it, Taylor. We should really consider changing your last name to Taylor. There are a lot of perks, like this store, for instance." I keep the playful, uninterrupted dialogue going.

We enter a store with amazing products. As we sift through the dresses and other items, I watch carefully for signs of things she might like. She comes upon a certain dress, and her eyes seem to beam. That's the marker—it'll be the dress we get, but it's too early in the day to make the purchase. What next? Go home? I begin fumbling through the dresses, holding one up to her.

"No, it's close, but that's not the one." I'm reading her expressions, looking for signs of what she might like. I hold another one up to her.

"No, this one's hideous!" I can tell she likes this one.

"Dad, I like that one." She looks at me sideways.

"Hideous, I tell you, hideous!" More weirdness to anchor the memory.

"Let's see this one." I hold up another dress that causes her to snarl just a bit.

"I think that one is in the lead. Oh, but wait! I hear another store down the street calling for you." I don't give her time to respond to the dress.

I lead her out the door.

"If you can't keep up, I'm going to get you a leash." Then it hits me—she doesn't know anything about our family. On some level, that has been by design. Maybe it's time to take the expressway through the family rather than the scenic route.

"When Cherie was young, they used to put a harness on her, which was kind of like a leash. No, it was a leash, just not connected to a collar." I chuckle as I remember Cherie's beach attire.

"Who's Cherie?" Katie seems intrigued.

"Cherie is my cousin, so she would be your second cousin." I watch her reaction to see if there's any interest in learning about her family.

"I want to know about my family." She bites the hook.

"Okay, we'll start with your great-grandma, Wanda. She was c-o-r-n-y. All sunshine and rainbows. You could say she pooped butterflies and puffy white clouds—until she wasn't feeling well." I start.

As we walk, a bus passes by loudly, disrupting our conversation. The noise briefly jolts me into a memory. I see my

364

grandma stepping off a bus, a few autumn leaves drifting at her feet. She had traveled all the way from Idaho with an angelic purpose.

"Jackie, they're not treating you okay here, are they?" Her voice is full of concern. She made that entire trip just to ask me that.

"Don't dig too deep, grandma. It'll only make it worse for me." The memory plays clearly in my mind.

"Okay, Jackie, I will respect your wishes, but I'm going to give you an owl to look out for you." The memory rewinds, and the bus fades into the distance, leaving us standing here on the sidewalk.

"Your great-grandma was in a lot of pain throughout her life. I remember her crying out, 'Mercy, oh mercy. Give me mercy.' She was in constant pain. She had diabetes, migraines, and later developed Parkinson's. She was catatonic before she passed away. I felt so helpless, watching her just stare off into space. I tried to get her attention. 'Come on, ski nose, pull out!' I used to call her ski nose because, for some reason, it made her laugh. It wasn't a nickname that made much sense. There was nothing particularly 'ski-like' about her nose, but she liked it. I'd like to think that as she sat there in that catatonic state, she wasn't in pain—she was just watching the movie of life happening around her."

I stop for a moment, collecting my thoughts, then continue.

"She was an artist and a poet. She even received a certificate of honor from Queen Elizabeth for her poetry." I glance at Katie, who is listening intently.

"Did she live in England?" The light turns red, and we stop at the corner.

"No, she lived here in Idaho. I think she was born in Montpelier, but don't quote me on that. It might have been Bear Lake." I've never been to Bear Lake myself.

As the flashing "don't walk" sign lights up, I take the opportunity to share a little more about her great-grandma, looking at Katie's face. I want to know that she's interested for two reasons: First, I don't want to bore her with conversations that don't hold her attention. And second, I want to see if she's truly making a connection to her family.

"I remember quoting one of her poems for a school project, and the teacher got all teary-eyed. She kept telling me how beautiful it was. The other kids in the class quoted famous poets, but the teacher really dialed in on your great-grandma's poem. I didn't say that 'Wanda Thornock' the poet was a relative. For all the teacher knew, it was just a poem I pulled from a book. I guess that was the moment when I realized how talented your great-grandma really was. It was like my DNA revealed a wonderful ornament passed down through the generations. I felt this deep pride, a wholesome, wonder-filled pride for her."

"Can I read some of her poetry?" Katie's eyes brighten with interest.

"Yes, you can. I have a few of her poems, but there are boxes of them at your grandma's house." I'm relieved and happy that she wants to read them.

We arrive at another dress store, but I already know what dress I'm going to buy from the previous place. From here on out, it's all about fun and theatrics, making this day truly memorable.

"Your great-grandma Wanda also painted," I continue, keeping her attention.

"Did she sell any of her work?" Katie's curiosity grows stronger.

"Probably a few, but when I was young, I collected those mirrors you get at the fair. You know, the ones with pictures of your favorite rock bands or whatever." I wasn't sure if she knew what I was talking about, so I glance at her for a response.

"Yeah, I know what you mean." She slips her hands into the pockets of her hoodie.

"Well, your great-grandma told me she would paint me one far better than any of those mirrors I had collected." This memory feels vivid and strong.

"Did she?" Katie looks at me, her curiosity piqued as we continue walking.

"Time passed, and I gave up on collecting them. I had forgotten about her promise. By then, her hands had started to tremor from the Parkinson's. The tremors got so bad that even if she wanted to, I knew she couldn't." I can see the disappointment starting to form on her face.

"That's too bad. It would have been nice for you to have a painting she made just for you." Katie's brow furrows with sympathy.

"She did, though." I pause, the memory growing more emotional. "Her hands were so bad that she couldn't even hold the brushes. But she had made me a promise, and she was going to keep it. She had my grandpa put the brushes in her mouth, and she painted me a scene. There were swans swimming on a mirrored lake, lily pads floating on the reflective water. In the background, there was a mountain scene, and above it, clouds filled the expansive sky."

I nearly tear up at the memory.

"Wow. That's amazing. Can I see it?" Katie's voice is full of wonder and excitement.

"I wish you could." My voice tightens with emotion. "When I was kicked out of the house in high school, it got ruined."

"That's horrible. You should have taken it with you." I can feel her sadness and empathy.

"I didn't have time to pack my things. I was too busy trying to outrun bullets," I joke, but it's the truth.

When we enter the store, I can almost hear the products calling out to her. Each one seems to be vying for her attention, but I focus on one in particular, acting like it's the loudest of them all. My enthusiasm is just a bit more than hers, keeping her energy slightly elevated, too. It's all part of the fun, to keep her engaged in the moment.

"I can hear it! Can you hear it? It's like the mystical voice of the angels calling out from the heavens to align you with the dress you were meant to have," I say with exaggerated seriousness.

"I… I don't hear it?" She tries to hold back a smile so big that it lights up the store, making the walls seem brighter.

"Don't tell me you didn't inherit the family blessing," I say, fighting the smile that wants to break free.

"What blessing? If it has to do with hearing voices, I don't think I want it!" She laughs, clearly entertained.

"Oh, my child, if you haven't discovered it yet, I don't know if you actually possess it," I tease, building the mystery.

"Well, tell me and I'll know if I discovered it," she replies, clearly intrigued.

"I can't just tell you. It has to be learned in deep, rooted ways, ways that can invade the resistance," I say, watching her absorb the words. The sales lady smiles at us, overhearing the conversation.

"Invade the resistance? Sounds like we're going to war," Katie says, picking up a soft scarf.

"In a way, we are." I smile, enjoying the game. "You see, your great-grandma on my dad's side—Ruby—she had powers."

"What do you mean powers?" Now Katie's hooked, the way I was when I first heard these stories.

"She could make dolls dance from across the room," I say, letting the mystery build.

"You're teasing me," Katie says, clearly amused but skeptical.

"No, it's true. I used to ask her how she made the dolls dance, and she always gave me the same answer: 'Jackie, out of all my grandchildren, you will be the one to know when it's time.'"

"So, did you learn?" Katie's curiosity is practically a physical thing.

I skip over that question for now, not quite ready to dive into that part of the story. "Your great-grandma, Ruby, she was a gem of a different color. She drank too much, played around with the boys, but she loved me. A big part of our communication was through riddles—mathematical ones, language riddles. Everything was a riddle."

"Like that movie... what's it called? Da Vinci Code?" Katie guesses, trying to make a mainstream connection.

"Sweetheart, this isn't a movie. And in spite of what you might think, the riddles are just beginning," I say, weaving the tapestry of our family's legacy. "But yeah, she would offer me like $10,000 if I could solve a riddle before morning. That riddle would be in my head all night, and when I fell asleep, I'd be dreaming about it. In a way, she was manipulating my dreams."

"Did you learn?" She won't let the question go.

"I've learned some extraordinary things," I reply, with just the right amount of mystery.

"That's so cool! It explains you so well." She smiles with pride, as if she's just figured me out.

"What do you mean?" I stop to listen.

"Well, you're a talented, gifted cornball who's a mystery," she says, with a gleam in her eye. Her words are playful, and I can tell she's proud of her observation, thinking she's wrapped me up in a perfect little package.

"Ah, so you think I'm talented?" I tease, pretending to be flattered.

"Don't let it go to your head!" she responds, throwing my words back at me.

"You are very cryptic," she says, giving me that head tilt, like a dog trying to understand a new command.

We continue to sift through the dresses, but I suddenly stop, sniff the air, and veer off toward the jewelry section. It's as if I've caught a whiff of exactly what we're looking for.

Awkward Silence

"So time went by, and I hadn't seen your great-grandma Ruby for several years. There was a family reunion, a family barbecue. Your great-uncle Kenneth was there. It was good to see him. Kenneth had once shared the stage with the man in black. Your great-uncle Kenneth kept asking me to play *Malagueña* on the guitar. Over and over, he asked me to play it. He was a musician himself. I guess you could have deduced that since he shared a stage with Johnny. Kenneth told your grandpa that he thought I was the best guitarist he'd ever heard."

I hold up a necklace with turquoise. This necklace may have belonged to Pocahontas. It has that Native American texture. Katie nearly trips over herself to get to me. Her eyes sparkle, and I can see everything she has ever learned or even pretended to know about Native American lifestyle reflected in that sparkle. And I continue with the story.

"As is frequent at these barbecues, the alcohol took effect, and animosity peeked through the curtains. It was time to leave. As I turned toward the driveway, your great-grandma stopped me. She said, 'Jackie, the word is love.' I replied, 'Oh yeah, Grandma, I love you.' She said forcefully, 'No, Jackie, the word is love.' No, I knew this was one of those riddles. It didn't have a lot of evidence to support that idea, but I felt it was."

I continue as she fondles the necklace.

"Well, go on, what did she mean?" Katie interrupted the natural flow of my story out of eagerness. I love that she is so interested.

"That, my child, is a mystery that I want you to explore. I'll tell you what I've figured out so far. First Corinthians 13 defines love in a way I've never known. I think it is key to become that definition of love. I looked up the dictionary definition, and it has a lot to do with affection. The letters are balanced. It is an energy

371

Jack Taylor

that flows through you. It can be a weapon to use against your enemies, and it can be the strongest magnet to hold relationships together."

"What does any of that have to do with making dolls dance?" She is trying to take it all in too fast.

"The first step is to purify your heart so that love can even live in that beautiful place. When love takes the throne in your heart, it commands the world around you." I stare deeply into her eyes when I say this so that it can be felt.

"There's a boutique down the street that is calling our names. Let's go, let's go. I swear, girl, I'm gonna get you a leash." I'm sidestepping to another mission.

"But Pa, I want to keep looking at the pretty jewelry." This is the beginning of us talking to each other like hill folk.

"No, it's time-sensitive. When these angels call our name, we need to hurry to catch them." I toy with her more to set more memory anchors.

"You are absolutely nuts!" She laughs, and it shows she is having fun!

"Thank you, but there's no time for flattery. Let's move it!" I'm trying to sound like a drill sergeant.

Katie and I run out the door so quickly that I worry for a moment that the store manager might think we're leaving with items, but the store manager waves with a big smile. I think she overheard our playful mission.

"Another thing about love: it is God. There aren't different types of love, as so many believe. There is love plus romantic desire. There is love plus friendship. But love is the same—

unconditional, overwhelming, always has been, always was, and always will be."

After I ran her tail off all day in and out of stores, we got some chocolates, encountered witches, warlocks, and angels, witnessed historical events, and experienced love, I circled back to the place we began. I walked right up to that dress, picked it off the rack, and took it to the counter. I said it had been calling for us all the time, from right here where we started. I know in my heart that she will never hate Valentine's Day again. I only hope that she holds this day as the bare minimum of what she expects from her future husband.

That night, Katie came in and put her head on my chest again. We watched a little TV, and then it was time for bed. I gave her a kiss on her forehead and walked her to her room. I went into the kitchen to get a glass of water and returned to my room. I heard the music of the spheres, as if an angel must've appeared to me. A few of these shattered memories became clear. Their pieces fell into place in that jigsaw puzzle. I can remember those floating boxes, and I made sense of God's love in the small, confined space that I called my brain.

Chapter 39
The Fear of Fatherhood

Romans 5:18 "Consequently one man's trespass resulted condemnation of all."

"The fear that I could be a monster that passes down a generational curse is a powerful fear and not without merit, I treated my brother poorly when we were still children."

The next morning, I pull myself out of the soft, cushy mattress and untangle from the web of sheets and covers wrapped around me. Once I'm free, I feel ready to take on any challenge the day might bring. Before long, the aroma of sizzling sausages fills the air, and the hotcakes are golden brown, ready to serve.

A song that had been stuck in my head escapes through my vocal cords, filling the room. I'm so filled with joy that I can't help but sing. My thoughts keep drifting back to yesterday—it was such a great day with Katie. Sharing those moments with her made me feel, in a way, like a super dad.

But then, I overhear Katie defending me.

"What does it matter? You're a liar! All those things you said about Dad—none of them are true." Her voice carries a mix of anger and resolve, and my heart twists, unsure how to feel.

"You're a horrible person! How could you even scheme like this?" I realize she's talking to Tonya. Though I wish it were a peaceful conversation, I'm touched by Katie standing up for me.

Awkward Silence

"He's nothing like you said. In fact, I think he's the kindest man I know. He cooks all my meals, talks with me, listens to me. He's fun, and he always looks for ways to encourage me."

Their argument goes on, but it doesn't seem to lead anywhere. I can sense Tonya's pressure weighing heavily on Katie, pressure I don't fully understand. Whatever Tonya is saying must be harsh because it's clearly causing Katie to battle both her mother and herself.

I realize I don't truly know what Katie's home environment with her mom is like. All I can do is try to bring her back to the joy I was feeling moments ago.

I begin singing, praising the Lord above, letting the music lift my spirits. I laugh as I sway from side to side, my version of dancing, though most people probably wouldn't call it that. While setting the table, I juggle and fumble the utensils, trying to make her smile. If there's anything I can do, it's to offer her a sense of spirituality and a spirit of joy for the day.

"Breakfast is served, my lady!" I announce, presenting her plate with an exaggerated bow, like a loyal servant.

"I'm not hungry," she says flatly, her body language speaking volumes.

"Let the record show that on this 15th day of February, Katie is not hungry," I say in mock seriousness, trying to lighten the mood.

"Dad, just stop!" she snaps, clearly frustrated, maybe even a little angry.

"Katie, whatever it is, you can talk to me," I say gently, dropping the act and grounding myself.

"Mom is being a bitch." Her bluntness startles me. I want her to respect her mother, but Tonya makes it hard to defend her.

"Okay," I say carefully, "but she's all the way on the other side of the country. There's nothing she can do to extinguish the love in this house today." I hold my palms up in a gesture of reassurance.

"You're right. Let's eat—I'm starving!" she finally says with a small smile.

That's my girl.

I'm starting to think I might be pretty good at this dad thing. I'm learning how to relate to my daughter in new and unfamiliar ways. I'm guiding her toward self-awareness and teaching her things she hasn't yet learned. I even taught her to talk like a hillbilly—one of our little inside jokes that never fails to make us laugh.

But despite my good intentions, I made a big mistake.

We were living near BSU, and I was all too aware of the statistics surrounding sexual assault on college campuses. One evening, I returned from a psychology class to find Katie outside, talking with a boy. I had made it clear that she wasn't allowed to be out after dark, even though, technically, she wasn't alone. Still, she knew what I meant.

"Get your ass in the house, now!" I barked, my tone overly aggressive.

I was being overprotective, and it showed. I automatically distrusted this boy, assuming the worst without knowing a single thing about him. That message—delivered out of fear, not love— was poorly received, as it should have been. My reaction was driven by my deep-seated fear of losing Katie or having something terrible happen to her.

Love would have taken a different approach. Love would have taken the time to meet the boy, to shake his hand, and to see him as a person rather than a threat. Love would have looked beyond my ignorance.

That night was enough to push Katie away. Of course, it wasn't just my outburst. She was already under pressure from her mom, dealing with the loneliness of being away from her peers, and struggling with homesickness. My reaction was the final straw, adding to her reasons to leave.

I am heartbroken. Shame surrounds me, and I can see nothing else. If only I had been better prepared to see my little girl growing up. In my mind, she's still just that—my little girl.

The truth is, no amount of preparation can prepare you for certain moments. It's not about preparation; it's about who you are at your core. If I were truly a loving man, then love would have poured out automatically, without effort. Instead, fear controlled me.

If love were engraved in my heart, my response would have been entirely different. I would have introduced myself to the boy, extended a handshake, and given him the benefit of the doubt. I would have had faith in Katie's ability to make good decisions. Instead, I assumed the worst. I failed her.

They say shame is a prison as cruel as the grave, and that's exactly how it feels.

Now, I'm wrapping manicotti in aluminum foil, trying to find solace in cooking. My stuffed manicotti is some of the best you'll ever taste—or so I tell myself. It's all in the process, the forbearance.

I start with a cheese blend: cottage cheese, ricotta, and mozzarella, mixed with an egg or two to make it light and fluffy. Next, I brown my meats—whatever I've aged to perfection—with diced onions, a touch of garlic, and chopped artichoke hearts. Once the meat is browned, I add sun-dried tomatoes—cherry tomatoes I dry myself, halved, lightly salted, and slow-roasted at 220 degrees. I throw in some olive slices, too, for good measure.

The sauce is made from fresh ingredients, and I like to mix a bit of homemade pesto into the marinara for added depth. Basil has a richness that makes everything taste brighter.

Here's where the magic happens: once the manicotti noodles are cooked, I stuff each one carefully, layer them with the marinara meat sauce, and sprinkle a little shredded cheddar on top. Each piece is wrapped individually in foil, and as they bake, the flavors stay snug inside, melding perfectly.

Cooking is therapy, but it's also a reminder of how much I care. Maybe tonight, this meal can be a small step toward healing—for me and for Katie.

With Katie no longer here, I don't cook every day. There doesn't seem to be much point. Cooking has always been something I enjoy—an act of creation and expression. Whenever I cook, I dance around and sing, making it a time of worship. I like to think it makes the food taste better.

But since Katie left, there's been a void in my heart. I can't help but feel that the manicotti I make represents more than just food. It feels like a metaphor for stuffing emotions, for trying to fill the emptiness she's left behind. Maybe that's a stretch, but I'm grasping for any analogy to help me understand how I feel.

Awkward Silence

There's a darkness hovering over me, an impending sense of unease. Yes, I'm sad about the fallout with Katie, but this feels deeper, heavier. It's as if I'm trying to fill an emptiness that looms larger than the loss itself.

Adding to this strange period is the reemergence of "Erica," someone who has been attempting to seduce me online for years. Her first message came through Myspace:

"Hi, I'm Erica. I don't know if you remember me, but my now ex-husband and I were in your music store about a year ago. Since then, I haven't been able to get you out of my mind. My husband and I were already on unsettled terms, but meeting you made me realize I had settled for someone whose values didn't align with mine. It was one of the factors that led to our divorce. I was wondering if, when I come out to Boise next week, you'd be willing to show me around."

The flattery was transparent, and while her profile picture showed an attractive woman, I wasn't emotionally available. Her message was unsettling in more ways than one.

I replied: "No, sorry, I don't remember you or your husband. I'm sorry to hear about the divorce—those things are never easy. My other half and I would love to show you around Boise. I realize that's not what you had in mind, but it would have to suffice if you come to town."

I used a fictitious girlfriend to make my boundaries clear. Still, something about her message didn't sit right with me. I couldn't pinpoint why, but it left me with a vague sense of discomfort.

A couple of days later, she messaged again: "My dad took a fall. I have to stay with him. I'll have to postpone my trip out there."

I replied politely: "I'm sorry to hear about your dad. Take care of him, and take care of yourself."

I assumed that would be the end of it. For a while, it was.

Months passed, then another message appeared: "Hi Jack, I just read your book. It's amazing what you went through and that you're willing to share it. I still want to see you, but I don't want to be placed in a position to become jealous. Will she be around next week?"

Her messages came and went like the tide, predictable yet sporadic. Each time, I deflected, batting her advances away with mentions of my imaginary girlfriend. This dance had been going on for three years.

But now, with Katie gone and the void in my life growing heavier, her timing was perfect—or perfectly terrible. I was feeling vulnerable, craving comfort. Against my better judgment, I replied:
"Erica, I just want a night of uncomplicated, stress-relieving sex."

As soon as I sent it, I read the words back to myself. They felt like an echo of something familiar, a recurring theme I hadn't fully confronted.

"I can do that. I'll be in Boise on Thursday." The message was sent.

"Seriously, I don't want anything complicated. I'll fix my famous manicotti. We can eat, hang out, and watch a movie, but after the weekend, I want to pretend like it never happened." I insisted.

"What would be so bad about you finding out you like me?" It was a legitimate inquiry.

"It's not that. I need a lot of healing in my life. If you read my book, you'd understand what I mean. I wouldn't be good for anyone right now."

"I understand what you're saying. Send me your address, and I'll see you about 6:00."

The kitchen was a disaster—every time I cook, it feels like I'm not the one who has to clean up the mess. I have a knack for making a meal like a freight train through the kitchen.

"The salad is done. The bread dip is ready. The bread will have to go in once the manicotti is nearly done. I have wine. I think I'm all set."

There's a knock on the door.

"Well, you're not who I was expecting." There were two unexpected guests—a federal marshal and a Boise cop at my door.

"Yeah, she won't be coming. Turn around and bring your hands slowly around to your back." The handcuffs went on. After they turned off the stove for me, the short federal marshal tried to push me down the stairs, using the handcuffs as leverage. I sped up, he lost his balance, and the Boise cop chuckled.

"You are being arrested under the authority of the United States federal government for non-payment of child support." He went on to read me my rights, but all I heard was blah, blah, blah. I knew this had been coming—something I even wrote about in my book—but it was still surreal. I was being charged as a federal felon for child support. There's supposed to be a level of understanding that if you commit a crime, this crime carries this punishment. If you rob a bank, you get a similar punishment to other bank robbers. That's the foundational idea of what is considered a "usual" punishment. The character of the criminal is also evaluated through past criminal actions. These things are meant to normalize punishment. This federal felony is certainly unusual for a child support matter, and it actually feels a little cruel.

As the marshal was transporting me to the federal building, we hit some road construction. A flag girl was standing there.

"I need to get through here. I'm transporting a federal prisoner."

"I don't care if you're transporting the president of the United States; you can't get through here." She made me giggle.

"Fucking bitch!" he yelled as he stomped on the gas, steering us back the way we came. A grown man—a representative of the U.S. government—acting like this. I have to suspect there's a demon pulling his strings.

Chapter 40
I Want Better

Romans 8:28 "All things work for the good of those who love Him and have been called according to His purposes."

"At some point you need to love yourself just so you can be sure that you can love at all."

They arrested me for willful non-payment of child support. They fined me $100,000 and locked me in a 6x9 cell for six months. Along the way, they trampled on every civil right I had. They filed a search warrant on my e-mail account. It was all-encompassing. Anything they found they could use against me. I fought that on the basis that if they were to serve a physical search warrant, it would have to be specific. They would have to detail what they were looking for. When the judge denied my motion, I fought again because it included attorney-client privileged communication. He couldn't deny that one, but his solution was to have a federal marshal—unrelated to the case—read through and filter out the privileged communications. That's indistinguishable from a lottery winner drawing the numbers. There's nothing in my e-mail or elsewhere that connects me to a crime, but it's the idea of them walking all over my civil rights and setting a precedent that makes it okay for them to continue with this all-powerful, almighty thought process.

The courtroom is filled with demons, but none more disgusting than Eric Hefner, better known as Erica. Somehow hiding in the shadows of online communication under the disguise of Erica is the lead investigator in the case. For years, they've been setting this up. Payments were made when 'Erica' first contacted me. If they hadn't been, then why didn't they arrest me then? More to the point, why? The effort they put into this case would have paid for three children to be raised from conception to eighteen. Lying is deception, and deception is the devil's tool. So why incorporate it in a courtroom that is supposed to be based on Godly justice? In God we trust and place your hand on the Bible. They don't do that anymore. They've completely turned their back on God.

"Jack, they've made an offer of six months in federal prison and a restitution payment of $100,000. There are other conditions they'll attach to it, like a probation period and counseling. And there's a condition to this plea."

"What would you do?" To me, that's a very strange request.

"Honestly, I would take the deal. It's obvious this judge wants your head. If we go to trial and you lose, he'll give you the maximum. There's that condition I mentioned. You have to read a letter that the court will write in open court upon sentencing."

"What does this letter I have to read say?" To me, that's a very strange request.

"I don't know, but he did say if you don't read it, he'll give you two years in federal prison." This felt like a setup.

I read the letter: "You are the honorable judge, and I am nothing but a low-life piece of garbage." My eyes swelled as I continued. I should have stopped and crumpled the paper up. I should have taken the two years. I felt like Meshach, Shadrach, and Abednego being forced to bow to this self-righteous, egotistical piece of shit.

It occurred to me back when I worked in drug enforcement that the system was not of God. Apparently, I knew they would come after me in some capacity. The demons that are incorporated and living within the system know that their time is passing. And as of today, it is coming to a screeching halt. I had given entirely too much power over to them. I didn't get it. I do now, and I'm going to share that with you.

The sound of the footsteps is bold, even though they are distant. It's remarkable how keen your senses can become when you practice them. That man coming this way weighs in at about 195 pounds and is using every bit of that weight to establish a perception of authority as he comes down the hall. I'm sitting on the bunk in my cell, listening to the footsteps and chatter. I give him no authority or headspace.

"Taylor, you're still in here? Wow, they must have forgotten about you."

Every day, one of these guards has to try to get under my skin. It worked once. One of the guards said he was going to take a picture that my daughter sent to me home with him to masturbate to.

"You filthy asshole! How about you come in here and clear up any misunderstanding we may have. I can recognize pathetic, so I'm not surprised by the fact that you'll be flying solo as you look at my daughter. Just remember she has my eyes. You're a sick little boy."

They kept me in that 6x9 until two weeks before my release. In those two weeks, there's enough time to get a little color back in my cheeks and gain back a little of the weight I had lost. I reckon they didn't want me to leave looking like I'd been mistreated. It may be a little funny to you, but guards, prison guards, stole my wallet and the money that was in it. I did get my wallet back, but the guard claimed, "On my life, there was no money in it."

Jack Taylor

Bitterness that churns in my stomach brings about the chunky projectiles that spray out every time I open my mouth. The bitterness is my takeaway from this experience. I lapped that up like a rescue dog. Seriously, they tried to feed me the greenest liver I'd ever seen while I was there. Every time I speak of it, I become more and more disgruntled. That bitterness is the oil floating on top of the water. It just keeps rising to the top of my conversations. I do think that it needs to be talked about and the justice system needs an overhaul, but it's a worldly system. The one that we place on the throne matters. I'm not speaking of the Republican or Democrat. I'm speaking of things much larger. That bitterness takes me further down the country road during the pitch of night, and I've been down that road enough.

Feelings move over me like a shadow that stretches out and lingers just before the sunset. Tonight, that emptiness has reached a new level. Sex has caused problems in my life. Federal prison is the most recent consequence. Child support is a direct result of my promiscuity. However, I'm happy for my daughter. I don't know if Faith is mine or not, which again is a direct influence of my immorality. I don't know, but she may even have a sister who is mine. I don't want to speculate about others I've brought into the world. I've never had a meaningful relationship. I want, with all my heart, a meaningful relationship. I feel like there's nothing left in my life to do except to change my direction and leave that way behind me.

"God, I'm tired of being immoral in my sexual conduct. I want something real and lasting. I'm done with one-night stands and sleeping around. God, I'm surrendering my promiscuity to you. Please help me! I no longer want to feel used and dirty. I want something real! I want to enjoy someone on truly intimate levels. I want so much more than what I've been giving myself. I know I don't deserve it, but God, you've told me that it's not by my works but by my surrender. I surrender my love life, my relationships, to you!"

I'm not emotional. I'm not led by an attachment to anyone. I'm not being led by some episode of infidelity. I just long for something more. I've decided to allow God to light my path. He knows what I need and who I need to be with. I've chosen many times and have always regretted my choices. I'm surrendering my heart to God! I will trust Him. I will place my hope in Him. I will move in faith with Him! There's been nothing exceptional about today that leads this decision. This decision leads to the day being exceptional. There is a fragrance, it smells like lilacs and lavender. This fragrance descends upon me like a mist. The aroma fills the entire motel room. God is speaking faith into my heart. I trust Him, and He returns that trust.

This decision is a pivotal moment. The events have been stood up, lined up, and twisted around. The decision reaches out beyond the borders and topples the first domino. About a month after I sat in the motel room, smelling the lilacs and lavender, I'm sitting in my truck, considering the restitution from my child support case. It seems like an impossibility. It's most certainly excessive—$100,000, a hundred thousand dollars. I laugh just a little, and that probably ascends to heaven as a groan. I get just a little reprieve from this deep thinking as I watch the people in the park. Again, I laugh, this time a little hysterical. "It doesn't matter." I think about how much even the thought of money has worn me down. I think of the countless hours I've spent trying to earn a decent living instead of actually living. This, whatever it is, has been stealing my life. I think of the frustrations I've felt when my bills are due. I think about how little control I have over my financial circumstances. I've been swimming upstream, and nothing seems to work. "Lord, all that I have is yours."

Jack Taylor

Chapter 41
Realm Beyond the Door

Acts 19:15 "Jesus I know, and Paul I know about, but who are you?"

"Spirituality becomes deafeningly real."

Flying overhead are winged creatures that bring turmoil to an otherwise peaceful community. They sweep down upon those who are fleshly connected but are unaware of the apparitions from other orbital realms, the spiritually blind. Most are not truly blind; they just can't see with the bright light shining in their eyes. They are distracted by the epistemology of the physical plane, these outward displays that impede their vision, warping their insights. It escorts their thoughts into perpetual motion and keeps them pinned down by a type of gravitational pull while they are free to soar with the foul.

It is a strange evening in Gresham, Oregon. All of the crazies are hovering closely to the borders that outline the spiritual lands. The spiritually dead are roaming the streets as if they are undead. I am getting out of the pickup when I notice a young woman sitting with just a shawl covering her otherwise naked body. She is in her early thirties and would be attractive if not for being destitute and hardened by a lifestyle of treachery. There is blood on her legs, and it takes me a minute to process that this is from her menstrual cycle.

I approach her with caution, but I know that I can't just ignore her desperation. After all, I have been desperate before.

"So, what gives?" I give a friendly smile.

"Some asshole brought me here. Then he left with all my clothes in his car," I can hear the beat-down, discouraged tone in her voice.

"Okay, so how can I help?" I notice a drug deal happening out by the road.

"I kinda need a shower," she gestures to the blood. I am slightly hesitant. I know she needs help, but am I truly the one for the job?

"Sure, follow me." I can't ask her what I can do to help and then avoid giving her that help. That would be the equivalent of picking up a broken heirloom. I have the glue to put it back together, but instead, I propel it to the ground to be sure it can't be fixed.

I led her through the motel lobby and up the stairs to my room. At the very crossing of the threshold into my room, it was as if this barrier had been broken that held back the lunacy. The shawl covering herself hit the floor with intention. She began to run bathwater as I got behind my guitar to hide. I played a few songs before,

"Won't you come in and talk with me?"

I took a few breaths to check myself. Can I go in there at this time to talk and keep my clothes on? Can I manage to talk and behave? Yes. She is an attractive young woman, but I have no desire to have sex with her. I sat down my guitar and sat on the toilet seat to talk. She told me that she had been living on the streets for about three years.

"It's different now. I used to be fine, but I don't feel safe anymore!" She opens an emotional dialogue.

"What do you mean? What changed? I mean, living on the streets could or should have never felt that safe." I attempt to be empathetic.

"I mean that it just feels like the more normalized it becomes, the more abnormal it feels. It seems like someone is always dying, and there is always a threat, and no one wants to do anything, like the whole world has given up. I just don't feel safe," she answers my question with a sense of a well-reasoned response.

"I can understand not feeling safe. I mean, you're a young lady, and that automatically puts you on the radar." I discern.

"Yeah, tell me about it," she replies.

Before I could process another word, everything changed. She began to speak as if there were others in the room with us.

"Do you think he's going to fuck us?" she asks.

"I assure you that I am not. Nothing could be further from my mind," Disgust is what prompted my response. That disgust isn't directed at her but at the misfortune that has her talking with a room filled with the invisibles.

"What's wrong with me? Ain't I pretty enough? Don't you like the way my pussy looks?" she asks.

"It has nothing to do with your appearance. However, You've stepped off trail into marshlands. You are not mentally capable of making decisions. All the others that you are talking to, um, what is that?" I take a deep breath to collect my thoughts.

Girl, I think you have a mental illness, and it does make me sad. I don't know what I can do to help, but I do know that I am not going to have sex with you." I begin to walk away.

She starts to shave her vagina, looking at me with each stroke as if that will entice me. It makes me so sad to think of this kind of thing. I could have gone my entire life without becoming so aware of this kind of thing. I'm sure there were drugs involved or that maybe some should have been.

Sweats and a t-shirt is the best I can do for her. They aren't going to fit her well but its gotta be better than a shawl. I lay them on the bed and leave her to her vises as I go to the front desk to rent her a room.

"Get some rest. I'm going to try to get you help tomorrow."

First thing in the morning, I begin to make call after call to find help for this woman. I don't know what to do. I can't believe that this reality can be connected to the realm I live in. I know it can; I just don't ever want to feel so helpless again.

"Knock, knock."

I open the door and allow her in. No sooner than she crosses that invisible barrier, her clothes drop to the floor again.

"Doesn't your room have a shower?" I say, sarcastically.

I do not know how to help this woman. I'm frustrated that I can't help. That frustration burns hotter with every failed attempt. That blazing frustration eventually leads me to abandon her. I leave Gresham to return home.

Angels fill the seats at a Bible study that I call together. Only the God of heaven and earth and His angels were there. One person shows up to study with me, but that is where two or more are gathered. The discussion I had intended was the correlation of the letters to the seven churches in the book of Revelation and the seven church periods. I think I have a sort of grasp on this subject that extends beyond normal teaching. I can lead a study on the subject.

The woman that came to the study is Lori. I have known Lori since we were in junior high. She is very eccentric and an incredible human being. Her son took guitar lessons from me when I had the music store. Little Mama's Music was between the Hong Kong Restaurant and Lori's hair salon.

"So, what have you been doing? I haven't seen you in a while," Lori asks.

"I've been working in Gresham, Oregon. The project just finished, but I've been there for about six months. How about you?" I answer.

"I just got back from a deliverance conference. It was very enlightening. Cindy and I went, and we both learned so much," she says.

"What did you learn?" I'm curious.

"Some of the indicators of someone that is demonized are using plural identity terms like 'us' or 'we' when they are talking about themselves. They cry excessively. They become vulgar— well, those are just a few things."

"When I was in Gresham, there was a young woman who said, 'Do you think he's going to F*** us?' I thought she was just mentally ill, but maybe she was demonized," I wonder.

"It sounds about right. It is so weird, but as you begin to speak deliverance in the name of Jesus over them, it is real. It's like the exorcist. There was a lady who came to me for deliverance, and there were facial contortions—it was so bizarre," she says.

"Wow, that's interesting."

As we talk, the conversation goes further and further from the predetermined outline. The content becomes about the commission of Mark 16. We are commanded to cast out demons. I never could have imagined where this conversation would lead. I feel enlightened a little to the possibility that the woman in Gresham is, in reality, demonized. Previous thoughts were only carnally directed. I just knew that she is mentally ill. I hadn't even considered the possibility of demonic influence. I should have weighed that on the balances. It has been many years since that boy said, "Get out of my world." Did the possibility just escape my attention, or did obstacles just get in the way?

"Hey Jack?" the phone rang.

"Yes, this is Jack."

"We need you in Woodburn, Oregon, to work on an Amazon project."

Woodburn is sort of near Salem and unfortunately another Oregon city taken over by the flying critters of darkness. The homeless community isn't as prevalent as the larger cities, but it certainly is within the stats per population. And though it is a smaller population of the flying minions, they are still hovering and bringing down the morale of the area.

After work, I am pulling into the motel parking lot. There is a convenient store lot connected. I look to the left, and there is a transformer set with short shrubs around it. Standing among the brush is a woman with her tits exposed. I can't blame her for having the "fun bags" out—it is 103 degrees outside. She is just trying to air herself out and be in some shade. She is just trying to cool down. I jaunt over to the convenient store where I grab a couple of waters and bring one back for her.

She has placed them back in the holster. They are no longer on display. I hand her the water, and I notice a Bible behind her sitting on the transformer. I don't know why that surprises me, but it does. I hand her the water.

"No one has been that nice to me for a long time," she says, her voice heavy with gravity as tears roll down her cheeks.

"I'm sorry to hear that. It's just water." I pause.

"You're looking a little flushed. If you want, you can come in and sit in front of the air conditioning. I go to bed by seven, and you're out before then."

"I couldn't do that. I don't know you."

"I understand. I only offer because it's so hot." I begin to walk away.

"I kinda need a shower, though."

A ton of bricks just fell over the top of me. It is with a clear conscience that I can say that the revelation of the abnormal petition is making the connection to the Gresham girl. What is it with me and this request? The demons have either been talking in the spirit realm, or this thing has followed me from Gresham. I am no longer thinking with such a constricted view. I have a pretty good idea of what I am inviting into my room, but I take a deep breath while I consider and say, "Sure, I suppose that will be okay, but the same thing applies: I go to bed by seven, and you're out before then."

She follows me to the room.

"I'm going to use the restroom before you get in here." I use it and flush it. As I reach for the doorknob to exit, I half expect to find her disrobed on the other side of the door. I am relieved to find that is not the case. She enters the restroom and closes the door behind her.

"This is a different circumstance than Gresham. It's just weird—a shower of all things. That's the same." I have a difficult time believing in coincidence. I tell myself over and again, "People living on the streets probably seek the opportunity to take a shower every chance they can. That's not really that strange." I still retreat to my safe place and hide behind my guitar. I play it until she exits the bathroom, fully clothed, I may add.

"You play beautifully." She again had tears pooling and leaking from her ducts.

"Thank you. Go ahead and take a seat by the air if you'd like." I gesture to a seat in front of the air conditioner.

She does elect to sit across the table as I gestured. She seems to be respectful and maybe even a bit timid.

"So, what do you know about that book you're carrying there?"

"Not much. I just got it last night."

"Would you like me to show you a few things about it?"

"Sure, I would love to learn."

Here's my chance to share what I had wanted to share at the Bible study a few weeks ago. After just a few minutes, I can see that what I am trying to share is just going over her head. I can assume or expect too much from others at times. For this study, I would do well to have pictures and graphs, but it is so interesting and, if you get it, it falls like an avalanche. You just can't help for it to open up the entire book in a new way. I decide to change the subject.

Awkward Silence

"So what is your name?"

"Amanda."

"I'm Jack, Amanda."

"Do you have a wife, Jack?" Amanda steps out of her shell about six thumb lengths, only to retract behind blushing cheeks.

"No, I'm not married." This is not the straightest answer. It is true, but in my heart, I was married the day that God confirmed He has someone for me.

"Does that mean that you're available?" Her facial expression is as one that seems to be overwhelmed by the vastness of the universe as she peaks through this tiny little window.

"No, I know this may sound funny, but I am faithfully committed to someone I haven't met yet."

"How can you be committed to someone you haven't even met?" She sort of scoffs this but she still presents herself timidly.

"I asked God to show her to me, and in a way, He has."

"Are you sure that God has shown you? I mean, how do you know that God doesn't have someone even better for you? I just don't want to see you get hurt. You may be passing up opportunities that He has ordained and that can be wonderful?"

This conversation reminds me point blank of a conversation I have read about. This is the same theme as the conversation that took place in the Garden of Eden. "Did God really say that you must not eat from any tree of the garden?"

"I am faithfully committed to what God has shown me." I answer the best that I can.

And the woman said to the serpent, "We may eat the fruit of any tree in the garden, but you must not eat from the tree in the middle of the garden, or you will die."

"You're telling me that if a beautiful woman were to come in here right now and want to have sex, that you wouldn't?" Amanda continued with this dialogue.

"No, I wouldn't." I respond.

"Why? I mean, surely you can have your cake and eat it too. Your future woman wouldn't even know about it. She wouldn't even care because she doesn't even know you. She doesn't love you and she never has."

And the serpent said, "Surely you won't die." In those words, the serpent has called God a liar. Just as Amanda is in opposition to what I know God has spoken to me. There are very few things in life that I will argue. There are some things that I just know. If I know it, I will defend it with the force of a raging sea. If you oppose that which I just know, then you are calling God a liar, and I won't have that!

"That is the whole idea behind being faithful. Giving in to my lustful desire would break the covenant that I have made with God. I will not jeopardize what God has shown me."

Then, right then, she leans toward me. I feel the shift in her energy.

She lifts her eyes from the ground in a jarring head movement, stopping to meet my eyes with hers. In a very deep voice that could not come from the same person as this timid sweet voice she had been displaying, she says, "You have beautiful eyes."

She stands up quickly and drops her clothing in one sweeping motion. She begins to masturbate as if she is driving nails on a construction site.

I jump back, feeling threatened by this shocking turn of events. It all comes forward in my mind—the girl from Gresham, the Bible study at home, and now I sift through the rubbish of the carnal view that I had regarding mental illness to this new perspective that this is demonic possession!

"Who are you?" I am stunned by my new reality. This reality will become my normal because a person cannot experience this just once and go back to being blind. It just can't happen that way.

"Come on, let's skip the pleasantries. Fuck me, you know you want to." I wonder if she/it knows that I am hearing the deep voice? I wonder if it is aware that it has been revealed to me that it is a demon? I wonder if it has the notion that it has been exposed? It is no longer hidden behind the partitions that divide the spiritual and carnal realms.

"That is the last thing I want to do." I repeat. "Who are you?" Now I am the one looking out the tiny little window into a universe that is opening in vastness, except I am not overwhelmed. You can't be prepared for this, and yet God has prepared me.

"I am Amanda."

"No, you are not! I ask again, who are you?" The expression of this creature changes as it does understand that it is no longer hidden from me.

"You may as well fuck me. Not every man can say that they fucked a demon."

"That is not going to happen." I speak out of knowing.

"Why? Your little commitment to God? You can never be faithful!" The demon now swings toward my confidence.

"I am the orb, Jack a puss. I am the one that struck you with the clog. I am Jezebel, the unfaithful whore. I am your worst nightmare."

"You don't seem very frightening to me. As far as nightmares go, you're about a two." I speak this with the calmness of a psychiatrist. I raise two fingers, "a two."

"You will think a two when we get into the climax," It lets out an orgasmic moan and then holds up the two fingers she has been pounding herself with. "The climax of the nightmare." It continues, and then continues to masturbate using those same two fingers plus one.

"Well, I may or may not be a prophet, but I most certainly have seen the flames that devour you. Something you should know, orb, when the flame first makes contact with your skin, it feels gentle and light. It may even take a moment to dance around showing you its beauty, its vibrant colors. Then, as it digs in a little deeper, you might understand that it is not there for your pleasure. You will at that moment want to scream at the top of your lungs. When you feel that scream building with intensity, that is when you will flash upon what eternity means. That reality will become more painful than the flames. You will want, with everything in you, to escape. The charring of your flesh is the replay in your vision. The combustion will give you moments of reprieve in that it will take your focus, but don't forget that the flames that expel from the combustion are the fire around you. It is devouring you in ways that you couldn't invent." It does no good to argue with a demon; their blindness to truth won't allow them to see anything but the bleakness of the darkness in which they dwell.

"Let the nightmare begin! I was there when you fucked your friend Travis' girl."

"Yeah, that was thirty five years ago and I know you were. I wouldn't have made any of the sinful mistakes I have made without a pervert circling in my head. Are you ready for the good news?"

"What about the time that you broke the driver's side window of Chris' Mustang? You stole the car from police custody."

"Yeah, it happened as you said, but the good news is that it's all been covered by the blood of Jesus. I am forgiven and you cannot be. I am not following you to the flames because God has delivered me from you, but I am not arguing with you anymore." I posture myself to connect to a different sort of dialogue.

"You need to leave Amanda alone. You are being evicted." I insist.

"I have been here far longer than you would know. I like this place; it feeds me well." The demon responds.

"Do you know me?" I ask this with a Biblical passage in mind. I need to know that it recognizes my authority in Christ.

"I know you." It answers with a turn of the head, a smile as if it is flirting. It has placed those fingers up on her lips. She, it, almost has a blushing schoolgirl shyness coming out again.

"Good, then you know who my father is. You need to go! Leave this woman alone in the name of my father. In the name of Jesus, get out." I feel the authority, the dunamis power of the Holy Spirit pour over me like oil. I get a shiver of reassurance. God is in the house!

There is a squirming in the seat. All the muscles of this woman's body flex, her arms extending outward as if to mock the crucifixion. I feel the hairs on my head begin to stand. I feel a chill down my spine. I am deafeningly aware of the presence of the Holy Spirit. And in this instance, I see her face become all contorted. I didn't realize the shapes a face could make. I may have seen this type of thing in horror movies, but this is as real as it gets. I am basically now just a passenger in this body as I listen and watch. I become grateful for these front-row tickets to something extraordinary! I watch intently as one demon after another discharges from her being. After about two hours of this flexing, shaking, trembling, and contorting, they begin to bow to me.

"Do not bow to me!" I speak up, offended that it is bowing to me because I cannot take credit for what is happening. This is the action of the Holy Spirit. It really has nothing to do with me except that I get to see the power at work. I am also fearful of the implication that the demon bowing to me is suggestive of a responsibility I have in this woman's freedom.

"Go and leave this woman alone in the mighty name of Jesus!"

"I have a legal right to be here."

It bowed again. She came over to give me a hug. I was dumbfounded. Then it left, bowing to me as it backed through the door to leave.

"That was some bedtime story!" So much for a bedtime of seven. It is now nine-thirty. I am awe-struck at what just happened. My view of life changed in this occurrence. I will never be able to view things the same again. What a rush. It was exciting. It was exhilarating. It was phenomenal. It is bizarre. I am not sure what to do with this, but it has to be done! It most assuredly is setting me towards something bigger than life, and now that I have had a taste, I need to exercise this.

"I kinda need a shower" will forever be an invitation from a demon. I kinda need a shower to clean the mist of vulgarity that sprayed from each directional change in that disgusting conversation. These demons were trying to trip me up. I surrendered my slut-like behavior, and they appeared from the street as zombies to be an enticement. Zombies are not enticing. Naked whore demons are no more enticing than the zombies that just keep invading my space. My sexual appetite was strained, if not devoured, the instant that, "you've got beautiful eyes" came out to play. In a big way, that made sticking to my commitment much easier. Anytime that one of these gals reaches out from her grave, all I have to do is think, "you've got beautiful eyes" and I'm all set. I don't need nothing!

When a dream of prophetic symbols and a "real" world demonic manifestation come together as transparency overlays it, it resurrects the flatlining spirit like paddles, and "clear." A crash cart for the spirit would ideally bring back the sharp details of my imagination. Oddly enough, the opening up to this world of crazy imagination is taking care of itself. Imagination does not hang out there by itself. It is not alone. It might be dulled from a hungry boy trying to cut through a can of hominy with eyes that shoot lasers, but if the detailed images of the mind's eye can be resharpened, there will always be hope.

Other than nursing a suffering spirit back to life, what purpose does this demonic conversation serve? I am absolutely positive that the Holy Spirit does not need me to cast out the demons. I watched and paid attention, but the Spirit of God and the army He commands fought the battle. So why was I there? Don't be mistaken by the question; there is a larger understanding that He has given me.

Jack Taylor

At six years old, when my traumas began, I was stunted in early childhood development. My imagination was all but destroyed—it was stunted as well during this period. I didn't have the capacity to use my imagination to connect with compassion. I couldn't see the world through someone else's eyes, except to consider that literally, and I didn't know how to do that. Now I stand in front of a woman demonized by countless demons. The Spirit is doing mighty work. But what is my purpose for being here? I did have compassion because it was that which invited her to cool down. I was down the wrong rabbit hole. Tempting the conviction with my faith is strengthening my character, but there is more. There is the revealing of the spiritual world, but that is not the gem I seek in this experience. My faith is strengthened through the event. There are many things that I can extract from this, and believe me, I will search every stone. But there is one element that has appeared on the map of my heart as the Holy Grail. It is a treasure that I have to find.

I refer to these things as gems because most often they need to be dug out of the earth, but when they are held in the hand, they have a high value. I consider what God would determine is valuable for me, and it would always have something to do with unearthing a mature man's honor, for the development of character, and for moral uprightness. There is some earth covering the objective, this gem.

When she first dropped her clothing and began to masturbate, I jumped back as if I were going to get some of the demon on me. I didn't see through my mind's eye, but I really didn't have to. This demon's presence is known by Amanda's behaviors and speech. I run through the scene again and again, searching for the gem, and then it dawns on me. Faith moves the mountains so that love can cut through. The mountains have nothing to do any longer with Amanda because she has bowed out, but I am still part of the equation that was part of that scene. I will soon have to dig deeper for this gem. If I set a mirror in front of me and that was Amanda staring back at me, I should look for that likeness. I should seek harder for self-love because even a demon said I have beautiful eyes.

In the book of Revelation an angel holds a small scroll that has been opened. It's hard to say what was written in that scroll. It may have had words meant to lead in healing from trauma and bitterness, a bitter sweet scroll. It may be a note of love so profound that it wakes the dead.

What is written becomes the message but the delivery is just as insightful. This angel has its left foot on land. The solidity of land is not like a dream. It is the firmness of the carnal realm. That firmness overlooks what can't be seen. My rigid diagnosis of the woman in Gresham was seated entirely upon land, the carnal diagnosis of mental illness may not have served her well.

The right foot that is in the water represents a realm that is more liquid, a spiritual realm. The waves that rolled into my understanding the day that I met Amanda, opened my eyes to a world that runs parallel to the land but is liquid and in a sense like water.

In either example there is a reality that is boldly standing out. Whether by land or by sea, that is whether it is mental illness or demonic possession the outbursts are the results of trauma.

I can think that I have achieved some level of spiritual understanding that causes these manifestations and things to happen. I can resort to assumptions regarding my sanity, but that would belittle my faith in Jesus and the things of the spirit. I stand not to test my faith. Or I can make another assumption. I can assume that there are things that I am being shown in a manner to get my attention so that I may learn and grow. I hope that I unearth something that will allow me to help others as I learn and grow in my moral code. I hope to be strong enough the next time that the "Amanda" is set free. I hope to reach through the parameters of the spirit world and cast aside the demonic influence in my life through this tree that keeps growing. I hope to have the courage to stand up where it is needed, and I pray that I am with God in what I am thinking. I hope that I will be a part of casting out the demons that are shadowing all life around me in some capacity.

Chapter 42
The Word of Knowledge

1st Corinthians 12:8 "To one there is given through the spirit a gift of knowledge."

"I have wondered, are you even listening at all?"

The colors swirling around are the sins blending together on the backdrop. The heaviness becomes too much once again to collaborate and feast at the table. When bitterness is in your thoughts, the weight of your thoughts is heavy. Bitter thoughts influence bitter behavior. That heaviness becomes a great excuse for escape.

I want to escape. I want to run. Sex has always been my great escape, and now I have made a commitment to abstain. There are so many of these blends swirling together—countless drops of color stirring in this potion. It is a numbing potion. It is a potion of invisibility. It is a temporal solution to the problems that still protrude from wounds cut long ago. The repetition and confirmations heighten the authority of fear over my life. This merry-go-round goes around and round, like all sin, with no end. It shows up as if the same story is written page after page, with the only difference being the name of the woman, or "I'll quit after this next cigarette, beer, whiskey..." The point is that it is unsatisfying and always leaves you wanting.

In a way, as I chew over the gristle of what happened in Woodburn and climb out from under the enclosure that has placed a lid on my understanding, a whole new world has been unveiled. I now live in a world of possibilities. All that I superficially believed has shown itself to be true. I may not be seeing the angels of heaven, but there is a certain deductive reasoning that can be administered here. If there is evidence in the captions of Amanda's dialogue and actions of demons, then by default, there is a world of angels. I believed in God—the Father, Son, and Holy Spirit—but I didn't see the angels. I didn't remember but spots on a billboard.

Everything that I wanted to believe has now been revealed to me. It's like I can't process it all. There is just too much. Amanda in Woodburn has reminded me of a four-year-old boy hunting with his poodle, full of life and imagination. She also reminded me of the other four-year-old later telling me to get out of his world. "I have experienced the realm of the demonic before," I remembered. That wasn't one of the memories that was shielded from me. I had just minimized that encounter to be the mental work of a very tired and very deprived man. But now, after this, I can no longer brush it off. There is a whole world out there that I know very little about.

At church, a man sits in front of me, noticeably tortured. He sits bent over, rocking ever so slightly. I raise my hand toward him and begin to pray. The sounds of the worship team sing words of deliverance. There is a baptism taking place in the loft. This man lets out a horrifying scream. That demon has no choice but to leave. The Holy Spirit allows each of us to have a seat in the front row to watch Him overpower and cast away that demon. The man has been delivered, and that is more reason to rejoice! And the praise and worship continues.

It is amazing to be a part of these experiences. When it seems to be happening all around you, if you're not careful, you might think that you are connected to the event. Keeping mindfully modest or humble is easy as long as you understand that the motives of the Holy Spirit are His alone and that He is just engaging you as a father might place his son at the steering wheel of the car. He has no intention of allowing you to drive; He just wants to include you as a sign of His love. I watch as others take the glory of His authority. I watch as others say, "We have teams trained for deliverance. We need you to not lay hands on him." That is so egotistical. I lay hands on him because that is what the Scripture tells me to do. I do it in obedience, but it is the Spirit that casts out the demonic. He does not need my hand on him to cast that demon away. Likewise, it is not by your training that it is done. You would do well to remember that.

The prophet that has come to speak at the church tonight has most certainly received the gift. He has carefully unwrapped it, taking off the wrapping paper to reveal a beautiful gift. It is such that I am seeking with desire for the prophetic to work through me.

Before the service begins, I walk down to the altar to give an offering for the ministry of this man. This offering is small, but I do it to support his travels. I don't know anything of his gift until I begin to walk back to take a seat. He stops me.

"Wait here, I have a word for you," he says as he retrieves a microphone. "Jesus is going to bless you with your hands in properties all over Idaho and the bordering states. You are going to see prosperity like you have never seen before. He says He is doing it for you because you said, 'Lord, all that I have is yours.' When you said that, you said it with sincerity and authenticity. Lead with generosity. People will want to sow into you because you have been generous. You are generous. You have always been generous."

A tear begins to pool as I look through this tear, knowing the exact moment He is speaking of, sitting in my truck, flabbergasted and tired, surrendering. It penetrates my heart at the deepest level to know that Jesus was in that truck with me. "He says this is going to begin to happen in six months. Some will be like leeches and try to attach themselves to your mantle, but you will just simply shake them off."

Everything from a thousand miles around begins to make sense. The shards of glass on the beach are reassembling in the same manner as my own shattered soul. The melodic lines of the glass dancing through the waves are more rhapsodic now. The anticipation builds. The audio is like a trumpet calling out to the fragments of memories. The scattered sweepings come out from every dark corner to muster and reform, reconvening from behind the walls of shame.

Enough light bounces from the mirrored splinters to resemble a kaleidoscope vision of a wizard surrounding the dripping stone with his cloak. The merging of the wizard and the stone is the beginning to beat the end. The lies that have tried to define my identity perpetuated the lies I have used to establish my identity. The sin of others calling me "Jack a puss" and treating me with zero respect as a human being connected me to sin that tried to counter my self-image with lies of inflated ego. Seeking the truth is melting the stone walls of false beliefs and leading the search beyond the confinement of the maze.

"I can remember!" The Cherubim have begun to lift their flashing swords. The fig leaves have fallen to the ground, and there is no shame. Jesus is redeeming me.

Chapter 43
Never Left the Room

Psalms 91:2 "He is my refuge and my fortress; He will cover you with His feathers."

"It is the inspiration I found in her that has led me back to where we began."

Six months later, we are back at the beginning. I gather the evidence in my mind, reinforcing the similarities between us. We are not so different, she and I. It's now that I take my dream into account—I must save her from the dragon. It's clear the dragon has been living around my heart. Saving her means extracting the dragon from within me. I won't leave her trapped in this endless curse.

The cherubim have lifted their flashing swords just enough for me to glimpse the life that was meant for us. I can see it through the words written on this tree of life, and I know what I must do.

"I want to learn everything there is to know about you." These words are untarnished. They are the words of absolute truth. In all my years, these are the first words I've spoken purely from the heart since I was five years old. Every word I uttered after that had been tainted by the toxicity of treachery.

I couldn't control the statement. I couldn't contain the words. There was no disguise to mask their purity or their resonance with the universe. My feelings, once numbed and filtered through my head, now surfaced unaltered. The innocence of the statement pierced the lava that had hardened around my heart. The formation of those words broke through the darkness in my soul. My thoughts and feelings aligned completely with the will that spoke them.

Jack Taylor

I am utterly vulnerable to love. And yet, a battle rages within me against this vulnerability. I cannot surrender to it and risk being as helpless as I was in childhood. But I am trying, because I feel an almost instinctive trust in her.

The bells are still ringing in my ears. Time stands still in these observations. I flash back to my youth, and the enemy artillery begins its assault again. The sounds of bazookas and machine guns rage through my mind as the internal war persists. The blood-colored tiles on the checkered floor, the stench of rotting flesh—these are the mental photographs that haunt me.

I remember the fruit cellar and the hand that covered my mouth, bruising my face. "Say a word, and you're a dead man." Those words pierced my flesh as the dirty sock stuffed into my mouth muted my cries, leaving a bitter taste I can still recall. The blaring music of Black Sabbath, meant to drown out my sounds, plays violently in my head. Everything from my past projects itself in my mind like a horror movie.

Now I stand here, unable to respond to the disrespect of this man. I see his vile behavior, his attempt to press his face against the zipper of her pants. I feel the event in my chest, my blood boiling with rage. Yet I can't react. No acceptable response comes to mind. All I can do is stand here, trapped in awkward silence.

Every word, every detail, crashes into me with brutal force. The debris scatters around the room. If my feelings were visible, there would be brain matter splattered and sticking to the walls. The image of this tree is overwhelming as I try to understand why I am frozen here.

Every cell in my body screams for release as I remain paralyzed. The explosion of thoughts and the numbness that consumes me are a crippling force. My insecurity, my social ineptitude, only add to the weight. Pain rises from the rubble, breaking through.

I stand next to the pool table, anticipating an eruption. The flashing sword illuminates my memories in vivid, painful detail. And yet, her emerald eyes shine through, inspiring the hope and healing that becomes my only objective.

"Why aren't you talking tonight?"

Chapter 44
The Serpent's Venom

2nd Kings 4:5 "She left him and shut the door behind her and her sons."

"Moving forward into the promised land is a treasure hunt!"

"Writing is therapeutic. Jack, I want you to write out the things that come to your mind. I'd like you to care about what you write. Articulate what you feel as much as you can." The counselor's suggestion makes sense, especially when I recall the story I once wrote for the angel so many years ago—a story that is now discreetly re-entering my awareness.

As I embark on this journey, I find myself staring at a blank field—a blank page—waiting for the words to magically appear. It feels as though they've already been written in invisible ink, and all I need to do is hold a flame beneath them to reveal their truth. What began as a seed of desperation has grown into a tree, a tree with many branches that symbolize so much of my life. The words are already there, tangled within the thorns and thistles of my mind.

I imagine a poetic theme nestled within an artist's view—vines of riddles and puzzles intertwining with clandestine messages from the depths of hell. There are walls of belief reduced to rubble. A prophetic dream introduces me to my inspiration, and with her, I rediscover hope, faith, and love. Each word I place is a deliberate act of defiance, intended to dismantle the childhood coping mechanisms that once held me captive, sending them spiraling out of the window to meet their doom on the pavement below.

Awkward Silence

This journey through the past is terrifying. Make no mistake—Pennywise, in all his horror, has nothing on the sense of dread that grips my shaking hands as I write this script. It is a journey down a dark, winding road that I've traveled a thousand times before. I've given guided tours of it to counselors. I've studied psychology in the hope of self-treatment. Yet now, I am guided by an inspiration that surpasses all understanding.

The words on the page are branches of the tree that is my life. They grow in many directions, far too many to explore fully. There are stories of trauma and survival etched into those branches. I've been mugged, leading to a CAT scan. I've survived a fire that left third-degree burns over 25% of my body. I once stopped gang members from assaulting a woman, earning stitches in my head as a result. I've stolen a car from police impound, endured motorcycle and car wrecks, and the list goes on.

Some branches have been pruned away, yet the tree remains—rooted in a once-blank, empty field, now standing as a testament to perseverance. Love is woven into its pages, though not always in ways that are easy to read. Sometimes, you have to search for it.

The shards of glass scattered on a beach create a mosaic impression—a fragmented beauty. Between the pages of my story lies the ongoing search for who I am. The trouble with blind spots or missing shards is their tendency to shape habits and beliefs in ways that feel inevitable. Beneath the ground, roots twist and turn, influencing the growth above. Yet as the tree rises, it offers glimpses into a less cluttered version of what's happening inside me.

The missing memories feel vital, as though they hold significance beyond what anyone could imagine—perhaps even biblical implications. Reviewing the design of these pages means turning each word inside out, examining them from every angle in search of new insights.

As I read this personal tablet of history, I am struck by the contempt I hold for myself. Why do I deliberately, perhaps subconsciously, sabotage everything that matters to me? The fire I inhale through the filter burns low, and the smoke rises—a screen for my insecurities to hide behind. I notice how fluently the cigarettes flow during precarious social moments, as if they're a silent companion to my discomfort.

Like fool's gold, there is also a fool's hope. We can hope for the brilliance of earthly wealth, for all the glimmer and shine of eloquent things. Or we can hope for joy, peace, and love to finally claim a place on higher ground in our hearts. Fool's hope, however, is rooted in unmoved soil. It has a glittery allure that draws your attention, but it lacks the substance needed to nourish growth. The key difference between fool's hope and true hope lies in their impact on moral character. Fool's hope does not inspire growth, whereas true hope does.

There is no shortcut to unearthing true hope. It reveals itself only when you are ready. Its power leads you toward becoming a better person, away from sin and selfish desires, and toward a purpose greater than yourself. In its purest form, hope inspires. It is not a fleeting wish. It demands dedication and long suffering. It requires the kind of faith that can move mountains—the obstacles that obscure your view of hope. The enemy will try to offer distorted views of hope, creating detours that masquerade as shortcuts, but there are no shortcuts.

For me, inspiration is my hope. I imagine myself running toward her in a meadow. The inspiration she has given me has set me on the path to healing from past afflictions. She has been monumental in guiding me toward forgiveness and repentance. She has made me want to become a better man.

Awkward Silence

Though she is not committed to me, from the moment I committed myself to her, I have avoided the stumbling blocks that lead to instant gratification. My commitment to her has strengthened my commitment to God. I am convinced He sent her to me as a tangible way to fulfill my devotion to Him.

She has become the force that holds me steady when avoidance tries to take over. Avoidance has many faces—writer's block, procrastination, or the urge to embellish the storyline. It has literally bounced me from wall to wall, had me pacing the floor, and muttering to myself. But my hope in her and the inspiration she provides have kept me grounded, focused on the objective of healing.

This writing—good or bad—would not exist without the hope she has instilled in me. Her influence has shaken my emotions and cut through the rock-hard barriers within me. She has opened my heart and inspired me to reach out and make a difference in the world.

To honor her, I have founded Divine Fortress Ministries, a safe place for people to heal from PTSD, CPTSD, and other trauma-related afflictions. It's a testament to the power of hope and her role in my journey.

The first demon I had to face in this process was fear—not the fear of surface-level dangers, but deep-rooted fears that creep in and out in unexpected ways. Avoidance is one such fear. It often disguises itself as writer's block or procrastination, attempting to pull me away from my purpose. I have had to fight it relentlessly, forcing myself to remain seated and committed to this path of healing.

This time, the journey through my past feels like the last time I'm willing to tread this pitch-black path. If I can't find resolution now, I will throw in the towel and accept that it simply is what it is. But don't worry—I am highly motivated. Still, I feel as though my soul has been through a paper shredder, my thoughts left behind as scattered strips in the waste bin. This time, the stakes feel transcendent—like it's the difference between running through the meadow toward hope or surrendering entirely, carrying someone in my arms.

The journey feels eerier than ever, as though a beast is stalking me in the shadows, waiting to pounce. A thick fog, smog, or mist hangs in the air—not just something you can smell but something that leaves a residue on the roof of your mouth, bitter and heavy, reminiscent of smoldering brimstone.

I've walked this road before with counselors. My original diagnosis was PTSD—more specifically, IBS linked to PTSD. At the time, I didn't understand the profound physical effects PTSD could have. It was like staring at a butterfly in the field, completely unaware that a baseball was hurtling toward me.

Complex PTSD is an even more tangled web. It occurs during early developmental periods, disrupting the normal growth and learning processes of a child. Many of us reach adulthood with certain stages of emotional and psychological development completely stunted. For me, the result was a diagnosis of dissociative identity disorder and severe apathy—a fishing net full of detestable things, a true hodgepodge of discombobulated emotions.

Dissociative identity disorder, as I've experienced it, isn't the dramatic multiple-personality portrayal often seen in media. It's triggered by stress and can manifest subtly, much like how someone might instinctively reach for a cigarette to cope with tension. In some cases, it's even helpful—detaching from oneself in emergencies can allow calmness to prevail. But more often, it's a disconnection from emotions that wreaks havoc, burning bridges and sabotaging relationships in reckless, destructive ways.

Awkward Silence

When you connect with someone who has been tortured by these experiences, you often see their truest self in moments of calm. In those peaceful settings, their genuine character shines through. But even mild stress can bring out a version of them that feels completely unfamiliar.

The world, for all its medical advancements and terminology, doesn't offer much to patch the potholes left by trauma. Terms like "dissociative identity disorder" may add credibility to the professionals, but they can also complicate a person's self-image. These big, clinical words often prey on vulnerability, inadvertently creating a reverse placebo effect. They fill the gaps in understanding with convoluted concepts that only deepen the confusion. While this isn't always intentional, the simplicity of how things began often gets lost in translation.

Still, I digress. The world does offer some helpful insights. Objective opinions can sometimes facilitate healing, even if they feel like looking at a snake on a pole. The biblical story comes to mind—God instructed the Israelites to look upon the bronze serpent for healing from venomous bites. Today, the snake on the pole remains the symbol of medicine. But while this path may offer relief, I long for total healing, free of scars.

For that, I can only look to God.

I send the incense up to the heavens, and the vapours drift back down. That's when the conversation begins with the Great Counsellor. At first, the voice feels indistinguishable from my own, but soon, His character sets it apart. He speaks with authority, wisdom, and knowledge that surpass my understanding.

"Jack, did you get any relief from writing out your story?" He asks, a raised brow punctuating the question.

"Honestly?" I pause, searching for the right words. "It's been a task."

"Of course." His tone dips, carrying a faint note of disappointment.

"Maybe a little," I admit, "but I still feel like I have a noose around my neck."

"You need to keep evaluating it and re-scripting it. In time, you'll understand its value."

"I definitely became aware of some things I've been avoiding." I manage a small smile.

"Good. Keep after those things." He flexes—an unexpected gesture that leaves me puzzled.

"I will."

"Looking at your story, Jack, I can see that you might be holding onto anger. You need to find a way to express it."

"I thought I was expressing it through my writing," I reply, uncertain.

"Jack," He says gently but firmly, "consider how you were beaten and mistreated. I'm shocked you're not as vulgar as the demon you encountered in Amanda."

"Well," I say cautiously, "I suppose it's a good thing I'm not a demon and have no desire to become one."

"Seriously, Jack," He presses, "bottled anger creates stress and tension that will rip you apart. Here—take this paper. Visualise what happened to you and tear it to shreds. Pour your anger into it."

I stare at the paper, sceptical. "But there's always more," I say. "It feels like a bottomless pit of anger, and I don't want to be stuck in a pit."

"Anger is a secondary emotion," He explains. "It stems from a primary emotion, often hurt. If you can't resolve the pain, it manifests as anger. Forgiveness can dissipate anger and redirect that energy constructively.

"When you feel powerless over the pain, you might avoid conflict altogether. But avoidance feeds anger, and that anger festers. Over time, it traps you. Without healthy ways to manage conflict, you either explode in a fight or avoid everything—becoming, perhaps, a doormat. And eventually, even a doormat snaps, turning passive-aggressive."

He turns slightly, as though embodying avoidance itself.

"Yeah, that hits home. That's me, times two."

"Good. This week, I want you to focus on expressing your anger constructively."

I take His advice to heart.

During the week, I threw myself into physical outlets. I spent hours at the gym hitting the bag, lifting weights, and running miles upon miles. I wrote angry music, releasing the turmoil into words and chords. Yet, I found that even small, destructive acts offered a strange sense of relief. I threw litter to the ground and smashed bottles—each shatter of glass soothing something primal within me.

Walking back into his office the following week, I felt a wave of dread rising in me. But this time, I refused to let avoidance win.

"So, Jack, did it help?" he asked the moment I entered, skipping any pleasantries.

"Like I said, it feels like a bottomless pit," I replied. "My anger actually seemed to grow stronger."

"Hmm," he murmured, tilting his head slightly. "Well, what did you do?"

"I punched the bag at the gym, ran extra miles, broke things, and pumped weights."

"Well, it sounds like it helped your workout," he observed, a faint smile playing on his lips.

"Yeah, it would be great if I wasn't still getting set off by triggers," I said, frustration creeping into my voice.

"Before we get to the triggers, I want to ask you—did you use more or less energy this past week?"

"I used more energy," I answered, feeling like the question was unnecessary given everything I had just described.

"Then there are two ways to look at this," he said. "You're either wasting too much energy on your anger, or when you focus on it, you can actually accomplish more."

"I see what you're saying," I admitted, "but until I learn to control it, I'm just wasting energy and destroying my relationships."

"How are you destroying your relationships?" he asked, leaning forward.

"Jealousy," I admitted. "It triggers me to act out—or, as you can see from my writing, to respond in awkward ways."

"Jealousy? What have you got to be jealous of?" he asked, as though the idea was absurd.

I hesitated, thinking it might have been rhetorical.

"Earth to Jack," he said, waving a hand. "What have you got to be jealous of?"

"Sorry," I said. "I thought it was rhetorical. Honestly, I could write books about what I'm jealous of."

"Jack, you're incredibly talented on the guitar," he said firmly. "And that's not just based on your writing—I've seen you play. You're an attractive man with a huge heart. You're a master electrician, and you didn't earn that by being dumb."

"I've studied nearly every topic under the sun," I said, brushing off the compliments, "but I'm so socially inept it's pathetic."

"I don't buy that," he said, shaking his head. "You're being social with me right now, and you carry a conversation better than most."

"Sure," I said. "But I'm comfortable in this setting. It's when I try to fit into other social environments that I struggle. My jokes are often misunderstood. Some of them are funny, but I feel like I need an interpreter to deliver them."

"Okay," he said, steering us back. "Let's return to the jealousy. What does it look like when you're jealous?" He gazed thoughtfully at the pencil he was holding between his hands.

"There are a few different faces it can wear," I explained. "The most common one, which I wrote about, is that I shut down and commit myself to defeat. I can act irrationally or weirdly.

Sometimes I speed off in frustration or become a massive pain to be around."

"Do you think you could train yourself to handle jealousy better?"

"I've thought about it a lot," I said. "Take the example I described in my writing—standing there shut down. I shouldn't have let it bother me at all. First, I shouldn't have been triggered by jealousy in the first place—I have so much more to offer than that guy. And second, I should've shown trust in her."

"I can see why trust could be a major problem for you. Jack, you haven't been able to trust anyone who's meant anything to you since you were six years old. You basically raised yourself and took on the responsibility of being the head of your family. Building trust has to be difficult. Now, here comes someone you decide you want to let in, and as you put it, you opened the door with no way to close it."

My eyes begin to well up, but I stop the tears before they can fall.

"If I could even remotely predict the feelings I was going to have, I might have been able to respond with poise. But like I said, it's irrational and almost always instantly triggered. If I could take a moment to breathe, I might be able to prepare for any possible scenario and handle it appropriately. It's so damn irrational, though. I mean, what could I possibly be jealous of with this guy who's so vulgar? The thing is, I immediately look past his shortcomings and amplify my own."

He looks at me with doubt in his eyes.

"I believe you amplify your own, but I don't believe for a second that you look past his. I think you immediately knew what his intentions were, and you'd already formed an opinion of his character. Hell, Jack, I think you probably already analyzed why he's that way. You probably knew his home life was unstable and that he had no respect for his mother. That all feeds into your protective instincts."

"You're right, I did."

"Of course you did. That's the protective part of your character. As the head of your house, this is the insight you've gained from being the protector. It's very instinctive for you to measure up any threat that might come. The only thing is, you need to learn acceptable ways of dealing with it." He pauses, watching my thoughts turn. "How might you have handled it differently?"

"The truth is, I don't know if I could have. I was really drawn into the heavy thoughts of my past—specifically, my aunt's hand over my face. I felt the anxiety of Nick coming down the stairs. It was just like how I portrayed it in my writing. If I could've gotten control of myself, it probably would've depended on when I gained that control. If I'd regained composure by the time she asked me why I wasn't talking, I'd have just been honest and said that I don't feel comfortable with his behavior toward her. I'd have hoped for my composure to never leave me. Maybe I'd have just been friendly with him and tried to talk to him as if he were a friend."

"Conflict resolution is a subject all on its own. Making a friend is probably the best approach. You don't have to agree with someone to be friendly. Let's play that out a little further. You become friendly, and you're free to express yourself in a kind way.

'Hey, can I talk to you about something?'
'Okay.'
'I didn't think we were going to be able to get along.'
'Why's   that?'

425

'I just think it's important to treat women respectfully, even in a bar setting. But it does seem like, otherwise, you're a pretty good dude.'

What do you think?"

"Ya keep your friends close and your enemies closer."

"That's not really what I'm saying. I think you have a loving heart and experience that can be shared. I believe you might have been able to form a bond that could've impacted him in a positive way. Who knows? He might've even become less obstinate." There's something about the way he says this that reaches me in an undefinable way. There's something here I need to process.

"That would be a long day to watch a sun that may or may not set."

"The ghouls that haunt you can teach you a lot." I smile.

"I look to drive a stake through the heart of all those experiences, and you suggest they might teach me something?"

"Sometimes we can acquire knowledge when we learn what not to do. What would Nick have done in this situation to deal with his jealousy?" This point is already pretty clear.

"He probably would've hit him from behind and just kept swinging."

"And your uncle? What was his provocation for shooting the man in the bar?"

"It was jealousy." I feel an urge to sink into the chair.

"The truth is, Jack, we're all going to experience jealousy at some point in our lives, but we can choose to handle it like Nick, like Ted, or we can try something neither of them would. We already know they're not good models for the man you want to become, so don't follow their footprints. Try to turn the other cheek and fight the evil intentions of the vulgar man with all the goodness in your heart." He's whittling down to a good point.

"It's easy to see now, sitting here without the threat in front of me." This sounds like resistance, but I don't want to resist this message.

"I think I remember hearing you were a state champion in martial arts. Am I remembering that correctly?" Wow, that was a long time ago. I was only twelve years old.

"Yes, but that was a very long time ago." I was just in junior high—how could he possibly have heard about that, let alone remembered?

"I was working with a high school student you went up against. I think you were only in the sixth grade, but you learned how to fight against bigger opponents."

"Yeah, I'd drop under their kicks and score a point with a groin shot. I used my short stature as a tool. Then I'd go for a sweep. I mastered that move and didn't often have to do much else that year. The next year, there was a senior in high school who went full contact with me. He caught me with a roundhouse that rocked my world. I got even with him. He kicked me in the face, so I did a dropkick and didn't stop contact. That groin shot could've been heard around the world. I did win the championship that year, but it was a pretty dirty match."

"That was the student I'm talking about. Anyway, you had to learn a style of fighting to compete with kids who were bigger,

427

older, and stronger than you. And any time you learn a new style of fighting, you have to practice. The methods you learned as a child to cope with jealousy, anger, or pain were to lock it up. You could've followed Nick or Ted's example, but that wouldn't have worked for you. You saw the other kids playing, but you weren't allowed to. All you could do was walk by and ignore the fact that you had feelings. I'm sorry, Jack, but you're human. You're part of the human race. You're allowed to have feelings. And sometimes jealousy gets thrown into the mix. We're going to do everything we can to help you realize what an amazing man you are, but you're going to have to learn a new style of kung fu."

"Yeah, I can't let jealousy trigger anger." I've been taken under by this before.

"Why not? We've already established that when you focus that anger, you can accomplish great things." His logic is sound.

"So I'm supposed to use his face as a punching bag?" I laugh, knowing that's not what he means, but I'm still not sure I understand his point—and I'm avoiding the intimacy of our conversation.

"Tell me, Jack. While you were analyzing the vulgar guy, did you start to justify his rudeness?" I'm all ears now.

"Yes. I first blamed it on the fact that he was high."

"Have you ever heard the saying, 'Hate the sin, not the sinner'?" He taps his pencil.

"Yes."

"How much easier would it be to make a new friend if you could separate the sin from the man and focus all that anger energy on intelligently showing him what's up?" The noise of a passing car sweeps in, momentarily taking my attention.

"From the moment he came in, he didn't make it easy to see anything other than the sin." I try to break free of this thought.

"Don't fight me on this," he says in a commanding tone.

"I understand. I really do. It would make it much easier to like him if I weren't looking through the lens of judgment. But it was the sin that so boldly heated up the room."

"Jack, what would happen if you apologized to him for being judgmental and forgave yourself for casting that judgment?" Once again, he fires from an angle I didn't see coming.

"It would release me from the chains around my judgment." I give a stiff smile.

"Then you need a strategy that fights the sin but loves the sinner. That's the new kung fu I'm talking about. And what if, instead of wasting energy on anger, you used it to show Candice how much you value her? Use the opportunity to tell her how much you appreciate her."

Wow, that strikes a nerve.

"Okay, I was out of control. But how do I fight the sin?" I'm acutely aware of my shortcomings—that's why I'm here.

"Don't let his raunchy behavior splatter on you. Counter his behavior with the antics of politeness and love. Let the man develop his own sense of morals." Again, the sound of a car momentarily distracts me.

"That's a tough one. How can I practice this when the situation isn't staring me in the eyes anymore? I'm going to need practice to get this into my heart."

"You may be misunderstanding. Remember how you said if it was appropriate, you would have marked her with urine. She was the target of his lewdness. She should be your target for politeness and love." I know what he says is true, but again, I felt I had no control over my reactions—or at least it felt that way.

"Actually, she should be the recipient of the feelings I have for her. I don't want to think that I'm targeting her with love and politeness. I should have just authentically expressed my love and affections for her. His actions had nothing to do with her, but somehow, I punished her." The disappointment I have in myself is beyond words.

"Does she know of your feelings for her?"

"That's a bit of a tricky question. She knows what I say I feel. She knows I'd do anything for her. But I'd still have to answer that with a no. After that night, my insecurities sat high upon my throne. It wasn't the only night I let jealousy out of the cage. I ran a trucker off who came into the bar. I was so insecure that I began to brag about who I am. I never really settled that. I became someone I'm not."

"So you didn't trust her with the real you?" Again, I hang my head.

"No, I had insecurities that took over, and no, I didn't trust her." Those are issues from your past. It would make it difficult for anyone to regain trust after that.

"Then you didn't love her, because without trust, there's no love." She's the inspiration that brings me here. That must mean something.

"I know you're right about that, but there were moments between the pages. There were some moments where I saw her— those times when her adventurous spirit came out. Those moments when I really saw the woman God created, and in those moments, I had complete trust."

"Do you think she was hiding behind a mask as well?"

"I don't think I created a safe place for her to be herself. I think initially, my insecurities rose up and took away her sense of security." There's something in this jargon—I'm reaching a pivotal moment.

"It sounds like she may have an issue with trust as well."

"How could she trust me? I didn't give her the real me to be trusted." I defend her.

"I agree, Jack. I think trust is the biggest culprit in the demise of that relationship. She sounds wonderful, and I know you're wonderful. I would love for you to learn to trust each other. I'd really like to work on your ability to trust this week, but I think until you can feel, in your heart, the trueness of your identity and know how amazing you are, you won't be able to trust. Too much trust has been given to those who tore you down—your family in particular. As long as you trust them at all, you may never trust anyone else because their words and actions contradict the truth." He looks over the top of his readers.

"No, I accept that they're liars. I've even analyzed what makes them that way. I don't talk to them other than I go to see my mom once a week." I hear someone in the outer office, which makes me consider trust even more.

"Do you trust your mom with personal information?" I feel a desire to avoid this.

"What do you mean? My mom knows me. She's my mom." He shuffles a couple of pages on his desk.

"Jack, I don't think your mom knows you as well as you think she does. I think you're putting entirely too much trust in a woman who allowed you to be tortured. Her vision of you is not reality. I'm sorry to be saying this, but her oblivious-to-the-world approach to life keeps you trying to take care of her." He again taps his pencil on the desk.

"Yeah, and now she's nearing eighty, and it's true. I go see her out of responsibility more than a desire to see her. I keep hoping that will change before she exits this world, but I'm truly afraid I'll be left with regrets."

"Those are some heavy chains," he says.

"Indeed."

"So, when you're talking with your mom, do you tell her about Candice?" He knows this is all with me wanting to avoid but he keeps pressing through.

"Yes, I suppose I do."

"Do you recognize that she speaks words of doubt and lack of trust?" He isn't going to let go of this bone.

"Yes, I suppose sometimes I catch those words. Those words have caused fights between us in the past with different situations." I recall getting pretty mad at her for this exact reason.

"Then you can see the point that I'm getting at. Her words do carry weight, and the words that she has spoken throughout the years have hurt if not demolished the man you see in the mirror." His point is more than valid.

"I can feel what you're saying is true, but God commands us to honor our parents."

"How do you give honor to them by sitting through their lies? No, simply by living an honorable life." He eloquently makes the point.

I know that most of the walls of the maze have been built by my family, particularly the walls that garble the picture I carry of myself. I declare that the picture has more holes in it than a block of Swiss cheese. Every peep at that picture is a look at someone different than who I know in my heart.

"Okay, Jack, I want you to write down the dialogue you have about yourself. If someone gives you a compliment, I want you to say, 'Thank you. God made me this way.' If someone tries to speak negatively, I want you to say, 'I reject that. God tells me differently, and God is not a liar. I rebuke that in the name of Jesus.' It doesn't matter how small the insult—rebuke it in the name of Jesus. Write down the exchanges as well."

Chapter 45
Covert Messages

Psalms 119:130 "The unfolding of your words gives light, it imparts understanding to the simple."

"Sometimes things aren't just as they appear."

To be honest, with the advancement of science and the naming of photons, the theories of old hold just as much value as anything else science has proposed. A belief in how light projects doesn't change its worth. Maybe, when you flip a light switch, it simply opens a portal of suction—like a vacuum, pulling in the darkness. The claws of the darkness, trying to avoid being sucked into the abyss, tear their way through flesh and bone.

No, I believe the light presents itself in battle, overtaking the darkness. The light lines up, ready for combat. The battle drums beat with rhythms that call to your heart, but until the trumpet blows, the light is merely potential energy—like an army waiting to be unleashed. Most of it is the wasted energy of anger and disgust, unfocused and without a clear battle plan.

Sure, some of your heartstrings may be tugged by issues laid before you, but you remain dormant. You might be frozen in fear. You might believe your life is meant to be lived behind a white picket fence, and because there's a semblance of peace in your world, you think nothing needs to be done. Meanwhile, the darkness actively consumes your neighbor, your brother, your friend.

The war is real. Once it devours your neighbor, your brother, and your friend, it will come for you. Unless we stand together, it will eventually consume us all.

Awkward Silence

I had many people who gave me hope. There was Miss Stanley, Reuben, the principal at Golfview, the nurse, and Mr. Flowers—all of them took the initiative. These were people who may have saved my life. Then there were the literal angels God sent to me. These are the people whose opinions should have mattered most. The light in their hearts was enough to overtake an army of darkness. These five people stood against the darkness and won, but their ability to remain consistent wasn't enough.

I'm not dead—and that may truly be because of their efforts.

The battleground, though, is in my mind.

"What the hell is this? A diary? What are you, a pussy? What's in it? It better not say my name once," Nick bellows, fire practically raging from his nostrils.

"I have to write in the journal for class. I don't even want to do this stupid assignment," I mumble.

He grabs it and starts to read.

"What's this? You can't even write. Are you even literate? This looks like—what are you, in the third grade?"

"I'm in the first grade," I reply.

"Well, it doesn't show."

The flashbacks hit me as I try to respond to the counselor's request. This isn't really what he asked for, but the assignment feels like a wooden spoon stirring a kettle of muck. The shadows rise up that quickly.

The counselor wants me to write the words that define my self-image. Just opening the journal and seeing the blank pages is discouraging. The words of the demon—possessing my cousin and tormenting me for years—bubble up, unbidden.

"I suppose I should tell you that I didn't submit your story for the contest," my teacher says. "I couldn't pick your story as the winner to submit."

I think maybe I'm a little disappointed. I think it even shows. I thought she'd grasp the meaning of my words. I thought, of all people, she would understand—maybe even relate, just a little.

Maybe Nick is right.

"Mom, listen to this. This is what Jack wrote for his class project," Nick says, pulling my journal assignment into his twisted spotlight.

He begins to read:

"When the lights turn off as I lie awake in bed, I can see the shadows of the furniture begin to rise. They are the monsters of darkness, uprising against the light. They are the enemy that walks in the damp, gloomy basement. The rattling of the boxes stored around me is nothing more than the souls sacrificed before I arrived. These are the cells where my cousin's childhood dreams were sent to die.

I can feel its breath behind me, and I shudder, anticipating its attack. The groaning of agony is the only sound I hear as its fist plunges into the back of my skull. The demons lurking outside guard the bones locked tightly in the closet."

Nick closes the journal and smirks.

"What the hell is that? That's not a journal. A journal has a date, then an entry. It talks about real things, like how the dog dragged me down the street chasing a squirrel. Do you even live in reality? You need to rewrite it like an actual journal," my aunt snaps, her voice dripping with condescension as she takes Nick's side.

Together, they rip the page—and my heart—into shreds.

I remember that day so vividly I can still recite the words exactly as I wrote them. I can still feel the sting of their laughter, the humiliation as they mocked what came from my soul.

"Your story is incredible. For a third grader to write like this is astounding. At first, I thought you might have copied it from somewhere," Miss Stanley had told me later.

"I didn't. It's my story," I replied, defensive but hopeful.

"I know, Jack. As I read it, I began to see glimpses of who you are. Then I started to piece together what experiences might have shaped it."

"Don't dig too deeply, Miss Stanley. Some of those bones need to stay buried—for now." But even as I said it, I could feel the backhoe already breaking the surface of those graves.

"I understand," she said gently. "I've thought about the discussions we've had about your gift, and I've decided to protect you as much as I can."

She was sincere but, in a way, clueless.

It doesn't matter how deep the grave is—some bones always find their way to the surface.

"Okay, Jack, I read what you wrote for this week," the counselor says, his brow furrowed. "I thought this assignment was supposed to focus on your self-talk. Was that not clear to you?"

He glances at me, puzzled, waiting for an answer.

"I can see where the voices of your cousin and your aunt might influence how you see yourself," he continues. "I can also see how Miss Stanley and others have played a positive role. But what does this all mean to you?"

I take a deep breath, forcing the words out. "I had to keep my mouth shut. I wasn't allowed to tell anyone what was happening in hell. So, I thought, if I couldn't speak the words, I'd write them. Since I was little, I've been trying to send covert messages to my teachers through my assignments. Message after message, bottle after bottle—I kept hoping that one day, someone would read what I wrote and rescue me from the deserted island I was stranded on."

The room is silent for a moment.

"I'm still doing it," I confess, my voice breaking. "Day after day, I write the same message, over and over, in a thousand different ways. And I'm still hoping to be rescued."

""It still isn't clear to me. What are the things that shape what you believe about yourself?" he asks me again.

"When Nick and Corine mocked my assignment and told me their version of what a journal is supposed to be, they didn't decode the message. They said I couldn't write, that my words didn't express anything of value, and, essentially, that I was worthless. Still, I held onto the hope that someday someone would decode my message. Every time I wrote, I expected someone to discover me. I even wrote music with the same S.O.S. embedded within it. I believed in my heart that I was meant to be a writer because I had to keep silent about everything else. I poured every ounce of magic I carried in my soul into my cry for help, but it was never enough." I took a deep breath.

"The truth is, I placed so much value on my ability to write. The message has always been clear to me, but if no one else understands it, then maybe I don't belong. Maybe Nick and Corine were right. If I can't write well enough to save my life, then maybe I'm not worth saving. Either the message I sent wasn't as evident as I thought, or they just didn't care enough to see beyond the grade. I put so much of myself into those messages that they became a part of who I am. I placed my trust in others to help me, only to be left empty-handed."

"I see. But Jack, how did you come to that conclusion this week?" he prodded.

"Because even as I was writing out the arguments presented at the boardroom table in my mind, it was the act of writing—how to express those arguments—that overshadowed the conflict itself." I paused, hoping my explanation made sense.

"Jack, give me a moment to think this through. There's a lot to unpack here, and I want to be sure I fully understand." He seemed to drift into another dimension for a moment before returning.

"Jack, you are more than the sum of your abilities or accomplishments. You are not defined by anyone else's judgment—only your own. If I were to define you, I'd place you on a pedestal as someone with the potential to change the world. But even my evaluation means nothing unless you choose to believe it." He tried to encourage me.

"I think what I've been asking you this week is whether I have to reject your compliment," I said hesitantly.

"Yes, Jack. And you see, the voices of people like your cousin or your aunt, the ones who stand against you, need to fall away. You must let go of their influence and allow them to rise or fall on their own."

"I know their opinions shouldn't matter, especially since I've seen how tormented they are. But somehow, their hurtful words still linger." I sighed, feeling the weight of it.

"Jack, you're trying to overpower their words. You're fighting them. But you heard those words as a child, and you're still trying to fight them as that same child. No. You'll struggle your entire life if you try to defeat them in a fair fight. The answer is forgiveness. When you forgive them, their words will lose their power. You're so busy trying to prove them wrong, yet you're still standing before them, absorbing their insults. Forgiveness is the answer. And Jack, you also need to forgive those who didn't understand your messages. Most importantly, you need to forgive yourself.

"You have to know that you can write, Jack. It wasn't your fault. Your words were never the problem. And you have to let go of the idea that it's anyone's fault—not the teachers, not the critics, not yourself. Forgiveness is not about judgment; it's about freedom."

There is a long moment of silence as I soak in the dialogue we just had. In some circles, forgiveness is considered weak. Some people believe that anger and resentment fuel a fire, one that will consume their enemies as long as it burns. But that's not what bitterness does. Bitterness turns inward, poisoning the self and those we truly care about. It shows up in passive-aggressive actions, subtle but damaging. It is a fire, but hell is not my destination.

"When you said you would place me on a pedestal, the first thought that came to mind was, 'Take my hand so I may help pull you up.'" The mental imagery felt arbitrary.

Awkward Silence

"Was there ever a moment when you thought about falling off?"

"Yes," I admitted, "but then I thought about the opportunity I'd have to help others." The conversation felt abstract.

"What if I took your hand and pulled you down?"

"Well, that's possible," he replied, "but since you have a heart for counsel, and you're the one who placed me here, I don't believe you would." The hum of the air conditioning filled the room.

"That raises a good point," I said. "People often see what they want to see in you, almost like a reflection of themselves. You can't control how others perceive you. When you said your insecurities hid your authentic self and made you boastful, would you say that was an attempt to control how she felt about you?"

"Yes," I admitted. "That's very clear to me now. In fact, I started to realize that a while back, but my pride got in the way. I painted a picture of how I saw Superman and hoped she would see me the same way. It was foolish. I was trying to protect myself from being hurt by how she might truly see me."

"Why is it so important for her to see you a certain way? I can see how it might have felt like protection, but it also shows a lack of trust. The Bible says that love always trusts. Perhaps this is what it was referring to."

"A lot has changed in me since then," I said. "I'm much more willing to be humble now. My pride is still there, but the part of it that keeps me from learning is fading. I no longer want to stand on a soapbox without the rest of the world standing beside me. We're all in this together."

"Jack, I feel like our discussion took a direction I hadn't expected today, but that's not a bad thing. We've uncovered a lot about where you've been, where you're going, and how forgiveness will play a part in that journey. The path wasn't as straightforward as I imagined, but the reason you want to write has become much clearer. We've also identified the obstacles—the venom of the serpent—that have discouraged your ability to communicate directly.

"I want you to remember this: while that venom left a powerful mark on your past, it no longer holds relevance. The past has shaped the present, and the present will shape the future. This week, I want you to deliberately and purposefully forgive anyone who stands in your way. If you find yourself doubting your capabilities, stop immediately and forgive the one whose voice stands against you. Does that make sense?"

I nodded, hearing his next appointment arrive in the outer room. "Yes, but what if I don't know where the 'I can't' is coming from?"

"Forgiveness is important," he said. "Seek it out, and the answer will come to you. You'll discover who or what is standing in your way." His confidence made me think he was right. The missing puzzle piece would reveal itself.

The vipers biting in the desert, as described in the book of Exodus, came from the Israelites' inability to grow into their new reality. They clung to the past, complaining without cause. They were given meat for dinner and manna each morning, protected from every enemy. Their complaints came from discomfort and a longing for the familiar, even though they had the God of heaven and earth leading them in ways greater than they had ever known. He would have healed them from the venom of the serpents if they had lifted their eyes to Him. For the venom of the serpents in my own life, I will lift my eyes to heaven. I will forgive.

Awkward Silence

"Jack, for our next session, I want us to refocus. Let go of the slithering words of those who represent the negativity in your life. Forgive them. Together, we'll work to uncover your true identity. You said your insecurities led to an inauthentic projection of yourself. I'd venture to say you may have never fully known who you are. Between now and then, read through your story and search for what feels authentically *you*."

Chapter 46
Finally Finding Identity

1st Peter 2:9 "But you are a chosen people, a royal priesthood. A holy nation..."

"Disagreeing with the venom of those that put you down."

I have been digging deeply into the soil of my story, turning shovels full of dirt upside down and clearing away thorns and thistles, only to uncover a few precious gems. That bear I scared off during my hunt with Snowball was a moment of identity exposure. God made me imaginative, creative, compassionate, loving, courageous, strong, generous, protective, and passionate. God made me amazing! This revelation brings me to my knees in gratitude. I embrace this identity with humility, giving God the glory. After all, I wouldn't know how to create such a being even with detailed schematics laid out before me. He sculpted me from the dust of the earth and infused me with the essence of who I am.

I don't believe this is the full disclosure of my identity, though. In this mining expedition, I've cleared away debris to uncover integrity, patience, and kindness as well. I will not stop this search because my identity is the person God created for fellowship with Him.

Just as the gems of my identity have surfaced, so has the temperament of a character formed by the pain and turmoil I've endured. This character is disruptive, hindering the natural growth of my true self and my spirit. I didn't have a psychologist who could articulate the damage, but I found solace within myself by separating who I am—the gems I've unearthed—from who the evil in my life tried to make me.

"Jack, I like how you've framed this as a mining expedition," he says, his voice warm with encouragement. "It shows your creativity and a stronger connection to who you truly are. In the Bible, hidden within its stories are also gems and nuggets waiting to be found. Did you know that a deeper revelation of who you are can be discovered in the very beginning?"

"I've often wondered what that means," I reply with a shrug.

"Well, one way to think about it is that you need to read more to uncover it. But there's something profound about how you've articulated that God is love. Love has a character—it's patient, kind, humble, and doesn't boast. You could say that everything describing love is a reflection of the characteristics you were created to embody."

"I see your point," I say thoughtfully. "So, abuse and trauma are meant to separate us from that identity. They cling to us to maintain that divide, and CPTSD becomes a battle over the soul. The violations and sins distort and contort the identity of the one enduring the pain."

"Exactly, Jack. You're right," he says, leaning forward. "The acronym CPTSD came long after the battle began. It always has been—and still is—an attack by the evil one. Evil connects to the aggressor through aggression, carrying out a diabolical and relentless crusade against the defenseless. It's a cowardly invasion."

"The dark forces would have defined the conditions that shaped my identity," I say, the words flowing freely now. "I could have walked through life as a man divided in moral character. That dissociation from moral character is also a dissociation from identity. But our true identity was established on the day of creation."

"Jack, it seems like you've already given this a lot of thought," he observes.

"To some degree, yes," I admit. "When I was uncovering those gems, I realized I might never have recognized them without this effort. Left to those dark forces, I would have defined myself the way they wanted me to. I would have buried myself in ignorance, believing that God made a mistake in creating me. My faith in God would have faltered constantly. I might never have understood the fight for my soul and my life. Instead, I might have accepted CPTSD as the disorder that defines me."

"Jack," he says gently, "CPTSD is a legitimate response to the conditions normalized by prolonged trauma. It's predictable in many cases, given the circumstances. But worldly diagnoses often try to fit people into boxes—defining them by symptoms rather than understanding their wholeness. Don't feel bad; they've been trying to fit God into a box they can understand too. You're in good company." He leans forward, his tone insistent. "The question is, who are you?"

I realize he's asking what I will allow to define me. I raise my sword once again to cut the gems free from the lava. It feels like serving divorce papers to the devil. Living under the same roof as toxicity hides the gems in stone. I exhume the precious ornaments of my character and uncover another treasure: God made me exciting and excitable. This revelation fills me with joy.

I continue turning the soil, mining for more gems, but I also notice that many of the attributes I lack are those that define love. I've been boastful, jealous, and envious. These flaws remind me that my excavation is far from over. But with every swing of the sword, I'm one step closer to the truth of who I am and who I was created to be.

Awkward Silence

In discovering that these writings conceal a wealth of authentication, we may also uncover where many demons hide. By reshaping how we write, therapeutically, we might flush more demons out onto the pages. There is a breadcrumb trail here, one that determines my perspective of the world. The walls of false beliefs build a maze in which I get trapped, leaving me in destitution. You must care about yourself, even a little, to desire healing. Compassion is essential for forgiveness. Healing from trauma requires tremendous effort, time, good nature, inspiration, and love. When you can extract enough love to get started, the treasure hunt becomes invigorating. It is exciting! It's the force that keeps the rock rolling downhill, becoming more engaging and fulfilling than any video game.

The "land of treachery" isn't grim enough to describe apathy. To be numb doesn't sound like a big deal—it might even seem helpful, like being numbed by a dentist for a filling. But apathy is more than detachment from feeling. Like me, you might try to simulate feelings, imagining what something should feel like, but that doesn't capture the grim reality of apathy. It takes a high voltage to restart a heart buried under layers of lava. It's harrowing to reflect on the relational encounters of an apathetic heart.

Collecting these gems of identity is often tedious work. Moving earth around resembles working in a landfill—unsightly junk conceals the gems, with creatures nesting in the debris. Some would love nothing more than to attach themselves to these treasures. The gems I've unearthed now rest on me as my mantle. A prophet once told me, *"Some will be like leeches and try to attach themselves to your mantle, but you will simply shake them off."*

Understanding the treasures unearthed in my soil has fueled my desire to help others untangle their vines. I want to invite others into this land of milk and honey with me. I don't want their

Pharaohs or personal Egypts to hold them back from God's promises. It all began in the simplest of ways: a mindful acknowledgment of God's power. God *is* power. That acknowledgment itself is a jewel. Recognizing God as the creator and ultimate authority exposes a treasure of hope.

"Jack, you have a good understanding of your lineament," he says, his voice steady. "I hope you'll hold on to the attributes of love in your heart and not let anything or anyone confuse the character of your identity again. We've tangled up your character and moral standing with your identity, but it's more important to determine who you are than what you are. So, Jack, who are you?" His face is serious.

I feel the weight of his question. "I know you're looking for something other than my name or character, but I'm not sure where to dig for that answer," I admit, feeling confused.

So often, we link our identity with what we do. I'm an electrical contractor—that's one of many things I do, but it has little to do with who I am. As I've pieced together fragments of myself, I've realized the devil's true mission: to hide, distort, and disguise my identity. For a while, I thought I had found it. But then I discovered I was even hiding my identity behind the treasure of my moral character. Treasures are brought to the treasury of the king, but they are not the king. The distinction is subtle but meaningful.

"You have to protect your jewels, your family, and the kingdom God has entrusted to you," he says.

Confusion washes over me. "How can I protect myself or anyone else when the enemy is everywhere? I want to help people with the trauma I've endured, but the words of battle are meant to cause separation," I say, feeling a familiar helplessness.

"I know it's difficult," he responds gently. "But there's a diamond of generosity in your heart. You will help lead others out of the checkered floor of confusion and darkness. You'll guide them out of their personal hell and into the battle for their identity. This, I know. But first things first—who are you?" He smiles, softening the intensity of his words.

"Yeah, I feel that," I reply. "But how do I maneuver around all the enemies?"

"You don't maneuver around them," he says firmly. "You walk in the authority given to you by Christ. It was never the intention for you to tiptoe around the enemy. The battle has been won, and you are part of the victory. When doubt surfaces and it doesn't manifest as unforgiveness, you may need to address it with repentance. Your conscience needs to be wiped clean in the understanding that, through Christ's work, you are forgiven. Your conscience can be the barrier that prevents you from seeing into the garden and looking directly at the tree of life."

He shifts gears, his tone steady but raw. "You sleep under the stairs, surrounded by garbage. You're treated with the same disregard as the contents of those boxes. The message is clear. You sleep and dream but can't escape the message that corresponds to your value—the clog meeting your head. You go through life as a subject of this dungeon."

"Yes, I would say that's accurate," I reply, hoping to avoid the sharp sting of his summary.

"You crawl out from the trash to begin your unpleasant day. Your self-image has been unwillingly determined by this message, taking root within you. Your actions reflect this message. The way you treat yourself is a product of it. And then, you feel bad for the actions that stem from how you see yourself," he says, pausing to let his words sink in.

"Smoking or eating unhealthily is a byproduct of how I feel about myself, and this begins the downward spiral into feeling less self-love." I feel overwhelmed.

"The need to be sorry for a behavior is self-defeating. Guilt and shame do nothing except extend your connection to the behavior. Instead, change the way you think about it. Don't allow it back in," he says. "Although guilt and shame might lead you to repentance, once you arrive there, repentance is simply about changing the way you think about the behavior—and, of course, changing the behavior itself from this new perspective." He concludes with a giggle.

"I like that," I respond. "I was always taught that repentance means being sorry, and I've felt sorry for everything." His giggle is almost contagious.

"Allow yourself to escape the message that was sent to you," he says, his tone elevated.
"Allow yourself to think differently about who you are." His voice is firm, almost commanding.
"Allow yourself to feel differently about who you are," he continues.
"Allow yourself to take authority over the messages you receive."
"Allow yourself to love and be loved despite the messages of others."

The series of commands feels like an order, but I listen carefully.

"When you love yourself as you are intended to, you love the beauty that God created. You won't let that forest burn. Your decisions will reflect that respect. Harmful habits you once latched onto will change and eventually fall away. You will no longer exercise self-defeating habits. Instead, you'll make healthy decisions based on the new message. At night, when you return to rest, you'll no longer crawl into an unmade bed," he concludes insightfully.

"How did you know my covers are always in disarray?" I question, curious about his uncanny perception.

"The message that was sent to you hasn't yet fallen away. I'd go further to suggest it's not just your covers. Your resting space probably holds onto other remnants of that message. I'd imagine there are still storage items or clutter surrounding you, compromising your rest." His insight astounds me, even though I understand where it stems from.

The love you feel for yourself—love for the creation you're meant to be—will naturally extend to others. Your communication will reflect that love, edifying and encouraging others in their growth while comforting them as they change. Your testimony, your story, is filled with words of edification. When you share that you were fearful but God delivered you from that fear, it edifies others. That might help you realize your conversations are not as limited as they seem," he explains.

"I get that," I say, nodding. "I think part of my social awkwardness is tied to how much I avoid exposure. I cringe when I hear a pastor reference movies or worldly influences in a sermon. It feels too close to the culture of the world. The vitiated morality of the church began slipping during the third church period when Constantine's vision merged church and state." I realize I'm deflecting to external issues, avoiding my internal opposition, which is where the real work must be done.

The walls of the maze collapse, one after another. These walls of false beliefs fall with each new gem I uncover. Most of the false beliefs were about myself—words and actions from those who sought to harm me. These lies contradicted the truth, keeping me trapped in this maze for far too long.

"Protect these jewels as if they are the most valuable treasures in the world, because they are. It's no coincidence you see your character as jewels. That is an indication of its worth. For our next session, I want to discuss hope and faith. Take this time to ponder what it truly means to be hopeful and faithful," he instructs.

The box of jewels is beginning to radiate with the contagious glow of reform. Repentance and forgiveness have moved the stone, exhuming these gems. I am making progress, moving swiftly toward my identity. The counselor asked me to consider hope and faith. I've churned that butter quite a bit this week, drawing conclusions I'm eager to discuss with him. I don't want to build any more walls of false beliefs, so I'm cautious about committing to any truths. Still, it's worth exploring

Like fool's gold, there is a fool's hope. We can hope for the brilliance of earthly wealth. We can hope for the glimmer and shine of eloquent things. Or, we can hope for joy, peace, and love to take their rightful place on the higher ground of our hearts. Fool's hope, nestled in the unmoved soil, has a glittery allure that can easily capture our attention. However, the key difference between fool's hope and genuine hope is that fool's hope does not encourage growth in moral character—whereas true hope does.

There is no shortcut to unearthing true hope. It reveals itself when you are ready for it. Its power inspires a desire to become a better person. It leads you away from sin and places selfish desires behind the greater desire to build up heaven. In its purest form, hope is inspiring. Hope is not a wish. You don't blow out birthday candles for hope. Hope demands dedication. It requires faith—the kind of faith that moves mountains, clearing the path that obstructs the view of hope. The enemy will attempt to distort hope, presenting false shortcuts and detours. But there are no shortcuts. Our only hope lies in Jesus.

Yes, inspiration is the hope I found in God. She means everything to me. She means the world to me. I envision running toward her in a meadow, surrendering together to the divine. The inspiration she brings has set me on the path to healing from my past afflictions. She has been monumental in guiding me toward forgiveness and repentance. She has made me want to become a better man. Though she is not committed to me, she has been the force that keeps me grounded, even as avoidance tries to creep in and show its ugly face. She has stirred my emotions, broken through the hardness of my heart, and provided the access point that inspires me to make a difference in the world.

Since committing myself to her, I have avoided the stumbling blocks of instant gratification. That commitment to her reinforces my commitment to God. I am convinced that He sent her into my life as a tangible means of fulfilling my devotion to Him.

I have stayed on track with my healing. I have been chipping away at the stone and dismantling the false beliefs that once held me captive. This singular focus on healing has grown into something greater. This writing—whether good or bad— would not exist without my hope of resolving the issues within myself that contributed to the loss of what could have been the greatest love of my life. She opened my heart, inspiring me to reach out and make a difference in the world. To honor her, I founded Divine Fortress Ministries, an organization dedicated to providing a safe space for those healing from PTSD, CPTSD, and other trauma-related afflictions.

For me, hope is boundless. I can hope for anything—a billion dollars, the perfect job, or an ideal life. Hope gives me the opportunity to explore these ideas and visualize their outcomes.

For example, let's say my hope is for a billion dollars. I can see how it might distance me from family or cause me to question whether someone I date is truly interested in me. I would need to accept that such wealth would consume a significant part of my life, leaving little room for boundaries.

I've read many tales of people consumed by greed, their lives shaded with arrogance and boastfulness. While I believe I could use such wealth to help others, I also recognize the potential for it to spark pride or hubris. Perhaps it would be better if such a sum were managed through a nonprofit, with decisions made by a volunteer board. Maybe by removing this from my hope list, I have extinguished a fire before it began.

The Bible conceals gems of wisdom. Just as rare stones are unearthed from my heart, the nuggets of Scripture are uncovered through interpretation. These treasures can be revealed through literal, allegorical, mystical, and moral readings of the text. The Bible opens corridors to the dimensions of spirit, soul, and body. Climbing out onto this branch reveals that the treasure found in the spirit permeates the soul and will soon conquer the body. What is loosed in heaven will indeed be loosed on earth.

Chapter 47
Gifts of the Spirit

1st Corinthians 12:1 "Now brother and sister I do not want for you to be uninformed."

"Listen carefully and never let them build walls in your house again"

The circus acts are spiraling out of control. Children demand litter boxes in schools, claiming they identify as cats. The absurdity doesn't stop there. There are women with beards, men identifying as women, and women identifying as men. It feels as though a coordinated attack is being waged against human identity and the divine image we were created to reflect. Politics has devolved into mere theatrics, bitterness saturating every corner of society. Social media amplifies and spreads this infection like wildfire.

Through the years, my dreams have unveiled layers of prophecy in surprising ways.

"The dragon is not evil. You need to accept it as a part of you. Have you ever tried shadow work?" A woman spoke these unsolicited words to me at a car show. Hearing her say, "The dragon is not evil," only affirmed that I am on the right path—a path deeply rooted in rejecting the dragon. Accepting the shadow of the dragon as a part of oneself is, in my view, as treacherous as accepting the mark of the beast. I have poured relentless effort and prayer into ensuring the dragon has no hold on me. I've searched tirelessly for the hidden cracks through which the dragon might have entered. I've taken a sledgehammer to the walls of my soul, uncovering jewels of truth and ultimately driving out the deceptions of the beast. Each deception removed seems to weaken the beast.

455

Jack Taylor

And yet, hearing those words—"The dragon is not evil"—in such a literal sense felt surreal. It challenges my understanding of the dream's symbolic nature. Still, I hold fast to the vision of a day of surrender in the meadow, where the world turns 180 degrees off its axis, and those who embrace their "shadow work" are torn from the earth.

The prophet's words guided me to that car show. It might not seem significant at first glance, but I wouldn't have been there without his guidance. His words acted like a radio signal, orchestrating every step that led me to that moment.

Each jewel I uncovered brought with it a memory long buried and a fresh epiphany. "Let us create man in our image," the scriptures say. My daughter is created in my image, just as I am my father's son. My Father happens to be the King of the universe. This makes me, by birthright, a prince. With the expansion of His Kingdom, my authority and identity also grow. I will always identify as the son of the King—that is my unshakable identity.

Memories swirl and shift like mist, blurring the lines of understanding. I see a sword and a decree of divorce. Clarity comes when a friend shares a poem about a two-edged sword. The poem speaks of those who discover their purpose later in life, yet they often take on the most significant roles.

Then, a grotesque image invades my mind: fingers as long as carrots, tipped with five-inch nails, curl around a door. The skin is reddish, bruised, splitting, and foul-smelling. A voice rasps through decaying vocal cords, "Little piggy, little piggy, let me come in."

"Don't let it in. Shut the door behind you!"

When the grave is opened and faith is exhumed, the obstacles of life scurry away like vermin exposed to light. Faith,

456

the evidence of things hoped for, is a gift from God. As we align ourselves with our genuine hope, faith overcomes the shadowing lies of the enemy. The gem of faith uncovered in the lava bed must be spent wisely, invested in the hope we've matured into—not squandered on selfish desires. The expansion of the Kingdom of Heaven brings abundant blessings, which is precisely why the enemy's attacks strategically target our faith.

These attacks often come disguised in common language, slipping by unnoticed. It is essential to reject and rebuke such assaults. Protecting your faith is critical, for with God, all things are possible.

Elisha further instructed the widow with the olive oil. He told her to gather as many empty vessels as she could. "Don't ask for just a few," he said. "Then go inside and shut the door behind you and your sons. Pour oil into all the jars, and as each is filled, put it to one side. When all the vessels are full, the oil will stop flowing."

The act of shutting the door behind her was a vital part of Elisha's instructions. As I reach for my own door to close it behind me, the enemy tries to wedge its foot in, resisting the closure. Residues of unforgiveness and unrepented sins attempt to keep the door ajar, threatening to invade again and again. The house must be clean.

The crowd grows hostile, angered by the words I speak and the implications of my message. I begin to run. Behind me, I hear the mob—those who once held power and their loyal followers—closing in. I can feel the walls of treachery collapsing as I flee. Ahead of me lies a trail leading away from the throne where the beast sits.

I stumble twice as I emerge from a mountain trail and look out over a valley that opens into a meadow. Glancing down to steady my footing, I lift my gaze again and see a horizon filled with people running toward me. The pursuers behind me are closer than those coming from the front. I keep running, but I have no destination in sight. Hopelessness begins to creep in.

Then, off in the distance, I see a glimmer of light. A woman is running toward me, and I notice the light flashing off her pendant. In that moment, an epiphany strikes: we are being driven together by the collapsing forces of emotion, united by a shared desire to be free from tyranny. Jesus is the light and our hope. If the pendant symbolizes hope, then running toward it is an act of faith.

The enemy, however, will stop at nothing to hinder this mission. It will even try to latch onto the mantle God has placed on me, seeking to prevent the filling of the vessels. The enemy fights fiercely because it understands the importance of the task at hand. I've had to shut the door in the face of those who emerged to oppose the healing process. Some of them even fight against their own healing. They come as empty vessels, yet reveal the lingering residue of unforgiveness, impatience, and hate stuck to the sides of their jars.

I lift my hands in praise, remembering all that God has done for me. I give thanks for His remarkable works and acknowledge that I have everything I need. My ambition to keep the ministry flowing remains steadfast, even as small demon-like forces attempt to attach themselves to the mantle God has poured over me. These attacks have become transparent because they target my faith directly.

But my faith is in God for all things. It is through Him that I find healing, provision, and strength. I do not look to the snake on the pole for healing, nor do I place my hope in doctors or pharmaceuticals. Those paths failed me. Instead, I followed the teachings of Jesus Christ, pursuing a heart of forgiveness. That has brought me remarkable healing. It is in God alone that I find my provision.

I feel no need to argue with anyone who challenges my faith or offers their ideas of how God provides through the resources of man. My faith rests in His promises, as revealed in scripture, and I have no room in my life for anyone who seeks to challenge or discourage that faith. I trust in what God speaks directly to me, and I do not need to defend His methods of communication. My only desire is to offer healing to those who seek it, even to those who resist the truth of His ways.

In Genesis 14:23, God tells Abraham not to accept as much as a thread from the spoils, ensuring that the glory for Abraham's prosperity cannot be shared or divided. The glory belongs solely to the Lord. In the same way, when you accept Jesus into your heart, you agree to His terms. The enemy, however, operates like the king who offers the thread—a thread of thought that threatens God's glory. If your successes are based on your own thoughts and efforts, you may miss the extraordinary blessings of His plan. Worse, you may unknowingly attempt to share in His glory. True glorification of God is achieved through the fulfillment of His will.

When His glory is upon me, it manifests as His mantle, a divine blessing others sometimes try to attach themselves to. The enemy, subtle as a whisper, works through our thoughts to undermine faith.

While I have no need for people disguised in spiritual camouflage who challenge my faith, I recognize their need for healing. These challenges are often driven by the demons they wrestle with—arrogance, pride, jealousy, or something else entirely. What other reason could they have to care so much about what I believe? To challenge my faith is, in essence, to challenge my relationship with God. I would gladly facilitate their healing, but once that journey begins, they must be willing to see it through.

Jack Taylor

I might give some consideration to those who challenge my faith if their perspectives made sense, but why must they challenge mine to express their own? My faith is of no consequence to them. They gain nothing if I believe my healing comes through Jesus Christ, nor do they lose anything if I refuse to take pharmaceuticals or trust in God's promises—whether delivered through scripture or direct communication. I rebuke anything that contradicts this faith. In the mighty name of Jesus, I cast away the demons that seek to darken my view with their shadows.

A prophet once told me that as I build up the Kingdom, some will try to attach themselves to me, but I would simply shake them off. I have come to understand the truth of those words. That realization has strengthened my faith, the very faith they sought to diminish. Interestingly, the enemy's relentless attacks on this faith have only deepened my conviction. If the enemy didn't fight so hard to cause me to doubt my connection to this new level of faith, I might have overlooked its significance. But because the attacks have been so orchestrated and unyielding, they've become like music to my ears—a reminder of the value of my faith. From now on, I will protect it with vigilance, refusing to let even the faintest whisper of the enemy's forces threaten it.

Just the other day, I had to shake off one of those attachments. I dismissed a friend from the board of directors of Divine Fortress Ministries. It became clear that anyone participating in this ministry must first go through the process of healing that we offer, guided by the Holy Spirit. They must believe in the vision and experience it for themselves. Without that foundation of faith and forgiveness, they cannot effectively contribute to the mission of this ministry.

"That's weird. You don't even take aspirin. Don't you think God instructed man to make pharmaceuticals?" the board member asked.

"Yes," I replied, "in the same way He instructed the Israelites to look upon the pole with the snake for healing from the viper bites. And you can call me weird if you'd like."

"Then I don't understand why you refuse medication," she pressed.

"The vipers bit them as a result of their complaining," I explained.

"Yeah, and they were dying because of it," she added.

"They were complaining because they still had one foot in Egypt," I said, pausing to let her connect the dots. But she continued.

"Yeah, and God gave them a way to live. What does that have to do with medication?"

"The way to remove their foot from Egypt was by forgiving the unsettling things that happened to them there," I said. "They were no longer bound by the shackles of misery. If they could forgive and release Egypt's hold on them, they wouldn't have been bitten by the vipers in the first place. Then there would've been no need for the snake on the pole. I will not look upon the snake for my healing. The snake on the pole is the medical insignia. By looking to pharmaceuticals and doctors, you are looking upon the snake for healing. I would rather plow the fields within myself, find forgiveness, and take my foot out of Egypt."

"But God instructed them to look upon the snake for healing," she countered.

"If God instructed man to make pharmaceuticals, it creates distance—an intermediary—between God and man. It's like seeking healing through a middleman. I prefer to go straight to the

Source. I would never imply you shouldn't go to the doctor if that's where your faith leads you. If your faith is tied to the idea that God placed the snake on the pole, then by all means, use pharmaceuticals. Your faith is yours, and I won't come between you and the direction of your faith."

I could feel her pushing against my convictions, her words carrying an air of doubt. Her energy was not seeking understanding—it was seeking to be right. Or perhaps to prove me wrong. In the process, I began to see how much unforgiveness was harbored in her heart.

"I just don't have much tolerance for my husband," she admitted, reflecting on an incident from the previous night.

"That kind of tolerance is an attribute of love," I said, hoping to shed light on the importance of patience.

"What are you saying? That I don't love my husband?" she shot back, her tone sharp, prying the conversation open further.

"No, that's not what I'm saying," I replied, feeling defensive.

"Then what are you saying?" Her irritation was not just with her husband—it spilled into our exchange.

"Keeping your composure is important, and I won't tolerate a lack of it being directed at me," I insisted.

"Okay," she said, stepping back momentarily.

But it didn't take long for her anger to resurface, this time redirected.

"So, what's up with you and 'Emerald Eyes'?" she asked, her voice dripping with provocation.

Awkward Silence

I should have kept my response short, but I didn't.

"It will all work out in God's time," I said.

"So, have you even talked to her?" she pressed, the taunt clear.

"I've shared part of the story with you, so why do you ask?"

"I just don't want to see you get hurt," she said, her words laced with doubt.

"God gives me comfort, and there's no reason to be concerned about my feelings. God gave me His word, so I have no concern. Everything will unfold in His time," I answered.

"It doesn't seem like she's into you," she said.

"Seasons change, but God remains the same—yesterday, today, and forever. Her season may be changing. Mine certainly has. I've relentlessly worked toward healing and becoming a better man. The work He has done in me makes me more suitable. When I'm ready, He will make the presentation."

"How do you know God doesn't have something better in mind?"

"That question implies that you think God is a liar. I know what God has said to me. Either you're calling me crazy, or you're calling God a liar. Either way, you're speaking with a forked tongue."

Her words echoed with a familiarity I couldn't ignore. The snake in the Garden of Eden had a similar dialect: *"Surely you won't die."* I could almost see her words leave her mouth with a hiss and a slithering motion.

"That's the second time you've referred to me as a snake," she said, her voice tinged with frustration.

"Do you think it's easy for me to keep hope alive?" I asked, my emotions bubbling to the surface. "Do you think I don't miss her every single day that we're apart? I'm not even sure why I feel this way, except that God placed her gently in my heart. There's evidence—strong evidence—that God is the one who put her there. Even if your words are meant to take me from my faith that God placed her there—"

"My words are *not* meant to take you from your faith," she interrupted defensively.

"I'm not going to argue with you," I said firmly. "I'm just expressing my feelings on the matter. If you don't think my feelings are valid, then you can leave."

"Well, you need to say, 'I feel dot, dot, dot,'" she said, as if invoking a universal truth from a self-help guide.

"So now you want to control how I express my feelings?" I asked, incredulous. "They're my feelings, and I'll express them however I choose. If you don't want to hear what I have to say, then you have options."

"No, go ahead. Finish," she said, leaning back in her chair with a touch of defiance.

"My faith says that God placed her in my heart. Nothing will deter that belief because I haven't reached toward sin. I've spent countless hours working to heal from dissociative identity disorder and all that's connected to CPTSD. God has led me into this healing. If I didn't believe God placed her in my heart, I'd probably do what I've always done—I'd be out looking for another woman to satisfy my desires. I probably wouldn't have been inspired to start the ministry or help those suffering the effects of trauma.

"Love is the true inspiration, but by placing her in my heart, God has highly motivated me. My relationship with Him has become everything. I'm leaning on Him because I know He is my only hope. He's the shimmer of light that keeps me moving in faith—the very faith you keep trying to challenge. When you challenge this faith, you're challenging the foundation of this ministry. It's being built on this faith.

"Words like, 'How do you know God doesn't have something better in mind,' make it clear that you don't believe in the ministry built on this foundation. Because of that, I have to dismiss you from the board. I'm sorry."

"I'm not challenging your faith," she protested. "I'm here because I believe in your vision. I believe in what Divine Fortress is doing."

"If you believe in what we're doing, then why do you negate everything I say?" I asked. "You're angry, and you need healing. As I've told you before, I'd love to facilitate some of that healing, but I can't force you. God has given you free will to hold on to unforgiveness and the things affecting your disposition. You can defend your demons, or you can surrender with humility. The choice is yours."

My decision to dismiss her wasn't solely based on her words—it was about her overall view of faith. She relies so heavily on her own abilities and intelligence that she leaves no room for God to perform the miracles that glorify Him. I can't tolerate this. It was my best thinking that created most of the problems in my life. I need God to achieve the plans He has for me, and I refuse to get in His way with pride or arrogance. I am present and willing to be used for His glory.

After this discussion, I had to take inventory of myself. My calmness grew thinner and thinner with each attack on my faith. My position should not have wavered, regardless of her disposition. My faith remained intact, but she rocked it slightly. That wouldn't have been possible if I hadn't placed trust in her.

From now on, I'll commit my trust only to Jesus. I will rely on the discernment of the Holy Spirit to guide me.

When your faith is unmovable, your actions rooted in that faith are unmovable too. That kind of faith grows out of complete vulnerability.

Chapter 48
Restoration of Faith

Ezekiel 36:26 "God replaces our hearts of stone with hearts of flesh."

"How could He know what I was going to write about with the lava surrounding my heart?"

From the barrage of challenges that have tested my faith, I have struggled to retain the temperament of a loving man. My patience has worn thin. Her lack of composure was one of the first signs that she was grappling with something deeper. Just as demons seek to leap from one soul to another, I find myself wrestling with my own endurance. My kindness has lost some of its sheen, and I may have even spilled some of my compassion along the way. I recognize the need to step back and recondition forgiveness in my heart.

Love cannot exist without tolerance or kindness. The qualities required to cultivate love are beautifully articulated in 1 Corinthians 13. This passage is not only poetic but also instructive, making it one of my favourites. To embody everything it describes is to aspire to the image in which we were created.

Reaching for the reset button has become essential for me, but it seems to have provoked the demons within her. Suddenly, they demand to be seen. I see her more often than ever, her presence becoming obsessive. To protect my peace, I block her on my phone and social media, yet she persists. Messages pour in from disguised numbers, laced with veiled threats. When that fails, she turns to email. Despite her relentless attempts, I stand firm in my need for time to regain my composure. Her actions only make it easier for me to entrust the situation to God and find peace in my decision to let her go.

467

Through my journey, I have learned that healing begins with removing all barriers that stand between God and me. Unforgiveness creates obstacles that hinder clear communication with Him. My sins kept me imprisoned in shame, blinding me to the possibilities of fulfilling the tasks He set before me. True healing comes with surrender—the willingness to be completely vulnerable to love. Perhaps this is the foundation of an unconventional, raw faith. The restoration of my thoughts, emotions, and will began with the single objective of reclaiming childlike faith.

The relentless assault on my faith has made me acutely aware of the changes that must be implemented. All future board members and faculty within the ministry will undergo a genuine process of healing. Though I still feel the sting of betrayal from her words and actions, God continues to lead me toward forgiveness. Obedience to Him demands that I release the residual unforgiveness that has crept into my heart. In doing so, I uncover other areas of unforgiveness that also need healing.

Her struggles remind me of my sister, as they share similar traumas and, consequently, the demons they battle. Both have control issues that influenced their choice to marry men they could dominate. Neither respects their husbands and both view their spouses as "stupid." Their similarities reveal that their true issue with me is their inability to control me. I see their demons clearly, and I am unafraid to call them out. Yet, I take the time to let the oil of forgiveness flow. I forgive them sincerely and pray for their healing. I long for the day we can share genuine connection once again.

Still, there remains an unfilled space in the ministry. I dream of that void being filled by the woman with the emerald eyes. To me, it would be the perfect vision—our knees on the ground in a serene meadow, surrendering together to the life God has appointed for us. I imagine us building a legacy and a life of richness, one that reflects God's glory.

As an electrician, the best I could hope for was to become the "best" in my trade. But through Divine Fortress Ministries, we can be part of something far greater than ourselves. Although there is more money to be made as an electrical contractor, life isn't about money. Despite the old cliché that "money makes the world go round," true fulfilment comes from aligning with God's purpose and contributing to something eternal.

"The one who dips his hand into the bowl with me will betray me."

In this scripture, I believe Jesus is offering profound insight into subliminal communication. Judas appears to be asserting his equality with Jesus by dipping his hand into the bowl. This action is a gesture of parity, as if he is saying, "I am worthy." If you follow my reasoning, you'll see that this act speaks volumes. I have concluded this interpretation to be true because Jesus could have simply said, "Judas will betray me," without the symbolic gesture.

Viewing scripture through this lens has provided me with valuable perspectives. If Judas's action is a statement of non-congruence—his action betraying his words—then I can use this understanding to discern the wolves in sheep's clothing around me. I observe subtle challenges in the behavior of others, especially those I consider for ministry roles. For example, I might place an object, like a pencil, on a table and watch for their reaction. Some people are indifferent to where the object is placed, while others feel compelled to move it.

One individual I removed from the board consistently displayed this need to challenge. She couldn't leave anything where I placed it. In my own home, she would reposition items I set down. This pattern of behavior revealed a deeper issue: a need to assert dominance. Looking through the "windows" of her actions, I could see the demon behind them, working defensively yet claiming control. It's a subtle but telling movement—a silent statement of defiance. Over time, this underlying theme of challenge often escalates into more vocal confrontations, such as dismissive comments about my faith or negating my words entirely.

When faced with such challenges, I remind myself to take authority over the enemy in the name of Jesus Christ, who holds all authority. By His will, the jars are filled. If you fail to recognize these challenges to your authority, you may face prolonged disruption. Demons aim to destroy your mantle, to prevent you from sharing the oil of anointing. Allowing them access before sealing the door is an act of self-sabotage.

This principle applies equally to the internal as it does to the external. You cannot seal the door to external attacks without first ensuring your own jar is clean. Shine light on the unforgiveness within you, and cast out your own iniquities. It is as Jesus said: "Take the log out of your own eye" (Matthew 7:5).

I cannot say with certainty what God has planned for your mantle or what path will lead you there. What I know is this: I placed my heart in a posture of surrender, and in that state, God revealed the power of forgiveness in healing. I repented and embraced a new way of thinking. He continues to expose the areas in my life that need transformation and guides me back when I stray. In surrender, I sought His will, letting go of my own ambitions and self-perceived intelligence.

I gave up aspirations of becoming a famous musician. I set aside the pride I once took in my own problem-solving abilities. Instead, I committed to being a man of integrity, striving to embody the attributes of love. Through all the enemy's attacks,

God worked with me. My growing humility became a marker of progress, especially given the arrogance I had once carried.

Time and again, I believed I was fulfilling His will, only to uncover that my motives were rooted in self-interest. Arrogance is deceptive, often disguising itself in the shadows of our thoughts. I thought my talent as a guitarist or my skill as a problem-solver should define my calling. But the truth is clearly stated in scripture: "He doesn't call the equipped; He equips the called" (Exodus 4:10).

It took time for me to realize that my purpose, in everything I do, is to build the Kingdom of Heaven by submitting to His authority. True fulfillment comes not from asserting my abilities but from aligning my will with His.

I have surrendered everything that I am to the Lord, and He may use it in any way that aligns with His will. If this is not my greatest aspiration and the driving force behind my actions, then I have missed the entire purpose. Without this understanding, I cannot walk freely into the promised land. My healing is secondary to His purpose. In truth, just as He can command the rocks to cry out in praise, He could heal me in an instant. Yet, through the process of working with Him in my healing, He has accomplished something far greater: He has drawn me into fellowship with Him.

Along this journey, He has given me precious gifts. These gems of spiritual enlightenment are invaluable, and I try to share many of them with you as we grow together. The essence of prophecy is to share God, and God is love. To be prophetic is to speak love over one another. I have also shared the gift of healing. While some mysteries are meant to remain veiled, I can assure you that behind that veil lies everything you could ever ask for. God is truly amazing!

Like Hosea, I see parallels between our individual experiences and the broader state of our communities, cities, regions, and nations. Warnings have been given, yet they are often ignored. The recent focus on the signs of the moon and sun is just one example. Our country has largely turned its back on God. From Monday through Saturday, it is difficult to distinguish Christians in their daily lives. Healing must begin with the individual before it can spread to communities. My love is no longer dependent on others or on those who were supposed to love me.

Pouring out the love of God through prophecy often goes beyond simple declarations like, "You're going to prosper." Sometimes, prophecy offers guidance to help avoid the snares of life. For example, "Taking the steps of healing will lead to that path of prosperity" is much the same as saying, "If you don't heal, you will remain stuck in the ruins forever." The difference is that love frames the message in a way that encourages hope and positive outcomes. That is the purpose of prophecy: to comfort, encourage, and edify. Ultimately, the greatest goal is to proclaim God's message to His people.

Not every prophetic word is meant to be rainbows and sunshine. Sometimes, the message is one of conviction. For example, "The prosperity you will achieve through healing will be the expansion of the Kingdom of Heaven" is far more loving than saying, "Your selfish pursuit of prosperity will always leave you unfulfilled." You can see that even now, I have just prophesied to you.

"Removing the thorns and thistles in your life through forgiveness and repentance will lead you to a prosperity beyond anything you can imagine. Through your generosity, you will witness the expansion of the Kingdom of Heaven, which in turn will create even more prosperity."

Awkward Silence

However, leaving the thorns and thistles where they lie will prevent this growth. Without addressing these obstacles, you will remain in the desert, never reaching the promised land. The burdens of these thorns and thistles will hinder your progress, and your prosperity will stagnate. Only through forgiveness, repentance, and the removal of these barriers can you walk freely into the life God has prepared for you.

Chapter 49
Anything For Those Emeralds

Luke 24:32 "Didn't our hearts burn within us as He talked with us and explained scriptures."

"The gems are dug out of the stone to resemble the waking of purity."

Elisha replied to her, "How can I help you? Tell me, what do you have in your house?"

This question resonates deeply with me. Do I have a house built on forgiveness, or am I still carrying the heavy burden of unforgiveness? Are the treasures within me—my virtues—enough to define who I truly am? When my house is free of debris, even a small jar of olive oil can go a long way. In other words, I strive to live in a way that allows me to fill empty vessels with the overflow of the olive oil that symbolizes the Spirit of God. But I can only reach this state by keeping my house clean.

Each day, I step outside of myself to examine the branches of the tree of my life. I trim away overgrowth, showing myself love through this act of pruning. If this tree is found in the Book of Life, it is also the tree of the knowledge of good and evil. As my life grows, its branches extend in many directions, exposing both light and darkness. One branch reaches through the pages of books and the carved wood of furniture. Another stretches into hell, wrapped in cedar walls. Yet another traces the contours of two women's faces.

I am driven. My focus is sharp, zeroing in on the faint elements—the elusive silhouettes of my life. Through mindful pruning, I ensure that the branches sprouting from darkness do not overtake me.

Awkward Silence

When I feel off balance or lose sight of the love rooted in my innocence, I remind myself that healing begins when I pay attention to subtle expressions. For instance, when my aunt said, "You reminded me of my brother," I listened. It wasn't my fault, but I chose to pay attention. "What did your brother do to you that was so horrific it justified what you did to me?"

Understanding that she wasn't walking alone in her sin helps me grasp that forces stronger than cannons can misdirect a person's behavior. Yet, it is not my role to justify her actions. My task is to obey—to love and forgive, as God commands. Realizing that her actions weren't truly against me but were instead a rejection of God makes forgiveness easier. I take comfort in leading with forgiveness.

Still, there's little reason to socialize with her. Not out of bitterness, but because time has made her a stranger to me. The ugly ship of our shared history has been docked in the harbor for years. If she ever needed help, I'd be there. And if you ever need anything, I'll be here for you too.

The opening move of chess—king pawn to king 4—sets the stage for the game. The pieces move across the board, each turn revealing strategy and misdirection. I'm no stranger to the schemes of the proverbial wizard. But I choose to prune that branch. I'm done with games. Authenticity is my only pursuit now.

Through practicing authenticity with myself, I've found greater tolerance for others. There are always new gems to uncover, and each one reflects growth. By treating myself with kindness, I've become kinder. Trading smaller gems for larger ones, I've discovered humility by embracing my truth. When I love myself, I am more loving.

Progress has been made, and the journey ahead feels shorter than the one behind me. The road has been long, but I've traveled farther from where I started than where I'm going.

Unforgiveness is self-serving, anchoring us to past dissatisfaction. It vocalizes itself through grumbling and complaints, keeping us trapped in sin. Forgiveness, however, removes us from the trauma of the past, propelling us into a state of peace. Living free from trauma dissolves dissatisfaction, silencing complaints and eliminating the desire for escape—escape being the seed of sin.

I am no longer wandering in the desert, complaining and being bitten by vipers like the Israelites. Instead, I wake each day excited to avoid the vipers and lean into the promises of God. Each day offers a new opportunity to learn about myself, and with that same enthusiasm, I grow closer to God. I'm no longer carrying the weight of Egypt in my backpack. Though Minnesota and its shadows have long been removed from me, it took nearly fifty years to climb out of that mindset.

This transformation has given me a deeper understanding of the pain others endure. I am no longer triggered to respond with self-sabotaging actions fueled by the enemy within. That enemy has been forced to retreat, driven out by the armies of heaven. I can now recognize the manipulative tactics of the enemy and stand ready to help those who want to heal. I am here to fill empty jars with what I have been blessed to receive.

Today began, as most of my days do, with a prayer of total surrender. I watched the rising sun, filled with hope that today might be the day. The day when I run through the meadow and embrace her in my arms, experiencing total surrender. I reflected on my dreams from the night, analyzing what fragments I could remember.

Awkward Silence

In my dream, I was in a house I didn't recognize, with Candice and her two boys. They were eating pancakes, devouring them as if they hadn't eaten in a week—or perhaps just with the boundless hunger of teenage boys. The syrup bottle stood out vividly, as if it were the Mona Lisa in a kindergarten art class. One of the boys reached for a soda and said, "Did you know that Log Cabin is making a soda pop?" I gazed into her eyes, and then I woke up.

The dream lingers with me. Could there be a log cabin in Soda Springs that needs my attention? The details aren't fully clear, but it feels like another riddle to solve and another adventure to embark on. I have a good sense of what I'll find and where it will lead me. I'm excited—this is just one of the many treasure hunts I'm currently pursuing. Sprinkled throughout this text are hints and clues, each as fun to plant as the actual quests are to follow.

I've been inspired again by those emerald eyes—this time, just seeing them in a dream. Perhaps it's because I see gems in the windows of her soul that I always refer to her eyes as emeralds. These gems have reached out beyond the internal barriers, lifting me from apathy and back into the vibrant, natural world.

As treasure hunts have become a source of joy and intrigue for me, I've also found new ways to express love and appreciation. The Spirit of God is love, and love is the greatest of all inspirations. This book is dedicated to that love, and so is Divine Fortress Ministries.

Divine Fortress exists to provide a safe place for healing from CPTSD, PTSD, and other trauma-based afflictions. Through the insights I've gained on my journey and the guidance of the Holy Spirit, we are now offering these services to others. With our newly obtained 501(c)(3) status, I am confident and faithful that this ministry is part of God's plan.

Jack Taylor

I remember the prophetic words spoken to me: "You will have your hands in properties all over Idaho and bordering states." Those words now ring with clarity. The timeline was precise—six months after the night I first met her, the snowball began to roll down the hill. Inspiration is indeed sublime.

I have committed everything I have to this ministry. I believe, without a shadow of a doubt, that God is doing great things.

Defending the childlike faith that God has restored in me has silenced the enemy's triggers. My identity is no longer fractured but fully restored. I am no longer burdened by the heavy net of unforgiveness. The gems of love and grace have grown over the hardened lava of my past, and my heart is now open to love and be loved. Through Divine Fortress Ministries, God has given me purpose.

I am filled with the oil of His Spirit, and it overflows into empty vessels across Idaho and the bordering states. Speaking engagements have become opportunities to release the hydrant of God's love, pouring out His blessings. I am in awe of what God has done in my life. Sharing prophetic words and helping others lean into His promises is a joy beyond measure. I am truly blessed.

Perhaps this chapter of my journey is the new brook flowing through the meadow. Recently, I had another profound prophetic dream, one that felt like the next step in this nearly perfect ending. My hope has been resurrected, and I know the story will soon conclude with nothing held back—no love spared.

Healing from CPTSD has always been the hope and goal of this book. Sorting through memories, thoughts, and emotions has been an integral part of this expedition. At times, this shuffling of the deck is evident in my writing. I spent years living in the past, rehashing memories that seemed to endlessly resurface in my actions. Triggers would plunge me back into the depths of hell, where I stared at the knotholes in cedar planks or the red-and-white checkered floor of old pain.

The only way to move beyond the past was to let it go—but for years, it refused to release its grip on me. It was only through forgiveness and repentance that I escaped the dragon's lair. The walls of false beliefs crumbled, exposing my tender heart—a heart I will never again allow to harden. The truth truly sets you free.

One by one, the barriers of faithless thoughts came down, overcome by the protection of my faith. With the aid of the Helper, I found my way out of the maze, and the truth became my key to freedom.

When Jesus died on the cross, He paid the price for sin, That price was more than enough to pay me to forgive those that have been against me. There is an unmistakable duality in the message of forgiveness. The devil seeks to cling to resentments, but that path leads only to destruction. Forgiveness is the merchandise bought at a very high price, and it must be delivered—to others and to myself. His sacrifice demands no less.

The story of Lot's wife turning into a pillar of salt serves as a powerful reminder of the cost of dredging up the past. I knew this was the last time I would travel that dark, familiar road. With inspiration in my heart and hope in my hands, I look forward to holding the future close as the brook cuts through the earth's crust.

In surrender, I have nailed this book to the tree with Christ. My old self has passed away, and I am no longer a slave to sin. I am a new creation. Though the details of the future are unclear and a little messy, I know it will not be dictated by my past. I will no longer respond to evil with evil. Instead, I will live for the image, identity, and purpose for which I was created.

Jack Taylor

Never again will I be trapped by the silence of unresolved pain.

Chapter 50
A Displaced Axis

Revelation 2:12 "These are the words of Him who has the sharp two edged sword."

"It has taken many humans to spawn a beast of this magnitude."

It is huge! It stands before us with its scales of armor protecting its decomposing flesh. That flesh is rotting away and oozing out from under the scarlet scales of its deceptions. There are many heads that spew the flames of these lies. Fires that burn through the generations are difficult to extinguish and it is so difficult to be aware of where they began. The truth is outnumbered by these lies but everyone knows that the truth will still be standing long after the dragon falls.

The entire beast has been formed piece by piece as it is extracted out of the hearts of the unhealed. It has taken many humans to spawn a beast of this magnitude and in the birthing process the human is devoured. The self righteousness of man, that arrogance, once again has erected a society enslaved. The need to control is a growth of fear, mostly from not having control at a time of trauma. The cathedrals housing the manipulative thoughts of the wizard are called universities, The smog is dense and once you can see through it you are already at the crossroad.

Surrender has placed me firmly in the hands of my God. My identity is restored, and my purpose is clear—climbing out of the pits of hell to serve as a weapon wielded by Him. *Swish.* The sword cuts through the vines that seek to bind my heart to this world. This is the final stage of complete internal healing, and paradoxically, it brings an even deeper surrender.

Jack Taylor

Complete healing has birthed the gifts of the Spirit, guiding me out of treachery. With the authority of my renewed identity, I wield these gifts to fulfill my purpose: to be the sword. A sword that severs believers from unbelief and casts out the demons that have relentlessly pursued us.

I thrust my cardboard saber into the earth, an inch from the beast's head. It was just me, the sword, and the beast. Yet, the treasure in this story—the gem I now recognize—is compassion. That moment was one of many imaginative expeditions with my toy poodle. A few years later, I was enraged after watching a film about a boy being abused. That day, I raised a stick as my sword and declared vengeance on Satan.

Those early adventures were prophetic in nature, though their fulfillment waited until now. Today, I raise my pen to declare compassion and protection over God's people. Under the tent of modern-day circus acts, I preach to those defending their own inner dragons. It is not for you to deflect, project, or blame in an effort to protect the sin of the dragon within you. The dragon is evil, and it must be confronted.

"These are the words of Him who wields the sharp, double-edged sword." As I stroke the ink across the page, I realize each stroke may echo the slash of Jesus' sword. The pen is mightier than the sword, and yet, this pen is wielded in the service of a higher calling. To be a sword in the hand of Jesus is to be His warrior. I stand here, pen in hand, against the modern-day weapons of the world, but with the confidence of victory.

Looking back at the tales of my imagination, I see prophecy coming to life. Now is the time for believers to separate from the beast, for the bear has been ruthless. The so-called separation of church and state is a myth. The incorporated church is wed to the state, a union that began long ago.

Awkward Silence

The marriage was arranged in 312 AD. The bride, the church, had long resisted, but the groom—the state—wore her down through violence and manipulation. She came to the altar battered and torn. Her martyrs had suffered for centuries. In her early days, the bride held to the hope of rescue and the promise of power. She dreamed of sitting on a throne, ruling with authority, and prospering in glory. It seemed a Cinderella story.

Enter Constantine, a Roman emperor who sought to officiate this union. Some call him the first Christian emperor, but he was a man marked by scars. I believe he wanted to understand the bride, but her raw principles eluded him. His baptism did not deter him from pursuing his mission of controlling the entire region—a goal that might have been impossible without the church's cooperation. Such an agenda hardly reflects the life of one who has died to Christ and been born again.

I suggest that Constantine acted in ignorance, though perhaps with good intentions. His mother, a Greek woman from Asia Minor, likely influenced him toward Christianity. Yet his father, a Roman officer, tied him to the empire's traditions. The desire to unite church and state may have had a political veneer, but I see a deeper yearning—a desire for unity.

Constantine's vision of unity extended to the entire region, a single authority binding all under one rule. Peering into his life from the outside, I believe this desire was rooted in the divisions within his own household. His struggle for unity reflected both his internal conflicts and the fragmented world around him.

The carnality of Constantine's choices is a story that reads well in its historical and political context, but the true elevation rises above the man and his earthly motivations. His actions are etched into the fabric of prophecy, particularly in the message to the church at Pergamum. Constantine's ambition perished with him, but the marriage he orchestrated—between church and state—was consummated in the sordid fornication with the kings of many nations. From that union, the bride's bed was defiled, and a prophetic landslide tore through the pages of Revelation, echoing through time.

This union may have been born of political expediency, but it unleashed spiritual ramifications far beyond Constantine's intentions. One might argue that the bride, scarred by centuries of persecution, made a decision rooted in trauma. Her compromise rippled into the fourth church period, where the adulterous and promiscuous behaviors of the church came into full bloom during the Crusades. Anniversary after anniversary, the church settled further into its role alongside the state. The church became the state's adornment, ruling not from a place of spiritual authority but as a diplomatic pawn.

Over time, the church reveled in its new status, rubbing elbows with the powerful, the wealthy, and the renowned. But this worldly connection came at a steep cost. The church lost sight of its identity and purpose, forsaking its calling to serve for the seductive allure of influence.

Meanwhile, demons clung to this union wherever they could. The decay of Christian integrity accelerated as the church welcomed corruption into its fold. No longer casting out demons, it began to invite them in, all under the guise of inclusivity. The uncomfortable message of supernatural deliverance was abandoned, and the church's moral standards eroded as it aligned itself with the offenses of the state rather than the life and character of Jesus.

If an ultrasound could have revealed the offspring of this unholy union, it would have shown the body of a dragon, sprouting heads that symbolized the fallacies of religion. Religious leaders sat on thrones like kings, preaching service while reveling in their elevated status. Their lives were a stark dissonance from their words, and their hypocrisy became another barrier between the laity and the truth. Without access to the written Word, the people were left to rely on the Spirit for guidance, even as the leaders constructed walls to obscure the voice of God.

The dragon continued to take form, adding new heads with each conquest. Religion joined forces with the state, aligning itself with sorcery and *Pharmakeia*. This dragon devoured everything in its path, growing in power and instilling fear. Its ultimate goal was the submission of all humanity.

The Industrial Revolution birthed another head. Men and women became willing participants in their own subjugation, laboring in oppressive conditions that soon became normalized. Families fractured under the weight of long hours and relentless toil, and worship began to fade.

Another head, gossip, emerged as control over information allowed the beast to manipulate perceptions. Printed news began the work of discrediting opposition while presenting a façade of ethical strength. This manipulation has only grown more insidious with the rise of social media.

Education became another tool of the beast, cloaked in arrogance and driven by an agenda of indoctrination. The systems of learning were designed to ritualistically program the masses, planting schemes in the soil of vanity and false intelligence. Just as apathy hardens the heart into stone, these schemes seek to entrap the mind, cutting off the lifeblood of truth.

The dragon thrives on fear and deceit, perpetuating its dominion through systems that bind humanity to its will. Its many heads symbolize the sprawling, interconnected forces of corruption, oppression, and control that challenge the faithful to stand firm in truth and grace.

The anticipation of a one-world order was once relegated to the realm of conspiracy theories, a fantasy imagined as government overreach on a global scale. Yet the reality is far subtler, far more insidious. Big business has already locked the world into an intricate web of control. If you're still searching for the rise of a one-world government, you've missed the main act. The consolidation of power isn't emerging—it's already here, hidden in plain sight. From this point forward, its grip will tighten, refined by governments defending the insatiable greed of corporate giants. Meanwhile, society's collective heart grows colder, more apathetic. The attributes of love—selflessness, compassion, and grace—are now rarer than sightings of Bigfoot or the Loch Ness Monster.

The dragon is no longer a fledgling. It has matured and embedded itself into the fabric of every societal system. Its influence pervades, indoctrinating us in ways so subtle and pervasive that to speak against it is to risk becoming a pariah. To challenge the dragon's grip on my soul and society's corruption is to declare myself a public enemy.

Even as I write my story—a tale of healing and redemption—the battle intensifies. By day, I encounter seemingly friendly faces, people whose bonds with me are rooted in self-interest rather than genuine connection. By night, the demons rise, striking from all directions. Their attacks aren't random; they're calculated, capitalizing on the weak points of faith and resolve.

The church, silent on spiritual warfare, leaves its flock ill-equipped to cast out demons or stand firm against the supernatural forces that oppose our healing. The disorder is palpable, leaving us vulnerable and unarmed.

A simple comparison illustrates this: imagine starting a diet, only to find everyone around you suddenly offering you cheesecake. This sabotage may appear harmless—a temptation to indulge—but it reflects a deeper dynamic. It is a subtle extortion of your willpower, a malignant force seeking to erode your resolve. The battle is not only against what is visible but also against unseen forces digging into your faith and determination.

When the reward is cheesecake, we may laugh off the assault, but the underlying truth remains. Just as we would hope our friends would support our goals instead of sabotaging them, we should expect the same encouragement in our spiritual journey. Yet the battle rages on, testing not only our resolve but also our understanding of what it means to stand firm in a world ensnared by the dragon's influence.

Chapter 51
Big Bang Huffing Chloroform

Genesis 1:1 "In the beginning God created the heavens and the earth."

"Let's take all of our lessons from the crack head down the street."

In a vision, I see two baskets filled with figs placed before the entrance of the temple. One is filled with good figs, while the other contains figs so rotten they wouldn't even be fit for mulch, as they would poison the earth. You reach your hand into the basket containing the good fruit and pull out a piece. You bite into it with anticipation, expecting sweetness, but instead, it is bitter. The fruit has been corrupted by the nutrients in the soil. If the soil remains untreated, it will continue to contaminate the fruit at the root. The question is: who picked the fruit?

One morning, I was driving to Lit'l Mama's Music when a cop pulled me over. I recognized him by his badge and gun, but there was no aura of enlightenment. To me, he was just a man hired to do a job. Spiritual attacks had been coming at me from every direction, firing upon me one after another. Late-night calls from the ghosts of my past kept coming—people I hadn't heard from in ten or more years suddenly decided to reach out. I knew I shouldn't be surprised. I was trying to cut away the bad fruit within me and treat the soil of my noesis. This inner work seemed to draw offenses that infringed on my peace from the outside.

"Do you know why I pulled you over?" the officer asked.

"Yeah, I think I do," I replied. "I was having a fantastic morning, and you couldn't stand to let that continue. You listened to the voice of your father, the devil, and decided, 'Hey, I'm going to ruin this man's morning.' It has to be the works of the devil because, in reality, I did nothing wrong. I know what you're going to say—that I made an abrupt lane change when I turned onto this one-way street. But you and I both know what I did was legal. Traffic laws are written for road safety. Did you see anything unsafe in what I did?"

"I suppose not, but I w—"

"Good. Then step back, Satan, by the power and authority of Jesus Christ, my Lord."

He literally stumbled backward as if the hand of God had nudged him. His perplexity was clear in his widened eyes. While he tried to process what had just happened, he signaled for me to leave.

As I drove away, I reflected on the event. Truth be told, the words had flown out of my mouth so quickly they seemed to leave fire trails. But that didn't stop the war. Later that evening, a kid stole my car. There was no damage, but I knew the kid needed to learn a lesson. I cut out all the goodness in me to intimidate him. I stared him down, watching the tremor of fear ripple through him. I made him contemplate his morality, and possibly his mortality. I didn't press charges, but he ended up sweeping my sidewalk for months.

Then, as I mentioned earlier, the US government wanted me to stand trial against Chuck. Just the phone call alone opened a Pandora's box. Memories of that time in my life brought feelings that were meant to remain submerged, bobbing up and down in the ocean until they finally drowned. These memories weren't supposed to be dragged out begrudgingly all at once.

The moment I began writing words that would promote my healing, the floodgates to the underworld opened. I was attacked daily. Those demons fired upon me relentlessly, but God protected me. Healing is not something the enemy desires—especially healing that inspires others to heal. With each symbol of recovery, the attacks came more rapidly. Yet, I continued to lift my sword to the page. I adjusted my trajectory, aiming for healthier subject areas as a defiant opposition to the darkness. Over time, I began to see the enemy clearly, beyond the carnal view. These were demons on a mission.

The double-edged sword is meant to sever worldly chaos from your identity. It separates you from the growths of moral decay. As it cuts you away from the vine binding you to wickedness, the world around you begins to feel the same liberation. The Kingdom of Heaven overtakes the kingdom of treachery. It will come to pass. The merchants will weep, for their wealth was built on the power of idolatry. These idols, though numerous and illustrious, will fall.

All the prophets of the past have carried the same core message: "Turn away from sin and back toward God." To truly turn toward God, you must heal from bitterness and anger. If bitterness drives your decisions, you are unlikely to move closer to Him. As the demons become entangled in the vines and are cut away, they fall into fiery depths, never to return. This is true freedom—the ability to make decisions that bring health and joy.

So, who picked the fruit? I allowed the soil to be cultivated by the media. I didn't regulate the trash that fed my mind. I let the education system fill my head with garbage. I allowed anything I found reasonable—or at least entertaining—to influence me. In this, I am not so different from my mom. I clung to cultural norms to absolve myself of accountability. When others are in control, I bear no responsibility.

But I've learned that I have the power to decide who or what I give my authority to. I can't simply hand over that authority to a man because he has a badge and a gun. If I do, the image in the mirror no longer reflects the truth of who I am.

The fruit in the basket may be rotted by my emotions, but I still have the power to choose what I submit my authority to. I alone can separate the good fruit from the bad. I cannot surrender the authorship of my life to fleeting emotions. I am more than the sum of my thoughts and feelings.

False beliefs remain a maze, but instead of focusing on myself and trying to find my own way out, I must broaden my perspective. Many people are lost, looping around and colliding with the walls of deception. Everywhere you look, there is evidence of the wreckage from this moral decline. Like me, others have been trapped by deeply rooted false beliefs perpetuated by those who use intimidation and false authority to force submission.

When you submit to God—the Creator of all things—there is no other author. He doesn't bully or rush you into rash decisions. Instead, He protects you and gives you the time to learn to trust Him.

Walking in the light of truth makes the walls of false beliefs crash and crumble. When you are surrounded by lies, the truth blends in and is hard to distinguish. But when you walk in truth, the lies stand out—like a red Corvette in a field of black hearses.

One of the heads of the dragon represents false information, primarily delivered through the news. It uses its influence to lend credibility to the other heads. The seven heads of the dragon work together, co-conspirators with one common goal: to deliver you into the hands of Lucifer.

Some walls of the maze were built by ignorant men consumed by arrogance. Freud was one such man. Common sense tells us that cocaine use is an attempt to escape inner turmoil, and that turmoil should be addressed—not masked. Freud's theories, such as the Oedipus complex, are deeply tied to his ideas of sexual development. These theories are taught in psychology forums, but I see them as the ramblings of a man strung out on cocaine, projecting his twisted desires.

There is a strong argument that society would rather listen to the drug-fueled delusions of a madman than confront the reality that such ideas are not normal. It is far easier for people to believe these are natural developmental processes than to acknowledge them for what they truly are: demonic influences.

Planted in the same soil is Carl Jung and his shadow work, which has furthered the work of the devil. Who in their right mind believes it is a good idea to embrace the evil within? I would argue it's far better to change the way you think and walk away from that dragon. Of course, the key phrase stands out: "Who in their right mind?" If I were in my right mind, I wouldn't follow Jungian idealism. Then again, if I were in my right mind, I wouldn't be seeking a shrink in the first place. If I follow anyone, it will be the One who created me. Even if that is viewed as mere ideology and God doesn't exist, it is still better to pursue the theorization of a perfect being than the ramblings of someone under the influence of LSD.

Jung's work often seems to exemplify—and perhaps amplify—the divide between the conscious and subconscious mind. While some aspects of his analysis carry a good fragrance, much of it reeks. My main issue lies in its ambivalence to what I know from God's Word.

Jung's idea of uniting the conscious and subconscious mind does resemble healing from the curse of mankind. It represents the desired wholeness that once existed before the effects of the fruit of good and evil divided us. Picture the tree of life, a beautiful entity at the center of the mind. It is guarded by cherubim, ensuring its safety from the demonic powers within—the dragon, the evil now residing in humanity.

If we could intellectualize our way into wholeness and the tree of life became visible while we still carried the fields and battle plans of the demonic, it would empower evil to overtake the human experience. If our motives were pure, we wouldn't try to enter illegally when a legal path is available. The result of such intellectualized infiltration would be an eternity of evil.

When you embrace and accept the evil within you, it becomes a permanent part of you that cannot access the tree of life. This is for your own good and the good of others. However, rebuking and rejecting that evil—and healing from its treachery— aligns you with the restoration of the garden's curse. The curse wasn't a punishment for Adam and Eve; it was a measure to secure the safety of Heaven.

Heaven is achieved by overpowering the evil within and sending it away by the authority of God. Returning to the Kingdom of Heaven means becoming undivided in your mind. It is the healing of the conscious and subconscious, bringing them back to their original state of splendor. Sin and evil cannot pass through the gate.

The jungle is dense, as is our guide. Swinging from branch to branch in the tree overhead is the spitting image of mom—Freud would be envious. In the distance, a shotgun blast echoes. It's the "big bang" that wakes young Charles Darwin and, supposedly, created our universe. This mythical explosion initiated the sequential splitting of cells that, over millions of years, transformed monkeys directly into men with no rest stops in between.

Did I forget to mention that Darwin had been unconscious from huffing chloroform for about twenty-five years? The visions it gave him were likely the lies he propagated.

It shouldn't surprise me that society bites into these apples. This is the same society that spends $150 billion per year on sex trafficking. The revenue from child pornography alone is estimated between $3 billion and $20 billion annually. Society, in general, isn't pursuing truth—it's too entangled in lies.

Finding truth requires looking into a mirror free of distortions. If you aren't pruning your own vines to escape these shocking realities, then your intelligence sits on the throne of ignorance—next to your "mother," the monkey. It's no wonder these concepts are packaged, wrapped in a bow, and sold as education.

The harm flourishing in these lies is theft—of hope, meaning, and truth. If the big bang is true, what hope can you possibly hold on to? It leaves you stranded in a universal desert with an empty satchel that once held hope. Worse still, we've spent fortunes learning about these drug-induced impressions of knowledge. The great institutions of education rake in about $100 billion a year to spread this nonsense.

Not everything that dragon preaches is a lie, but truth within its message is engulfed by non-sustainable, twisted information. Like a python, these lies constrict your growth and obscure reality. These institutions aren't fostering understanding; they're building walls akin to the Tower of Babel, and these so-called insights become barriers to the truth.

I've sat across from shrinks who insistently wielded the theories of their craft. I did the footwork, engaged with their methods, but I often left those sessions feeling as though I'd tied their logic into straight jackets. This is not to antagonize people in these professions. On the contrary, I may have even picked up a few tools for dealing with others in the process. But what I truly learned is this: I am speaking a language that most of the world no longer understands.

My language—the language of integrity, honor, and glory to God—has been confused by theories that obscure truth. I wouldn't have been in those sessions if I hadn't bought into the idea that psychology held answers. In fact, psychology was my major in college. I took to it with enthusiasm and was even recruited into an honor society.

But the more I learned, the more closed off my thoughts became, as I began placing others in boxes of judgment. What I didn't see at the time was how much of what I was learning contradicted the spiritual principles of Christianity.

Desperate to release the pressure that built up in my mind before it imploded, I clung to these teachings. But when I finally grasped the reality that I was created to love and be loved, the chains of falsehood broke, and I was set free. That realization returned my heart to God—a heart that had been so polluted it resembled the streets of San Francisco.

Theories, taught as truths, filled my education in anthropology, psychology, and virtually every discipline I encountered. But theories can be twisted, manipulated to serve agendas far removed from truth. I don't want theories. I want truth.

Chapter 52
The sword to Divorce

Revelation 12:9 "And the great dragon was cast out, that old serpent called the devil."

"You are the only one that can cut him out of your life by choosing God."

A smog so dense envelops the air that you can not only smell it but also taste it—like the smoldering fumes of brimstone. Litter clogs the streets, and you must tread carefully to avoid stepping on an infected needle. The zombies don't shuffle slowly like in the movies. Instead, they either lie motionless on the sidewalk, appearing dead, or suddenly emerge with their hands outstretched. The factory fires and the haunting sight of vandalized, empty buildings serve as bitter reminders of better days. It feels like a picturesque version of hell, if I were to judge.

We have arrived here by following the rantings of lunatics, and soon we'll need to make amends for that. Freud's iceberg theory comes to mind. Psychology suggests that our minds are divided into three parts: the subconscious, the preconscious, and the conscious. The subconscious plays hide-and-seek with information, much like hiding your keys in the refrigerator while your conscious mind wastes all day searching for them. It resists certain basic movements and functions presented by the conscious mind, which explains why you might trip over a gumball wrapper.

I agree these divisions of the mind exist, but a divided mind is an enemy to itself. The mind was never meant to be fragmented. Psychology has normalized this fractured state, calling it "dropped" or "broken." Yet, until the divisions are lifted, the pieces unified, and the mind made whole, the game of hide-and-seek will persist.

Awkward Silence

Some functions, like blinking and heartbeat regulation, are automatic, driven by the subconscious. However, if a mystical hypnotic trance can grant access to the subconscious and retrieve hidden information, then perhaps no trance is truly necessary. Entering this trance-like state is simple—deep relaxation is the passcode. Clearing the debris of your conscience and maintaining a state of peaceful ease allows you to walk in that wholeness. Perhaps the mind has never been divided but merely bombarded with clutter, creating artificial boundaries and hiding places.

It's difficult to send messages to the front lines during war, and battling yourself is no different—it's still war. If you choose to remain divided, the internal conflict will continue to be self-destructive. But if you arrive at your destination whole and intact, the swords will be lowered, and you may finally glimpse the tree of life.

Greed and lust are like arrows shot into your conscience, piercing it and creating the divisions we've been discussing. These arrows are also the drivers of social decay. Greed, wielded with relentless force, pushes us closer to destruction. We cling to systems we know are failing, desperate to preserve the illusions we've built about ourselves. Even as we see the lies of the media, we hesitate to let them taint our self-image.

If we examine our inner sketches deeply enough, we'll see the demons hiding within. The unnatural allure of lust permeates everything, even fueling human trafficking. I can hardly fathom that human trafficking is a $150 billion-a-year industry. The scale of involvement in such an atrocity is incomprehensible to me. Knowing this amount of money circulates within and around human trafficking makes me look at the world—and my neighbors—differently.

Greed rages across the land, striking fiercely at anyone who refuses to bow to it. It affects everyone, but especially those who resist adopting its values. To take greed's "number" is to allow it into your habits, thoughts, and feelings. Once greed becomes part of your soul, it entrenches itself and throws you off balance—both as an individual and as part of society. It corrupts your morals, turning a small beast into a monstrous force.

This insidious force is often bolstered by the ideas of Adam Smith, who emphasized self-interest as the driver of a competitive economy. But while self-interest may fuel capitalism, I believe the true father of greed is Satan himself.

At night I lie awake listening to the wails of the beast. It never sleeps, It paces back and forth along the freeways, highways, and roadways. It silences the crickets chirp and replaces it with the painful shrieks and squeals of Torment. The city light is a thick pasty smog that blocks a third of the stars from view. The grumbling sound is especially noticeable as the day should be winding down. It is unsightly. The tar paved roads circle around leading nowhere. It is supposed to be progress but it comes at a steep cost.

Scripture overpowers the rantings of lunacy. I have never seen the words so clearly before. I see the angel with the small bittersweet scroll that is described in the book of Revelation. His right foot in the water and his left on land. One foot is on the seemingly solid ground of carnality while the other is placed in a more liquid realm, the spiritual. He sees the beast's uprising in the spirit and tries to relay this understanding in the carnal realm but it is a bittersweet gesture. This beast has been built brick by brick to satisfy an unquenchable thirst. There are armies made up of young people that will kill and die to protect this master.

You would think the nearer we get to the flames of Hell the more that would turn away but that just doesn't seem to be the case. The heat can be felt. It begins to singe their hair. They can smell it. Thgey can hear, taste, see, and even sense the evil but they continue to justify the demons. They pretend that they can't see them. They pretend they don't exist. There is nothing written on this scroll that we have not been warned of before. The beast is rising out of the liquidity of the sea of molten lava that solidifies in the carnal world around our hearts.

The thriving spirit of capitalism is greed, but united with that greed is idolatry. The very essence of selfishness aligns perfectly with Satan's plan. There is little about the economic system that promotes anything endorsed by God. You cannot serve both God and mammon—you will love one and hate the other. It's a false belief to think you can have both God and money unless that money is being used to build up the Kingdom of Heaven. Otherwise, you've fallen into the wayside of greed. Be honest with yourself: are you trying to sit on a throne above others? If so, the fall from that height will be long and hard.

Healing begins with painful honesty. This honesty doesn't come crashing in like a freight train, though at times it feels that way. It requires an inward reflection that decides it's time for change. The culture of change is one of repentance. It demands that you turn from the direction you are traveling and find a new path. When I caught the scent of the slaughterhouse ahead, I turned away. For me, that meant changing course as soon as I realized where I was headed. Society, it seems, has lost its sense of smell. Many can no longer recognize where their choices are taking them.

When we think of the sounds of war, we often imagine machine gun fire, exploding missiles, and RPG blasts. But the loudest sound of war is the quiet weeping of children who learn their mothers or fathers won't be coming home. That sound lingers for a lifetime, echoing across generations. War has many tragedies, but let's be clear: every war is the same war. Since the beginning, we have fought against powers and principalities. It's the same war you fight within yourself and the same one reflected in the world around you. There have been countless battles, yet I wish we could finally arrive at the war that ends all wars.

What happens inside you influences what happens outside you, and vice versa. If you are living in internal peace, choosing to go to battle isn't a decision you'd make lightly. Fighting the battle within changes the outside world because it sharpens your personal decisions. That's one reason you encounter so much resistance when you try to change. It's not just about you—your life influences others, and your transformation creates a ripple effect. By confronting the daily pains within, you can change the world.

Every death on the battlefield, regardless of the side, is caused by the same enemy. That enemy is the one who abducts children for slavery, justifies battles with lies, and manipulates sympathy for its own ends. The evil of Epstein's Island is the same enemy that distorts your thoughts and prevents you from standing up for morality. It's the same force that pushes families onto the cold, hard streets. It's the same one that beats a child bloody and feeds them filth. That same enemy lives within you if you harbor resentment, bitterness, or unforgiveness.

Victory over small battles, like individual healing, prepares us for greater triumphs. Personal healing separates us from the intolerable marriage to worldly ways. Unity in the mind brings clarity, and suddenly, you'll remember where you left those keys. Injustice will become intolerable. Greed will become intolerable. It's the same enemy that slams a gavel, claiming to be god over the moment. It's the same one that hides authenticity behind the insecurities of lies. When these things are revealed, many of the worldly pursuits that people chase will no longer seem desirable—or tolerable.

The whip cracks, but the outcry is silenced by the muffling of a pillow pressed against the face at night. Most people know this is not what life was meant to be, but they also know the comfort they hold dear can be taken away in an instant. Circulating Christian prophecies speak of a time when people will face the choice to take the number of the beast or die. There are many assumptions about what this means.

When I reflect on this, I think of how many Jewish people still await the Messiah. The time has come and gone, yet they remain fixed on a vision of what they believe His coming will look like. I would argue that, much like this prolonged expectation, the mark of the beast has already come and gone. What difference does it make whether you're stamped with a number on your forehead or your right hand if you've already allowed bitterness to take you by the hand and direct your will? What difference does it make if your thoughts are consumed by revenge? In my opinion, if you've given yourself over to such things, you've already been marked. The world forming before your eyes is the hell you've created—or allowed in.

You built your personal maze by accepting certain lies. I don't know who first told you those lies—about yourself or the world—but if you want to escape the maze, read the words I've written on every mirror within it. That house of mirrors and its twisting maze can no longer hold you. You are stronger than the sum of all evil. You are a child of God. I have declared your identity. I've left you treasure maps to help you find your gems. There is no reason to ever look back again.

The lava has been bubbling for a very long time. You can feel it in the air—the temperature of wickedness is rising, glowing red-hot like molten magma. Nothing in this world feels truly right anymore. I wonder how long it will be before pedophiles demand more than basic human rights. Accepting the human being and loving them is fundamentally different from embracing their sinful pedophilia. Such acceptance would be like shadow work from an external perspective. There is nothing within me that will ever tolerate that beast.

Child marriages remain prevalent in parts of the world, such as India, where pedophiles are implicitly celebrated through cultural practices. In the West, we have month-long celebrations of certain lifestyles and identities. Yet we don't declare a month to celebrate being heterosexual. Why, then, must sexual preferences be shouted from the rooftops? Fill in that blank for me. No, I get it—you're trying to add insult to injury. It's a fire of bitterness, insisting on rebellion against the nature of creation.

What's twisted is that the same force that oppressed and shamed you is now standing beside you, holding symbols of your pride. Satan is cunning. He first sowed confusion in the fields where you would plant your seed, perhaps generations ago. He trapped you in the closet, compounding your shame, and now he exploits you to burden love itself with your pain. He exploits your defiance, using your rebellion to mock God as you wave the flag of immorality.

But what happens when pedophiles unite under the rainbow flag of the LGBTQ community, adding a "P" to the growing acronym? Imagine pedophilia becoming a "recognized" identity—a new member of the PLGBTQ circus. It's a performance, but even the best tents must eventually come down.

As a sword wielded by God, it is not my purpose to sever the ropes holding up the tents. My purpose is to free those who wish to escape the wrath to come. The lava will consume those who continue to dance around it. Humble yourselves. Step away from the flames.

The chains that once bound you have fallen. They lie broken on the ground. Nothing can hold you back now—unless you allow it. Let go. Heal from your past afflictions by changing the way you think. Rebirth your ideas and submerge the old ones in repentance. Take a new path. Let go of the heavy backpack you carry. Let your burdens fall beside the chains. They only slow you down, and time is of the essence. Heal from your past wounds by forgiving those who were misguided in their actions.

I can hear the patter of feet behind me—a deep, hybrid hum that rises from the pounding of countless steps against the earth's surface. Anger fuels their rhythm, a pulse of hostility stirred by my words. My confrontation with their demons has placed pitchforks in their hands. It seems my message has struck a nerve, provoking this furious response. Still, I wish to see them heal. I long to mend the displaced animosity that echoes throughout the world. But for now, I move quickly, escaping the wrath my preaching has ignited.

As the sword swings overhead, words of judgment pour from its edge, flowing like ink onto the page. Time is of the essence. You thieves and liars, beware—the sword is swiftly descending upon you. You nearly fooled the entire world with your embellishments and deceit. Each person alive has been given the breath of life, and with it, blessings ordained for them. Yet, you steal these blessings and place them on the market, seizing what is not yours.

You sought power over others and, through trickery, convinced them they must become indentured to you to possess what I have already given. You take wives—the women I formed from their own flesh—and blind them to the gift God has bestowed, prostituting their beauty and purpose to another. Your deception has sown confusion throughout the world. Marriages have walked the plank, drowning in divorce, because so many unions are not what I have endorsed.

You have led them to lean on their own understanding, and the truth is obscured by smoke and mirrors. What God created was perfect, destined to bloom in His righteous timing. Yet lies and deceit have tainted the soil. By clinging to the heavy backpack of sin and ignoring the compass of truth, they have allowed deception to rule. Surrender, forgiveness, and repentance are what they need to rekindle hope.

I lower my gaze to focus on my footing but stumble twice. Anxious to escape those who thirst for my blood, I press forward. They are a lynch mob—nothing more than the demons of bitterness and anger pursuing me. I run to stay ahead, but I still hear them behind me, their whispers promising destruction.

These are the same liars who once told me I was unworthy of God's blessings. When my blessings lay unclaimed, these thieves came and took what was rightfully mine. They are the same deceivers who distorted humanity's understanding of what they are truly entitled to—not the entitlement of selfish desire, but the divine inheritance from our Heavenly Father.

Imagine this: A father gives his eldest son a gift—a Tonka truck, perhaps. But the envious neighbor devises a way to take it for himself. In his jealousy, he not only destroys his own chance to receive the perfect gift from his own father but also ruins the stolen gift in the process. The gift a father gives is not random; it comes from his heart and carries his plans for his child's future.

Yet envy blinds the thief, driving him to seize what was never meant for him. By doing so, he forfeits both the stolen blessing and his own.

Thieves and liars, repent before it is too late. The sword swings overhead, and its descent is near.

The sword strikes again, slicing through another head of the dragon. The Nicolaitan spirit—the desire to conquer the laity and make them subservient to religious authority—has deeply wounded the relationship Jesus desires with His followers. There are layers to this deception. In the fourth letter to the church of Thyatira, Jesus is described as the one with feet like burnished bronze. These are not the feet of a statue of Peter. Over centuries, tears and the wiping of Peter's statue have worn its feet down from size eleven to size three. But even Peter would oppose the worship of his image. He knew God, and you have the same opportunity— yet you seek Him through the conventions of tradition.

Jesus is alive. Speak with Him. Cry out, "Jesus of Nazareth, hear me, O Lord!" Let the sword fall, severing your unhealthy marriage to tradition. Do not let any man stand between you and God. Let those who sought power over you face their own repentance. They have used their numbers to consolidate authority, appropriating your devotion for their gain. They've united with worldly corruption, now apparent in the pope's approval of same-sex blessings. While I hold compassion for those caught under the dragon's wing, God's position has not changed. His promises endure—yesterday, today, and forever.

The path to His blessings remains simple: repent, forgive, and surrender. Yet liberal theology leads us astray, moving us from Thyatira to Laodicea. In Laodicea, we build aqueducts to bring water from distant hot springs, but by the time it reaches us, it is lukewarm. We are self-satisfied, believing in our own sufficiency, and blinded by the arrogance of our wealth. The sword is raised to sever the vines of pride and sin that bind us. Surrender, so you may live victoriously.

As I look across the field, I see figures on the horizon, much like those chasing me from behind. Their heavy breathing is close now, and the pounding of their feet nears. Delay even a moment, and they will catch me. Those ahead block any hope of escape, yet I must press forward.

The sword rises again, cutting the vines that threaten to trip me. It wields the truth, freeing not just me but anyone entangled by lies. The sword was never meant solely for my benefit—it was always meant to serve you. It exposes conspirators, articulates the truth, and urges you to cut your own vines, leading to freedom. This blank page staring back at me is not empty; it is a field of purpose, meant to do the will of the Father. His will is for you to experience the freedom found in truth.

I run, my pace quickening as I approach those ahead, even as I feel the breath of those behind me. I am trapped, the meat between two slices of bread, with nowhere to go. The baggage I have carried serves no purpose now, so I release it. It has weighed me down, tethering me to sin. Nothing it contains can help me when the demons catch up.

Just as despair sets in, I see a shimmer—a slight glimmer of hope. Perhaps when people read my words, they will recognize my failures as deeply as their own, or even more so. Maybe they will follow me toward hope with the same fervor they have followed bitterness and despair. Perhaps they will realize the enemy is real, but also that it can be subdued by a change in perspective.

These words may guide someone to release the animosity they have carried toward those who hurt them. Perhaps they will see that forgiveness is the key to breaking the chains of bitterness. If these words, growing like branches on this tree, bring even a glimmer of hope to combat the schemes of misdirection, then my efforts have been worthwhile.

In the middle of the meadow, she and I finally meet. We are surrounded on all sides, nowhere to run, nowhere to hide from the aggression of our enemies. There is but one choice left to us. I thrust my pen into the ground and embrace her. Together, we drop to our knees in surrender.

Awkward Silence

Suddenly, the world begins to quake—not along fault lines, but with a deep, earth-shaking force that defies comprehension. The poles themselves are shifting, the north becoming the south, the south becoming the north. With eyes closed, the last image imprinted in our minds is of our enemies closing in, their faces twisted with rage. We hold each other tightly, bracing for the end as the thought of impending doom fills us.

Around us, chaos erupts. Screams of anguish pierce the air as those clinging to worldly ways are torn apart by their own resistance. In the midst of the commotion, He appears—not as a figure we can see, but as a force we can feel. He takes back the sword and wields it with divine precision, cutting away every vine and shackle that bound us to a corrupted worldview. With one final swish of the blade, the truth is revealed: we have been living in an upside-down world, enslaved by its lies. Now, those chains are broken, and the world as we knew it is no more.

For so long, I had believed that intellect or sheer willpower could lead one to wholeness of mind. I see now how untrue that is. No amount of reasoning or effort can bridge the gap. True wholeness comes only through surrender. When love is elevated in your heart as your master, a sincerity arises that restores your intended sight. No meditation or self-deception can overcome the obstacles of the soul. Only through repentance, forgiveness, and surrender to God can you be led out of the maze. By the name of Jesus, your vision will be restored—not through pretense, but through a genuine willingness to change. To enter the kingdom of truth and righteousness, you must be truthful and righteous yourself.

Then, all at once, the quaking stops. For a moment, we do not dare open our eyes. Fear grips us—the fear that the enemies who pursued us might still be standing here. But as we hesitate, the gentle sounds of nature filter through. The aggression is gone.

They are gone. We are alone—but I realize now that we were never truly alone.

With a newfound awareness, we rise slowly to our feet. The ground beneath us feels steady, but we are reluctant to move too quickly. What just happened? The thought no sooner enters my mind than the earth begins to quake again. Yet this time, the fear is different. It is mixed with wonder, a sense of anticipation for something greater.

Before our eyes, a brook springs forth in the meadow, a symbol of renewal and life. The water glimmers, alive with promise. Surrendering to the will of God has brought us here, to a place beyond what we could have ever imagined. We are alive, open to His love and the precious gifts He bestows. Rubies, onyx, opals—riches beyond compare. Gold paves the ground beneath our feet. But none of these treasures can match the most valuable gift of all: the ability to truly love and to be loved.

This began in a moment of silence, born from an awkward circumstance. It was a blank page in an empty parcel, but the branches have grown in many directions. Each branch reaches out to flip a switch, illuminating the light that sparks your inspirations and aspirations. The pen keeps returning to the poetic chorus of the song I play as you sit upon the swing—a song that calls out from a relational grave. It carries a message cloaked in transparency, a message of hope, faith, and love.

It is a traditional courtship, once wagered to death by the actions of our sin, laid to rest in a tomb, and left to decay. Yet, when the stone is rolled away, it reveals a risen King—a King whose dominion shines beyond the shadows, lighting every crevasse and leading us on an adventure, a treasure hunt to uncover the gems you've hidden and buried. Innocence and safety are bundled within this proposal of traditional courtship.

Awkward Silence

Traditionally, I would never show up at your doorstep empty-handed. In my hand, the pen holds flowers, chocolates, and more wealth than words can express. In this, I reflect the image of my God, who holds a deeply romantic nature. He has equipped me with the province of your hand and filled me with treasures so vast that, if not shared, they would burst from my chest. With the pen, I draw a map to treasures both within and beyond this field, uncovering the gems you hold—more precious than you may ever know.

I am with you in battle, wielding the sword of ink and the capacity of my soul. I am here to rekindle the light on your gem of courage whenever it grows dim. You can navigate life's difficulties with nobility and integrity, steering through even the deepest and roughest waters. With every word, I have longed to carry you in my arms toward the door—not to set you down, but to protect you, to hold you until we step safely over the threshold. Together, I dream of entering the magnificent Kingdom of Heaven.

This is one way—perhaps not the best way—to express my love for the same woman and to set myself apart from the normalized practices of modern dating culture. I am cutting myself free from a world filled with sin, wielding the sword upon myself, reverting to biblical impressions of a time when courtship was sacred. Even if it means standing apart from cultural norms, I choose this path. Good things are worth the effort and the wait. There is nothing, short of death, that will hold me back from finding yet another way—perhaps not the best way—to love you.

For now, I would love for you to join me for a glass of sweet tea and conversation on the porch. I have missed you so much that it feels as though the very oxygen has been sucked from the air. No pain I've endured comes close to your absence. Though I feel untangled, I am still twisted with desire. I feel as if I cannot go on another moment—but I know I will find a way.

Jack Taylor

I just thought you should know.

Chapter 53
Final Attempt

Genesis 3:4 "You will not certainly die."

"Eating the fruit was the affirmation that they believed the serpent when he called God a liar."

I stood at the threshold, looking directly into the eyes of love. My gaze absorbed the mighty presence of a passionate manifestation of God and His love. Inspiration stood before me, the physical embodiment of my deepest desires, yet I was immobilized by the cursed souvenirs I carried with me. Speechless, I was called to take accountability for my life. I knelt before the things I had placed on the throne of my heart—and it was not love.

I might have been permitted to enter heaven, but my backpack was full of insidious creatures. I don't know if I will get another opportunity. If only I had taken the time to heal, perhaps this paralysis would not have overcome me. Love came upon me like a thief in the night, and I was unprepared. I walked back through hell and emerged with the keys, trying now to hand them to you.

From the very first sentence formed in the otherwise blank field, I have been calling out to one individual in the spiritual realm. You can see that the long game has been played; patience has been exercised. But time is nearing an end. Inspiration is sublime, yet there appears to be a subliminal proposition within it. You may want to look closely every time inspiration is mentioned, so you can decode its deeper meaning.

The beginning of this message was shaped by the actual words I spoke to her, protecting the overall message from those who might maliciously invade heaven through their works or understanding. Only she will be able to fully comprehend the directive. The rest of you may find pieces missing from the puzzle. Love will reveal those missing pieces at the milestones of your healing.

She must remember the words I spoke into her heart. She felt them when I said them. Those words seeded her field and will break through the soil's surface as she removes the thorns and thistles of her understanding. I have no doubt that this message will untangle the vines, leading her to the water. In that clearing, she will find everything she desires, but only through surrender. God is love, and so it comes only through surrendering to love. Take a drink of the living water—I don't want to see you thirst to death. Continuing to war against God will only lead to torment and death.

Through my empathetic comprehension, I now understand that, in my unforgiveness, I was battling against God. You reap what you sow. It may seem like the natural law of karma, but it is, in truth, the response of heaven to your defiance. Anger and frustration will reach new heights as you take these things out on yourself and those around you. Taking it out on me is like kicking a dog because you had a bad day at work. That dog did nothing but love you.

I have some final words. Earlier, I said I want to speak plainly, so I'll reiterate: there is no earthly reason you should listen to me. I have accomplished nothing of worldly significance. I am not a celebrity whose words are exalted by fame. But I will no longer hold my tongue to appease your sin. I do not see sin as a mistake; I see it as an enemy. That enemy can become your master, holding you back from the blessings of heaven.

Turn from wickedness and return to God—all you people, in all nations. The alterations to your thoughts and feelings through the works of wicked hands have not been lessons. They have been corruptions of your soul. They lead you away from the attributes of love, steering you from trust, damaging your patience, and hindering your kindness.

The bio portion of this script has been my personal war—a battle waged with death itself from the depths of hell. It has been my personal Armageddon. There are parallels that leap out of the chaotic barrel of transgression, running side by side with the sin of the world. The oppression I encountered mirrors the tyranny we stumble into as a population. The unfaithfulness, disloyalty, and lack of integrity we experience from others directly reflect the unfaithfulness, disloyalty, and lack of integrity we demonstrate toward God. It is a great mirror. What happens inside you is reflected outside, and what happens outside reflects back to you.

I am here to tell you: if someone steals from you, it is because somewhere, somehow, the gates of treachery have been compromised. *Shut the door.* Those beasts have infiltrated your land. They will rummage through your treasures, taking what does not belong to them. They will pillage and plunder until nothing remains. The infection that moves through your actions and invades the world around you only gives you more cause for change. The suffering the world faces is no different from the torment I endured. I was raging within, trying to control every situation, never happy, paranoid of everyone's intentions. I was corrupted by an enemy that lived inside me.

You don't have to wait until death for heaven to arrive—it is already here. Heaven is a domain you can step into by letting go of sin. You cannot enter if you are carrying the moldy spores of sin, for they would seek to spread their defilement throughout this promised land. Clean your house and shut the door behind you. True friends will not encourage you toward destructive choices. Rebuke those who enable promiscuity and passivity—they are acting out something broken within themselves through you. Don't anchor yourself to this world and its endless cycle of demise. Heaven is worth the effort.

Heaven is the wholeness of mind. It is the connection of spirit to soul and soul to body. It is the pearly gates, the golden streets, the harmonious vibrations of peace—the angels singing. It is an eternity of joy and fulfillment, victory over the carnality of the demonic monarchy. It is the giddiness of late-night laughter, the simple, overwhelming happiness that stirs your spirit. Heaven is beautiful. To me, it is how I imagine the Garden of Eden: vibrant plant life, peaceful wildlife, and every kind of critter, all under your authority. They pose no threat because you are a child of the King. Take my hand and walk through the gate with me. You can drop your baggage outside the gate. If you decide to leave, your burdens will still be waiting for you—but you don't have to carry them anymore.

I love you. I truly do. I don't want to stand idly by as you self-destruct. Don't defend your demons—face them with boldness, or they will destroy you. Confess them and change your path. Forgive those who have hurt you, because your life truly begins when you let go of the past. Don't just hunt for an open gate; guide your heart into submission. Seat Jesus on the throne of your heart, and love will prevail.

The dream I had has been integral to my journey. It showed me the darkness of my wandering and gave me insight into the enemy within. It gave me the hope of inspiration and, through faith, directed me to love. It turned my world upside-right. With all the words in this message, I've tried to share with you a gift that was given to me. I want you to prosper from what Jesus has given to me.

You can do with it what you want. I am not trying to control you. I'm only trying to share my soul with you. Take it or leave it—it's your choice. However, rejecting the sword meant to cut the vines that entangle you in the arms of the enemy may be the same as rejecting the one who wields it. You can continue running further into the field and risk being overtaken by the demons that pursue you, or you can surrender with me and enjoy the blessings of a transformed life. You can wake up to a different story.

You don't have to rely on your sense of smell to know that the end is near. It can be seen. When you imagine what hell might look like, you can recognize that it is being constructed in the streets of every major city. Small towns across this nation are not immune—they, too, are striving toward that same wretched growth. The relentless economy demands it, forcing people to do whatever it takes to keep food on their tables. This is extortion through inflation.

If bitterness sits in your mind, you may as well have 666 written on your forehead. If that bitterness leads you into sin, it is as though 666 is engraved on your right hand. The end can be heard in the echoes of past treachery. You can feel its eeriness as you travel down a pitch-black country road, perhaps for the last time. You can taste it in the smoldering brimstone of chaos and destruction—the collective bitterness of a population misled by political agendas. Donald, you are bitter. I understand why. You are up against raw evil. But to be most effective, you must let go of that bitterness. Replace it with joy.

The beauty of this moment is that we are perfectly positioned for transformation. Let love guide you by the right hand, away from the marriage of convenience and the entanglements of the state. Allow love to shower you with a fresh perspective. Share your kindness and patience. Cast aside your pride, boasting, and arrogance. Learn to embrace your individual blessing so you may prosper in your unique calling, and in doing so, free yourself from envy.

Jack Taylor

Hold yourself in high regard—you are a child of the righteous King. Seek not for yourself, but offer yourself as a blessing to the Kingdom. Walk in honor, spreading honor to others. Forgive instantly and completely when wronged, holding nothing back. Use your gift of discernment to humbly distance yourself from those who defend their own demons. Shake the dust from your sandals and move on. Keep no record of wrongs and rejoice in truth. Love never fails. Love is the force that defeats the enemy, inspiring healing and triumph over opposition.

Short of hitting you with a cast-iron skillet, I have given you all I have. If you have eyes to see, the picture should now be clear. The more truth you carry within, the easier it becomes to see the falsehoods around you. One day, and I suspect it will be soon, there will be a call on your life. You will face a decision that will feel like an exercise of free will, but it will be influenced by the roaring voices of past events, voices that have poisoned your judgment. In that moment, you may find yourself staring love in the face. You won't be thinking about the small bitterness or anger that flows through your veins. Your life will flash before your eyes, revealing the dust that never settled.

Let's hope you can cut through these influences and make the right choice. Now is always the right time to seek healing for your soul, because when you stand before Jesus—whether in death, at the call of the trumpet, or in some other divine encounter—you won't want to be caught in the snare of awkward silence.

Awkward Silence

Any one suffering from CPTSD that wants
information on how we might help
or any jars wanting to be filled step forward in faith!!!

Divine Fortress Ministries 208-810-5111.

www.ingramcontent.com/pod-product-compliance
Lightning Source LLC
Chambersburg PA
CBHW051128120626
46547CB00012B/717